To...

Many...
for y...
hr

Wolaitta Evangelists

Paul & Lila Balisky
2023.

American Society of Missiology Monograph Series

THE ASM MONOGRAPH SERIES provides a forum for publishing quality dissertations and studies in the field of missiology. Collaborating with Pickwick Publications—a division of Wipf and Stock Publishers of Eugene, Oregon—the American Society of Missiology selects high quality dissertations and other monographic studies that offer research materials in mission studies for scholars, mission and church leaders, and the academic community at large. The ASM seeks scholarly work for publication in the Series that throws light on issues confronting Christian world mission in its cultural, social, historical, biblical, and theological dimensions.

Missiology is an academic field that brings together scholars whose professional training ranges from doctoral-level preparation in areas such as scripture, history and sociology of religions, anthropology, theology, international relations, interreligious interchange, mission history, inculturation, and church law. The American Society of Missiology, which sponsors this series, is an ecumenical body drawing members from Independent and Ecumenical Protestant, Catholic, Orthodox, and other traditions. Members of the ASM are united by their commitment to reflect on and do scholarly work relating to both mission history and the present-day mission of the church. The ASM Monograph Series aims to publish works of exceptional merit on specialized topics, with particular attention given to work by younger scholars, the dissemination and publication of which is difficult under the economic pressures of standard publishing models.

Persons seeking information about the ASM or the guidelines for having their dissertations considered for publication in the ASM Monograph Series should consult the Society's website—www.asmweb.org.

Members of the ASM Monograph Committee who approved this book are:

Paul Kollman, *Notre Dame*
Michael A. Rynkiewich, *Asbury Theological Seminary*
Wilbur Stone, *Bethel University*

PREVIOUSLY PUBLISHED IN THE ASM MONOGRAPH SERIES

Ken Christoph Miyamoto, *God's Mission in Asia: A Comparative and Contextual Study of This-Worldly Holiness and the Theology of* Missio Dei *in M. M. Thomas and C. S. Song*

Edley J. Moodley, *Shembe, Ancestors, and Christ: A Christological Inquiry with Missiological Implications*

Roberta R. King, *Pathways in Christian Music Communication The Case of the Senufo of Cote d'Ivoire*

Auli Vähäkangas, *Christian Couples Coping with Childlessness: Narratives from Machame, Kilimanjaro*

W. Jay Moon, *African Proverbs Reveal Christianity in Culture: A Narrative Portrayal of Builsa Proverbs Contextualizing Christianity in Ghana*

Wolaitta Evangelists

A Study of Religious Innovation in Southern Ethiopia, 1937–1975

E. Paul Balisky

American Society of Missiology
Monograph Series

6

PICKWICK *Publications* · Eugene, Oregon

WOLAITTA EVANGELISTS
A Study of Religious Innovation in Southern Ethiopia, 1937–1975

American Society of Missiology Monograph Series 6

Pickwick Publications
A Division of Wipf and Stock Publishers
199 W. 8th Ave., Suite 3
Eugene, OR 97401

www.wipfandstock.com

ISBN 13: 978-1-60608-157-0

Cataloguing-in-Publication data:

Balisky, E. Paul

   Wolaitta evangelists : a study of religious innovation in southern Ethiopia, 1937–1975 / E. Paul Balisky

   xx + 390 p. ; 23 cm. Includes bibliographical references and index.

   American Society of Missiology Monograph Series 6

   ISBN 13: 978-1-60608-157-0

   1. Missions—Ethiopia. 2. Ethiopia—Church history. I. Title. II. Series.

BV3560 .B35 2009

Manufactured in the U.S.A.

Contents

List of Figures and Photographs

List of Maps

Foreword

ANYONE WITH A NODDING interest in Ethiopia will at once associate the country with the Ethiopian Orthodox Church, a venerable institution tracing its roots back to a micro-calamity that took place some seventeen centuries ago. Accompanying their uncle Meropius on a voyage that was to have taken them from Tyre to India, two young Syrian brothers were the only survivors of a massacre that took the lives of all hands on board—retaliation for the crew's miscreant behavior at an Ethiopian Red Sea port where the ship had stopped the day before to take on fresh water. Frumentius and Aedesius were taken to Aksum, where they became tutors to Prince 'Ezānā, first-born son of Emperor 'Ellä-'Améda. They could not have been aware that their protégé was destined to become the Aksumite Empire's greatest ruler and its first Christian emperor. Frumentius was subsequently consecrated bishop by Athanasius, then patriarch of Alexandria.

From then and on to the present time, the heartlands of Ethiopia would remain adamantly and profoundly Christian, despite relentless, at times severe, pressure by Muslim invaders who succeeded in obliterating all traces of Nubian Christianity. The first four centuries of the Ethiopian church were marked by an impressive scholarly productivity that included the translation of the Bible into Ge'ez. For the next eight hundred years (700–1500), the country was effectively cut off from the rest of the world. Academic speculation tends to the view that it was during this period that the Church's theology and practice became suffused with the distinctively Hebraic and monastic traditions that continue to distinguish it from all other Christian traditions. Today, as the official religion of the only country to successfully resist nineteenth century European colonization of the continent, the Orthodox Church continues to be inseparable from ethnocentric self-definition, particularly among highland Ethiopians.

Unfortunately, while surviving Ahmed Gran's religiously driven campaign of religious and cultural genocide in the mid-sixteenth century, the Orthodox Church suffered enormous losses, particularly throughout the

South. Thousands of its churches were destroyed and, with them a vast millennium-old accumulation of liturgical and historical vellum manuscripts. Confronted with the stark alternatives of conversion or decapitation, a majority opted to keep their heads.

It was only toward the end of the nineteenth century that faltering efforts were mounted by the Orthodox Church to recoup its losses. These attempts were only partially successful, however. For despite its longevity, and possibly because of its close ties with Ethiopian imperial power— at times brutally imposed on subject peoples—Orthodoxy was less than welcome, even in parts of the country not directly affected by the Muslim Armageddon. For many southerners, religious Orthodoxy and imperial oppression were inseparable, since conversion to Orthodoxy was often both legislated and coerced. Among these large populations of unwilling converts were culturally, religiously, and linguistically distinctive peoples in Harerge, Bale, Sidamo, Gamo Gofa, Kefa, Ilubabor, and Welega provinces. Difficult to pacify and on the margins of mainstream Ethiopian cultural and political life, these peoples became the imperially sanctioned province of foreign missionaries from the West, through whom, it was hoped, pax Ethiopiana could be attained throughout greater Ethiopia. Pacification would come by means of missionary education and medicine, offered in Amharic, the lingua franca of the country's political and religious power.

Roman Catholic and Anglican missionaries arrived in the mid-nineteenth century, cooperation with the Orthodox Church in Tigre as their modus operandi. By 1935, eight Protestant mission agencies—some denominational, others non-denominational, most of them evangelical—were at work in southern Ethiopia: the Sudan Interior Mission (SIM), the Bible Churchmen's Missionary Society (BCMS), the Seventh Day Adventists (SDA), the United Presbyterian Mission of the USA, the Church Mission to the Jews, Evangeliska Fosterlands—Stiftelsen (EFS—Sweden), Bibeltreue Freunde (until 1911, part of EFS), and Hermannsburger Missionsanstalt. These were forced to suspend operations when the Italians briefly (1935– 1941) but brutally occupied the country during the Second World War. Following the war, and to their great surprise, missionaries returned to discover communities of evangelical faith that had not only survived but flourished in their absence. Between 1950 and 1975 these agencies were joined by numerous others, variously engaged in evangelism, education, and community development.

Today the largest Protestant denomination in the country is the Word of Life Evangelical Church (Kale Heywet), related to the SIM. While other significant Protestant churches in Ethiopia include the Evangelical Church Mekane Yesus (Lutheran), the Seventh Day Adventists, and a number of dynamic groups tracing their roots to missionaries from the Reformed, Baptist, and Pentecostal/Full Gospel tradition, this book is about the Kale Heywet Church. More narrowly, but significantly, it is about the largest and arguably the most dynamic of its many culturally delineated branches, the Wolaitta Kale Heywet Church, without whose hundreds of dedicated evangelists the astounding growth of Christianity throughout the South would be inconceivable.

While there is some awareness that the number of evangelical churches in Ethiopia has increased exponentially over the last fifty years, less well known are the Ethiopian missionaries (evangelists) and their mission-minded congregations whose dedication, perseverance, and sanctified ingenuity gave rise to the statistics. This is both regrettable and potentially fatal, since, as American poet laureate Robert Pinsky reminded readers in the October 1999 issue of *Atlantic Monthly*, "a people is defined and unified not by blood but by shared memory, [and] deciding to remember, and what to remember, is how we decide who we are."

Paul Balisky has here produced an exemplary study of one of the twentieth century's most dynamically missionary churches. It is a book that could have been written only by someone steeped in the culture, the language, and the church. Balisky's unlabored and appreciative familiarity with the work and accomplishments of some three hundred evangelists and their families who left their homes to carry the gospel throughout southern Ethiopia, transforming the region into one of the most Christian regions in the world, makes this book a rarity in the annals of African church history. Rich in detail and replete with information available only to an insider, the book is a model of historical, religious, and cultural investigation and interpretation. It is the work of a mature scholar, but by no means one of the all-too-common ivory tower variety. Paul Balisky and his wife, Lila, spent nearly forty years in Ethiopia, their lives intimately intertwined with the people and the churches that constitute the book's subject matter. Supplemented by numerous maps, figures, photographs, a glossary, and five appendices, this book is a model for hundreds, even thousands of stories across Africa that remain to be chronicled and shared with the larger Christian church.

One hope is that this book will be a kind of first-fruit, a model that will be emulated elsewhere in Ethiopia and across the African continent, where, it is clear, Christianity has found a home.

Jonathan J. Bonk
Director of Overseas Ministries Study Center
New Haven, CT
April 14, 2009

Acknowledgments

THIS THESIS HAS COME to fruition through the labors of others. It was through the commitment and dedication of the Wolaitta evangelists, their wives and their children, that the seed of the Gospel was sown through much of Southern Ethiopia. I am grateful to many of them who spent hours telling me their inspiring stories.

And I want to thank the SIM pioneers in Ethiopia who wrote their stories into the lives of many Ethiopians by persuasive teaching and loving deeds of kindness. Theirs is truly the "story behind the story." I am grateful for the 61 SIM colleagues who provided extensive information through letters, interviews, and personal correspondence.

I would like to thank my SIM colleagues in Ethiopia who willingly took on extra work responsibilities during my several study leaves from Ethiopia. Bruce Adams, Bruce Bond, Tim Fellows, Steve Strauss, and Tim Jacobson deserve special mention. And Brian Fargher inspired me through the example in his career of disciplined and scholarly writing.

My study at the Centre for the Study of Christianity in the Non-Western World (initially at the University of Aberdeen, then at Edinburgh) was partially sponsored by financial assistance from SIM International. For this affirmation, I thank Ian Hay, our former SIM International General Director, as well as the SIM Office in Canada. I am also grateful for the support of many friends and churches—McLaurin Baptist in Grande Prairie, Alberta; Delbrook Baptist in North Vancouver, British Columbia; Westminster Chapel in Seattle, Washington; and Colonial Church in Minneapolis, Minnesota—for their encouragement and commitment to recording the development of the church in southern Ethiopia. For the friendship and fellowship of Newhills Parish Church near Aberdeen and of Bellevue Chapel, Edinburgh, I am grateful. Also to the SIM archival staff personnel, Marge Koop and Betty Harrison, who served me so skillfully at SIM Toronto, ON, and to Tim Geysbeek and staff at SIM International Archives, Charlotte, NC, I extend my thanks.

It is difficult for me to single out Wolaitta Kale Heywet Church leaders and personnel for special thanks because nearly 100 people contributed oral and documentary information for this research project. Three deserve special mention from during the late 1980s: Markina Mäja endured three months of freezing Scottish weather writing his memoirs in the New College library, and Wolaitta church leaders Desalegn Enaro and Waja Kabato generously assisted in providing informants and helpful counsel. Also, in 2008, Eyob Denio, Séta Wotango, and Mälkamu Shanqo provided me with current information on the status of Wolaitta evangelists serving beyond the borders of Ethiopia.

Woyita Woza spent over seven months in Kamba, Gämo Gofa, transcribing Wolaitta taped interviews within the secure confines of our Landcruiser during the difficult years of the *dergue* when there was limited religious freedom in Ethiopia. I am grateful to him.

Family members deserve special thanks. Sons Allen, Loren, and Kevin willingly shifted from their high school in Kenya to Aberdeen, Scotland, in 1985 and patiently taught their father the wonders of the computer during their evening hours. And my heartfelt thanks to Lila, my wife, for listening enthusiastically to many historical discoveries and evangelists' stories, and for tough love in telling me to quit researching and get to writing. Her affirmation, support, and skillful editing through this long process have been immeasurable.

Those associated with Wipf and Stock Publishers deserve special thanks for bringing further readability and order to this work; each individual I have corresponded with has been very cordial and professional.

Professor Andrew Walls not only served as my mentor but indeed was the "hound of heaven" who kindly and persistently drew the many strands of the Wolaitta evangelists' story into a coherent, glorious history. I am deeply indebted to him for his patient professional guidance through this pilgrimage.

Undergirding all other acknowledgements, I thank God for his enabling and the privilege of serving in Ethiopia for nearly forty years.

Introduction

IN DECEMBER, 1927 THE Sudan Interior Mission,[1] under the leadership of Dr. Thomas Lambie, arrived in Addis Ababa in response to "our call to the regions beyond . . . where Christ has never been preached."[2] After a decade of missionary activity in southern Ethiopia, the SIM personnel were evicted by the invading Italian army. From less than 100 baptized believers in 1936, this religious movement exceeded several thousand by 1945, when SIM missionaries were allowed to return to the South.

During the past thirty years three serious studies on the emergence of the Kale Heywet Church in Southern Ethiopia have been undertaken by SIM personnel. Each writer has told his story well, attempting to explain why there was rapid growth during the Italian occupation (1936–1941) and subsequent years. The reasons put forward are as follows:

Raymond Davis in *Fire on the Mountains* writes, "The phenomenal growth of the church and the effectiveness of the Gospel in Wallamo can only be attributed to the work of the Holy Spirit."[3] He then continues in the preface, "At the same time, however, there are factors that we can discover. We owe it to God, the church, and the world to investigate the means God used in Wallamo."[4] At the conclusion of the book, eight significant "means" or reasons why the Wolaitta responded to evangelical Christianity are suggested.[5] However, following the advice of Ethiopianist

1. The Sudan Interior Mission was founded in 1893 by three Canadians with the purpose of evangelizing those residing in the hinterland of Africa, north of the equator, known then as the "Great Sudan." After 1980 the Sudan Interior Mission changed its name to SIM (Society for International Ministries), and after 2001 SIM was legally registered as "Serving in Mission." Throughout this study, the abbreviation "SIM" will be used.

2. Quoted in Cotterell, *Born at Midnight*, 17.

3. Davis, *Fire on the Mountains*, 9.

4. Ibid.

5. Ibid., 240–49. Davis was challenged by J. B. Toews in 1959 to try to uncover the reason(s) the Wolaitta people experienced such a turning. See Toews, "Excerpts." Reflecting on the factors contributing to a mass movement toward Christianity in

scholar Donald Crummey,[6] a much broader investigation, taking into account the historical, political, religious, and socioeconomic situation of southern Ethiopia, must be undertaken if we are to adequately understand the "means" God used in Wolaitta.

Peter Cotterell in *Born at Midnight*[7] outlines three strands that answer for him "Why the unusual growth?" He states, first of all, there were cultural reasons. The gospel spread through peoples of similar culture and similar language. Second, the early missionaries adhered to uncompromising indigenous principles.[8] And third, there was the removal of the missionaries at a unique time. The clue that assists Cotterell in understanding this unique growth is that the gospel spread mainly in a linguistically homogeneous triangle from Hosanna in Kambatta/Hadiya, west to Soddo in Wolaitta, and south to Homacho, in Sidama.[9]

Brian Fargher's Ph.D. thesis, "Origins of New Churches Movement of Southern Ethiopia, 1927–1944,"[10] describes the process in which SIM missionaries penetrated Southern Ethiopia and were given the opportunity to "fill the religious vacuum in the South."[11] The focus of his research is, by and large, on the expatriate missionary who acts as a catalyst or, to use his image, as a "choir leader." We are not told with any degree of satisfaction what this "religious vacuum in the South" really was and why the Ethiopian Orthodox Church or the Muslim faith could not fill this vacuum. Fargher very carefully and meticulously describes how the "new

---

Wolaitta, Professor A. F. Walls comments, "It is as if God sometimes removes the blocks which appear to prevent a person or a group from hearing the Gospel, or at least from considering response to it an open option. Was the Italian occupation of Ethiopia, and the subsequent resistance, for instance, a factor in the remarkable story told by R. J. Davis in *Fire on the Mountains?*" "Recent Literature," 222.

6. Crummey says the Wolaitta religious response "must surely, have been a resistance movement against the Italian occupation." "Review of *Fire on the Mountains*," 156.

7. See also his seminal articles "An Indigenous Church in Southern Ethiopia" and "The Case for Ethiopia." Cotterell states, "The two primary factors involved in the growth of the church in southern Ethiopia are indigeneity and the involvement of the masses in the church." "Case for Ethiopia," 22.

8. The early SIM pioneers in Ethiopia were influenced by Roland Allen's writings, as Malcolm Forsberg comments in *Land beyond the Nile*, 63.

9. See also Cotterell, "The Case for Ethiopia," 12–23, where, among other reasons, he discusses the "remarkable cultural homogeneity" (16) of the ethnic groups within this triangle.

10. Recently Fargher's thesis has been published: *The Origins of the New Churches Movement in Southern Ethiopia, 1927–1944*, Leiden: Brill, 1996.

11. Fargher, "Origins of New Churches Movement," 995.

churches" were established in southern Ethiopia from 1927 to 1944 under the tutelage of SIM missionaries. The reasons why the Wolaitta accepted the gospel of Jesus and were motivated to proclaim it to others were beyond the parameters of his study.

The Wolaitta evangelists announced their new found faith enthusiastically, not only to those of their own Omotic language group but also to surrounding ethnic peoples in southern Ethiopia, because they discovered that Jesus Christ was their King—their divine king. It was the worship of Christ within their newly established communities that brought hope and meaning to their disorganized society.

This disorganization had resulted after King Menelik II and his armies conquered Wolaitta in 1894. King Tona was humiliated and eventually retained in Addis Ababa and given the Amhara title "*Balabat* of Wolaitta." This struck a devastating blow to the psyche and thinking of the Wolaitta, who perceived *Kawo* Tona as their divine king, the mediator of *Tosa*, the Wolaitta high god. *Tosa* is the one who fed, nurtured, and cared for not only the Wolaitta people but creation: the forest, the crops, the animals, and the birds. The Wolaitta were disgraced and subjugated by their colonizers, who called themselves Orthodox Christians. Consequently the demoralized Wolaitta found little attraction to Orthodox Christianity. How could they accept the religion of those who had decimated and carried off captive their kith and kin? Officially the Abyssinian Christians did not condone slavery, but they allowed the prestigious Wolaitta Malla and Tigre clans to unashamedly sell off their Wolaitta clansmen to Arab slave traders.[12] "We are poor and miserable"[13] was the lament of the Wolaitta, who were longing for salvation and deliverance.

Ésa, a prophet from the southern province of Gämo, brought hope when he called the people to repentance in the 1920s. In Wolaitta, entire families would go to an open field and worship the Creator God, *Tosa*. While the head of the family would flick pure white honey into the sky as an offering to *Tosa*, together they would recite the Decalogue and repent of past sins done against others and of their practice of sorcery and divination. Ésa had a profound influence upon the Wolaitta by expanding their

12. Bogalä Wälalu, *YäWolamo Hizb*, 49, 50. Bogalä writes as an insider of the cruel conditions of slavery inflicted by *Lij* Iyasu (reigned 1913–1916), grandson of Menilek II, in Wolaitta and southern Ethiopia.

13. Chiatti, "The Politics of Divine Kingship," 340. See also Werner J. Lange: "The economic exploitation, political subjugation, and cultural humiliation subsequent to Menilek's conquest had remained fresh in the consciousness of the Kafa people." *Domination and Resistance*, 50.

cosmology.[14] They began to leave off the worship of their deities and ancestor spirits to worship the high God, *Tosa*.

The Wolaitta were thus prepared by Ésa for the coming of the expatriate evangelists—both the Capuchin Catholics and SIM evangelicals. They introduced Bible portions in the Wolaitta vernacular. But an even more significant introduction by expatriate evangelists to the Wolaitta was the person of Jesus Christ. The Wolaitta discovered his authority and power over the minor deities that were disturbing them. They were given an opportunity to be released from fear.

The Wolaitta experienced changes that brought vitality and a wholeness into their newly formed *amanyoch* (believers) communities. In gratitude they sang this song of praise to their divine king, Jesus:

> You have exalted those who were in a poor lowly state;
> You brought low those who were proud,
> And destroyed the work of the evil one.
> You opened the eyes of the blind,
> Straightened the humped back child,
> Made the ignorant wise,
> And now the poor man has become rich.[15]

The Wolaitta evangelists crossed mountain ranges and forded rivers, preaching and teaching. Why they went and what they did is the story that will be told.

We conclude this section by affirming that this research has not been undertaken merely to satisfy our curiosity of how the Wolaitta evangelists went about their missionary enterprise. In another context David Bosch reminds us that studies of this nature are done primarily with a view to gaining deeper insight into what mission might mean for us today. After all, every attempt at interpreting the past is indirectly an attempt at understanding the present and the future.[16]

It is the aim of this study that, in the process of probing the Wolaitta Christian past, we may be challenged to explore new concepts for mission within Ethiopia.

---

14. Robin Horton relates the effect of the prophetic leader Kinjikitile in German East Africa during 1905–1907 in expanding the cosmology of some twenty ethnic groups who previously operated within "fairly strongly bounded microcosms, with a religious life correspondingly focused on the lesser spirits rather than on the supreme being." "Rationality of Conversion," 230.

15. EPB collection: Early Wolaitta Hymns, *Oh Why Do You Ignore?*

16. Bosch, *Transforming Mission*, 183.

Abbreviations

AAU	Addis Ababa University
AFM	Abyssinia Frontiers Mission
EC	Ethiopian Calendar (follows the Julian calendar)
EECMY	Ethiopian Evangelical Church Mekane Yesus
EPB	Paul Balisky Collection: personal letters, newsletters, reports, documents, and transcriptions of taped interviews
EOC	Ethiopian Orthodox Church
IAMS	International Association for Mission Studies
IES	Institute of Ethiopian Studies (Addis Ababa)
JES	*Journal of Ethiopian Studies*
KHC	Ethiopian Kale Heywet Church
MAF	Missionary Aviation Fellowship
SIM	Serving in Mission (formerly Sudan Interior Mission)
SIM Ar	SIM Archives
WBP	Wolaitta Bible Project
WKHC	Wolaitta Kale Heywet Church

Orthography

VOWELS:

The seven different vowel sounds that may be attached to an Ethiopic *fidel* are represented and pronounced as follows:

1st form:	ä	as in "bed"
2nd form:	u	as in "too"
3rd form:	e	as in "bead"
4th form:	a	as in "sod"
5th form:	é	as in "state"
6th form:	i	as in "his"
7th form:	o	as in "cone"

The following equivalents for the five explosives in Ethiopic and Amharic have been used:

q = the explosive form of "k"

t̠ = the explosive form of "t"

p = the explosive form of "p" (No special symbol has been used for the letter "p" because it only occurs here in its explosive form.)

s̠ = the explosive form of "s"

c̠h = the explosive form of "ch"

Historical Background of Southern Ethiopia and the Emergence of the Wolaitta Kingdom

"The establishment of Christianity cannot be studied in isolation:
it must be viewed in the whole context of events."[1]

Introduction

THIS CHAPTER WILL ATTEMPT to uncover the distant past of Wolaitta. In order to provide a historical background, first, there will be a brief account of the planting of Christianity in Aksum and the southward movement of Christianity to the present geographic position of Wolaitta. The rich hagiographical material describing the activities of Ethiopian Church evangelists of the fourteenth and fifteenth centuries will be referred to. There are also the Ethiopian Royal Chronicles, which relate the story of the Solomonic kings and their military exploits in southern Ethiopia against the Muslim kingdoms that bordered on Wolaitta.

Second, there will be an exploration of the questions about northern Damot and southern Wolaitta that bear on this thesis. European historians, travelers, missionaries, and contemporary Ethiopian scholars have contributed useful written documents and maps that are helpful in the attempt to differentiate between the fourteenth century kingdom of Damot and the Wolaitta kingdom that began to structure itself in the middle of the seventeenth century.

Third, we will briefly survey the findings of several linguists with the intention of locating Wolaitta in a linguistic scheme for southern Ethiopia. And fourth, an outline sketching the rich oral tradition of the Wolaitta kings will enable us to gain an understanding of their historic past, mythology, and worldview. The chapter will conclude by identifying the many

1. Pirouet, *Black Evangelists*, 113.

Wolaitta clans and their place of origin, the diversity of which may provide us with a further clue to understanding the Wolaitta past.

The Advance of Ethiopian Christianity into Southern Ethiopia

According to the report of Rufinus, Christianity was introduced into the northern city state of Aksum (spelled "Axon" on map 1.1) in the fourth century by two Syrian youths, Frumentius and Aedesius.[2] It was through the evangelistic activities of the Syrian Church, specifically through the Nine Saints during the fifth and sixth centuries, that Christianity took root in the Aksumite kingdom.[3] These Syrian evangelists made a significant contribution to Bible translation, to church government and forms of worship, and to the evangelistic expansion of the Aksumite church.[4] One of the Nine Saints, Aregawi, preached in Debre Damo where a serpent was worshipped. Eventually a church was built on the site of the serpent shrine. As these sixth century evangelists moved into pagan territory, they encountered opposition, and some may have been martyred.[5]

In the tenth century the Christian kingdom of Abyssinia—roughly correlating to the present-day geographic area of Ethiopia—was besieged by a pagan queen from the South. An Arabic source records that shortly after 979 A.D. the king of Abyssinia wrote to the king of Nubia, George, asking for permission that his letter be sent on to the Coptic Patriarch Philotheos. The Abyssinian ruler was in dire straits because a queen of the Bani I-Hamuya was devastating his country, hunting him and his followers down like animals. The Christian population, including the clergy, were in danger of being wiped out.[6]

A contemporary Arabic writer of that time, Ibn Hawqal, also refers to a queen dominating sections of Abyssinia:

> As regards Abyssinia, for many years it has had a woman as its ruler. It is she who killed the king of Abyssinia who was known un-

2. As found in Sergew Hable Selassie, *Ancient and Medieval Ethiopian History*, 98–99. See also Kaplan, "Ezana's Conversion," 101–9, for the truly religious perspective of Ezana's conversion.

3. Sergew Hable Sellassie, *Ancient and Medieval Ethiopian History*, 115–21.

4. See also Balisky, "Expansion of the Ethiopian Orthodox Church," 9–19.

5. Sergew Hable Sellassie writes, "They suffered suppression and persecution." *Ancient and Medieval Ethiopian History*, 115 n. 1.

6. Budge, *Saints of the Ethiopian Church*, 1:233–34.

der the title of *hadani* (Ethiopian *hade*), and she continues to this day to dominate her own country and the neighboring regions of the land of the *hadani* in the west of Abyssinia. It is a vast limitless country, rendered difficult of access by deserts and wastes.[7]

Taddesse Tamrat, following others, suggests that this pagan queen was probably of Damot (Sidama)[8] origin.[9] Taddesse continues the discussion of this above-mentioned queen elsewhere, stating:

> The queen's territories are specifically located "in the southern part of Habasha," which fits in perfectly with the general pattern of development in the medieval history of Ethiopia.[10]

Francisco Alvarez, a Jesuit priest travelling through the northern (Amharic) kingdom of Shoa in the seventeenth century, recorded this rather fanciful account of a kingdom in the South once ruled and dominated by women.

> They say that at the end of these kingdoms of Damute and Guorage, towards the south, is the kingdom of the Amazons. . . . They have not got a king, but have a Queen; she is not married, nor has she any particular husband, but still she does not stop having sons and daughters, and her daughter is the heir to her kingdom. They say they are [very strong] women of a very warlike disposition, and they fight on [very swift animals that resemble] cows, and are great archers, and when they are little they dry up the left breast in order not to hinder drawing the arrow. They also say that there is an infinite amount of gold in this kingdom of the Amazons, and that it comes from this country to the kingdom of Damute, and so it goes to many parts. They say that the husbands of these women are not warriors, and that their wives excuse them from it. They say that a big river has its source in the kingdom of Damute, opposite to the Nile, because each one goes to its own direction, the Nile to Egypt, and as for this other no one of the country knows where it goes to, only it is presumed that it goes to Manicongo. They also say that they find much gold in this kingdom of Damute; I tell as I heard it.[11]

7. As found in Trimingham, *Islam in Ethiopia*, 52.

8. See glossary entry.

9. Taddesse, *Church and State*, 39. Also see Ullendorff, *Ethiopians*, 61.

10. Taddesse, "Ethiopia," 103.

11. Alvarez, *Prester John*, 455–57.

The geographic detail is worth noting. The "big river" mentioned must be the Gibe that flows into the Omo River.[12] Alvarez makes a distinction between this river and that of the Abbaye River, which he indicates is "opposite to the Nile," flowing to Egypt. And then there is the mention of gold.[13] One of the significant and outstanding gold fields of southern Ethiopia is located in the Kibre Menghist area, near Agär Sälam. Other rivers in western Ethiopia, such as the Baro and Didessa, are also sources of gold.

Another source of recorded history for southern Ethiopia are the chronicles of the southern military excursions of the Solomonic kings, beginning with Amdé Seyon (1312–1342). The chronicler of these military exploits lists such place names as Damot, Ganz, Hadiya, and Bali. From the *Glorious Victories of Amdé Seyon*,[14] one is able to gain further insights and knowledge about the Sidama region from which the cluster of Sidama aristocracies/kingdoms developed in succeeding centuries.[15]

The background to this fourteenth century chronicle is that the Muslim king of Ifat, Säbrädin, who formerly paid tribute to the Ethiopian Emperor Amdé Seyon, revolted in 1329 A.D. and took to the field against his former overlord. Säbrädin arrogantly challenged Amdé Seyon, saying, "I will be king over all the land of Ethiopia; I will rule the Christians according to my law, and I will destroy their churches."[16] Of the twenty-five provinces listed by the chronicler over which Säbrädin managed to establish his own governance, two were the southern provinces of Damot and Waj. And these former southern strongholds of paganism were at that time acknowledged as being Christian. This is why Amdé Seyon was so vexed and accused his enemy, saying:

12. Ibid., 457 n. 1.

13. "The reputation of Damot as a source of gold probably goes back to the sixth century at least, for the Adulis inscription seems to refer to this region." Crawford, *Ethiopian Itineraries*, 80.

14. Huntingford, *Glorious Victories*, 29–32, regarding "Place-names of the period." See also Beckingham et al., "Ethnology and History," liii, where the name "Wolamo" is mentioned in the fifteenth century hymn of Yeshaq. Could it be that this refers to the Gafat title of their ruler, Awolamo?

15. Some of these Sidama kingdoms were Jimma, Käfa, Conch, Gooma, Qucha, Wolaitta, Kambatta, Hadiya, Alaba, and Koyra. See Hassen, *Oromo of Ethiopia*, 84–113, for a historical development of the Gibe River kingdoms.

16. Huntingford, *Glorious Victories*, 54.

Of a truth, did you or did you not burn the churches of God and kill the Christians? And those who survived, did you make them turn to your religion, which is not as the religion of Christ, but (is) that of the Devil your father?[17]

There is also reference in the *Glorious Victories* to the conquest of the southern kingdom of Hadiya, around 1329 A.D. A false prophet had deceived king Amano of Hadiya, advising him to rebel against Amdé Ṣeyon. But King Amdé Ṣeyon, "strong like Samson, a great warrior like David, a conqueror in war and himself unconquered, rose up in anger, set out for the land of Hadya, slew the inhabitants of the country with the point of the sword."[18]

In the *Soldiers' Song in Honour of King Amdé Ṣeyon*,[19] the minstrel eulogizes Amdé Ṣeyon's ability to conquer the frontier outposts. The conquered kingdoms are mentioned with their kings. Reference is made to several Sidama kingdoms, such as: Waj, whose king was Zebedar; Hadiya, with its king Amano; and Damot, together with its notorious king Motolämi.[20] The song concludes with the refrain:

> Who is left for you at the frontier?
> Whose face have you not disfigured?
> Whose wife and child have you not captured?
> Hero, Amdé Ṣeyon
> To and from the frontier.[21]

In 1520 A.D. Emperor Läbna Dängal wrote to the Portuguese asking for their assistance to help stave off the devastating attacks of Ahmed Gragn, who was armed with Turkish matchlocks. The Portuguese, detained from coming for several years because of warring factions along the Red

---

17. Ibid., 56.

18. Ibid., 58. The present day administrative center of Kambatta/Hadiya *awraja* is Hosanna, 325 km. southwest of Addis Ababa. See also Huntingford, *Glorious Victories*, 132, where Hadiya and Gudéla are mentioned together in a *Soldiers Song*. To this day the people of the Hadiya administrative region will refer to themselves as "Gudéla." See also Cerulli, *Peoples of South-West Ethiopia*, 85, for a brief history of Hadiya; see 118 for comment on the name Gudéla.

19. Ibid., 129.

20. Ibid., 132–34. Huntingford suggests in his brief commentary on this song that *Mota Lami* is possibly derived from the Amharic *meta* "guard" and *lam* "cattle" and is thus a synonym for the title "guard of the cattle." This seems incredible, as it goes against the tenor of this song, which accepts as fact that these were actual names of defeated kings.

21. Ibid., 128–29.

Sea coast, were unable to use the port of Massawa and were delayed. Läbna Dängal asks in his letter: "Why were you not able to come by sea by way of Damot, rather than to Massawa?"[22] It would seem from the Emperor's question that he is referring to the southern section of the country, Damot, which extended far to the south and possibly as far east as the Red Sea.

The next sources of information about medieval Southern Ethiopia are the hagiographies of several evangelists of the Ethiopian Church. Täklä-Haymanot (1213–1312 A.D.) is one of the better known evangelists of this period. His biography was compiled by his disciples based in the monastic center of Däbra Libanos.[23] He was born in Shoa province to devout Christians. His *gadla* (biography) suggests that even before his birth he was destined to become the spiritual antagonist of Motolämi, the pagan king of the southern province, Damot.[24] As a young lad, Täklä-Haymanot was commissioned and empowered by the angel Mikaél "to catch many souls . . . given power to heal the sick, and to drive out unclean spirits in all the world."[25]

The hagiographers of the Däbra Libanos version list the various countries and localities of Täklä-Haymanot's spiritual activities during his ninety-nine years. Damot, one of the nine countries named, is where he spent twelve years engaged in spiritual battle against diviners, magicians, and the wicked machinations of King Motolämi. Eventually the forces of evil in Damot were overcome by the preaching and miracles of Täklä-Haymanot. Finally King Motolämi himself became a Christian,[26] and churches were built throughout his kingdom. It is not clear to what extent and depth northern Christianity penetrated the belief systems of the Damot kingdom at that time in history, but we are told that churches were built and the Christian rites of baptism were administered.[27]

In the *Life of St. Anoréwos*, which was written in 1478, it is recorded that St. Anoréwos, a disciple of Täklä-Haymanot, was exiled from Däbra

---

22. As quoted in C. F. Beckingham, "Achievements of Prester John," 23.

23. Budge, *Takle Haymanote*, 28.

24. Ibid., 29–30. On a raiding expedition into Shoa, Motolämi captured Täklä Haymanot's mother before she was wed to Zaga Za'ab, a young man from a family of priests. The mother was miraculously rescued from the evil clutches of Motolämi and returned back to her betrothed, Zaga Za'ab.

25. Budge, *Saints of the Ethiopian Church*, 1242.

26. Budge, *Täklä Haymanote*, 361.

27. Ibid., 110, 133.

Libanos to the South.[28] He first went to Zway, then travelled further south to Gämo. It is noted in this biography that Gämo is on the extreme south of the Damot territory. Anoréwos, along with others, played a significant part in spreading Christianity in the entire region south of the Awash River. It is recorded that he built a large monastery somewhere in the province of Damot at a place where pagans worshipped and held religious ceremonies.[29]

Another disciple of Täklä-Haymanot was *Abba* Zena Marqos.[30] Like his master, he was born to a Christian family of Shoa. He rejected marriage to become a missionary and evangelist and was the first missionary to Guragé and to the area north and northwest of Lake Zway. According to his biography, *Abba* Zena Marqos found the people of Guragéland worshipping their idol Gärdan, who was believed to bring rain. He destroyed the idol and was protected by an angel of God from the subsequent anger of the Guragé. Because of this rather evident supernatural intervention and protection, the Guragé accepted the Christian faith.[31]

Historical Reports and Comments by Europeans and Ethiopian Scholars about Southern Ethiopia

The Venetian geographer, Zorzi (writing in 1523 A.D.), recorded information from a certain Portuguese Franciscan Brother Thomas who had completed a journey from the southern Shoan highlands to Jerusalem around 1520 A.D.[32] Zorzi's maps and information are helpful to us because southern Ethiopian kingdoms, rivers, and lakes are identified with some degree of accuracy. He refers to a large province called *Ulamo* (in subsequent years referred to as Wolamo, now as Wolaitta), commenting that it "is very great and goes . . . to the sea, but he knows not its size."[33]

28. As cited in Chiatti, "Politics of Divine Kingship," 53. This exile probably took place during the reign of Amdé Şeyon. The clergy at Däbra Libanos strongly protested his second marriage; as a consequence, Amdé Şeyon took punitive action against the clergy.

29. *Life of Anoréwos,* as quoted in Taddesse, "Traditions of Pagan Resistance," 140.

30. Budge, *Täklä Haymanote,* 80.

31. As cited in Kaplan, *Monastic Holy Man,* 92.

32. As compiled in Crawford, *Ethiopian Itineraries.*

33. Ibid., 187.

Fig. 20. Names mentioned by Zorzi on ff. 48 to 58ᵛ. and in Iters V, VII and VIII.

Reprinted from O.G.S. Crawford, *Ethiopian Itineraries 1400-1524*, Hakluyt Society, 1958, opposite p.9

He describes the Wolamo as "Ethiopians with curly hair, idolaters . . . ."[34] In other words, by the sixteenth century they had not yet been Christianized. In the same document he refers to another distinct area called "Damot, a very great province where the climate is very hot and torrid because of being under Capricorn; which province was rich in very fine gold."[35] A traveling companion of Brother Thomas was Brother Antonio, a Dominican monk, a native of Damot, "who is very black with a long beard and long hair, and beautiful face."

34. Ibid.
35. Ibid., 149.

He was born in this province of Damot, where he says it is very hot from being under Capricorn. The said brother says that in the province of Naria [Inarea] they are of an olive color and have bigger noses than others.[36]

According to the map sketched by Zorzi and his detailed narrative, some of which is quoted above, the countries of Damot and *Ulamo* were separated by two kingdoms, *Naria* and *Sicondi*.[37]

Zorzi's map is significant to our study for several reasons: First, a country by the name of *Ulamo* (Wolamo) is accurately located on the western edge of the Rift Valley escarpment and south of the Guragé. Zorzi includes a notation beside the Rift Valley lakes: "A very great lake of sweet water with a church of St. George." It would seem that he is referring specifically to Lake Zway because by the sixteenth century there were several Orthodox churches and a monastery located on the Zway Islands.[38]

Mention has already been made of Francisco Alvarez's vivid description of the "Amazon inhabitants of the South." Alvarez paints this picture of sixteenth century Damot, just prior to the Galla invasions.

> To the west of the kingdom of Xoa, there is a big country and kingdom which is called Damute. The slaves of this kingdom are much esteemed by the Moors, and they do not let them go at any price; all the country of Arabia, Persia, India, Egypt, and Greece, are full of slaves from this country, and they say they make very good Moors and great warriors. These are pagans, and among them in this kingdom are many Christians.[39]

Alvarez makes no mention of Wolamo or Wolaitta but comments on Gämo, mentioning that "they are pagans, little valued as slaves; they have no king, only chiefs who rule separately."[40] We will note that he describes "Damute" lying "to the west of the kingdom of Xoa."

Manoel de Almeida, who in 1624 arrived in Ethiopia,[41] described in detail the travels and experiences of Jesuit Father Antonio Fernandez

36. Ibid., 177.

37. Ibid., 187. This may be an indication of the prelude to the ultimate demise of the expansive Damot kingdom and the proliferation of the Sidama kingdoms.

38. Taddesse, *Church and State*, 189 n. 3, makes mention of Abba Sinoda, founder of a monastery in Gojam, who attended a monastic school at Lake Zway by the end of the fourteenth century. There is no evidence of pre-Menilek Orthodox churches on the shores of Lake Abbaye, located one hundred kilometers south of Lake Zway.

39. Alvarez, *Prester John*, 455.

40. Ibid., 454.

41. Ullendorff, *Ethiopians*, 6.

in the province of Damot. At that time, the former domain of Damot
was called Enarea, and was described as "the most southerly of all those in
this empire."[42] Fernandez had heard reports that this kingdom was much
larger in former days; Almeida records Fernandez's assessment that "this
kingdom is not as big as some have said."[43] The priest and his companions
continued their journey south to Janjäro, and after a precarious crossing
of the Gibe (he called it *Zebee*) River, they had an amiable audience with
the king of Janjäro (his spelling, *Gingiro*). In the neighboring kingdom of
Kambatta they were not so favorably treated because the court of Kambatta
was suspicious "that they were going for no other purpose than to fetch
Portuguese troops who would take possession of the Empire of Ethiopia
and force them to change their faith."[44]

LUDOLF'S MAP OF ABYSSINIA, 1683

Showing Damot south of the Abbaye River
Reprinted from W. Foster (tr. and ed.), *The Red Sea and
Adjacent Countries at the Close of the Seventeenth
Century*, London, 1949, opposite p.184.

42. Almeida, "History of High Ethiopia," 164.
43. Ibid.
44. Ibid.

The travelers continued their journey by way of Alaba and "through the inhospitable country of the Galla." Wolamo or Wolaitta is not mentioned. This may be an indication that in the early seventeenth century Wolaitta had not as yet emerged as an independent power.

Ludolf's 1683 map of Abyssinia, assisted by the Ethiopian scholar, Gregory, is included because it locates both Damot and Gafat south of the River Abai, or Blue Nile.[45] The country south of Inarya identified as Zen may be the kingdom of Janjäro. The present-day location of Kambatta is southwest of Guragé, not southeast as shown on the map. Neither *Ulamo* nor Wolamo (as on Zorzi's map above) is not included on Ludolf's map.

In 1696, Englishman Michael Geddes compiled a *Church History of Ethiopia*. He described the area south of Lake Täna not as Damot but as Inarea:

> Narea is the most Southern Country of Ethiopia, and is about thirty or forty leagues in compass; its inhabitants are reckoned to be the best and honestest of people in the whole Habassin Empire; they are well shaped, and not very black, and have thin lips and long noses; the country is fertile and populous, and its chief trade is in slaves. . . . They were first converted to Christianity by Malac Saged, to which they had always been well disposed.[46]

Geddes no doubt compiled his *History* from a source document written much earlier. The local population of Inarea had not yet been decimated by the Galla. But he does indicate that the Janjäro (he refers to them as *Gingiro*) had already established their kingdom as had the Kambattan.[47] It is significant that Geddes makes no mention of the Wolamo. It could well be that Wolamo at that time was under the suzerainty of the kingdom of Konta, located just north of the Omo River and south of the Gojeb River.[48]

From 1839 to 1842, missionaries Isenberg and Krapf of the Church Missionary Society were based in Shoa province. Through information

---

45. Ludolf, *New History of Ethiopia*, map.

46. Geddes, *Church History of Ethiopia*, 294. It could be that Geddes was not aware that "King Saged" could have been any one of five kings who reigned between 1294 and 1299 A.D. within the newly established Solomonic dynasty. It is significant that this was the period in which Täklä Haymanot was involved in evangelistic endeavors among the Damot. See also Taddesse, *Church and State*, 120, 121, 176–82.

47. Geddes, *Church History of Ethiopia*, 296.

48. See Mohammed Hassen, "Oromo of Ethiopia," 391, where he says the Wolaitta state "was founded sometime between 1650 and 1700, centered around Kendo."

gleaned from informants, they recorded the history and geography of much of Ethiopia. The traditions of the conversion of Damot ruler Motolämi by the preaching of Täklä Haymanot were known to the people of Shoa. By 1840, the population of Damot had fled their homelands in what is now known as Wälläga, going north across the Abaye River, and were residing south of Lake Tana. Isenberg and Krapf explain the reason for this:

> Formerly the province of Damot extended across the Nile south-ward to the confines of Enarea; But since the conquests by the Galla, Damot is now confined to the north bank of the Nile.[49]

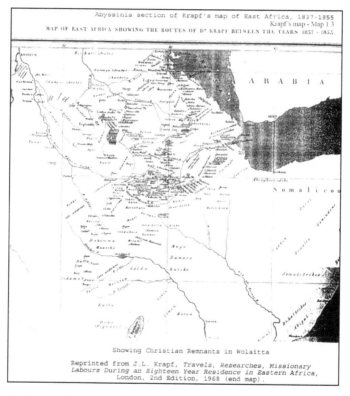

Reprinted from J.L. Krapf, *Travels, Researches, Missionary Labours During an Eighteen Year Residence in Eastern Africa*, London, 2nd Edition, 1968 (end map).

---

49. Isenberg and Krapf, *Journals*, 61. James Bruce also makes mention of Christian Käfa, Nariya, and Janjäro in his *Travels to Discover the Source of the Nile* (1790). Bruce did not personally visit the southern section of Ethiopia but was dependent on Ethiopian informants for his information. His references to Damot province place it north of the Blue Nile. See 3:533, 546, 549, 584. This would confirm that a section of the Damot population fled their homeland from the plains south of the Blue Nile River, away from the ravages of the Oromo, and settled farther north. It is feasible that some Damot fled south to Wolaitta, carrying the place-name Damot and the fourteenth century Motolämi and Täklä Haymanot tradition with them.

A Guragé priest, interviewed by Isenberg and Krapf in 1842 made no specific mention of the Kingdom of Wolamo. He stated that the populations of Inarea and Käfa were generally Christian but of late years had become "intermixed with Mohamedans and with pagans."[50]

Another informant told them that the currency of *Wolamo*, with the capital located at Wofamo, was salt[51] and that it once was a Christian nation but that now there were no resident priests. Circumcision was practiced and several church festivals were celebrated during the year. It was confirmed that the Omo River does flow through the country.[52] Isenberg and Krapf's 1843 map of Africa locates Damot south of Lake Tana but north of the Blue Nile. The southern Ethiopian kingdoms of Kambatta, Janjäro and Käfa were quite accurately placed. Though mentioned in the text, Wolamo is not shown on the map.

In concluding this section, we will look at two additional maps drawn by Charles Beke, a linguist and geographer functioning under the umbrella of the British Consulate located in Shoa. His research was conducted in southern Ethiopia from 1841 to 1843.[53] The maps he produced of central and southern Ethiopia in 1843 and 1844 are important because he confirms Isenberg and Krapf's description that the Damot and Gafat populations had shifted to the north bank of the Abbaye River. Beke travelled extensively in the Damot district from March 8 to April 8, 1842, and was impressed with the dense Damot forests, compared with Gojam to the north, which was nearly deforested because of overpopulation.[54]

Information for Beke's second map (p. 15) was obtained from a Muslim trader who had returned from a trading expedition in the vicinity of the Rift Valley lakes of Zway, Langano, and Abbaye.[55] As indicated on the map, "Countries South of Abyssinia," Beke collected additional oral

50. Ibid., 62.

51. Metal strips called *marchwa*, about two feet long, were also used as currency in Wolaitta in pre-Menilek times.

52. Isenberg and Krapf, *Journals*, 157–58.

53. The following three articles were written by Charles T. Beke subsequent to his Ethiopia tour from 1841 to 1843: "On the Countries South of Abyssinia," "Routes in Abyssinia," and "On the Languages and Dialects of Abyssinia and the Countries of the South." See also the reference to Beke's "reliable information about the Gibe region" in Mohammed Hassen, *Oromo of Ethiopia*, 84.

54. Beke, "Routes in Abyssinia," 15.

55. Beke writes, "I only regret this map is not fuller. . . . I succeeded in getting from him this hurried sketch." "Countries South of Abyssinia," 254.

information from Gojam traders who had traveled in the south country. On the map, Wolamo, or Wolaitza, is clearly located in approximately its present position, except it is placed north of the Gojeb River.[56] Apparently Beke's informants did not have a clear understanding of the location of the Omo River, or they may have confused it with the Gojeb River. The kingdom of Woranta is noted twice and probably refers to what was, until recently, known as the district of Boroda. Damot is placed as a village on the caravan road, north of the Käfa kingdom and east of Jimma. This would seem to indicate that when the people of Damot were forced to disperse from their homeland by the intruding Oromo, not all fled north. Some of the Damot population chose to move south, as is evidenced by this Damot village.

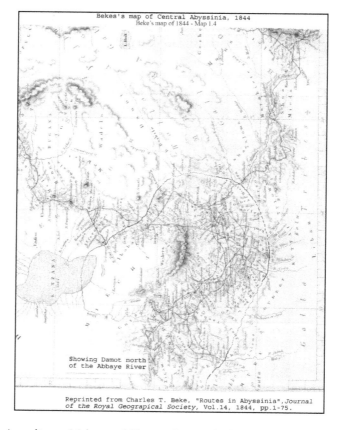

Bekes's map of Central Abyssinia, 1844
Beke's map of 1844 - Map 1.4

Showing Damot north
of the Abbaye River

Reprinted from Charles T. Beke, "Routes in Abyssinia", *Journal of the Royal Geograpical Society*, Vol.14, 1844, pp.1-75.

56. According to Mohammed Hassen, *Oromo of Ethiopia*, 28, a sizable population from Damot, known as the *Tsadacha* (the Religious or Holy Ones), migrated to the south, settling near the Gojeb River.

Beke learned from his informants:

> Respecting Wolaittza—this is the native name, Wolamo being
> the Galla designation—I have not been able to learn any par-
> ticulars, except that it is on the way to this country, and that not
> between Jimma and Kaffa, that the Gojeb is crossed in boats.[57]

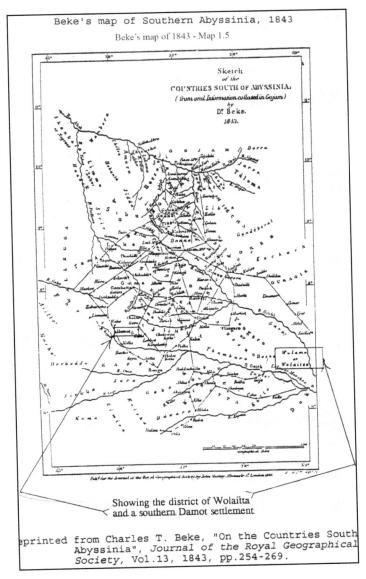

Beke's map of Southern Abyssinia, 1843

Beke's map of 1843 - Map 1.5

Showing the district of Wolaïtta
and a southern Damot settlement

Reprinted from Charles T. Beke, "On the Countries South
Abyssinia", *Journal of the Royal Geographical
Society*, Vol.13, 1843, pp.254-269.

57. Beke, "Countries South of Abyssinia," 262.

Beke correctly identifies what others called Wolamo with the name "Wolaitza."[58] Although not all names are placed in their recognized geographic locations, Beke's map is of value to us in locating Wolaitta north of what is identified as "lakes or marshes," which is no doubt the present-day Lake Abbaya.

The Geographic Location of Damot

On one side of the argument, the country of Damot may have been located deep in the South, adjacent to Lake Abbaye, one of the Rift Valley lakes. From the previous section it has been shown that written documents place fifteenth and sixteenth century Damot near the Abbaye River. It has also been pointed out from Beke's maps of 1843 and 1844 that Damot and Wolaitta were located in two distinct geographic areas; Damot situated north of the Abbaye River, Wolaitta located some 400 kilometers south in the Ethiopian Rift Valley. But on the other hand, there is contemporary oral tradition within Wolaitta that insists that Damot was located in the geographic area of present-day Wolaitta. The Wolaitta oral tradition is bolstered from three sources. First, the Täklä Haymanot *gadla* mentions rivers and place names presently found in Wolaitta. Mt. Damot towers over the city of Soddo, the administrative center of Wolaitta. Other names, as Abbaye, Bilaté, and Gärar, well known in Wolaitta, are names of places Täklä Haymanot visited in the fourteenth century.[59] Second, there is a commemorative plaque at Täklä Haymanot's grave at Däbra Libanos with this eulogy written in Amharic: "During his preaching ministry Täklä Haymanot evangelized Wolamo."[60] And third, the tradition linking Damot with Wolaitta has now become part of Ethiopia's written tradition. Emperor Menilek's chronicler, Gäbrä-Selassie, writes, "The land known as Wälamo was once ruled by a pagan called Motälami."[61] *Aläqa* Tayyä compiled an Ethiopian history at the request of Menilek II around 1910a Contemporary scholars acknowledge that *Aläqa* Tayyä's work includes tradition and chronological inaccuracies, but *Aläqa* Tayyä confirms that his information about "Damot of Wolamo" was accurate and substantiated because of historical documents found within the island churches

---

58. In 1974 the Ethiopian Government officially recognized that the name "Wolaitta" identifies both the language and the people of Wolaitta.

59. Budge, *Täklä Haymanot*, 355.

60. EPB, personal observation and translation from Amharic.

61. Gäbrä-Selassie, *Chronicles*, 218.

at Lake Zway.[62] Another contemporary written source confirming that Täklä Haymanot was the "Apostle to the Wolaitta country" is found in the Amharic-Amharic dictionary defining the word, *Echagé*. Author Kassate Berhan Tessema indicates that the title *Echagé* was given to Täklä-Haymanot by Motolämi because "*Abun* Täklä Haymanot converted the land [of Wolaitta] from paganism to Christianity."[63]

On the other side of the argument, two recent scholarly articles published in the *Journal of Ethiopian Studies* present strong evidence that the Damot kingdom of the thirteenth and fourteenth centuries was located in the upper regions of the Gibé River, just east of Shoa, not in Wolaitta, some 300 kilometers south. First we will look at the evidence that Taddesse Tamrat presents.[64] He argues that many of the place names mentioned in the Täklä-Haymanot hagiographies were in the kingdoms of Damot and Gafat country. For example, Bilat refers to both a mountain and a river just southeast of Däbra Libanos, present-day Shoa Méda, where Täklä-Haymanot engaged in bitter spiritual struggles with the pre-Christian religious leaders. Another argument presented by Taddesse Tamrat is that the name Awälamo," found in a praise song sung to the famous warrior King Amdä-Seyon (1314–1344), originally was the title of a Gafat political leader, not the political kingdom of Wolamo that King Tona eventually ruled in the late nineteenth century.

> From Gafat, Awälamo;
> From Damot, Mot Lami;
> Whom have you spared on the Border-land?
> Amdä-Seyon, the patriot,
> Restorer of the frontiers,
> Amdä-Seyon who spread his name,
> As far as Értra.[65]

At present, the name "Awälamo" has been altered slightly to "Wälawumo" and designates a small district on the banks of the Blue Nile River, directly north of Däbra Silalo. And another argument advanced by Taddesse Tamrat is that significant movements of the Gafat and Damot populations took place throughout much of Ethiopia during the Ahmad Gragn (1531–1543) conflict. This was soon followed by the movement

62. *Aläqa* Tayyä, *History*, 69.

63. Kassate, *Yamarinya Mazgaba Qalat*, 1012.

64. Taddesse, "The Case of the Gafat."

65. Ibid., 129.

of large numbers of Oromo from southeast Ethiopia to the central and northern highlands. It has been verified that certain clans from both the Gafat and Damot populations found refuge on the northern banks of the Abbaye River by the seventeenth century and have integrated with the local Gojam population.[66] And it would seem there was also a southern migration of the Gafat and Damot into localities further south such as Inarya, Käfa, and fertile Wolaitta. If that was the case, some of the place names like Damot in Wolaitta and Bilaté river (that serves as a dividing boundary between the Arsi and Wolaitta) could well have been transferred to the South by the eighteenth century.[67]

The second writer, Tsehai Berhane Selassie, after correlating oral information from Wolaitta sources and fourteenth century hagiographies concluded, "The fragments of evidence to link Wälamo with the historic Damot, St. Täklä-Haymanot, Zär'ä Ya'eqob, and Enarya provide us with only the makings of a legendary past."[68] Dr. Tsehai confirms that the Wolaitta oral tradition designates Motolämi as a king from the Wolaitta Malla dynasty. But this dynasty was acknowledged to be of local people, and their original place of ruling was on Kindo Mountain, on the southern banks of the Omo River. As stated above, this is some 400 kilometers south of Jebat and Mécha *awraja*, which seems to be the center of the historic Damot. Dr. Tsehai suggests the following reasons why there has been a linkage of the Wolaitta oral history with the fourteenth century Motolämi of Damot and evangelist Täklä-Haymanot. First, there was the propaganda tactic taken by Menilek II to identify the Wolaitta ruler, *Kawo* Tona with the pre-Christian Motolämi of Damot.[69] According to Menilek's chronicler, Gäbrä-Sellassie, Damot was once part of the Christian nation of Ethiopia, therefore it must be brought back to Ethiopian sovereignty again.[70] And, second, it was the Christian settlers within Wolaitta (Menilek's *näftänyoch*)

66. Ibid., 138–42.

67. Dawaro was one of the seven Islamic principalities located in eastern Ethiopia in the fourteenth and fifteenth centuries. Because of seventeenth and eighteenth century migrations of the Dawaro into Kullo Konta, a large district is now called "Dawro." See map in Trimingham, *Islam in Ethiopia,* 64. Bartels, "Studies of the Galla," 32, recounts why the Boräna Galla named a prominent mountain in Wälläga "Tullu Wallel," which means, "the mountain we forgot." In a similar manner, could it be that Mt. Damot in Wolaitta is reminiscent of an ancient tradition concerning the country of origin of some Damot population who migrated to Wolaitta?

68. Tsehai, " Question of Damot and Wälamo," 45.

69. This will be further developed in chapter 2.

70. Gäbrä-Sellassie, *Chronicles,* 218. Frenchman J. G. Wanderheym follows the same propagandist line of thought in *Une Expédition,* 180–81.

and their descendants who linked their own northern history to that of Wolaitta and have continued to transmit this prestigious folklore to their descendents.[71]

We conclude this section by acknowledging that the kingdom of Damot was extensive and that until the Ahmad Gragn wars of the sixteenth and seventeenth century Oromo invasion, Damot referred to the region immediately south of the Blue Nile and extended south to the kingdom of Inarya, as far east as the headwaters of the Awash river and maybe to the borders of Hadiya. During the expansion and contraction of the kingdom of Damot through the centuries, Damot Christians may have sought refuge as far south as Wolaitta. It could well be that a remnant of northern refugees from Damot took their place names with them to Wolaitta. The Damot oral tradition would have been kept alive in Wolaitta among the Damot Christians through their clergy. Succeeding generations in Wolaitta accepted a "symbolic history"[72] that gave them an identity with Damot.[73]

A Brief Linguistic Survey of Southern Ethiopia

Beke pioneered a linguistic map of southern Ethiopia. He collected extensive vocabularies of the Käfa, the Boroda (*Woratta*), Wolaitta (*Wolaitza*), and other ethnic groups of the Southland. He discovered a marked similarity between these languages and postulated that they were cognates of the Gonga languages still spoken in a portion of Damot, now located on the northern side of the Abbaye (Blue Nile) river. He, along with other ethnographers, was struggling with the historical connection of these various Sidama[74] ethnic groups and arrived at this conclusion:

71. Tsehai, "Question of Damot and Wälamo," 37. It has been stated above that some northerners may have migrated to Wolaitta in the seventeenth century. But Dr. Tsehai's point is still valid; post-Motolämi Christian settlers have been passing down their own folklore.

72. Tsehai, "Wolayta Conception of Inequality," uses the term "symbolic history" to represent functional stories, anecdotes, or myths in a historical sequence.

73. Conti Rossini is quoted to state that the former kingdom of Damot once incorporated the geographic region of Wolaitta. See reference in Taddesse, *Church and State*, 121, n. 1. For further references to Damot, see also Taddesse, *Church and State*, 65, 84, 91, 122–24.

74. According to the report of Bahrey of Gämo, the appellation *Sidama* was a word used by the Oromo to designate those who were Christians. It became the tribal name of those living in the expansive area south of the Abbaye River to the Rift Valley Lakes. Later it acquired the meaning of "stranger," that is, one who is not a Galla. See Beckingham and Huntingford, *Some Records of Ethiopia*, li.

Hence it is not unreasonable to conclude that, previous to the irruption of the Gallas, one single language in various dialects prevailed throughout the table-land now occupied by these invaders as far eastward as the limits of the dialects cognate with the Amharic.[75]

Of the various expatriate travelers, geographers, and linguists of southern Ethiopia, it was Charles Beke who attempted to go beyond the recording of basic data. Making use of linguistic analysis, he was able to gain new insights into the historical past of the various ethnic groups of southern Ethiopia. He postulated that the many clusters of ethnic groups in southern Ethiopia were at one time in a much closer relationship to one another than previously perceived.[76]

After Beke's research from 1841 to 1843, only limited linguistic study was undertaken in southern Ethiopia for nearly one hundred years. It was in 1940 that Enrico Cerulli made a study of several Gonga dialects as well as the Wolaitta, Janjäro, Baskéto, Sayse, Zala, Chara, Shé, Na'o, Shéko, Burji-Sidama, Ari, and Masongo languages. He formally classified all these southwestern languages under a general heading "Sidama".[77]

More recent research by Harold Fleming and others indicates that the southern Ethiopia classification "Sidama" may be too inclusive. He has coined the term "Omotic" to refer to the body of languages in the watershed of the Omo River and has refined his classification into several Omotic groups. What is significant to us from Fleming's research is that he has grouped together the Kafa, Janjäro, Ometo (Wolaitta is in this language cluster), and Gimira-Maji to form the North Omotic branch.

After linguistic research on the Ganjule Island people of Lake Chamo and the Harro of Gidicho Island out in Lake Abbaya, Fleming classified these ancient languages as Omotic. He was amazed at the close linguistic affinity these isolated island people had to other Omo valley ethnic groups. This led him to postulate that there may be a long historical connection between the various Omotic groups in southern Ethiopia. He comments:

Yet one would expect such ostensibly ancient peoples to be each highly divergent from the rest of mankind, linguistically as well as culturally, rather like the bush people of East and South Africa.

75. Beke, "Countries South of Abyssinia," 265.

76. Ibid.

77. As found in Fleming, "Omotic Overview," 303.

The fact that the lacustrine hunters are not at all divergent linguistically thus contains an interesting problem for future research.[78]

Bruce Adams (following Fleming) explains that within Ethiopia there are three major language clusters: the Omotic, the Cushitic, and the Semitic, Wolaitta being classified under the Central Ometo cluster within the western Omotic family tree and having a "dialect cluster with possibly more than forty varieties."[79] We can assume from this linguistic analysis that there is no strong evidence of a linguistic connection between the Wolaitta and the former Gafat and Damot populations[80] and that the effectiveness of the future Wolaitta evangelists about whom this thesis is written was greatest in the Omotic language groups situated near the Omo River.

To show the inter-relatedness of the languages of southern Ethiopia, in 1972 Peter Cotterell analyzed the results of Bender's language survey of Ethiopia. Relying on Bender's work, Cotterell listed seven of the forty varieties of languages from the Central Ometo cluster of southern Ethiopia.

The point that Cotterell makes is that the Wolaitta evangelists were able to communicate throughout much of southern Ethiopia because of the similarity of dialects. His study showed that there was not only a similarity of vocabulary but also a similarity of syntax and grammar.[81] Further linguistic comparisons between Wolaitta and other Omotic languages such as Käfa, Ghimira, Chara and Gonga would be helpful.

In summary it can be said that the Omotic language family has great diversity within itself. Most languages within this family are spoken within the geographic area of the Omo river system, from which the name is derived. The two regional sub-families of the Omotic are the Northern and the Southern Omotic. The Northern Omotic includes Wolaitta, Gämo, Gofa, Malle, Zalla, Kullo Konta, Zayse, Dorze, Koyra, Gidicho, Kachamo, Baskéto, and others. The Southern Omotic families include the Aari, Dime, Bänna, and Hammär. Linguists are not in agreement about the Ometo cluster. Some place Ghimeera, Janjäro, and Na'o in the Ometo cluster.

78. Fleming, "Recent Research," 270–71.

79. Adams, "Wolaitta Language," 30.

80. Linguists have not been able to verify Beke's language analysis that there is a relationship between the language of the Wolaitta and that of the Damot people who in 1840 were residing north of Lake Tana in Gojam.

81. Cotterell, *Born at Midnight*, 107–11.

Wolaitta Oral History

Attempting to recover the history of Wolaitta by oral research is fraught with hazards.[82] What does emerge from their oral tradition is that two successive dynasties ruled in Wolaitta. First there was Motolämi,[83] the Damot ruler converted to Christianity by Täklä-Haymanot in the late thirteenth century. The Wolaitta tradition states that Motolämi established the Wolaitta Malla dynasty, and successive rulers were Ansé, Buré, Oché, and Lanché.[84] Bogalä Walälu, a Wolaitta writer, mentions that Täklä Haymanot gave his special blessing to Motolämi as the first *kawo* (ruler) of Wolaitta.[85]

The oral tradition then recalls that the Wolaitta despised their name, so they changed it to Arujé.[86] But all did not go well for them. The Arujé argued among themselves, and instead of achieving a spirit of unity and oneness they splintered into many small groups and scattered. Only seven of the Wolaitta clans remained intact, and these forsook the fertile Wolaitta plains and sought refuge in the Kindo mountains.[87] One of their oral traditions identifies these as: Wolaitta Mallaa, Woshesha, Bubula, Hiziya, Womghira, Zirgo Mallaa, and Gezo Mallaa.[88] For survival they foraged in

82. A current example of attempting to correlate oral traditions and historical records in southern Ethiopia is given by Ulrich Braukamper. He affirms oral tradition because "the collection of oral tradition can open new information sources and historical perspectives offering precious contributions to the enlightenment of the past of illiterate peoples." "Oral Tradition and Historical Records," 49. The research for this thesis seems to reveal that the prestigious Shoan Christian history, especially that of Täklä Haymanot, was borrowed by the Wolaitta and has now become part of their living history, allowing them identity and cultural unity with greater Ethiopia.

83. Beckingham and Huntingford, *Some Records of Ethiopia*, lxv, indicate that the name Motolämi is derived from two Oromo words, *Moti* and *Lami,* and may have been a title for Damot rulers meaning "the king's prosperity."

84. The names of these successive rulers seem to be of Oromo derivation, not Wolaitta.

85. Bogalä, *Yäwolamo Hizb Tarik ina Barnätim Indét Indatäwägädä,* 24–25.

86. The following Wolaitta elders generously contributed their understanding of the Wolaitta past: Alaro Hajeso, Laliso Täntu, Malaqo Dängo, Sorsa Wäqamo, Täsäma Täntu, Tushé Tagasha, Wakuno Waläna. I have attempted to correlate their varied strands into a coherent sequence.

87. One tradition claims that the Wolaitta Malla originated in Dämbe in Käfa Gomära. The expression, *Käfa Gomära ayka* (Go back to Käfa Gomära), is based on this myth of origin.

88. Alaro Hajiso, personal information, September 25, 1987. Another list produced by informant Täsäma Täntu is Qésiga, Lonta Malla, Kominiya, Zantala, Gaurarwa, Argama, and Woshesha. Four of these clans are said to be from Shoa.

the forest, eating the fruit of the *doqima* and other trees. Instead of properly made clothes of cotton, they dressed in animal skins. They lived like this for many years, longing for their former days of peace and plenty.

It is difficult to ascertain what the situation was among the Wolaitta during the Ahmed Gragn wars and subsequent Oromo migrations. It could well be that the Arujé period of the Wolaitta history was their dark ages, when their relationship with greater Damot in the north was severed and internal disintegration took place. The second dynasty to rule Wolaitta was the Tegré clan,[89] conjectured to have arrived in Wolaitta during the seventeenth century.[90] As to the manner in which they took up residence in Wolaitta, research done in Guragé may be helpful for us. Oral research carried out in the Silti Guragé area from 1956 to 1968 by Philip Lebel indicates that because of land pressure and the Oromo invasion of the seventeenth century, a number of families from the Silti group, called the Soddo Guragé, were uprooted and settled to the west on the fringes of Chaha.[91] The Guragé traditions claim that they migrated from a place called Gur'a in Tegré.[92] It could well be that part of this migrant Tigre group continued their journey further to the south and eventually occupied the spacious plains of Wolaitta, taking their name with them. Tsehai Berhane Selassie reported a similar tradition about the Tegré dynasty in Wolaitta. But present Tegré clan members insist that their ancestors came from Tambén in Tegré. According to oral tradition collected by Dr. Tsehai, an entire colony of Christians accompanied the first Tegré ruler, Mikaél, to Wolaitta. The present Qésiga clan claim to be descendants of those Christians.[93]

89. Beckingham and Huntingford, *Some Records of Ethiopia*, lxvi, include the Arujé as a ruling dynasty of Wolaitta. With Chiatti, "Politics of Divine Kingship," 310, it would seem that only the Wolaitta Malla and the Tegré dynasties ruled in Wolaitta.

90. Trimingham, *Islam in Ethiopia*, 164 n. 2, refers to various migrations from the north in search of better fortunes because of famine. In "Solomonic Monarchy at Gondar," 359–62, Laverne Berry presents evidence that the southern Ethiopia monarchies developed because northern control was broken after the Oromo migrations of the sixteenth and seventeenth centuries. The Oromo east/west corridor across Wellega allowed the south to develop politically without northern interference.

91. Lebel, "Oral Tradition," 100.

92. Ibid., 101.

93. Tsehai, "Question of Damot and Wälamo," 41. Merid, "Southern Ethiopia," 433–34, defines "Tegre" as anyone carrying arms as a soldier. "They were soldiers of fortune from Tigre, Bagemder, Gojam. For some reason they no longer wanted to serve their local lords."

Contemporary Wolaitta historians are adept at reciting the Tegré line of kings.[94] The king list reproduced below was set down in writing by Borelli, a European traveler to southern Ethiopia in 1888.

1. Mikaél
2. Gärma
3. Gäzenja or Gäzenya
4. Addayo
5. Koté
6. Lebäna
7. Tube
8. Sanna
9. Ogato (1761–1800)
10. Amado (1800–1835)
11. Damoté (1835–1845)
12. Gobé (1845–1886)
13. Gaga (1886–1890, limited authority under Gobé)
14. Tona (1890–1893, son of Gobé)[95]

Of the various traditions that have developed around the Tegré rulers, we will mention several that will be relevant to our future discussion. Koté reinstated the former name "Wolaitta" and foretold that the Wolaitta would once again extend their eastern borders to the Bilaté River. During Koté's rule, the Wolaitta kingdom had been confined to the Kindo Mountains. He warned them that if they were to return to their old Arujé manner of life, they would again disperse and come to nothing. This fifth ruler of the Tegré dynasty was the first to be designated *kawo*.[96] To this day, Koté is remembered by the Wolaitta as "righteous Koté."

Kawo Tube, the son of *Kawo* Lebäna, an aggressive warrior-king, extended the borders of Wolaitta to Ofa but was disliked because of his "vile and wayward manner of life."[97] He was called *arämawe* (non-Christian) because of his many wives. Tube was the first ruler who wore the golden

94. Bureau, "'Tigre' Chronicle of Wollaita," transcribed the history of the nine Tegré dynasty kings from the account of Wolaitta historian Afework Gebre Sellasie.

95. As found in Beckingham and Huntingford, *Some Records of Ethiopia*, lxvi. Spellings of several names have been altered to comply with Wolaitta pronunciation. Research in Wolaitta from 1987 to 1994 confirms all fourteen Tegré rulers except the first, Mikaél. Afewerk Gebre Selassie shortens the Tegré dynasty list, omitting the first four rulers, and begins with Koté. See Bureau, "'Tigre' Chronicle of Wolaitta," 50.

96. Bogalä, *Yäwolamo Hizb Tarik*, 29, states that it was Tube who was first designated *Kawo*.

97. Ibid., 27–29.

ring, designating his authority to rule within the Tegré dynasty. Before he died of malaria in the lowlands of Boroda, he named his son Sanna to succeed him and under oath entrusted the golden ring to a faithful servant.

Kawo Sanna was reluctant to begin ruling in Wolaitta without the golden ring. He told his court, "If the golden ring is lost, this means the demise of the Kingdom of Wolaitta."[98] It was discovered that the faithful servant had swallowed the ring prior to being searched by the Boroda ruler. After the servant was given a purgative, the ring was retrieved. Because of the power of the ring, *Kawo* Sanna pushed back the border of the Gudéla in the north and the Dawro in the west.

Before he died he asked that he be buried in a shallow grave facing their enemy, the Gudéla. His right arm was extended from the grave holding a strong spear. He charged his followers that when they went to battle they should shout no other name but Sanna.

Kawo Damoté expanded the Wolaitta borders to Bodete and controlled the mountain that he named after himself. He established his residence at Wofana, on a lower southern slope of Mt. Damota.[99] *Kawo* Damoté was an industrious builder of defense ditches and stone walls, some of which are still evident on the southern Wolaitta borders. This ditch and wall building, as well as military campaigns, eventually eroded his subjects' loyalty. There was a rebellion and *Kawo* Damoté was imprisoned.

During the forty years that *Kawo* Gobé (1845–1886) ruled Wolaitta, there was peace and justice. Laws were made so that personal rights and life itself would be honored and protected. And in order that the laws not be broken, the king took an oath on the spear of Giorgis, on certain *qalichawoch* (traditional functionaries), and on the clan of Qésiga. To ensure that the oath be carried out by the king, eight officials were selected, one each from the following districts: Boloso, Damota, Duguna, Humbo, Kindo, Koysha, Ofa, and Soré. These eight constituted the *Hospan Dana*, whose duties were to assist in administrating the kingdom of Wolaitta. It is said that because the eight carefully monitored the activities of *Kawo* Gobé, the kingdom of Wolaitta enjoyed peace for forty years. During the time of *Kawo* Gobé, the kingdom of Wolaitta reached its zenith. He extended the eastern Wolaitta border to the Bilaté River and recovered Koyra and Gämo to the south.

---

98. Ibid., 30.
99. Isenberg and Krapf, *Journals*, 257, mention Wofana of Wolamo.

The lengthy Tegré presence in Wolaitta was a factor in developing the hierarchical structure within Wolaitta society. Through the centuries these northerners were assimilated into Wolaitta culture and language. The Tegré may have lost their northern language, but their prestigious clan identity was retained. Wolaitta proverbs and sayings portray the Tegré out-smarting the other clans. One Wolaitta proverb describes the Tegré feasting on the tubular root of the potato and offering the bushy but inedible leaves of the potato plant to the local Wolaitta. Another proverb portrays the Tegré lavishly feeding on nourishing ears of corn, while members of the non-Tegré clans in Wolaitta are fooled into eating the corn stock, ordinarily fed to the animals.[100] These and other Wolaitta proverbs and mythology, in which the ruling Tegré usually outwit the other Wolaitta clans, display the deference shown to the prestigious Tegré. The following discussion will survey the various clans within Wolaitta and demonstrate the hierarchical relationship between them.

The Wolaitta Clans

A study of the Wolaitta clan system (see appendix 1) is helpful in understanding the origins of Wolaitta and the various clan relationships. As already stated, Wolaitta society is hierarchical.[101] It is structured in at least four levels. On the first level are the rulers, the Tegré. Within the second level are the farmers (goqa), who are given a significant place in society because they own and farm the land, and in the third level are the artisans (chinasha).[102] They own no land but make their living producing pottery, forming metal tools, tanning hides from which they make leather products, and singing and playing horns at funerals and other celebrations. On the lowest level are the slaves (ayele). People in this class have no rights and, together with the artisans, are marginalized in Wolaitta society.

Appendix 1 is a listing of 88 Wolaitta clans. Seventeen of the eighty-eight Wolaitta clans have their origin in Shoa.[103] There are fourteen clans

100. Sorsa Wokämo, personal information to EPB, October 20, 1988.

101. Tsehai Berhane Selassie states, "The society is rigidly hierarchical, this being in the basis of occupation and access to political position and land." "Wolayta Conception of Inequality," 342. This is not unlike the social stratification of the Oromo dwellers in the Gibe states described by Mohammed Hassen, *Oromo of Ethiopia*, 92–93.

102. Abebe Arka differentiates between the *chinasha* (potters) and the *dogella* (tanners). Personal information to EPB, June 15, 1996.

103. For other listing of clans, see Chiatti, "Politics of Divine Kingship," 114–18; Bogalä Walälu, *Yäwolamo Hizb Tarek*, 12–13; and Babanto, *Origin of Wollaita and*

from Kullo Konta and twelve from Gämo Gofa. From Kambatta there are nine. There are four each from Qucha, Kindo, Käfa, and Tämbaro. Two are from Sidama. Of the remaining twenty clans, seven are uncertain as to their origins. Thirteen are from a diversity of places.

In Wolaitta the prestigious clans incorporate the appellation "Mallaa" into their clan name, for example, Wolaitta Mallaa, Boroda Mallaa, Gaömo Mallaa, Zirgo Mallaa, Gura Mallaa, Lonto Mallaa, and so forth. They comprise over 40 percent of the Wolaitta population.[104] These Mallaa clans claim that they are the original Wolaitta, with their roots in Kindo. This is unlikely, because many of the Mallaa clans migrated to Wolaitta from various locations such as Boroda, Gämo, Qucha, and Kullo. The Wolaitta claim that their name means "mixed together." This claim is compelling when one observes the diverse origin of the many clans that comprise the Wolaitta.

The Wolaitta seem to place significance on the clans for the following reasons: First, marriage must be outside of one's clan because clan members are perceived as belonging to the same family. Second, the clans are in a hierarchical relationship to one another. Traditionally, certain taboos and regulations were adhered to in order to retain the hierarchical structure of society. And third, clans are dispersed throughout all districts of Wolaitta. This no doubt came about because of population movements during Wolaitta battles against the Arsi, the Kambatta, the Maräqo, and the Tämbaro. Wolaitta soldiers settled in their newly gained territories. It is significant that Wolaitta, though composed of over eighty diverse clans originating from various geographic areas of Ethiopia, has retained her unity and corporate identity.

Summary and Conclusion

After reviewing the emergence of the Wolaitta Kingdom, we conclude that the domain of the former kingdom of Damot did not extend south beyond the Omo River into Wolaitta, even though Wolaitta oral tradition and several recent writers favor the view that the fourteenth century Damot king-

---

Revolutionary Modern Ethiopia. See also Trimingham, *Islam in Ethiopia*, 141, 157, where reference is made to the Beit Malla clan residing in northern Tegré. Appendix 1, Wolaitta Clans, in this thesis has been revised several times by leaders at the Wolaitta KHC center in Soddo. There appears to be some uncertainty as to the origin of some clans. Marriage among the Wolaitta clans could be a factor in this uncertainty.

104. Abebe Arka, personal information to EPB, June 15, 1996.

dom did extend to the south and include present-day Wolaitta. From other written documents and oral sources it would appear that the Wolaitta state, as presently known, did not come into existence until the late seventeenth century. It appears that the history of the Wolaitta people reflects not only the mixture of various clans and divergent groups of people but also the fusion of their stories, mythologies, and symbolic histories. Historical evidence favors the view that the glory and zenith of the Wolaitta kingdom, under the rule of *Kawo* Gobé, was just over a century ago and does not extend back to the fourteenth century. Unless further documentary or archaeological research confirms otherwise, we will assume that the sphere of activity of the Damot ruler Motolämi and evangelist Täklä Haymanot was not within the confines of present-day Wolaitta. However, the northern Christian connection to Wolaitta is important to this thesis, as we shall see in the following chapter.

The Imperial Expansion of Menilek's Army into Southern Ethiopia and the Effect on Wolaitta

Amara yazäzal inje aytazäzim
(The Amhara is to rule, not to obey).[1]

Introduction

THIS CHAPTER WILL EXPLORE two competing forces that affected the Wolaitta population from 1894 to 1937. One of these forces was the imperial expansion of northern Ethiopia into the South at the end of the nineteenth century. The other force was the attempt of the Wolaitta king and his counselors to retain their own independent sovereignty. The interchange of these two rival factors, the national and the local, the center and the periphery, are important to the story of the Wolaitta because this precipitated the Wolaitta crisis of identity. When *Kawo* Tona and his Wolaitta counselors resisted the peace negotiations of King Menilek, they involved the Wolaitta in severe consequences. First, there was the humiliation of military defeat. Second, the Wolaitta were reduced to supplying slaves for the northern nobility and for export. Third, they had to live under the burden of paying heavy tribute.

In 1890 *Kawo* Tona succeeded his grandfather, *Kawo* Gobé, as ruler of Wolaitta. At this time, the boundaries of the Wolaitta kingdom extended to the Bilaté River on the east, Kambatta on the north, the Omo River on the west, and Lake Abbaye on the south. Qucha, Gämo, Boroda, Kullo Konta, and Koyra had become independent of Wolaitta some fifty years before.

---

1. Amhara proverb.

At the turn of the century, the many clans within Wolaitta were residing in a harmonious relationship with one another, retaining their social status and function. The artisan clans, the *chinassa,* produced their products for the community. The majority of the Wolaitta were farmers, the *goka,* who understood themselves to be the real people of Wolaitta. They were dependent upon their small plots of farmland for their livelihood. There were other specialists within the Wolaitta society such as minstrels and religious functionaries who were also dependent upon farming. News of the peace and prosperity within Wolaitta spread to adjacent areas such as Boroda, Gämo, Qucha, Koyra, and Kambatta. Disgruntled families who had been mistreated within their own districts, those who were unable to pay their taxes, and those who were attempting to escape from false criminal charges were welcome to migrate and settle in Wolaitta and start a new manner of life.[2]

Because of a surplus of goods within Wolaitta, trade links were developed with distant areas. Exported products included butter, honey, beeswax, coffee, some ivory, and slaves. Salt and spices for their diet, metal for their ploughs, hoes, axes, and spears, and some cotton for their clothing were imported. But at the end of the nineteenth century all was not stable beyond the Wolaitta borders. When a delegation from Menilek was sent to the Wolaitta court demanding submission and tribute, *Kawo* Tona, along with his counselors, made a decision to resist.

Menilek's position of expanding the Shoan center to the periphery followed a pattern established by fifteenth and sixteenth century Ethiopian sovereigns.[3] During the time of Zär'a Ya'qob (1434–1465), the borders of Abyssinia were pushed well into Shoa to gain a rich fertile base.[4] Menilek desired to control the rich resources of the South and incorporate them advantageously into his kingdom. Subjugation by his Shoan army was the means of attaining this goal. Those on the periphery who submitted and paid tribute, as did *Abba* Jifar of Jimma, were allowed a measure of autonomy.[5] For those who resisted, the consequences were defeat, humiliation, and subjugation.

---

2. Dana Mäja Mädäro, elder of Wolaitta, related that his ancestors migrated from Koyra in the middle of the nineteenth century. Personal information to EPB, September 22, 1987.

3. Taddesse, *Church and State,* 99.

4. Bartnicki and Mantel-Nieko, "Religious Conflicts and People's Movements," 10.

5. Bahru Zewde, *Modern Ethiopia,* 62, 63.

Menilek's Military Subjugation of Wolaitta

We begin this section with a discussion of Ethiopian myth and its significance to the national life and ethos of Ethiopia. This will be followed by describing the developing Täklä Haymanot mythology within Wolaitta and how the northerners manipulated that mythology for their military advantage.

The Ethiopian epic myth *Kibrä Nägäst* (*The Glory of Kings*) was, until the Revolution of 1974, the center pole of Ethiopian society that upheld the basic structure of the monarchy. Eike Haberland describes the *Kibrä Nägäst* as "the Magna Charta of Ethiopian monarchy."[6] This legendary narrative is based on the Old Testament account found in 1 Kings 10:1–13. The Ethiopian epic story describes, with some embellishment, the queen of Sheba's visit to the court of Solomon in Jerusalem. The Ethiopian account relates how the queen accepted the religion of Israel, how she slept with Solomon and, consequently, gave birth to a son called Menilek, and how this son subsequently stole the Ark of the Covenant from the temple in Jerusalem and transported it to the new Zion, Aksum of Ethiopia, thought to be the capital from which the queen of Sheba reigned.

That the *Kibrä Nägäst* was important to Ethiopian life was vividly illustrated when, in 1872, Emperor Yohanis IV asked the British Government to return a copy of the *Kibrä Nägäst* to Ethiopia. Many significant Ethiopian manuscripts were taken to England in 1868 subsequent to the Napier expedition. The Ethiopian emperor's letter states several reasons why this document must be returned, including the following:

> I pray you will find out who has got this book and send it to me,
> for in my country my people will not obey my orders without it.[7]

It appears from the request of this former Ethiopian Emperor that the legitimacy of his leadership and kingship was being challenged by a rival power. And he had adequate reasons to distrust the imperialist motives of the British. This is why it was so important for him to have this document returned to him by the British imperial power. When the British complied with his request, he regained his symbolic authority among his own people. And his subjects were also able to share in the greatness of a noble genealogy—that of God's elect people Israel.

---

6. Haberland, *Untersuchungen zum Äthiopischen Konigtum*, 320.

7. Ullendorff, *Ethiopia and the Bible*, 75.

Contemporary Ethiopianist Donald Levine writes that the *Kibrä Nägäst* contains "a myth of the founding of the Ethiopian nation."[8] He continues:

> It is thus a national epic in the conventional, dictionary sense: an imaginative work that embodies a conception of crucial formative events in the national history. As such it has aptly been compared with the *Aeneid*, another effort to glorify one nation's beginning by linking it to an earlier, prestigious nation's history and epic.[9]

Scholars acknowledge that even though this document was committed to writing early in the fourteenth century, the oral tradition probably dates back to the sixth century.[10]

Just as the people of northern Ethiopia linked their history "to an earlier, prestigious nation's history and epic,"[11] the Wolaitta have accepted the description and detailed account of the traditional ruler of Damot, King Motolämi, and fourteenth century evangelist Täklä Haymanot, as their founding story. It appears that the short historical account, compiled by Wolaitta author Bogalä Walälu,[12] is representative of the founding tradition of Wolaitta. Throughout this chapter, this founding tradition will be referred to as "Wolaitta oral history."

---

8. Levine, *Greater Ethiopia*, 101. See also McCann, "Ethiopian Chronicles," 47–61. "The *Kibrä Nägäst* served as the foundation on which legitimacy [for the Amhara] was to rest" (50).

9. Levine, *Greater Ethiopia*, 101.

10. Budge, *Queen of Sheba*. See also Hubbard, "The Literary Sources of the *Kibrä Nägäst*," 52–60, where Hubbard verifies that the Old Testament quotations used in the *Kabrä Nägäst* are from a text of a very early period. Ethiopian historian Dr. Sergew Hable Sellassie presents evidence that confirms for him a historical connection between the Queen of Sheba and contemporary Ethiopia. See his *Ancient and Medieval Ethiopian History*, 34–41.

11. Ibid.

12. Bogalä, *Yäwolamo Hizb Tarik*. I am not aware of any other Wolaitta who has published the indigenous history of Wolaitta. Abraham's *Lämlämetwa Wälayta* is a rather thin ethnology that borrows heavily on the Bogalä document as well as the ethnographic findings of the Wolaitta Bible Project. See also Bureau, "'Tegre' Chronicles of the Wolaitta," 49–64. My recorded accounts from informants Toshé Tagasha, Alaro Héjeso, Täsämma Täntu, and Laliso Täntu do not differ substantially from the account compiled by Bogalä Walälu. *Ato* Bogalä acknowledges indebtedness to *Fitawrari* Bäqalo Sälfaqo and other Wolaitta elders for his information.

The *Life of Täklä-Haymanote*, as compiled by his disciples at the monastery at Däbrä Libanos,[13] depicts Motolämi as an ungodly warrior-king of the frontier territory of Damot who takes captive innocent women, one being the betrothed woman who would become the mother of Täklä Haymanot. This account relates how the mother was miraculously protected and rescued from the evil intentions of the pagan ruler Motolämi by the divine intervention of the angel Michael. On the other hand, the Wolaitta oral history depicts Motolämi as a brave, benevolent warrior. Bogalä describes this episode as follows:

> Motolämi arose from Wolaitta and cutting across untraveled terrain and uninhabited country, followed the captives to Bulga. Without any mishap the mother of Abuna Täklä Haymanot was rescued from captivity. After she was returned to Wolaitta, with great honor a suitable house was built for her and she was settled in a special place. Even to this day the elders [of Wolaitta] continue to talk about how she was treated with such great honour.[14]

The Wolaitta account therefore describes Motolämi as a generous, gallant gentleman. Even his soldiers and retainers were depicted as being kind and benevolent (chäwa) individuals who would not treat others in a cruel or contemptuous manner.[15] The inference is that even if the Wolaitta people were not yet Christians, they were a civilized and gentle race.

It appears that the Wolaitta account contradicts, molds, and reshapes the Däbrä Libanos story to create the Wolaitta idyllic past. The two hagiographies of Täklä Haymanot, written at the monasteries of Däbrä Libanos and Wäldäbra, both depict Motolämi as a despotic pagan ruler who is the arch-enemy of the people of God and thus the prime focus of Täklä Haymanot's preaching and spiritual ministry.[16]

Concerning Motolämi's conversion, the Wolaitta oral history and the Däbrä Libanos account differ little. Both affirm that when Täklä Haymanot became of age he journeyed from his home in Shoa (Bulga), and began preaching in Damot. This preaching was not without resistance. Motolämi tried to kill Täklä Haymanot by several different violent means.[17] But eventually the Damot ruler, being overpowered by various

13. Budge, *Täkläa Haymanote*, 21–33.

14. Bogalä, *Yäwolamo Hizb Tarik*, 14.

15. Ibid.

16. Budge, *Täklä Haymanote*, 359–61.

17. Bogalä Walälu attempts to underplay the violence of Motolämi and describes

miraculous signs, believed and, together with thousands in his province, accepted baptism.

> And having performed signs and wonders before the governor and destroyed the soothsayers, he made the governor believe on Christ, for he raised up before him many dead persons."[18]

What is significant for our thesis about the conversion of Motolämi and his subjects in the thirteenth century is that it was accomplished by the preaching and miraculous signs of Täklä Haymanot, not by the military exploits and coercion of the Abyssinian army. Both the Wolaitta and the Däbrä Libanos accounts attest to this.

The Abyssinian campaigns to conquer Wolaitta by Menilek II and his generals beginning in 1890 revived the Motolämi myth. These were some of the reasons: First, the initial Wolaitta campaign of November 1890 that was led by Ras Mängäsha ended in defeat. Second, in 1892 a famine was devastating Shoa province, thus weakening Menilek's power base. And third, in 1893 when Menilek and his soldiers conquered the Lake Zway islands, many sacred manuscripts and historical writings were brought to Addis Ababa.[19] These documents, which would have included both Scripture and a history of Ethiopian saints such as Täklä Haymanot, somehow filled a spiritual and psychological vacuum among the Abyssinian elite. From the Zway documents, Menilek's weary soldiers were reminded of Abyssinia's heroic past when Christianity penetrated southern Ethiopia some 300 years previously. Prior to the 1890 military campaign against Wolaitta, Menilek had laid claim to all the territory south of Addis Ababa as far as Lake Rudolf. Because Wolaitta successfully repelled several attempts by the Abyssinian armies, Menilek himself, acting against the advice of his wife Taitu and others, in 1894 decided to lead the final assault. Wolaitta must be conquered. According to the official memoirs of Menilek, compiled by Gäbrä Sellassie, the Abyssinian monarch read about the evangelizing

---

his pre-conversion activities in a rather positive manner in *Yäwolamo Hizb Tarik*, 14. Similarly, in the dramatic presentation of the *Life of Téwodros* at the Addis Ababa National Theatre in 1982, Téwodros was portrayed not as the cruel, despotic, and tragic hero described by Donald Crummey in "The Violence of Téwodros," but rather as a brave warrior and champion of the oppressed. Wolaitta informant Täsämma Täntu related the tradition of Motolämi's becoming a hermit and joining the monastery at Däbrä Libanos subsequent to his becoming a Christian.

18. Budge, *Saints of the Ethiopian Church*, 4:1243.

19. Rosenfeld, *Chronology of Menilek II*, 146, 162.

activities of Täklä Haymanot in southern Ethiopia and believed he must reclaim this territory for the crown and the cross.[20]

> *Atse* Menilek, having heard the story, and somewhat saddened by the existence of Wolamo, where Abuna Täklä Haymanot had accomplished many miracles, had baptized Motolämi, but where religion had been destroyed, was waiting for a suitable time to make the matter right. As it (the Bible) says, "What God wills will indeed happen. And when the right time comes for it to be made right, it will happen." So, aroused by the Holy Spirit he took his soldiers close at hand and went to campaign in Wolamo.[21]

This narrative account by Menilek's biographer transfers the historical data of the exploits of Täklä Haymanot into mythic story. The rightness and justness of Menilek's military campaign against Wolaitta has the authority of holy Scripture and the third person of the Trinity.

According to Jan Vansina one must understand narratives as significant myths. "Any myth refers to a dualistic structure of basic symbols which express, not only the fundamental values cherished by that particular society, or indeed any human society, but also the working of the human mind itself."[22]

---

20. Gäbrä Sellassie, *Tarek Zemen*, 360–80. According to *Aläqa* Tayyä Gäbrä Maryam, *History of the People of Ethiopia*, 69, the documents discovered in the island monasteries of Lake Zway were an important source of forgotten Ethiopian history of the south. Braukamper, affirms that at the beginning of the imperial occupation of the south by Menilek II, "only a thin *firnis* of Christianity was left." "Correlation of Oral Traditions," 46.

21. Gäbrä Sellassie, *Tarek Zemen*, as found in Tsehai Berhanie Selassie, "Political and Military Traditions," 327. It appears that the Lake Zway documents as read, studied, and prayed over by the Orthodox priests, who were close confidants of Menilek, played a significant role in the re-creation and re-shaping of the fourteenth century Motolämi mythology and its application to the Wolaitta King Tona. Frenchman Leon Chefneux, connected with the Djibouti-Addis Ababa railroad and an advisor to Menilek, expressed the ethos of soldiers, generals, and the clergy of Addis Ababa in affirming the Wolaitta campaign: "Menilek's sole aim is the reconstitution of the ancient empire of Ethiopia. . . . The emperor has no claim on territories which have never been Christian." As quoted in Marcus, *Life and Times of Menelik II*, 151. See also McCann, "Ethiopian Chronicles," 53, in which he observes that Gäbrä Sellassie "was an ecclesiastic commissioned by the emperor specifically to prepare the document. . . . Gäbrä Sellassie chose consciously to portray the emperor in traditional terms . . . reflecting a look backward into Amhara tradition."

22. Vansina, "Once upon a Time," 455. See also Eliade, *Myth and Reality*, 18–19, for a comprehensive description of the structure and formation of myths.

It becomes evident that Menilek mythologized fourteenth century Abyssinian history to portray himself, not as a military commander attempting to extend his empire, but as a modern Täklä Haymanot on an evangelizing mission to Wolaitta.

The final military campaign against Wolaitta in November and December 1894 was documented by J. G. Wanderheym, as he accompanied the troops of Menilek.[23] Because most of Menilek's generals, along with their armies, were asked to participate, this was no small battle. The most notable of these were: *Däjazmach* Haile Mariam from Wälläga, *Liqwa* Makwas Abätä from Shoa, *Däjazmach* Bälcha of Guragé origin, *Ras* Mikaél from Wällo, and *Ras* Wäldä Giyorgis of Käfa fame.[24] Recently appointed governors of provinces contiguous to Wolaitta, together with their armies, joined Menilek's massive military entourage. *Däjazmach* Tässäma of Arusi and Kämbatta joined forces at the Bilaté River and donated a large consignment of cattle to help feed Menilek's troops who had been on the march for nearly one week.[25] *Abba* Jifar II of Jimma assisted in attacking from the direction of the Gibé River. And *Däjazmach* Lulsägäd with his army from Sidamo and Därassa joined the battle near Shoné.

Wanderheym was impressed at the wealth and the wellbeing of the Wolaitta countryside in comparison to territories such as Guragé and Kambatta, through which they had just marched. Unlike Wolaitta these territories had been preyed upon by the northerners for several years. Wanderheym writes:

> Wolamo is extremely fertile; numerous plantations of corn, wheat, barley, coffee, tobacco, cotton, and millet surround the compounds of huts and make the country's appearance rich. Vegetation is abundant with figs, palms, spindle trees, sycamores, etc. . . . Skins of animals, gazelles, lions or leopards, hung in the inside of the huts show how hunting was a major activity. They

---

23. Wanderheym, *Unédition*. Wanderheym, a Frenchman on business in Ethiopia as inspector of Franco-African Company's three offices in Djibouti, Harrar, and Addis Ababa, accompanied Menilek from Addis Ababa to Wolaitta on this 1894 military campaign. His detailed battleground account is rather lurid: "It was a terrible butchery of living and dead flesh . . . by the soldiers drunk from blood." As quoted in Marcus, "Imperialism and Expansionism," 449.

24. Tsehai, "Political and Military Traditions," 328–29. See also Bahru, *History of Modern Ethiopia*, 64, 65, for a similar account of the Menilek military campaign against the Wolaitta.

25. Rosenfeld, *Chronology of Menilek*, 167.

were a happy population, very self-sufficient, still living a biblical style of life.[26]

One may question whether Menilek's extravagant military campaign against Wolaitta was only to re-establish Christianity, as his chronicler Gäbrä Sellassie would have his readers believe. Prior to the 1894 military campaign to the South, war preparations were being made for the northern battle against the Italians. Menilek believed the wealth of the entire South was his to be used as he thought best. A future northern campaign against the Italians would demand thousands of robust porters and cattle in abundance for army rations. Livestock throughout central and northern Ethiopia had been drastically depleted by the 1888–1892 rinderpest epidemic, drought, and famine.[27] The Ethiopian monarch no doubt saw Wolaitta as a rich resource of both food and labor. When Menilek and his armies reached the border of *Kawo* Tona's domain, a message was sent to the Wolaitta ruler to submit peacefully. Menilek's chronicler recorded this retort of Tona's, "No Christian is to come into my country. I will not submit. I will fight."[28] Prior to the final assault on the Wolaitta capital, Dalbo, situated at the foothills of towering Damota mountain, the Ethiopian chronicler records Menilek's further negotiations.

> Noticing the fertility of the land, and the number of the population and the cattle, and in sympathy with the country and the people, so that they do not become destroyed, he sent word to the balabat (King Tona) saying, "It is difficult to build up the country once it is destroyed. Your money will not totally be relinquished, if you pay your taxes willingly. So why not bring your tribute and submit. Do not have your country destroyed." But T'ona stayed away and did not submit.[29]

The account then describes Menilek ascending the foothills of Damota, near the place where Täklä Haymanot supposedly baptized

26. Wanderheym, *Une Expédition*, 162–63, as found in Remi Chiatti, "Politics of Divine Kingship," 334–35. See also Marcus: "Wolamo was a rich resource and provided an oasis." *Menilek II*, 139 n. 3.

27. Pankhurst writes, "Menilek indeed was said to have lost around 250,000 head of cattle, while some of the richer Gallas each lost 10,000 to 12,000 head." "Great Ethiopian Famine," 103. It appears that the areas of southern Ethiopia were not adversely affected during this tragedy that devastated much of eastern Africa.

28. Gäbrä Sellassie, *Chronicles of Minilik*, 220, as found in Tsehai Berhane Selassie, "Political and Military Traditions," 331.

29. Tsehai Berhane Selassie, "Political and Military Traditions," 333.

Motolämi centuries before. Menilek issued orders to his army to begin the offensive.

Here we see Menilek depicted in a dual role. First, he is seen as an Old Testament warrior/king regaining lost territory, with spoil and loot being consecrated to the Lord. And second, he is depicted as the renowned evangelist, preacher, and baptizer Täklä Haymanot advancing into pagan territory. The people of Wolaitta must be baptized and re-Christianized because they had lost their former faith.

This military campaign had taken on a mythic dimension and quality. There was a sense of moral rightness that pervaded the thinking of Menilek and his elite, which provided a strong motivation for his ordinary soldier. A new dynamic had been released. Malinowski's description of "a narrative resurrection of primeval reality, told in satisfaction of deep religious wants, moral cravings, social submissions, assertions, even practical requirements," echoes this phenomenon. Malinowski continues:

> Myth fulfills in primitive culture an indispensable function: it expresses, enhances, and codifies belief; it safeguards and enforces morality; it vouches for the efficiency of ritual and contains practical rules for the guidance of man.[30]

It would appear that Menilek's skillful use of mythology was a determining factor in the military conquest of Wolaitta.[31] But the morality of this mythology's outworking and reshaping is open to question.[32] The devastation and pillage of Wolaitta brought terrible consequences. Wanderheym estimated that over 20,000 were killed, 18,000 captives marched to Addis Ababa as slaves, 18,000 cattle taken as booty, and countless houses burned.

---

30. Malinowski, *Magic, Science and Religion*, 101.

31. Jacob Loewen says, "The integrating function of myth is closely linked to a society's ethnocentric orientation, i.e. each society puts itself and its way of life in the center of universe." "Myth and Mission," 302. The 1894 imperial campaign against Wolaitta was another example of the northerners imposing themselves upon an established indigenous population, as they had done in Harar in 1886. See Zewde, *History of Modern Ethiopia*, 64–65, for his brief but factual account of the Menilek military campaign against Wolaitta.

32. We are not attempting to discredit the sincerity of Menilek's spirituality. Marcus comments, "There was something of the prophet, something of the mystic, and something of the modern man [in Menilek]." *Menilek II*, 214. Again, Marcus writes, Menilek "was a spiritual man, in 1903 he arose between 5:00–7:00 AM and immediately went to one of the three adjacent churches in the *Ghebbi* for devotions," 218.

Even children and mothers were butchered.[33] Wanderheym describes the massacre as follows:

> One had the feeling of witnessing some kind of infernal hunting where human beings rather than animals served as game.[34]

It appears that the soldiers were out to kill and to collect as much loot as they could transport back to their respective provinces. It was a bloody slaughter of the Wolaitta, whose means of defense were spears and long knives. When Ṯona was finally captured in Boroda, south of the border of Wolaitta, and brought bleeding and humiliated before Menilek and his court, he was rebuked for his stubborn resistance and defiant rebelliousness. He penitently replied:

> It has been the madness of my stomach which suggested to me to resist this great enemy. The death of my people is on my head. Only I am responsible for this extermination, because of my pride. I should have submitted to you, so I could have avoided the devastation of my country and the massacre of my nation.[35]

In the myth Menilek used to motivate his soldiers, Wolaitta King Ṯona was seen as a modern pagan Motolämi in need of conversion. The baptism of the penitent Ṯona was, in fact, witnessed by Menilek prior to the mass exodus of prisoners, slaves, and animal loot to the capital city. Another significant symbol of the former Christianization of Wolaitta was re-enacted when Menilek's soldiers discovered the ruins of an ancient church that supposedly dated back to the time of *Abuna* Täklä Haymanot.[36] For soldier and general, this verified that the southern campaign was for a noble purpose—the re-evangelization of Wolaitta.[37] The legitimacy of this major

33. Wanderheym, *Une Expédition*, 182, as found in Chiatti, "Divine Kingship in Wolaita," 335.

34. Ibid., 181, as cited in Zewde, *History of Modern Ethiopia*, 65.

35. Wanderheym, *Une Expédition*, 182, as found in Chiatti, "Divine Kingship in Wolaita," 336–37.

36. *Aläqa* Tayyä writes, "Furthermore, with investigation in cave after cave are found church robes for a long time eaten by insects and torn by bats, and sacred objects and books which were put there and hidden when the Galla plundered them." *History of the People of Ethiopia*, 67.

37. See Eliade, *Images and Symbols*, 119–24, which deals with the interaction of symbolism and history. See also Haberland's "Influence of the Christian Ethiopian Empire," where he records relics of former Christianity preserved in eight Orthodox churches within Wolaitta. Haberland acknowledges that the Wolaitta "reverted to paganism, but still show the places where Takle Haymanot preached in front of the mythical King Motolomi" (ibid., 236).

campaign against the pagan kingdom of Wolaitta was now established. Menilek could now say, "See, this part of Ethiopia was formerly Christian but had lapsed into paganism. We were doing our duty to bring it back into Christendom."[38] Ṭona Gobé died in Addis Ababa in 1917, a defeated and demoralized monarch.

The mythology that was imposed upon the Wolaitta by their northern conquerors in one sense was inadequate and deficient. The Wolaitta could not accept the fact that the monarch of imperial Ethiopia, Menilek II, was a modern Täklä Haymanot coming as an evangelist for their salvation. They did, however, accept the fact that they once were Christianized[39] but that through the centuries they had lost the teachings of Täklä Haymanot. Now with heads bowed down, all they could say was: "We are poor and miserable."[40]

The after effects of the Wolaitta defeat were not unlike those experienced by another southern Ethiopian monarchy, that of Käfa, in 1897. A contemporary writer described the lot of the Käfa in this manner: "The economic exploitation, political subjugation, and cultural humiliation subsequent to Menilek's conquest remained fresh in the consciousness of the Kafa people."[41]

---

38. Tsehai Berhane Selassie, "Political and Military Tradition," 328. She points out the significance of the religious motive of this military campaign for the predominantly Amhara army. She asks, "Did Menelik use a very strong evocative myth, 'Restoring Christianity to Walamo,' only as a ruse to get his soldiers to fight, or was he really after economic gain?" 338. Contemporary historian Harold G. Marcus seems to indicate that the motive was, rather, material gain: "The emperor returned to Addis Ababa from his Wolamo campaign in 18 January, 1895, having added to his empire a large, rich, kingdom, with the acquisition of much booty and glory." *Menelik II*, 156.

39. See Tsehai Berhane Selassie, "Question of Damot and Walamo," 37, where she notes that Borelli discovered the Motolämi and Täklä Haymanot tradition in Wolaitta in 1888, six years prior to the Menilek campaign.

40. Chiatti, "Divine Kingship in Wolaita," 340. Since 1894, the name "Wolamo" evokes the pejorative meaning "slave" to the Wolaitta elite. "Wolaitta," the term traditionally used to describe their language, is now used to designate all people formerly called "Wolamo." As mentioned in chapter 1 (pp. 13–15), Dr. Charles T. Beke collected language data about fourteen ethnic groups of southern Ethiopia from 1841 to 1843, one of which he noted as *Wolaitsa*. See Beke, "Languages and Dialects of Abyssinia," 94.

41. Lange, *Domination and Resistance*, 50. See Bahru Zewde , *History of Modern Ethiopia*, 65–66, for his description of the northern expansion into Käfa. Because the king of Käfa, *Tato* Gaki Sherocho, and his soldiers strenuously resisted Ras Wälda-Giyorgis's military advance, there were heavy casualties. In 1897 *Tato* Gaki Sherocho was taken prisoner to Addis Ababa in chains—but in gold chains befitting royalty.

The Wolaitta were now deprived of the prestige and well-being they had once experienced. They no longer controlled their own center. Along with other southern kingdoms, they now became a periphery frontier of the northerners. The human and agricultural resources contained within Wolaitta were subject to exploitation by their subjugators. The following section will discuss the negative effects of slavery upon Wolaitta.

Wolaitta and Slavery

The war of 1894 reduced Wolaitta to a vassal state. Now that northern troops were allowed to occupy the conquered area of Wolaitta as *näftänya*, the possibility of slave trading became very real.

Within Ethiopia, slave-raiding and the sale of slaves had a long established history. During the reign of King 'Amdä Seyon (1314–1344) the rich hinterlands west and south of Shoa were annexed and conquered. The victorious king gave credit to his high God for assisting him in enslaving the people of the periphery. He boasts:

> God gave me all the people of Damot into my hands; its king, its princes, its rulers, and its people, men and women without number, whom I exiled into another area [country].[42]

Slave raiding appears to have been an accepted by-product of 'Amdä Seyon's military campaign. Information is lacking as to where the people of Damot were exiled. Whether it was to foreign lands or within 'Amdä Seyon's domain, it certainly meant a major disruption and dislocation to those who were subjugated.[43]

Slavery was accepted as a national institution, as evidenced in the Ethiopian legal code, *Fetha Nägäst*. There are some fifty-seven references to slavery in this Ethiopian legal code,[44] making it appear that the practice of trading in humankind was indeed sanctioned by church and state. Donald Levine describes the function of the *Fetha Nägäst* as that which "served not as a working code for the adjudication of court cases but as an embellishment of *de facto* decisions."[45] In the twentieth century, Bartleet observes

42. Taddesse, "Abbots of Däbrä-Hayq," 96.

43. Taddesse states, "It appears that this island port [Dahlak] supplied particularly Yemen with Nubian and Ethiopian slaves. It is reported for the year A.D. 976 that an annual supply of 1,000 slaves, of whom half were Ethiopian and half were Nubian females, used to be sent to the Ziyadite rulers of Yemen." *Church and State*, 86 n. 2.

44. Pankhurst, *Economic History*, 129 n. 38.

45. Levine, *Wax and Gold*, 269.

that even the clergy of the Orthodox Church sanctioned the institution of slavery:

> Negus Tefari has done his best to carry out the requests of the League of Nations, but the great hindrance to the entire fulfillment is the clergy. They hold that according to the Mosaic Law, slavery is morally justifiable and economically necessary.[46]

In the *Fetha Nägä*st two parallel concepts of how a slave functioned in Ethiopian society existed side by side. On the one hand, slaves were perceived as chattel and could be bought and sold as animals.[47] On the other hand, they were viewed as people with rights and privileges. The *Fetha Nägäst* encouraged Christians to use all means to promote the conversion of their slaves and to prohibit the sale of baptized slaves. The demands of everyday living made such ideals difficult to put into practice.

W.C. Harris, writing of Emperor Sahle Sellassie's reign (1841–1855), notes that there were some eight thousand slaves serving the king's court in various subservient capacities.[48] The Christian monarch Sahle Sellassie would invoke history to defend the practice of slave trading. Former Ethiopian rulers utilized all available resources to accomplish a given task.

Harris makes mention of Wolamo as a Christian province under an independent sovereign lying just south of Kambatta and southeast of Janjäro. He heard it said that "twenty pieces of *amolé* would buy a Wallamo slave of fair complexion who spoke a distinct language."[49] But slave trading was one aspect of life in Ethiopia with which Harris never made his peace. He viewed the entire business as degrading. "The Christians, moreover had become so corrupted by evil example, that in lieu of opposing a barrier to the advance of slavery, they shortly adopted and encouraged the debasing traffic."[50]

Menilek, prior to being crowned emperor of Ethiopia (1889), presented himself to western governments with whom he desired to trade as the champion against slavery. In 1878 he responded to a letter from the Anti-Slavery Society in England in the following manner:

46. Bartleet, *Land of Sheba*, 159.

47. At a place called Yejubbi, a slave merchant begged medicine from Dr. Beke for his sick slaves, saying, "They are our *käbt* (cattle) and we cannot afford to lose them." See Beke, "Routes in Abyssinia," 21.

48. Harris, *Highlands of Aethiopia*, 1:78.

49. Ibid.

50. Ibid., 1:308.

Dear friends, you formerly wrote to me and advised me that for a Christian King the institution of the slave-trade in his kingdom was an inconsistency. Herewith I send you the joyful message, as answer, that I have abolished the slave-trade in my whole kingdom and in its borders, for I am a Christian. Therefore, consider me, henceforth, with good will as your friend.[51]

Commodities from Europe that Menilek very much needed for Shoan expansion and for defense against foreign aggression were arms and ammunition. He desired to portray himself as a "Christian king" to the European powers and so denounced slavery within his domain. On the other hand, the export of slaves to Arab markets provided a lucrative commodity and hard currency with which arms and ammunition were purchased. In July 1893 Menilek ordered 100,000 rifles and 1,000,000 rounds of ammunition from a Hamburg firm. They were never supplied because the German government prohibited their shipment. But through French agents, Menilek did receive a large shipment of French arms and ammunition in 1895.[52]

Menilek's official chronicler, Gäbrä-Sellassie Wäldä Arägai, is silent about his monarch's involvement in slave trading. Ironically, Wolaitta writer Bogalä Walälu confirms that Menilek upheld the spirit of the *Fetha Nägäst* when he made an *awaj* (proclamation) against slavery in 1894, at the Wolaitta village of Jäge. Bogalä Walälu describes the release of certain captives just prior to his march back to Addis Ababa.

Many small children, women, and men who had been taken captive were brought before Menilek. At that time *Asé* Menilek allowed the small children with their mothers, the old widows and the old men to remain in their homeland.[53]

Bogalä is careful to point out that this *awaj* was made with empathetic compassion and concern for the well-being of the individual as well as for

51. British Foreign Office 407/11, Menelik, 14.12.1878, as cited in Pankhurst, *Economic History*, 101.

52. Rosenfeld, *Chronology of Menilek*, 161, 169. See also Richard Pankhurst's enumeration of costly weaponry: "By 1894, the year before the war with Italy, Menilik is said to have had 82,000 rifles, as well as 5.5 million cartridges. . . . Which made them 'by far the strongest native power in Africa.'" "Menilik and the Utilization of Foreign Skills," 43.

53. Bogalä, *Yäwälamo Hizb Tarik*, 48. That Bogalä was concerned about the past evils of slavery in Wolaitta is evident from the translation of the Amharic title of his book, "A history of the Wolamo people and how slavery was driven out."

the future of Wolaitta.[54] Nevertheless, Menilek marched 18,000 healthy, able-bodied Wolaitta captives to Addis Ababa to join his work force. Bogalä Walälu makes reference to two anti-slave proclamations in 1926 and 1930, which basically curtailed slave raiding in Wolaitta. The following action was taken against known slave traders in Wolaitta. *Fitawrari* Dändo's son, Tito, was apprehended and hanged in the Bodete market. Aluté Shanka was hanged from a tree next to his own house. Slave trader Haloboloha was captured and hanged in the Saturday market in Soddo. Others such as Bärata Gota, Wachena, Andäbo, Ali Wäda, and Aru Tema were hanged in the very location where they were involved in slave trading.[55]

The SIM missionaries who served in Wolaitta from 1928 to 1937 were cautious in speaking about or against slavery.[56] However, some mention is made of it in personal diaries and letters. George Rhoad records during a trip through southwestern Ethiopia in 1931:

> The people are Galla speaking and Mohammedan, but by repute are more interested in secret slave hunting than in anything else. We had our first "close up" view of the traffic today, when at a

54. Be that as it may, it is a historical fact that in 1915 Ras Mikaél, governor of Wällo and father of *Lij* Iyasu, was exporting many caravans of slaves to the Red Sea coast, as was *Abba* Jifar of Jimma. See Pankhurst, *Economic History*, 106. Bogalä himself acknowledges that during the 1894 Menilek campaign against Wolaitta, the greatest destruction was not the slaughter of war; rather it was the looting and plundering of villages for slaves that denuded the country of people. Bogalä, *Yäwälamo Hizb Tarik*, 48.

55. Bogalä, *Yäwälamo Hizb Tarik*, 56.

56. That slavery was practiced in Wolaitta during the pre-Italian period is acknowledged by SIM writers such as Malcolm Forsberg, *Land beyond the Nile*, 74. Clarence Duff also mentions pre-Italian slave raiding near Soddo. Walda, an SIM employee, lost his sister and her baby when slave raiders fired the house, killed the husband, and made off with his sister and her baby. Duff, *Cords of Love*, 208. In her diary, Vi Roberts notes the Italian anti-slavery proclamation made in the Soddo market. The February 4, 1937, diary entry reads: "All people are alike. Walamos, Amharas. . . . No more slaves." And in her March 13, 1937, entry she records another proclamation made in the market: "Slaves [are to be] released—could live on masters land or leave just as they felt like." Roberts, "Personal Diary." Officially, SIM's position in a host country was non-political, which usually meant compliance with the host government's policies. This non-political stance is evident in the Lambie March 5, 1932, letter to Mr. E. Grimwood of the SIM London office (SIM Archives). "We have the Slavery Commission here with us and we are afraid of becoming involved. Perhaps this has too much influenced us. We feel our duty is to preach Christ crucified. If we were to give full information as to the slavery question it would, perhaps, react unfavorably on our work and it might even mean the leaving of the country. We are sure His Majesty is earnestly seeking to do away with slavery, but there are others in the country who are profiteering from the slave labor [trade] and are opposing him."

turn of the trail we suddenly came upon two burly men, carrying guns, with a crying boy, who was quite frightened to speak, and whose every demeanor suggested late seizure, between them. They disappeared into the bushes ere our interpreter came up. We did not attempt to do anything lest . . . opposition would cause a tedious delay.[57]

At a 1931 inter-mission prayer meeting in Addis Ababa Miss Ferron reported:

We might mention the matter of slave-raiding in Wallamo country. Perhaps you are not troubled with this in the parts of Abyssinia where you are working. The Governor of Wallamo is doing all he can to put a stop to it, for which we are thankful. Not so very long ago, only about a quarter of a mile from the station [SIM, Soddo], a woman and two men were killed and two children were taken away by slave raiders, although the children were later recovered.[58]

In 1935 Vi Roberts wrote about a young girl who went missing while herding cattle near her home. The family and friends set about doing a lot of shouting and wailing when the cattle came home but she was nowhere to be found. It was assumed that she had been stolen and taken off as a slave. Vi Roberts cautioned her family in Canada, "Please do not tell this to anyone outside for it wouldn't look good in print."[59]

As a parallel to the SIM statements, French Canadian Capuchin priest, Paschal de Luchon, resident missionary in Wolaitta (1927–1947) made some rather straightforward comments in his journal entries regarding slavery in Wolaitta:

The capture of children is frequent. Two of our neighbors had seen the disappearance of two of their children. Others are sold by their close relatives. Terrible moral poverty which can disappear only by a change in customs, i.e., by faith. Wolaita, as a prolific race, has kept alive the slave market. A consistent part of the population is composed of slaves. When the master dies, the

---

57. Rhoad, *Wayside Jottings*, 15.

58. As found in Cotterell, *Born at Midnight*, 50. This incident is also mentioned in the Selma Bergsten, Raymond Davis, and Earl Lewis transcribed interview of 1961, p.55. The Lewises adopted one of the children, named Assala, later changing it to Yohannis. Percy and Vi Roberts letter to family, June 29, 1933, confirms that Yohannis was taken into the Lewis household.

59. Vi Roberts, letter to family, August 23, 1935.

slaves are the best part of the inheritance. The group increases continually, either because of the introduction of new slaves or because of new birth among existing slaves. They surpass the need of the house in such a way that they are a burden more than a positive asset. . . .

The *mälkinya* [Abyssinia soldiers] are in this country only temporarily. Their concern is not the improvement of the country or of their tenants; no, they worry only about making money by extortion. . . . They double the tax when they foresee a change.[60]

It is somewhat problematic to define what slavery really meant in Ethiopia immediately prior to the Italian occupation. Fan Dunckley, living in Addis Ababa from 1926 to 1934, wrote: "Slave-trading itself is punishable by death. Domestic slavery, however is still a recognized institution and practiced in a beneficial form."[61] Ethnographic researcher McClellan interviewed a significant number of Gedeo people in 1974. He ascertained that domestic slavery was not exceptionally cruel. "Internal domestic slavery had been a popular institution in many areas, and was not particularly harsh, nor characterized by perpetual bondage. Children of slave parents often acculturated and were freed."[62]

Slave-raiding and domestic slavery died a slow death in Ethiopia. In an article commemorating the coronation of Haile Sellassie, Rowland Bingham, Director of SIM, wrote in *The Evangelical Christian*:

Slavery has existed and serfdom is the condition yet of the overwhelming majority of its people. . . . Haila Selasi has already given his pledged word that he will seek by processes to become effective in a course of years the elimination of slavery from his land. It is for other nations . . . to exercise patience.[63]

After the coronation of Haile Sellassie in 1930, reform bills and various laws passed for the abolition of slavery did substantially reduce the number of slaves.[64] But it was the Italian occupation that brought about the final demise of Ethiopian slavery. This came about in the following

60. de Luchon, "Journal of 1931," 72–73, as quoted in Chiatti, "Divine Kingship in Wolaita," 201–2. Because of Paschal de Luchon's efforts in exposing Ethiopian slavery, he was expelled from the country in 1947.

61. Dunckley, *Eight Years in Abyssinia*, 54.

62. McClellan, "Reaction to Ethiopian Expansionism," 22.

63. Bingham, "Long Live the King," 575–76.

64. See "Law Passed for the Abolition and Protection of Slaves on 31st March, 1924," as found in Sandford, *Ethiopia under Hailé Selassié*, 135–44.

manner. First, the majority of the Amhara *näftänyoch* from the South and a significant number of their retainers and domestic slaves went off to battle. The ethnic groups in southern Ethiopia experienced a liberation from Amhara dominance during the war with Italy. Second, the Italians introduced wage labor from 1935 to 1941 on their road construction and house building activities.[65] This created a different relationship between worker and supervisor. The worker was shown dignity and rewarded for his labor. And third, the Ethiopian Red Sea ports were now controlled by the Italians.

In summary, slavery imposed a terrible stigma and burden on much of southern Ethiopia and particularly on Wolaitta. The *Fetha Nägäst* was ineffective in granting the rights of the individual and in recognizing the personhood of the Ethiopian citizen. Evidence indicates that the imperial domination of central Ethiopia over the provinces of the South seemed to promote slavery rather than curb it. Southerners lost control of their corporate ethnic destinies and the cohesiveness of their families, as well as their own personal rights and freedom. They bore deep psychic scars, feeling inferior and alien in their own culture.[66]

The Exploitative Tax System in Wolaitta

Another form of exploitation that encumbered the Wolaitta when the northerners took up residence among them was excessive taxation imposed upon the farmers. There had been a form of taxation under the Wolaitta kings, which was administered by the local *sangadanna* (the local judge and tax collector).[67] The levy on each household seldom exceeded that which would be consumed at the annual Mäsqal celebration. But after Menilek's conquest of Wolaitta, the *gäbbar* (farmer) and *näftänya* (northern rifleman) system was introduced to Wolaitta. Under this structure, for each *näftänya* anywhere from five to one hundred *gäbbaroch* were allocated. It was reported that around five hundred *näftänyoch* were settled in Wolaitta after the Menilek conquest. The *gäbbar* continued to hold the land (*rist*) by inheritance from his forebears, but he was obligated to pay various kinds of tribute to the *näftänya*. And to add a further burden to the *gäbbar*, because Wolaitta was classified as *mädäbét*, a certain amount of

65. Perham, *Government of Ethiopia*, 233–34.

66. Levine, "Ethiopia," 248 n. 1.

67. Chiatti, "Divine Kingship in Wolaita," 427.

additional tribute was exacted from each *gäbbar* and sent to Addis Ababa annually.[68]

Another form of tribute was the *asrat,* the tithe which was a tenth of the peasant farmer's income. And over and above these, the farmer was obliged to provide extra provisions for officials and visitors who were passing through the countryside. He was also obligated to provide firewood for his *näftänya* overlord and was expected to provide honey by which the northern ruling class could make their *täj* (a refreshing drink of slightly fermented honey mixed with water). Other gifts could be extracted from the *gäbbar* at the time when a new governor was appointed.

The *näftänya* could also appropriate labor from the *gäbbar.* This was usually done by forcing the *gäbbar* to cultivate state land under the control of the Orthodox Church or to maintain the roads. Often one-third of the farmer's time might be spent in this kind of compulsory work away from his own plot of land. Other tasks imposed on the *gäbbar* by the *näftänya* were the grinding of grain and repairing of granaries and fences. The *gäbbar* could be conscripted to carry personal effects for his overlord when he travelled to distant places or to transport the annual tribute of grain, butter, honey, or coffee to Addis Ababa.

The exploitation that took place in Wolaitta was not dissimilar to that which was taking place in other southern provinces. Administrators assigned by Menilek to these provinces were both exploiters and protectors of the local population. Frank de Halpert visited Käfa in 1934 and wrote this account:

> It is estimated that a fourth of the land in Kaffa was owned by the great Amhara land owners. *Ras* Walda Giyorgis, *Ras* Getachew, last governor, *Dejazmach* Taye, *Ras* Gatachew's sister, and the Minister of Finance in Addis Ababa, were all large land owners. The land is fertile and rich in coffee, and these nobles drew large revenues from it, as it was let to tenants who paid as rent a third of their crop and supplied their own oxen.[69]

68. *Däjazmach* Balcha served intermittently as governor of Sidamo Province from 1897 to 1927. He utilized the market tax from Wolaitta, which was estimated at 50,000 *Maria Teréza* annually. "Wolamo served as the Emperor's [Menilek's] *mädäbét* (a kind of private estate designed to provide staples for the Imperial table)." McClellan, "Reaction to Ethiopian Expansionism," 173 n. 14. See also Zewde, *History of Modern Ethiopia,* 87.

69. As quoted in Perham, *Government of Ethiopia,* 320. See also Levine, who says, writing in 1974, "Slavery was widespread in greater Ethiopia until 1930 and today ex-slaves, children of former slaves, and *de facto* slaves in some regions occupy social positions much like their predecessors." *Greater Ethiopia,* 54. Explorer and geographer George

As has been stated, land ownership was by heredity, and the majority of land was occupied by small Wolaitta farmers. There were common grazing areas that were left uncultivated. But with the intrusion of the northerners into Wolaitta, the peasant farmer faced the new danger of losing his land to his overlord. If he was unable to pay his annual taxes on time, he would be imprisoned and a tax receipt would not be issued to him. Evidence of unpaid taxes was indication that the ownership of his land was under question. If he lost his land, he would become a tenant farmer who was obligated to pay one-third of his produce to the *näftänya* overlord.

Exploitation was inherent in the *gäbbar/näftänya* system.[70] The *näftänya* took little interest in assisting the *gäbbaroch* under his jurisdiction in the means of production. Crop rotation, planting of trees, or introduction of new varieties of grains was entirely left to the wisdom and innovation of the farmers. There was little incentive for over-production. The *näftänyoch* were there "to skim off as much surplus as possible from whatever the peasants themselves happened to produce, in whatever way they happened to produce it."[71] The rights of the *gäbbar* were unprotected. The only freedom a *gäbbar* could exercise was to transfer his family to another district and become a tenant farmer for another *näftänya*.

This is the reason why *The Times* of London on April 18, 1937, called the *gäbbar* system "a far worse evil than slavery."[72] In 1947 Capuchin Pashal de Luchon was expelled from Ethiopia when he criticized the *gäbbar* system, which he viewed as another form of slavery.[73]

The exploitation and oppression in Wolaitta were rooted in the class distinction between the *gäbbar* and the *näftänya*. The Wolaitta *gäbbar* was anchored to his social standing for several reasons. First, because of his inability to speak Amharic properly, he was relegated to the status of *balagär säw* (a person from the countryside). Secondly, he was described religiously as *arämawe* (he who has no religion) because of his participation in Wolaitta traditional religion. Neither he nor his relatives could be buried within the confines of the Orthodox Church. He was not allowed

---

Montandon described the social status within Ethiopia as follows: "If the Abyssinian is master everywhere, one may say the Galla is a domestic, the Kafficho and the Wolamo a serf, and the Gemira, like the Negro, a slave." "Journey in South-Western Abyssinia," 383.

70. See Alaro, "Political History of Wolayita," for a description of serf exploitation.

71. Donham, "Old Abyssinia," 92.

72. Quoted in Bahru Zewde, *History of Modern Ethiopia*, 14.

73. Chiatti, "Divine Kingship in Wolaita," 188.

to be an active participant of the Orthodox Church *mahibär*. A third mark of the *gäbbar* was his physical features. They were pejoratively called *shanqila* (black ones).

All of these pressures caused the Wolaitta to lose confidence in their glorious past. With little opportunity of changing their social status, they could only lift hands to *Tosa* and beg for deliverance.[74]

Conclusion

When Menilek's northern army marched into the South at the end of the nineteenth century, the Wolaitta were in control of their own destiny, with a king and a noble history. *Kawo Tona* and his counselors made a deliberate decision to resist the northern invaders, miscalculating their own military strength, and suffered a humiliating defeat by Menilek's modern army. The Wolaitta defeat brought an end to *Kawo Tona*'s reign and the Tegré dynasty. Their confidence in an earthly kingdom was smashed, and they were left disillusioned and confused.

The northern subjugation of Wolaitta should have meant that the Wolaitta would be incorporated into greater Ethiopia, but the Wolaitta now found themselves forced to respond to a burdensome historical force beyond themselves. Menilek's military subjugation of Wolaitta, motivated by the myth of a former evangelization, did not bring revitalization to the Wolaitta people; rather it promoted disillusionment and despair. The effects of the military subjugation of Wolaitta were slave trading and the imposition of excessive taxes, which reduced them to serfdom and poverty. But their Christian past not forgotten. The Wolaitta had in their possession their own critical consciousness and potential for action. Could it be that their quest to be whole and to become full citizens of Ethiopia might be met through a religious solution? This will be developed further in succeeding chapters.

---

74. On May 7, 1928, a Wolaitta farmer confided to the SIM staff at Soddo, "We Wolamo are ignorant people and very wicked; we steal and kill and do so many bad things. But some of us know a little about *Tosa*, and we have been hoping that someone would tell us about Him and teach our people the way of *Tosa*. Now you have come and when we heard it we were very glad. My home is far from here, but when I heard you had come, I came all this way to see you. And when the people all around this country hear about you, they too will come, many, many of them." As recorded in Duff, *Cords of Love*, 61–62.

3

Primal Religion of Southern Ethiopia

Perceptions and Understanding of Wolaitta Religious Beliefs

"African primal religions form part of the common
spiritual heritage of mankind."[1]

Introduction

AN EXPLORATION OF PRIMAL religion in southern Ethiopia and specifically
the pre-Christian religious beliefs of the Wolaitta may be undertaken from
several angles. We will first look at the hagiographies of several Orthodox
evangelists of the fourteenth to sixteenth centuries who encountered pre-
Christian populations of southern Ethiopia. In many instances the biographies depict sharp conflict between the evangelists and the local religious
functionaries. In some instances there is appeasement, with the result that
there is a continuation of former religious belief and practice. It appears
that the biographers, writing a century after the religious exploits of Täklä
Haymanot and his disciples, wrote from a perspective that the Christian
faith had triumphed over primal religion.

The second perspective on southern Ethiopia's primal religion will
be that of early twentieth century Ethiopian historian *Aläqa* Tayyä. His
Christian beliefs had been shaped both by historic Ethiopian Christianity
and the Swedish Evangelical Mission. As he "documents" the history of
southern Ethiopia it is evident that he reflects a northern perception of
the South. Northerners saw little of value in the belief systems of the "pagan" South; therefore, the pre-Christian southerners were called *arämawe*
(without a religion) and were in need of conversion.

---

1. Turner, " Religious Study of African Primal Religions," 14.

Islam in southern Ethiopia demands brief mention in the third section of this chapter. The growing influence of Islam along the Red Sea coast culminated in the devastating Ahmad Gragn attacks of the sixteenth century on the Ethiopian Christian heartlands. This has a bearing on our study because populations such as the Wolaitta, located on the southern periphery, found themselves isolated from the Christian North. It appears that Wolaitta sympathies continued with the Christian North during this period of isolation, therefore Islam made negligible inroads into this kingdom.

The fourth section deals with Wolaitta primal religion. Wolaitta cosmology is similar to that found among the other Omotic populations of southern Ethiopia. The degree to which beliefs and practices were affected through centuries of interaction with northern Christianity will be explored. Reasons will be given for the active practice of primal religion among the Wolaitta, since they themselves admit to once being evangelized by the disciples of Täklä Haymanot in the fourteenth and fifteenth centuries. We will explore the extent to which northern Christianity was assimilated into the primal religion of the South. This chapter will conclude by affirming the positive contribution primal religion does make when understood as the context into which the Christian faith was introduced.

The Response of the Solomonic Evangelists[2] to Primal Religions in Southern Ethiopia

During the thirteenth century the Ethiopian kingdom known as the "Solomonic" dynasty, founded by Yikunno Amlak (1270–1285), began to expand southward into the area populated by speakers of Cushitic languages. Yikunno Amlak's grandson, 'Amdé Seyon (1314–1344) was successful in curbing the commercial trade activities of the Islamic kingdoms of Ifat, Dawaro, Bali, Hadiya with the resource-rich Sidama.[3] Through military strength he gained control of the important trade routes to the Red Sea as well as political hegemony over much of what was then known as Damot. But this Ethiopian expansion into the South was not limited to the military sphere. Christianity sometimes preceded and sometimes followed this secular advance. This section will attempt to survey the

---

2. "Solomonic evangelists" is the term that will be used to designate those evangelists who were actively involved in evangelism during the Solomonic dynasty founded by Yikunno-Amlak (1270–1285).

3. Taddesse Tamrat, "Revival of the Church," 19.

Orthodox Church's responses and understanding of primal religions in southern Ethiopia from the fourteenth to the sixteenth centuries.

From the extant hagiographies of various Ethiopian evangelists and saints who preached in southern Ethiopia, one is able to ascertain their perception and understanding of primal religions. The writers of these hagiographies represented the point of view and cosmology prevalent among the adherents and leadership of the Orthodox Church.[4]

Taddesse Tamrat cautions against trying to construct a cosmology of primal religion from the hagiographies of the fourteenth to sixteenth centuries.[5] "From the purely hagiographical records at our disposal, it is very difficult to give an adequate reconstruction of the pre-Christian beliefs of the regions in which Täklä Haymanot and his followers began to work."[6] At best we are given a general picture of traditional religious practices and worship. Taddesse Tamrat also cautions regarding the accuracy of these hagiographies. Usually written by the disciples of an evangelist or monastery founder, these documents decrease in accuracy as the time period between the death of the subject and the date of composition of the *gadla* increases. The miracles and spiritual exploits performed are no doubt exaggerated far beyond what was actually accomplished. New editions would introduce additional apocryphal material.[7] Bearing these cautions in mind, we will now look at these rich resources describing the perceptions of these pioneer evangelists and their activities in southern Ethiopia.

Mention has already been made in chapter 2 of Täklä Haymanot (d. 1313), the disciple of Iyasus Mo'a of Däbrä Hayq, the island monastery located in Lake Hayq.[8] After some years of evangelizing and preaching in

4. Zär'a Ya'iqob (1599–1693), renowned philosopher of Ethiopia, enumerated world religions as the Catholics, the Copts, the Muslims, the Jews, and several religions of India. He then asked, "How can all these different faiths come from God?" Apparently he did not consider the traditional religions of southern Ethiopia worthy of mention. See Sumner, *Ethiopian Philosophy,* 2:31–32.

5. For the first section of this chapter I am indebted to Ge'ez scholars Taddesse Tamrat, G. W. B. Huntingford, Steven Kaplan, E. A. Wallis Budge, and others for their gleanings from the Ge'ez hagiographies. I have been made aware (through Dr. Sergew Hable Sellassie's lecture "Ethiopian Church Manuscripts") that there are many other Ge'ez manuscripts from Ethiopian monasteries recently microfilmed by the Institute of Ethiopian Studies and awaiting scholarly research.

6. Taddesse Tamrat, *Church and State,* 178–79.

7. Taddesse Tamrat, "Hagiographies," 15–18.

8. Taddesse Tamrat has confirmed by personal research that there was Christian habitation on the islands of Lake Hayq as early as the ninth century. See his "Abbots of Däbrä-Hayq," 107.

Shoa, Damot, and other regions of southern Ethiopia, Täklä Haymanot eventually established a monastic centre at Däbrä Libanos.[9] From Däbrä Libanos Christianity continued its southern movement, with staging centers being established at the edge of the crater lake on Mt. Zäqwala and on several islands of Lake Zway.[10] The evangelization of the South was not always done in a systematic, pre-planned manner. The biographies of *Abba* Anoréwos and *Abba* Filipos indicate that King Säyfa Ar'ad (1344–1371) banished these two illustrious teacher/preachers from Däbrä Libanos to the southern monastery on Lake Zway because they opposed his polygamous marriage. These same hagiographies indicate that the native population on the Zway islands had no religion because they ate the meat of dead animals and the meat of animals improperly slaughtered.[11] Biographers of *Abba* Gäbrä Mänfäs Qädus, who was head of the Mt. Zäqwala monastery and a contemporary of Täklä Haymanot, depict their religious leader doing battle with innumerable devils. It is reported that in one day Gäbrä Mänfäs Qädus conquered 7,200 devils.[12] This account appears to confirm the oral tradition that Mt. Zäqwala was a significant primal religious center prior to the coming of Christianity. In 1964 Otto Meinardus made a lengthy study of religious shrines on Mt. Zäqwala. He saw evidence of numerous pre-Christian cultic sites around the crater lake situated at the summit.[13] There is a still lingering belief that the crater lake has therapeutic qualities. To the Cushites inhabiting the valley floor below Mt. Zäqwala, this volcano, enshrouded with clouds in the rainy season, was the cosmic meeting place of the gods with men. M. de Coppet assessed the significance of Zäqwala thus: "Most of the shrines of Ethiopia have a long pre-Christian

---

9. Unless otherwise indicated, this study will refer to Budge's 1906 English translation of *The Life and Miracles of Täklä Haymanote, Version of Waldäbrä*.

10. For a thorough treatment of the expansion of the Orthodox Church into southern Ethiopia in the fourteenth and fifteenth centuries, see Taddesse Tamrat, *Church and State*, chap. 5, "Evangelization."

11. Taddesse Tamrat, "The Abbots of Däbra Hayq," 107. See also Blundell, "Exploration in the Abai Basin," 531, where mention is made of the Christian influence of the monasteries of Lake Zway on the Sidama hinterland.

12. Meinardus, "Zequala," 34–37, tells about the *Abba's* birth in Egypt, his miraculous transport to Mt. Zäqwala, and his spiritual exploits. See also Taddesse Tamrat, *Church and State*, 161 n. 2, regarding Gäbrä Mänfäs Qädus.

13. Meinardus, "Zequala," 39. In 1964 Meinardus observed lepers making the strenuous ascent to the Zäqwala crater lake, believing that healing would take place if they dipped themselves into the cold water.

history. With the introduction of Christianity, the cultic functions of the site were filled with new theological meaning."[14]

The Solomonic Evangelists' Description of the Unseen

Devil(s)

When Täklä Haymanot was preaching in Katata, a district of Shoa, a devil was seen living in a tree and was worshipped by the entire population.[15] In the country of Ensedsete was a mountain called Wifat, inhabited by devils.[16] When Täklä Haymanot drew near, "the devils departed in the form of black men and others in the form of apes [baboons] and fled to the rocks and the crags and promised that they would never return to their former habitation."[17] And in the country of Damot, on the mountain of Zeba Fetan,[18] the population worshipped Satan.[19] He was described as black, with red eyes like coals of fire, and with hands and feet all twisted and misshapen.[20] There is also the account of the governor of the district surrounding the high Mt. Dada who had a relapse of faith and returned to his former worship of the serpent. Täklä Haymanot would have nothing to do with this apostate until he changed his allegiance. He admonished him to, "forsake the worship of Satan."[21]

Steven Kaplan observes that Ethiopian society has a tendency to believe in devils, especially when the future is uncertain. This is especially true for those who reside in the royal court, near the centre of power.[22] King Zär'a Ya'iqob (1434–1468) was very zealous for the purity of the Orthodox Church and for the perpetuation of the royal Ethiopian court. Because of his intense zeal there were unusual tensions created within his court. As a result of these "pockets of uncertainty and competition,"

14. M. de Coppet, *Chronique du Régne Ménélik II, Rois des Rois d'Ethiopie,* Paris: 1931, I:291 n. 11, as found in Meinardus, "Zequala," 39 n. 1.

15. Budge, *Täklä Haymanote,* 77–78.

16. Huntingford, "Saints of Mediaeval Ethiopia," 229, suggests that Mt. Wifat may be the present day Mt. Zäqwala. The evidence seems tenuous.

17. Budge, *Täklä Haymanote,* 99–100.

18. Huntingford, "Saints of Mediaeval Ethiopia," 300, makes the rather fanciful suggestion that fourteenth century Zeba Fetan is the present day Mt. Damot in Wolaitta.

19. Budge, *Täklä Haymanote,* 106.

20. Ibid., 164.

21. Ibid., 192.

22. Kaplan, *Monastic Holy Man,* 71–74.

there was an increased evidence of satanic activity. A hagiographer of Zär'a Ya'iqob wrote:

> There was a great fear and trembling on all the people of Ethiopia because of the severity of his judgment and his power and especially because of the people, who admitted bowing to Däsk and the Devil, and caused the death of so many innocent people by speaking lies.[23]

Apparently the security and tenure of the court officials and other office holders was greatly reduced during the reign of Zär'a Ya'iqob. Uncertainty seemed to elicit bizarre religious activity.

The chronicler infers that the spirit of Satan operates through people. A son of Zärä Ya'iqob, Bätärgéla Maryam, was the pawn of unusual intrigue while residing at the royal court.

> There arose against the child envious and corrupt people whom Satan used as lyre and horn. They accused many of the children of the ruler, and many were destroyed by the accusation of the cursed Satan, some with flogging and some with imprisonment. Many of the messengers of Satan accused him to the ruler saying, "This child is at one with them: he did not separate from them." When the ruler heard this from many fraudulent people, he imprisoned the child. The child remained with his two imprisoned brothers.[24]

Satanic activity was curbed and put under control when Evangelist Filipos used the Trinitarian formula, "In the name of the Father, the Son and the Holy Spirit." The spirit came out of the possessed barking like a dog.[25] "An example of such a confrontation is the episode on Mt. Wifat, where Täklä Haymanot found himself surrounded by many devils. When he made the sign of the cross the devils "vanished like smoke before the wind."[26]

Diviners

When Filipos was still a boy living near Däbrä Libanos, his parents took him to a teacher so that he would be instructed in the Christian faith.

---

23. Ibid., 72
24. Gatachew Haile, "Power Struggle," 52.
25. As quoted in Huntingford, "Saints of Mediaeval Ethiopia," 310.
26. Huntingford, "Saints of Mediaeval Ethiopia," 308.

Young Filipos was full of questions and asked his tutor why it was that people in the neighborhood worshipped "stones, wood, the lake, magicians, and diviners, and hold them for a god." His tutor replied:

> They venerate magicians because these men invent and display to them false imaginings in order to deceive them. In them is the spirit of Satan. When they see him sitting in the fire which does not burn him, holding in his hand red-hot tongs, they leap and turn round as if possessed by devils. When they see this false wonder, they bow to the ground and ask, "Shall we live for many years or die? Shall we be rich or poor?" And the diviner, being a liar, answers to those who will soon die, that they will live long; and to those who will live long, that they will soon die; to those who will become rich, that they will be poor; and to those who will be reduced to poverty, that they will be rich. Speaking thus he seduces them.[27]

Täklä Haymanot preached in the districts of Enareet and Wayrage. He discovered many diviners on the hill of Bilat, which was their main abode and the center from which they itinerated.[28]

After King Motolämi of Damot was converted certain of the diviners refused to believe. These were called "evil and wicked priests" and were consumed by fire.[29] But other diviners in the domain of Motolämi believed and were made preachers and priests in the church.[30]

After the conversion of Motolämi, diviners (some of them women) throughout the domain were sought and destroyed by fire.[31] Anowéros found a woman *marit* (diviner) and rebuked her, saying, "Woman, why do the people sacrifice to you and bow down before you?" Upon hearing this question from the evangelist, she asked to be converted and was baptized.[32] A special proclamation of Zär'a Ya'iqob was issued throughout the Ethiopian Christian realm, which now extended far into the Cushitic South, in order to root out traditional religious practices:

> At that time a herald read out the following proclamation: "Learn, O you Christian people what Satan has done. We prohibit the

27. Huntingford, "Saints of Mediaeval Ethiopia," 312.

28. Budge, *Täklä Haymanote*, 101.

29. Budge, *Täklä Haymanote*, 131.

30. Ibid., 142.

31. Ibid.

32. Huntingford, "Saints of Mediaeval Ethiopia," 316. Huntingford defines the Ge'ez term *marit* as "sorcerer".

worship of idols and the adoration of Dasek and Dino, but Satan has insinuated himself into our house and has led astray your children." He then ordered the latter to be punished; they were whipped before a crowd who gathered to see their wounds and sufferings.[33]

It is difficult to determine what English word or words best depict those who practice witchcraft, magic, and divination. One and the same person, in a given society, may practice all of the above-mentioned without any seeming contradiction. Kaplan cautions, "Any attempt to establish a precise English equivalent such as 'witch,' 'sorcerer,' 'diviner,' or 'priest,' for each of the Ge'ez terms is doomed to failure."[34] Sixteenth century Portuguese Jesuit priest Paez, writing his *History of Täklä Haymanot*, translated from the ancient sixth century Ge'ez Bible such words as *maryan, masaryan,* and *haras* (which can mean witchcraft or magic) with the Portuguese word *feiticeiro,* which is derived from *feitico,* the root for the English word "fetish."[35]

Spirit Possession

Stories of spirit possession abound in the accounts of Täklä Haymanot and the other evangelists. The son of the governor of Adamo was brought to Täklä Haymanot to be delivered from demon possession. The spirits asked Täklä Haymanot, "Why have you come to this country to disturb us?"[36] In another instance Täklä Haymanot cast out a devil from a harlot in the city of Zorare.[37] A man residing in Amhara who had an evil spirit asked Täklä Haymanot why he had left his place of work in Shoa and come to Amhara to torment him.[38] Because of the preaching activity of Täklä Haymanot in Tamaryo, the evil spirits began to move elsewhere. One spirit said he was going to Gojam because "a stronger man is coming."[39] A young lad who had formerly been possessed by an evil spirit eventually became a monk.

---

33. As quoted in Pankhurst, *Ethiopian Royal Chronicles*, 30.

34. Kaplan, *Monastic Holy Man*, 110.

35. Huntingford, "Saints of Mediaeval Ethiopia," 321–23, attempts, with little success, to find the Ge'ez equivalent terms of "witchcraft," "divination," "sorcerer," etc. in the Authorized Version of the Bible.

36. Budge, *Täklä Haymanote*, 109.

37. Ibid., 147.

38. Ibid., 158.

39. Ibid., 195.

Täklä Haymanot's fellow monks were greatly offended at their leader for permitting this.[40]

When one of Täklä Haymanot's disciples was walking along the shore of a lake, a wicked spirit ascended out of the water and tried to enter the disciple. When Täklä Haymanot made the sign of the cross the spirit-possessed man stood beside the lake shore. The account relates how Täklä Haymanot captured the possessed disciple and "circumcised and (he) baptized him with the name of Krestos Haraya, and finally gave him the monk's habit."[41]

There is no doubt that the Solomonic evangelists believed in the reality and efficacy of primal religious practitioners. But they were committed to the belief that their God, *Egziabihir,* the God of the Old and New Testaments and the God of the Christians, was more powerful than the god of the traditional religionists. Unabashed, Täklä Haymanot could challenge the non-Christian cult practitioners of Motolämi to heal their ailing ruler. The practitioners explained their impotence to cure their king: "We are unable to heal him because your magic is stronger than ours."[42] It was then that Täklä-Haymanot put his hand out and touched the king, called on the name of Christ and healed him. The magicians were then destroyed by fire. The exaggerated accounts of the evangelists' feats over the practitioners of witchcraft and sorcery exhibit the firm belief and faith of the evangelists in their God and in the reality of the forces of evil.

Places and Objects of Worship

Location of Shrines

Täklä Haymanot observed that there was a shrine on a high hill of Bilat.[43] And in the lofty mountains of Jama and Ambusha, Täklä Haymanot pulled down many false altars.[44] Usually the shrine was located within

---

40. Ibid., 200.

41. Huntingford, "Saints of Mediaeval Ethiopia," 309.

42. Budge, *Täklä Haymanote,* 50.

43. Ibid., 101.

44. Ibid., 197.

the confines of a sacred grove or at the foot of a large tree.[45] In the city of Katata the people offered their sacrifices in a grove of trees.[46]

The evidence seems to indicate that the traditional cultic shrines and religious centers of southern Ethiopia were converted to Christian places of worship. We have already mentioned the religious significance of Mt. Zäqwala in the primal past. Däbrä Libanos, formerly known as Asbo, where stone shrines were the focus of some kind of Cushitic worship, became a significant evangelistic center for much of southern Ethiopia.[47] A picture emerges that the evangelists of the thirteenth to sixteenth centuries seemed to stress continuity rather than rupture by retaining former places of worship.[48]

Objects of Worship

Snake worship has had a long tradition in northern Ethiopia. On one of the fallen stelae at Aksum there is a relief picture of a serpent called *Awré* in legendary stories of the pre-historic past.[49] During the Solomonic period, on Mt. Wifat located in Damot, Täklä Haymanot killed a serpent that the local population had been worshipping for some years. After this event the people were converted to Christianity.[50] On the high mountain of Dada, Täklä Haymanot discovered a greatly feared sorcerer called Gudit, with

45. Heldman, "Christ's Entry into Jerusalem," 51–52, describes the sacred nature of the *shola* (sycamore) tree. She suggests that this veneration goes back many centuries. Around each Orthodox church in Ethiopia is a grove of trees. These may be cedar, eucalyptus, *shola*, or *zigaba*. Priests told Heldman that the groves of trees surrounding the churches were "necessary for providing shade, incense, and wood for repairs for the church." See also Trimingham, *Islam in Ethiopia*, 260, for the mention of sacred groves and their use in traditional religion.

46. Budge, *Täklä Haymanote*, 357.

47. Budge, *Täklä Haymanote* (Duäbra Libanos version), 196–97. See also Huntingford, "Lives of Saint Täklä Haymanot," 37, and Lange, *History of Southern Gonga*, 297 n. 57.

48. Sergew, *Ancient and Medieval Ethiopian History*, 116–18. Mention is made of four of the nine saints of Syria establishing churches on pre-Christian holy places in and around Aksum. But see Taddesse Tamrat, *State and Church*, 180, where reference is made to the "bitterness of the struggle" when pagan practitioners strongly resisted the Orthodox Church because the evangelists insisted on building churches on the sacred places.

49. Sergew, *Ancient and Medieval Ethiopian History*, 95–96. It has been suggested that serpent worship, rooted in Persia, eventually found its way to Ethiopia.

50. Budge, *Täklä Haymanote* (Waldäbrä version), 362. See also Taddesse Tamrat, "Traditions of Pagan Resistance," 143–45, in which the ruler of the Agäw is described as a staunch worshipper of the serpent.

whom was associated a very large snake. When Täklä Haymanot made the sign of the cross, the snake was cut in two.[51] That the veneration of snakes was widespread in southern Ethiopia is also evident from the *Lives* of Anowéros and Zä'Yohanis.[52]

Cultic objects of primal religion were often consecrated by the church and were eventually used in the churches. In the district of Geraya, Täklä Haymanot had a confrontation with a powerful diviner. Täklä Haymanot held high his cross and quoted Psalm 27:2: "When evil men advance against me to devour my flesh, when my enemies and my foes attack me, they will stumble and fall." A great victory was won and all the items previously used for sorcery were then made holy and were transferred for use in the church.[53] In the region of Katata, the inhabitants worshipped various objects that were part of the created order. When asked what they worshipped, the people took Täklä Haymanot to a tree, where a voice spoke to them, "I created you, I am your god."[54] Täklä Haymanot cut down the tree and used the wood to construct a church.[55]

The Evangelists' Attitude toward Primal Religion

The Solomonic hagiographic accounts emphasize the sensational and the confrontational when Christianity interacts with traditional religions.[56] Evangelist Täklä Haymanot is depicted in his *Lives* as doing battle against devils and the evil kingdom of Motolämi. Täklä Haymanot destroyed the cultic places at Bilat and Enar'et.[57] When Täklä Haymanot came to the country of Damot, to the mountain of Zeba Fetan, he found idols of stone and wood and observed people offering sacrifices and pouring out

51. Budge, *Täklä Haymanote*, 190. Huntingford, "Saints of Mediaeval Ethiopia," 318 n. 3, suggests that Gudit may refer to the pagan queen who did much damage in Christian Ethiopia, destroying churches and holy objects during the Zagwé dynasty. *Gudit* may also be a primal designation for all witches.

52. Kaplan, *Monastic Holy Man*, 120.

53. Budge, *Täklä Haymanote*, 197–98.

54. Ibid., 79.

55. Ibid., 31.

56. Huntingford admits that we possess "scanty information . . . about paganism in medieval Ethiopia." "Saints of Mediaeval Ethiopia," 296. What information we have is gleaned from the *Lives* of Täklä Haymanot and his followers Filipos, Anoréwos, Basalta Mika'él, Feré Mika'él, and Täklä Hawaryat. The chronicles of King Zär'a Ya'iqob and *Life* of Evangelist Ewostatéwos are also helpful.

57. Huntingford, "Saints of Mediaeval Ethiopia," 297.

the blood of beasts as libations. When he saw "these graven images, he took a stone and broke them in pieces therewith, and he turned their altars upside down."[58]

A confrontational attitude toward primal religion was evident during the reign of Zär'a Ya'iqob (1434–1468). He believed evil spirits were "the manifestations of malign forces of the Fallen Angels."[59] He took strong measures to root out every form of primal religion from his realm. "If you see anyone sacrificing to Satan, kill him with a spear, or with a staff or a stone."[60] His uncompromising and rather extreme attempts to purify the church are further evidenced by his proclamation that "whoever kills pagans has committed no sins."

In the middle of the fourteenth century Christianity began to penetrate the Sidama territory. Mention has already been made of evangelists Filipos and Anoréwos being banished to the island monasteries of Lake Zway. That these two were not content to be confined in solitude on their island fortress is made clear from the account of their *Lives*. Anowéros began to search for a suitable place from which to begin his evangelistic outreach some distance from the serenity of his island monastery. A local chief, Bäragban, invited Anowéros to establish a Christian center in his domain of Sigaga because he had heard of the positive effect of Anowéros's preaching and teaching ministry. Later when there was organized resistance to these Orthodox evangelists, the chief Bäragban sided with his guests and routed out the magicians in a rather final and drastic manner.[61]

From the above account and other similar evidence, it appears that the burden of traditional religion became a heavy yoke for the Cushitic people of southern Ethiopia to bear. As an indicator that the Sidama were continually placating the practitioners of traditional religion, we have the account of Täklä Hawaryat quoting the local traditional practitioner Mäqawzay thus: "If you fulfil my wishes you shall live, and I shall bless you; if you refuse to obey me you shall die with all your sons, your daughters and your wives."[62] It is evident that every family lived in a state of fear and dread lest an angry spirit strike death if there was the slightest divergence from the traditional ritual form of worship. This fear is further illustrated

---

58. Budge, *Täklä Haymanote*, 107.

59. Taddesse Tamrat, *Church and State*, 234–35.

60. Ibid., 238.

61. Taddesse Tamrat, *Church and State*, 180.

62. Ibid., 234.

in the *Life of Täklä Haymanot*. The biographer describes the activity of a certain diviner, the *marit*.

> A man said to our father Täklä Haymanot, "When I was in my country I went to a *marit* and asked him how I could gain riches. He answered me, 'Kill your wife, and take out her liver and kidneys and eat them; and in this way you will increase your possessions.' I said, 'She will prevent me from killing her.' He answered, 'Put poison in her drink and when she has become weak, kill her.' I did what he said."[63]

It appears that the northern evangelists anticipated that the divinities of the South would eventually fade away through ongoing contact with the Orthodox Church. Addressing a similar situation in contemporary Africa, Kwame Bediako writes:

> Yet, it has also to be pointed out that whenever this happens in the spread of the Christian faith, it has been through a process of the demonization of these divinities in the Christian religious consciousness.[64]

There were those in the South who were unwilling to demonize their divinities and ancestors. It was for this reason that the Orthodox clergy were willing to make concessions. And to this topic of compromise and concessions we now turn our attention.

Compromises and Concessions Made by the Orthodox Church to Primal Religions

Throughout southern Cushitic Ethiopia the population displayed a diversity of cultural and linguistic characteristics. It appears that the Orthodox evangelists did not expect the local population to turn immediately from their former traditional religious practices. Täklä Haymanot was given permission by the Archangel Michael to serve mass early on a Friday morning to comply with the rural activities of the new converts. His concession contravenes the established Orthodox practice of celebrating the mass on Friday afternoon, after some seven or eight hours of a rather rigorous fast.[65] *Abba* Filipos, who was evangelizing in southern Shoa, instructed his own disciples not to be overly harsh or zealous in imposing stringent

63. As quoted in Huntingford, "Lives of Saint Täklä Haymanot," 38.

64. Kwame Bediako, *Christianity in Africa*, 98.

65. Budge, *Täklä Haymanote*, 54.

Christian practices on the new converts. They were to be lenient with the new catechists.[66] It seems that *Abba* Gäbrä Mänfäs Qiddus, leader of the religious community located on Mt. Zäqwala, was compromising in his requirements for baptism. He allowed his disciples to delay their baptism and continue worshipping their deities, giving priority to a more lucrative tradition—the *täskar*. Observance of this commemorative feast required the family of the departed to bring the priests an abundance of meat, money, and *ṯaj*. "Even murderers . . . and even those who worship idols and even those who commit perjury shall be pardoned for your sake if you observe the *täskar*."[67] It appears that the *Abba* allowed the elaborate *täskar* feast for the dead to take the place of baptism.

Towards the end of the sixteenth century, there was a strong movement towards Christianity from among the Cushitic people of the South. After a military victory by Sarṣa Dängäl (1563–1597), the king of Inarya and the majority of his subjects were baptized. The chronicler records:

> At dawn the baptism began. King Sartsa Dengel baptized Badancho . . . he was his godfather . . . and said to him, "As from today you are my son and I am your father!" They gave him the name of Zamaryam which is a Christian name, because believers take a new name on the day of their baptism. . . . After he had received baptism the king dressed him with magnificent clothes. . . . Finally the inhabitants of the country, from small children to old people, men and women, young and old, all received baptism; their numbers were unknown.

The chronicle continues with a description of a large number being baptized:

> Because of the multitude of converts there were not enough priests to baptize them or to put their hands on their heads: they therefore went into the water and baptized themselves without looking for a priest for there was such a crowd.[68]

It is unlikely that the clergy were really able to communicate the beliefs, the ethos, and the spirit of the Orthodox Church that would bring about any lasting conversion to the ordinary non-literate peasant residing on the peripheries of the Amhara domain.[69]

66. Taddesse Tamrat, "Traditions of Pagan Resistance," 147.
67. Ibid.
68. Pankhurst, *Royal Chronicles*, 88.
69. Taddesse Tamrat, *Church and State*, 232.

The Conceptualization of Primal Religion in Southern Ethiopia as Expressed by Aläqa Tayyä Gäbrä Maryam (1860–1924)

Tayyä, born in Bägämdär, educated by the Swedish Evangelical Mission at Imkullu, Eritrea,[70] was commissioned in 1905 by Menilek II to write a history of Ethiopia. His shortened edition was first published in 1922 and has subsequently been reprinted seven times. In the foreword to the 1987 English translation, Harold Runblom comments:

> The significance of the book is due less to its accuracy than to the perceptions of Ethiopia and Ethiopian society which were prevalent in Ethiopia in the 1920's. . . . Its value for historians, students of languages and cultural anthropologists hardly can be exaggerated.[71]

Recognizing that *Aläqa* Tayyä's account is more an "ethnography" of Ethiopia than a systematic history,[72] it is, nevertheless, a valuable interpretation of how a Northerner viewed the traditional religion of the southern Ethiopian periphery.

There is basically a negative view of the *arämawiyan* (literally, those who have no religion) life and practice.[73] An underlying assumption evident in the writing of Tayyä is that the ancient Christianity of Ethiopia is authentic and that a true religion is good for all. He understood the kingdom of Inarya, prior to the Oromo invasions, to encompass the entire Cushitic South, which consisted of the inhabitants of Wolaitta, Sidama, Kullo, Konta, Koyra, Janjäro, Hadiya, Damot, Kindo, and so forth.[74] He acknowledged that Christianity penetrated into the Inarya domain during the reign of 'Amdä Ṣeyon (1314–1344) through the preaching of the disciples of Täklä Haymanot. But when the power and influence of the Ethiopian kings declined, the Oromo invaded the country, killing priests and teachers, burning churches, destroying Bibles and holy writings. Those

70. Arén, *Evangelical Pioneers in Ethiopia*, 287.

71. *Aläqa* Tayyä, *History of the People of Ethiopia*, 3.

72. Sergew, *Ancient and Medieval Ethiopian History*, 5.

73. *Aläqa* Tayyä, *History of the People of Ethiopia*, describes the practices of the *arämawiyan*, 19, 25, 29, 65, 69–73, 85, 87. *Aläqa* Tayyä acknowledges (p. 69) that the source documents for his history of the Inarya were from the island monasteries on Lake Zway.

74. Ibid., 69. According to *Aläqa* Tayyä, the Damot people inhabited Wolaitta, but no mention is made of the pagan ruler Motolämi or his conversion to Christianity through the preaching of Täklä Haymanot.

who survived had no one to teach them. It was for this reason, Tayyä stated, that the inhabitants reverted to paganism.

> Having lost their Christian religion they worshipped serpents and the *zar* spirit. What shows today that the Enariya country was Christian in ancient times are the ruins of the church buildings, fragments of crosses, censors, other sacred articles and shreds of books found in many parts of the country. In some places in cave after cave are found *tabots*, books, vestments, and other sacred objects.[75]

It was the traditional religious practice to which the people of the South had reverted that was so abominable to the Christian Amhara of the North. Not only were the Southerners worshipping the serpent and the *zar*, but they allowed their lives to be directed by fate and by chance. *Aläqa* Tayyä described how the Janjäro chose a new king from amongst the many ill-conceived male children of the royal household. First there was a wild celebration of dancing by the people, and then they slaughtered and feasted on many animals. At the height of celebration the serpent finally came out of his hole in the earth, tasted the blood of the slaughtered animals, and then selected the future king by coiling itself around one of the young men. All the other children came running and worshipped the newly chosen king.[76]

A significant observation made by *Aläqa* Tayyä relates to the growing power of the *zar*-chief. Initially power resided in the secular official, the newly appointed king. Even the *zar*-chiefs would pay homage to the new king, saying, "Immortal king."[77] Apparently, however, there had been long-standing jealousy and competition between the kings and *zar*-chiefs

---

75. *Aläqa* Tayyä, *History of the People of Ethiopia*, 71. See also p. 67, where the writer states that another reason for this terrible destruction and decline of the Ethiopians was "the conceit of leaders and the lack of love among themselves and disagreement among the people."

76. Ibid., 71. The accounts of how the Janjäro chose their king in times past are as varied as the fertile imagination of the Amhara. Father de Almeida was told by his Amhara informant that the cry of a bird in the forest identified exactly where the future king was hiding, as found in Beckingham and Huntingford, *Some Records of Ethiopia*, 158–59. See also Harris, *Highlands of Ethiopia*, 57, for a similar account. The Maale of southwest Ethiopia have a tradition that the "king bee" identified who the next king would be by climbing up the future king's leg, his body, and finally "his chest, to his forehead, where it danced about in circles and then flew back to Bussa." Cited in Donham, *Work and Power*, 42.

77. *Aläqa* Tayyä, *History of the People of Ethiopia*, 73.

of the many smaller kingdoms of the South. Eventually the secular and the sacred offices were coalesced into one. Tayyä's account indicates that it was inevitable that this should happen because the same kind of power transferred onto the newly chosen king through the serpent could be transferred by the *zar*s to other kingdoms. "Therefore in our time, since the *Zänjero* [serpent], the king who reigns in Käfa today adds the *zar* chieftaincy as well and has become *zar*-chief and king."[78]

Aläqa Tayyä concluded his discussion by describing the *arämawi* practices of the people of the South. First, they did not observe strict dietary rules and regulations. They "serve things to eat according to their different customs."[79] And second, they were people without decent ethics. Even the kings of the South, once established in their palace with multiple wives, have "no other activity but fornication."[80] Tayyä ended on what he considered the optimistic note that Menilek II was able to put a stop to all this *arämawi* practice when he sent his powerful armies into the South and defeated the kingdoms of the *zar*-chiefs.[81]

Islam and Its Impact on Wolaitta and the Cushites of Southern Ethiopia

Early History of Islam in Ethiopia

During the eighth century the spread of Islam into Ethiopia was by way of the Red Sea coast. By the ninth century the Red Sea port city of Zeila was a significant slave trading center, noted for its influence in the propagation of Islam.[82] By the twelfth century the Muslim states of Adal, Mora, Hobat, Jidaya, Ifat, Dawaro, Hadiya, Fatajar, and Bali controlled the southeastern periphery and some of the highlands of Ethiopia.[83] It was during this period that the city of Harrar became a powerful centre of these sultanates, from which Islam was spread throughout the region both by propagation

78. Ibid., 75.

79. Ibid., 73.

80. Ibid.

81. Ibid., 75.

82 83 Taddesse Tamrat, "Abbots of Däbrä-Hayq," 113. After the reign of Al-Yaqubi (872–889) Zeila became an important commercial outlet for the entire Ethiopian region.

83. Trimingham, *Islam in Ethiopia*, 62. See also Taddesse Tamrat, "Abbots of Däbrä-Hayq," 113, where mention is made of the southward shift of the political and economic center of Ethiopia.

and by coercion.[84] The city of Harrar is an innovative and vibrant Muslim worship center to the present day.

Islam and Its Impact on the Sidama

The extent of the impact of Islam on the Sidama populations in general and the Wolaitta in particular during the past six centuries is difficult to ascertain. Taddesse Tamrat quotes from the fourteenth century hagiography of Qäwiṣṭos, an evangelist to the Cushites of southern Ethiopia:

> He found the inhabitants of the country worshipping the devils at the foot of *kobäl* [?] tree. They were sitting there eating, drinking and amusing themselves in the fashion of the Muslims. They fanned the fire with their hands and held hot flames in their mouths and chanted saying "O people of Galan and Yäy, see what your god Qorké [can] do! . . . And they brought for [Qorké a daily present of] two fat cows, five sheep, five goats and twenty-one baskets of white bread.[85]

This seems to indicate rather superficial Islamic influences on a population that were very much involved in their own traditional religion. Trimingham noted in 1965 that "Islam then is still rare amongst the Sidama."[86] Except for the Alaba, Ṭämbaro, and the Hadiya ethnic groups, the Kambatta, Sidama, Gédéo, Amaro, Burji, Ghimeera, Na'o, Janjäro, and the various Omotic tribal groups in Gamu Gofa, Kullo Konta, and Wolaitta were not receptive to Islamic penetration. Only small Islamic enclaves had been established in the larger trading and administrative centers of southern Ethiopia, with their own cultic practitioners, sacred shrines, and burial places. Trimingham, writing in the 1960s, notes, "Islam is not spreading among the pagan Sidama tribes, but considerable movements to Christianity are taking place, notably amongst the Wolamo."[87] Islamizing amongst most of the southern Ethiopia population, if it took place at all, was by gradual process of individuals marrying into Muslim families.

Islam and Political Expediency

There is evidence that former kings of Wolaitta did form marriage alliances with the more powerful and prestigious Muslim rulers of Jimma and

84. Trimingham, *Islam in Ethiopia*, 205.

85. Taddesse Tamrat, *Church and State*, 184.

86. Trimingham, *Islam in Ethiopia*, 180.

87. Ibid., 185.

Hadiya. Around 1865, Wolaitta *Kawo* Gobé married Dägetu, the daughter of *Abba* Jommol, King of Jimma. *Kawo* Gobé's own daughter, in turn, was given to *Abba* Jäfar, successor to *Abba* Jommol.[88] During the eighteenth and nineteenth centuries Jimma was the prestigious trade centre of southwestern Ethiopia. New ideas, modern products, world news all emanated from the Muslim stronghold of Jimma. About 1700, Wolaitta *Kawo* Tube formed a marriage alliance with Hadiya.[89] And just prior to Menilek's invasion of Wolaitta in 1894, *Kawo* Tona married Madde, a Hadiya princess, attempting to strengthen a military liaison with this former Muslim stronghold.[90]

The impact of the sixteenth century Muslim incursions on Wolaitta is difficult to ascertain. Ernesta Cerulli states categorically that "Though it was invaded by Moslems during the war with Gragn, Walamo never came under Moslem control."[91] Very evident in Wolaitta today is the fact that there is a minimal Muslim population. These are contained within the urban trading centers at Soddo, Bodete, Areka, and Bedéssa.

Traditional Religion within Contemporary Wolaitta and Surrounding Environs

We have already seen that the Orthodox evangelists of a former era had a certain understanding of the traditional religion of the South. In the section following, a description of contemporary traditional religion in Wolaitta will be presented because it is in "the daily pieties of the group one

---

88. Chiatti, "Politics of Divine Kingship," 487–88. Based on information collected through oral research in Wolaitta.

89. Bogalä, *Yä Wälamo Hisb Tarik*, 57.

90. Chiatti, "Divine Kingship in Wolaita," 488–89.

91. Cerulli, *Peoples of South-West Ethiopia*, 86. It appears that Peter Cotterell heightens the historical impact of Islam on Cushitic Ethiopia when he states, "The region was left with a Moslem mantle." *Born at Midnight*, 111. Also, evidence is rather slim to support his claim that Wolaitta was brought "into a Galla confederacy" (ibid.). To the contrary, oral tradition and the defensive ditches and walls still visible along the northeast and southwest border of Wolaitta witness to a heroic repelling of Oromo encroachment. Merid W/Aregay, "Southern Ethiopia," 435–37, argues that the kingdoms in the mountain fortresses of southern Ethiopia, such as Wolaitta and Käfa, were refuges for Christians from Harrar as well as sections of Wollo, Bägämdär, Gojam, and Tigré during the Oromo invasions. If these areas were predominantly Moslem, it is not likely they would have been a welcome haven for these Christian refugees. See also Trimingham, *Islam in Ethiopia*, 180, for an account of the Inarya Christians fleeing to the mountain strongholds of Käfa.

is studying, their common observances, the unique and special skills and knowledge of the experts" that one gains appreciation for their historical tradition.[92] New religious forms will inevitably be built upon that which has been practiced in the past. Some years ago W. Robertson Smith wrote in *The Religion of the Semites*:

> No positive religion that has moved man has been able to start with a *tabula rasa* and express itself as if religion were beginning for the first time; in form, if not in substance, the new system must be in contact all along the line with the older ideas and practices which it finds in possession. A new scheme of faith can find a hearing only by appealing to religious instincts and suscep-tibilities that already exist . . . and it cannot reach these without taking account of the traditional forms in which all religious feel-ing is embroiled, and without speaking a language which men accustomed to these old forms can understand.[93]

Wolaitta Cosmology

The Wolaitta cosmology appears to have four tiers.[94]

The highest level is where the Wolaitta high God *Tosa* dwells. He is the creator God who lives high above his creation and is greatly feared by all. He created the sun and moon for light, the earth to provide for all the needs of humans and animals, and the fertility in women, cattle, and birds. *Tosa* is not the object of sacrifices or offerings because he lives in the sky, far above the sinful behavior of people and their arrogance. One account says that because of the bad behavior of two arrogant men who quarreled and insulted one another, *Tosa* fled to his house in the sky. It is not known exactly where this place is.[95] Cerulli writes, "Although he lives in the sky, he is not clearly identified with the vault of heaven."[96]

Several characteristics of *Tosa* should be mentioned. A Wolaitta prov-erb says that the creator God who dwells in the heavens is righteous, just, and good—*"Guzo säluwan dé eya Tosa."* The Wolaitta have a strong faith

92. Walls, "Primal Religious Traditions," 256.

93. Smith, *Lectures on the Religion of the Semites*, 2.

94. Geoffrey Parrinder, *African Traditional Religion,* suggests the following categories for an understanding of African traditional religion: the Supreme Being, divinities, ances-tors, and objects of power.

95. Chiatti, "Divine Kingship in Wolaita," 71.

96. Cerulli, *Rivista degli studi Orientali,* 7, as cited in Chiatti, "Divine Kingship in Wolaita," 70.

that the God of heaven will send them many blessings.[97] When blessings are withheld because of community sins, the entire community must gather together at the *dubusha* for confession.[98]

Tosa is also all-knowing. Because of this, all wrongdoing must be confessed to the creator. The Wolaitta pray, *hana Tosaqo gäku* meaning, "God, let this be known to you." In other words, God will not forget the punishment that is due to someone. Even if the elders do not mete out correct judgment, one can leave the matter with God because he alone knows all and will deal justly with the matter.

The creator God did all things well from the beginning and continues to judge fairly and justly in all things.[99] In Wolaitta there is a saying, *bolay ira imin sa'aye ayfiya imés.* This means, "When rain comes from the highest heavens, the earth will give forth abundant fruit." When one clan offends another, it is as if the creator is offended or sinned against, and he may withhold the rain. The community must endeavor to restrain corporate as well as individual evil.

Further explanation of the qualities and character of the high God, *Tosa* is made difficult because, for the Wolaitta, he remains beyond their depiction. What is known about him is that he is the creator, the first principle, and the explanation of everything. But he is far away in his home in the sky.

The second layer of the Wolaitta cosmology is complex. It consists of benevolent spirits or deities known by general names and hierarchically arranged.[100] These are the spirits to whom invocations are made and rituals performed. To receive a blessing upon one's wealth, children, and general circumstances, a thanksgiving offering must be offered to the above-mentioned spirits. Families will meticulously practice this form of worship in order to receive wealth, peace, and offspring. The spirits or divinities are not equal in power or ability. For this reason, in times of crisis or rapid social change, worshippers will offer their sacrifices to various spirits, attempting to gain assistance. The spirits or deities in some way have the

97. Yosef Menna, "*Yätinsaéw Näsibiraq*," 32.

98. Tätämqä Yohanis Shondé, personal information, December 12, 1995. The *dubusha* also is the place where the *mäsqäl dämära* is lighted each year in September.

99. Bediako says, "It is significant that from the evidence adduced, the differences between pre-Christian and Christian understandings (of the divine) are almost negligible." *Theology and Identity*, 238.

100. See appendix 1 for a list of some thirty-seven different spirits. Chiatti defines *ayana* spirits as "the active principles of human daily life." "Divine Kingship in Wolaitta," 344.

ability to infuse a person with authority and power. When this happens, the person is said to have *ayana*. A commonly held belief, not merely in Wolaitta, but also in much of southern Ethiopia where a similar word is used, is that the *ayana* is transmitted to the religious functionary, to the family head, or to the clan leader.[101]

John Hamer did extensive field research among the Sidama of southern Ethiopia in the 1960s. He describes the *ayana* as "good fortune" but qualifies this by referring to the good fortune of the ancestors as *anu-iyani*. This term always implies positiveness or goodness, in contrast to *shätani*, which has reference to malevolent spirits that dwell in trees and water and connotes the power of evil, disease, and death. It is believed that the *shätani*, who came after the southern invasion of Menilek, are the possession spirits and make excessive demands of gifts in exchange for health and welfare.[102]

The third tier of religious worship within the Wolaitta cosmology is the ancestor spirits called *wuqabé*.[103] Mälkamu Shanqo, a Wolaitta evangelist, made a study of Wolaitta traditional religion within the Boloso district in 1985. He argues that each clan in Wolaitta has its own *wuqabé* (ancestor spirit) that is unchanging.[104] The following is a sample of several Boloso clans with their respective *wuqabé* deities.

a) The Qésiga clan, with priestly connections to the Orthodox Church in a former generation, worship in large groves of trees and in caves. They follow a regimented pattern of worship. An animal is sacrificed to their *wuqabé* annually, every month, or every fifteen days. Those who sacrifice regularly will receive much honor.

---

101. See Knutsson, *Authority and Change*, 53–59. Knutsson describes *ayana* as part of the divine being as well as a human quality. It could also refer to the guardian divinities of the family. See also Ronnie Sim's description of the *jarra*, a class of spirits among the Hadiya people, as found in Fargher, *Origins of the New Churches Movement*, 180, n. 154.

102. Hamer, "Myth, Ritual and the Authority of Elders," 336.

103. Dansa Dana, personal information, July 2, 1997, relates that within present-day Wolaitta there appears to be a fusion of the function of the deities and the *wuqabé* (ancestor spirits). Chiatti confirms this ambiguity: "But the question as to whom the cult is addressed evokes complex and, at least from present-day Wolaita, even indefinite answers regarding the spirit of the house (for clans with a totem), or the ancestor, or God, or all of them together. What is certain and is unanimously stated, is the belief that there can be no well-being without the performance of rituals, because the ancestors and spirits (*ayana*), or the supernatural in general, want them." "Politics of Divine Kingship," 345.

104. Mälkamu Shanqo, "*Hulum Ades Honwal*," 6–11.

b) The Zaminiya group, who are contained within the Wolaitta Malla clan, worship the *gammana wuqabé* and offer payment at regular times with the hope that honor will be generously proffered.

c) The Tegré ancestral deities are the moon and the *yafäno*. Each year the worshippers bring an animal for sacrifice with the hope that they will be carefully guarded and protected.

d) The Agärshwa *wuqabé* is the lightning and the thunder. Offerings are presented in the groves of bamboo and other stands of trees.

e) The Boroda Malla clan have the open plains as their *wuqabé*. Unless they present a satisfactory offering, they will be inflicted with leprosy. This clan will not eat sheep, goat, ox (cattle of any kind), or small deer unless they first offer a sacrifice to their deity. If they do eat without appeasing their deity, they believe they will die.

f) The Qalicha clan claim their roots are in Kambatta, but they may have migrated from beyond Kambatta, from the Muslim area of Silti Guragé or beyond. Their ancestor spirit is *qaydara* or *alahi*.

Research within Wolaitta continues to yield a variance of opinion as to names of the ancestors (*wuqabé*) and the names of the deities who may infuse the practitioner with *ayana*. This is no doubt an indication of the dynamic forces of adaptation and change within the primal religion of Wolaitta.

The last layer of the Wolaitta cosmology is the malevolent spirits that must be appeased and are very much involved in the everyday affairs of humans. It appears that some of the formerly benevolent deities may have become harmful. They no longer speak the truth or bring blessing, therefore they are to be appeased lest they exercise a pernicious influence. Of all the malign spirits, it is *tälähéya*, the spirit of the Omo River, who is greatly feared.[105] It is thought that the creator *Tosa*, the many benevolent deities, or the *wuqabé*—the ancestor spirits—will give fair and equitable judgment on a certain matter, but it is *tälähéya*[106] who will mete out this judgment upon the person. It is thought by some that this spirit rides the

---

105. See Fleming, "Recent Research in Omotic Speaking areas," 270–72, where he describes the few but traditional and ancient people residing on the island of Ganjule in Lake Chamo who revere the crocodile. Fleming is convinced that the Gangules' "passivity toward the crocodile is grounded in reverence for his sacredness" (ibid., 270).

106. Bogalä, *Yä Wälamo Hizb Tarik*, 23, makes use of a curious Ge'ez word *sälatälaté*, used in reference to Satan or *diabolis*.

hyena and can move very rapidly from place to place. The Zala ethnic group, residing in Gofa, believe that the crocodiles living in the lakes and rivers serve as *ṭälähéya's* horses, who work these waterways for the detriment of all. After the conquest of Wolaitta by Menilek, this spirit came to be identified with *shayṭan*.[107]

Religious Ritual Practices

Correct ritual must be assiduously observed in all traditional forms of worship. *Gométea*, a strong system of taboo, is a means of reinforcing specified forms of worship. For example, if one's cow becomes suddenly sick or dies, it is said that so-and-so has got into the back yard and because the eye is evil, *higishä* or *buda*, that is why the cow became ill or has been "eaten." It is possible for the dead to be raised with an application of special medicine. For this reason a person will go to the house of a religious practitioner called the *sharechewa* and will return with a special potion of traditional medicine, with which he will anoint the sick person or animal for protection. And extra precautions are taken to protect the calf of the sick animal as well as the udder of the sick cow. When the sick cow fully recovers, a suitable gift is given to the *sharechewa*.[108]

The practice of offering a white bull or cow as a special offering in southern Ethiopia has a long documented history. Täklä Haymanot observed that a white cow was used as a sacrifice at the water's edge where people came to receive a blessing of wealth and healing as they ate the flesh of the sacrificed animal.[109] In the 1930s Thesiger saw the Danikil nomads of the Awash River basin slaughter a white as well as a red bull. The blood was caught in a pan and ritually poured over the head of the chieftain. This was followed by the entire clan's smearing blood upon themselves and anointing their bodies with butter.[110] Dana Mäja recalled that prior to 1935, at the annual *Mäsqäl* celebration, he and his relatives would slaughter a white ox as a sacrifice in the morning and in the afternoon celebrate

---

107. Cerulli, *Peoples of South-West Ethiopia*, 114. Captain M.S. Wellby refers to Wolaitta as "a fairyland . . . 'devil haunted.'" He said that he and his Ethiopian assistants personally experienced "the devils of Wolamo." "King Menelik's Dominions," 297. See also Trimingham, *Islam in Ethiopia*, 18.

108. Yosef Menna, "*Yätinsaéw Näṣibiraq*," 46.

109. Huntingford, "Lives of Saint Täklä Haymanot," 39.

110. Thesiger, "Awash River and the Aussa Sultanate," 8.

with a feast.[111] But before anyone would begin feasting, choice parts of the slaughtered animal would be roasted and placed on two ensette leaves at the head of the family bed in each household. This was to satisfy the ancestor spirits.[112]

SIM pioneer Alfred Roke reported a similar phenomenon in Sidama back in the 1930s. After the ox was slaughtered, the blood would be flicked up to the sky with a shout, "*Muguno,* may it reach you."[113]

Some of the many clan deities of southern Ethiopia are of interest in relation to possible vestiges of an earlier Christianity.[114] *Giorgisan* most certainly alludes to St. George, who killed the dragon. This powerful deity is claimed by eight Wolaitta clans: Agowa, Amaara, Angotiya, Badaadriya, Badigadalaa, Fategaraa, Maraqua, and Masha. For the Ayfarssuwaa and Hiraytwa clans, *Kitosa* (said in Wolaitta to be a corrupted form of the word "Kristos") is their deity. Other clans claim *mariam* and *mäsqälia* (*mäsqäl—* "cross") as their clan deity. These clan deities seem to indicate a synthesis of Christian and primal religion. This dynamic openness to change has been in continual process within the primal religions of the South. If a deity is unable to perform its duties or if another deity appears much more powerful, the individual or family household can opt to change without fear of recrimination.

The *mäsqäl* holiday in September, which celebrates the finding of the true cross by St. Helena, is a significant annual event in Wolaitta. It is unknown when this practice originated in the South, but Haberland claims that his research shows it to be of a pre-Menilek period.[115] He bases his evidence upon the manner in which the Wolaitta traditional religious practices are so deeply embedded into what was once a Christian celebration. The cult of the Wolaitta primal religion is very evident at the *mäsqäl* celebration. This may be the reason members of the new churches in Wolaitta refuse to participate in the *mäsqäl* celebration.[116]

According to Wolaitta traditional religion, the annual worship to the clan *wuqabé* is performed at a sacred place called *mitta*. They sacrifice

---

111. Dana Mäja, personal interview with EPB, September 8, 1987.

112. Markina Meja, *Unbroken Covenant,* 15.

113. Roke, *Indigenous Church in Action,* 48.

114. See appendix 1.

115. Haberland, "Influence of the Christian Ethiopian Empire," 236.

116. Dick McLellan pejoratively describes this celebration as a "sacrifice to the idol." "Wallamo Church," 8.

various kinds of animals, such as oxen, bulls, sheep, and goats. They also offer the first fruits of their crops, usually as a specially cooked meal. Those who perform this religious ceremony to the *wuqabé* are from the Zomboro clan. This ritual continues to be practiced. If all goes well, the offerer and his family are blessed by good crops and honor in the community. If there is abundant blessing, there will be peace from war; there will be no starvation. That is, no one will have to eat wild berries because of hunger, and the men of the various clans who bring sacrifices to be offered to the *wuqabé* may be elected to sit as honored judges.[117]

In Wolaitta the goat has special significance for certain kinds of sacrifice. Those who believe in the guardian spirit of the goat say, *"mechä peatin taw metua imopa,"* which means, "Except for laughter and joy, do not bring any trouble against me." There is no special name for the guardian spirit of the goat except for the general word in the Wolaitta language *"mecho,"* meaning that which makes one happy or makes one laugh for joy. Therefore the deity of the goat is accepted and believed in as the one who can bring happiness to all of life. When pestilence and trouble come against a family, they will make their vow to the *mecho* spirit of the goat. After the difficulty has passed and happiness returns, a thanksgiving offering is made to the same *mecho* spirit. A goat, set aside for this ritual and carefully kept and fed, is found in every Wolaitta home practicing traditional religion. The ritual goat cannot be sold or traded.[118]

Circumcision

In Wolaitta traditional religion, circumcision has significance for several reasons. It is a means of determining a man's status within his clan and tribe. It is carried out several years after puberty.[119] At death, a circumcised man is granted a special burial. The grave is dug about two meters deep, then a special shelf is made into the side of the vertical wall where the body that has been wrapped in three *buluco* (a heavy cotton blanket) is carefully placed. A makeshift retaining wall is made of bamboo sticks to protect the

117. Tushé Tagasha, personal interview with EPB, November 1987.

118. Yosef Menna, *"Yätinsaéw Näṣibiraq,"* 42–43. It is evident that SIM authors have missed the significance of the fact that Wolaitta new churches' adherents no longer keep goats. It was not merely a misinterpretation of the scriptural "separating the sheep from the goats," as Davis, *Fire on the Mountains,* 148, and Cotterell, *Born at Midnight,* 162, indicate. In Wolaitta traditional religion, the goat was used for cultic purposes.

119. Wolaitta informants revealed that circumcision is performed on the young men several weeks before the *mäsqäl* celebration. At *mäsqäl,* the recently circumcized eat raw meat and are involved in licentious acts.

body from loose dirt. An uncircumcised man is simply laid on the bottom of the grave and loose dirt thrown on him.[120] Uncircumcised people are not regarded as full members of the clan and are not allowed clan burial, nor are they allowed to assist in raising the center pole when a new house is being constructed.[121] Only circumcised men are allowed to make offerings to the clan deities.[122] Clitoridectomy is enforced upon the young ladies prior to puberty. It is believed that only the women who have this operation will be fertile.

Ritual Practitioners

In Wolaitta there are two significant ritual practitioners. These are the *sharechewa* (the magician) and the *qalicha* (the diviner). Their activities are often interactive, and sometimes it is difficult to determine their specific roles. Generally, the *sharechewa* lives isolated from the ordinary citizen. He does not shave or cut his hair and wears a conical black and white hat made of the skin of the colobus monkey. In Wolaitta, it is those of the lower strata clans such as the Adda, the Agarshuwa, and the Maraqua who have the highest percentage of *sharechewa* practitioners.[123] For various rituals, the *sharechewa* is called by different names. For example:

1. *Borodeyaga* is a person who speaks or utters things in a strange language or who is a "mutterer."[124] When a special spirit comes upon a *sharechewa,* induced by means of a frenzied dance or the ringing of bells, he or she is said to be *borodés.* When possessed by the spirit, that person is able to utter prophetic words that will come against certain persons or to reveal people's sins and predict their subsequent punishment.[125] Usually the *borodeyaga* has an

120. Cotterell, *Born at Midnight*, 69, 131.

121. Dana Mäja, personal information, September 8, 1987.

122. McLellan, "Wallamo Church," 7.

123. John Hamer and Irene Hamer, "Spirit Possession," 399–401, suggests that the lower strata of clans become functionaries in order to break out of their clan stratification.

124. Ruth McCoughtry, letter to prayer partners, November, 18, 1958, describes a well-known *qalicha* who predicted the future while possessed. She gained this information from one of her students at the SIM Waka Elementary School, who served as the *qalicha's* spokesperson.

125. John and Irene Hamer reported in 1966 that "possession has been declining in frequency [among the *qalicha*] and that the spirits themselves have lost power since the coming of the Amhara and the Italians. Even the *qalicha* . . . have lost all power to make predictions." "Spirit Possession," 406.

assistant (*maga*) who interprets the utterances spoken in a trance to the listeners.[126]

2. *Märächiyateleya géta* is one who is able to predict the future by reading the entrails of an animal. These practitioners can do this at any time, not just when an animal is sacrificed, but whenever entrails from any slaughtered bird or animal are brought to them.

3. *Shucha qoräyagétä* is the one who predicts the future or has the ability to discover the cause of a misfortune by counting stones. This specialist *sharechewa* is highly skilled in interpreting the human dynamics within a family and the extended family.[127] The more the *shucha qoräyagétä* knows about the dynamics within a family, the more effective will be the diagnosis.

The second significant religious practitioner, the *qalicha*, does not live in complete isolation but involves himself in farming and going to market. According to Trimingham, the word *qalicha* may be linked to the Oromo *qallu*, who was a traditional man of religion practicing ritual slaughter.[128] There is a strong tradition that the *qalicha* practitioners originally came from Jimma.[129] According to Täsämä Täntu, the ancestor spirit of the *qalicha* was *alahi*—a name that sounds very much like that of the God of Islam.[130] Chiatti collected oral history about the positive activities of the *qalicha* in Wolaitta. During the reign of *Kawo* Tona one well-known *qalicha* was Moché Borago. His responsibility was to look after the health and well-being of the king and royal family. His predictions were thought to be nearly infallible by those who remembered his activities.[131] But not all *qalicha* have the same ability. The services of some are sought after from a very wide area; others have a limited clientele.[132]

John and Irene Hamer observe that in Sidama the *qalicha* has a much stronger spirit than that of any other religious functionary. He has the abil-

126. Garo Minjo of Goba Chara, Käfa, used an assistant to interpret his messages. EPB personal observation, August, 10, 1974.

127. Dana Mäja, personal information, September 22, 1988. Täsämä Tänto enumerated the same three practitioners, with the addition of the *tänqway*, who predicts the future by dreams. Täsämä Täntu, personal information, September 22, 1988.

128. Trimingham, *Islam in Ethiopia*, 336.

129. Cerulli, *Peoples of South-West Ethiopia*, 114.

130. Ibid., 35.

131. Chiatti, "Divine Kingship in Wolaita," 411.

132. Neal, "Arsee Story," 6.

ity to distinguish between the various spirits and can make contact with his *shätana* any time he so desires. He prefers to make contact with his deity at night, when he beats his drum and others join by clapping. He is able to predict the future and can prescribe treatment for ills generally related to inter-personal problems. But there is a financial burden connected to this ritual. The spirit must be fed, and this may be more than the client can manage financially.[133]

Those who are inflicted with a malevolent spirit go the *qalicha* who claims he has the power of exorcism. The *qalicha* identifies the spirit by name and through incantations and ritual will deliver that person from the molesting spirit. The *qalicha* is also called upon to assist those who suffer a physical ailment. A burning coal is applied near the spot where there is an ailment. Many Wolaitta children have their stomachs and temples seared with a hot coal to rid the patient of the molesting spirit. The *qalicha* may prescribe a special potion that he himself has concocted.

The *qalicha* boasts that he has the power to send rain if there is drought. He may ask for a black goat or some payment for his services. If it does not rain on the specified day he tells the people that they have committed a great hidden sin for which they have not repented. Then all the people will gather together and offer a large ox or a ram, and with hands raised high they will cry, "Oh, spirit, we beg of you." Dana Mäja testified that after corporate repentance it soon rained.[134]

Among the Wolaitta, offering sacrifices, making an invocation or expressing a prayer of thanks are religious activities not limited to the domain of special religious functionaries. The head of the family can function as the priest of the family because he is the eldest member. While serving in a priestly function he is considered a sacred person. The well-being of his family, the fertility of women and cattle, the abundance of his crops are assured by his regular performance of ceremonies. For example, the head of the house must offer the first fruits from the land to the ancestor spirits. When the corn gets ripe the head of the house will take a small portion of the ripened corn, cook it carefully, and offer it on an ensette leaf together with a young calf for the ancestor spirit to feast upon. Only after this is done will the family be allowed to eat of the produce of the fields.[135]

133. Hamer and Hamer, "Spirit Possession," 395.

134. Dana Mäja, personal information, September 8, 1987.

135. Ibid.

Purpose of Traditional Religious Activities

Retaining the peace and the equilibrium within the community appears to be an important function of the ritual practitioners. Before going off to battle a warrior will visit the *qalicha*. The *qalicha* will get the warrior to make restitution with all concerned before departing for war. Should there be some tension or aberration in the warrior's mind, he would not be successful on the battlefield. He must experience total peace and serenity within himself.[136]

Wolaitta writer Yosef Menna describes how the people of Wolaitta attempt to achieve security from pestilence. They gather together at a designated place and offer an animal as a sacrifice and then repent of their sins, begging *Tosa* for forgiveness. In the Wolaitta language this ritual is called *sigétä*, meaning "reconciliation," between God and the people. All must beg to be reconciled. All who have sinned must daub some of the blood of the sacrificed animal on their forehead or sprinkle it toward the creator, *Tosa*. While this ritual is being performed, the people, with hands held high, will call out to *Tosa*, "*Yarshuwa!*" which means, "Accept our sacrifice to you."[137]

Before a battle one may call down a curse upon the enemy. The *sharechewa* curses the enemy by the various ancestor spirits.[138]

The Wolaitta are very careful to appease *Tosa* and keep him from getting angry. The religious practitioners and the elders take many precautions because, if for some reason the hearts of the people are lifted up in pride or anger against *Tosa*, he may bring a terrible pestilence against them. It is because of this possibility that they will go to the *qalicha's* house and make inquiry. They will then offer their sacrifice to their clan spirit and say, "*moreda*," which means, "I have sinned against you and I know I must repent."[139]

When disaster strikes a family or community through sickness,[140] pestilence, or famine, the services of the *sharechewa* are sought. Dana Mäja described the process of counting pebbles:

---

136. Yosef Menna, "*Yätinsaéw Näṣibiraq,*" 45–46.

137. Ibid., 38.

138. Täntu Badécho, personal interview with EPB, October 21, 1988.

139. Yosef Menna, "*Yätinsaéw Näṣibiraq,*" 38.

140. The smallpox spirit can be appeased through the mediation of the spirit *womba*. See Yosef Menna, "*Yätinsaéw Näṣibiraq,*" 37.

When he takes two by two, one will remain. Next he will lay them down one by one and one will remain. He continues this for awhile and then will say, "You have wronged your father or your father's family. You must go and slaughter an ox or a bull and atone for that sin by placing some of the meat on the grave of your father (providing he has died)". After that the man's sins will be atoned for. If the husband has wronged his wife he must make things right. If it is his deceased mother, he must do the same as he did to his deceased father's grave. This also would apply to any wronged neighbor or former landowner who may have been evicted unjustly. The important thing is to make restitution.[141]

Another function of traditional religion is to protect or ward off the malefic influences of the *gomé* (spirit of prohibition). Strict regulations are imposed on what a person may or may not do to be protected from the *gomé*. If one comes in contact with the blood of a relative who is giving birth, that is *gomé* and it is thought that a terrible calamity will befall that person. If there are several deaths in a family, it is believed that *gomé* is present; therefore, the family must vacate their farmstead.[142] It is thought that a piece of goat's hair in the pocket, an amulet worn around the neck, or tobacco stuffed into the lining of a coat could provide protection from the negative effects of *gomé*.[143]

There is also the influence of *gormotia,* the malign power of witchcraft activated by medicine. To combat the effects of witchcraft the *qalicha* prepares some counter-medicine, which is worn as an amulet around the neck for protection. Even though religious practitioners attempt to ward off the malign forces of witchcraft, the fear of sickness, disease, and death is very real among the Wolaitta.

An Assessment of Primal Religion in Southern Ethiopia

Within the religion of southern Ethiopia, the basic primal religious attributes of variety, color, involved emotion, fearful reverence, and sacrifices have not been readily discarded. Steven Kaplan acknowledges that it was easy for fourteenth and fifteenth century southerners to convert

141. Dana Mäja, personal interview with EPB, September 22, 1988.

142. From 1986 to 1989 the author observed that several prosperous farmsteads were abandoned in the Kamba, Gamo, area.

143. Dana Mäja used tobacco as a protective power when he first went to the SIM clinic at Soddo in 1935. Personal information to EPB, September 8, 1987.

to Christianity by adding something to their primal beliefs rather than replacing them.[144]

Before concluding this discussion of primal religion, we will highlight a significant concept that Kwame Bediako calls "primal imagination." He explains that to appreciate "primal imagination," one must have as a starting point primal religions themselves.[145]

> Because primal world views are fundamentally religious, the primal imagination restores to theology the crucial dimension of living religiously for which the theologian needs make no apology.[146]

Basic religious issues such as human identity, living together in community, peace and justice, and non-exploitation of ecology are addressed within primal religion and can be of service to Christian theology. Bediako pleads that primal religion be taken seriously and that the continuity between primal religion and Christianity be appreciated. Another writer says of primal religions, "They have always been the most fertile soil for the Gospel. They underlie, therefore, the Christian faith of the vast majority of Christians of all ages and all nations."[147]

The manner in which primal religion is tenaciously adhered to in southern Ethiopia is verified by Haberland, who spent a number of years researching among the Omotic people of southern Ethiopia. His prior perception of Ethiopia was that it was unique among African countries because of a long history of being a "Christian land." After his field research, he made this assessment of the incorporation of Christianity into the southern cultures.

> This laid however only a thin veneer over a solid African core and affected the popular culture but little. For the Ethiopian peasantry, Christianity means obeying a number of Old Testament rituals and prescriptions and living by the Christian festival cycle. Often the forms of older pagan rituals remained in these feasts.[148]

From the evidence that has been presented, it appears that Solomonic Christianity made little lasting impact on the primal religion of south-

---

144. Steven Kaplan, *Monastic Holy Man*, 132.

145. See Bediako, *Christianity in Africa*, chap. 6, "Primal Imagination and the Opportunity for a New Theological Idiom."

146. Bediako, *Christianity in Africa*, 105.

147. Walls, "Africa and Christian Identity," 213.

148. Haberland, *Untersuchungfen zum Äthiopischen Konigtum*, 319.

ern Ethiopia. Christianity and primal religion have elements in common. Both religious communities have a concept of the high God, the need for sacrifice, a code of moral behavior, communal repentance, a reverence for the cycles of nature, specified ritual in worship, and a strong belief in the power of evil.[149]

It is evident that the primal religion of southern Ethiopia is indeed a living religion that is vitally involved in all aspects of community life. It represents that which is basic and elemental to all human experience.[150] How Wolaitta adherents to primal religion continued to be impacted and changed by several Christian traditions after 1928 will be the study of chapter 4.

149. See Whaling, *Christian Theology*, 165–66, for a model suggesting eight commonalities in all religions.

150. See Walls, *Missionary Movement*, chap. 10, "Primal Religious Traditions in Today's World."

4

Catalysts for Religious Change in Wolaitta

Ethiopian Orthodox Church, Prophet Ésa, SIM Evangelists,
Italian Soldiers, and Catholic Priests

> The chief actor in the historic mission of the Christian
> church is the Holy Spirit. He is the director of the whole
> enterprise. His mission consists of the things that he is
> doing in the world. In a special way it consists of the light
> that he is focusing on Jesus Christ.[1]

Introduction

THE IMPERIAL CONQUEST OF the South in 1894 was a catalyst for religious change in Wolaitta. In this chapter we will consider the dynamics of the Orthodox Church and primal religion between 1894 and 1941, as well as the impact of new outsiders, namely, the SIM and the Italians.

We commence with a discussion regarding the substantial impact of the Ethiopian Orthodox Church on Wolaitta. The positive and negative effects of the imposition of the northern colonizers' state church within the context of the Wolaitta religious beliefs will be discussed. Because of the exploitation and domination the Wolaitta experienced at the hands of the northerners, any overt attempts to spread the Orthodox faith among the Wolaitta were less than successful.

The primal religion of Wolaitta was viewed with condescension by the clergy of the Orthodox Church. But subsequent to 1920, the followers of traditional religion received a special message from Ésa, who was one of their own. He was like a "John the Baptist" to the Omotic-speaking people of southern Ethiopia. His message was, "Repent, worship only *Tosa.*" An

---

1. Taylor, *Go-Between God,* 3.

option for change was thereby presented to the followers of traditional religion. The negative attitude of the state church toward traditional religion, on the one hand, and the reforming initiative of Prophet Ésa, on the other hand, served as catalysts for change.

But the state church and Prophet Ésa were not the only catalysts for religious change in Wolaitta and southern Ethiopia. SIM and Catholic missionaries located in Wolaitta in 1928 and 1930. Both groups claimed Prophet Ésa as their precursor. The extent of Ésa's religious impact on Wolaitta may never be fully substantiated. But an attempt will be made to understand the extent to which he shaped the religious terrain of Wolaitta.

From 1928 to 1937 the SIM evangelists were involved in preaching, teaching, and healing within Wolaitta. Some may assess the ten years of SIM activity as less than successful, for there were only forty-eight baptized *amanyoch* (believers) by the time the missionaries left in 1937. The goal of the SIM evangelists was to establish new religious communities with the capacity to develop and replicate themselves. To achieve their goal, the SIM expatriate evangelists announced the gospel of Jesus, translated scripture passages into Wolaitta, and taught the nascent community of believers the basics of Christian belief and practice. By doing this, the SIM evangelists were, at best, mere catalysts for religious change in Wolaitta.

From 1930 the Catholic contribution to religious change within Wolaitta was fostered by the Capuchin missionaries through schools and catechism classes. The Italian occupation from 1937 to 1941 shifted the stance of Catholic missions from servanthood, under the Abyssinian government, to colonialism. The Italian military war machine was bent on power and conquest. But the Italian presence in southern Ethiopia inadvertently brought liberty to those oppressed by serfdom and the exploitative taxes imposed by the northern colonizers.

This chapter will conclude by narrating how this freedom allowed the Wolaitta to pursue their own spiritual itinerary.

The Ethiopian Orthodox Church and the Northerners in Southern Ethiopia

As was delineated in chapter 2, the evangelization of southern Ethiopia in the fourteenth and fifteenth centuries was through the impetus of the monastic clergy. Orthodox monastic centers at Mt. Zäqwala and Lake Zway provided the spiritual nurture and motivation for evangelization in the southern environs.[2] Filipos and Anowéros, disciples of Täklä Haymanot, transferred to Lake Zway in the fourteenth century, and evidence indicates that they evangelized further "south and south-west of Lake Zway."[3] This evidence of the evangelization of the South in former centuries is significant to our present chapter in showing the possible vestiges of early Christianity within Wolaitta. Oral tradition gathered from Wolaitta sources for this study indicates a long tradition of Christianity.[4] As was pointed out previously, the major reason why Orthodox Christianity lost its foothold in the South was due to the Oromo expansion into the central highlands of Ethiopia in the sixteenth and seventeenth centuries. In the initial stages of the establishing of Solomonic Christianity in the South, the newly established churches relied on the resources of Gojam and Gondar to provide their professional clerics. When communication was severed between the southern frontier and the Christian North, much of the South reverted to their former traditional religion.[5]

The northerners made several lasting contributions that served as a catalyst for change in the Wolaitta culture. The Ethiopian Orthodox Church and the imperial government located in southern centers such as Wolaitta Soddo were purveyors of a literate society in southern Ethiopia. For those from oral societies, a written document had a certain power and mystery about it. The power of the written page impressed the Wolaitta who, themselves, functioned only in an oral society.[6] In traditional Wolaitta culture, the entrails of a goat, sheep, or chicken were read by a religious

2. In reference to the evangelistic outreach of the monastery at Lake Zway, Taddesse Tamrat writes, "By the middle of the fourteenth century, therefore, the Ethiopian Church had already begun to make direct contacts with what is today a predominantly *Sidama* country." *Church and State*, 189.

3. Taddesse Tamrat, *Church and State*, 189. See also his map 5, p. 204, which indicates that Wolaitta was evangelized prior to the sixteenth century.

4. Some of the "Fathers of Wolaitta" who contributed were: Alaro Hajeso, Albazo Agaw, Bädécho Bala, Dana Mäja Mädäro, Hajeso Toshé, Laliso Täntu, Malaqo Déngo, Sorsa Wäqanu, Täntu Bädécho, Tässäma Täntu, and Wagänu Waläna. It cannot be verified if the vestiges of Orthodox Christianity are indeed from the long past or from the more immediate past, originating with the Menilek *näftänyoch* who were assigned to Wolaitta in 1894. But Haberland, after four years of research in southern Ethiopia, states, "Legends concerning those apostles [fourteenth and fifteenth century] are still conserved in the folklore of Wolamo." "Influence of the Christian Ethiopian Empire," 236.

5. Jones and Monroe, *History of Ethiopia*, 103–5.

6. Earl Lewis, resident missionary at Otona, Wolaitta, in 1932 related sending a note by the hand of one of his workers to fetch a certain tool. When Mrs. Lewis received the note she read it and responded immediately. This caused unusual consternation to the workman because it appeared as magic to him.

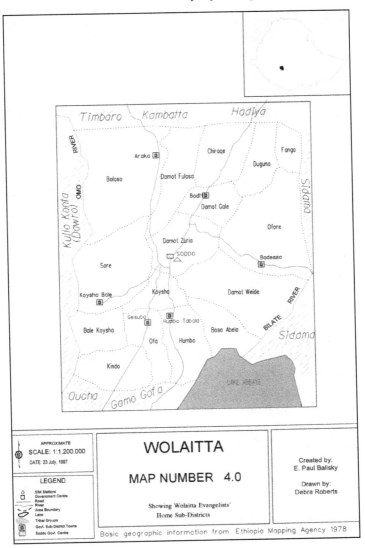

Timbaro   Kambatta   Hadiya

Araka   Chiraqe   Fango
Duguna

Baloso   Damot Fulosa

Bodi   Damot Gale

Ofore

Damot Zuria

SODDO

Sore   Badessa

Koysha Bale   Koysha   Damot Weide

Gesuba   Humbo Tabala   Bosa Abela

Bale Koysha   Sidama

Ofa   Humbo

Kindo   LAKE ABAYE

Oucha   Gamo Gofa

APPROXIMATE
SCALE: 1:1,200,000
DATE: 23 July, 1997

LEGEND

△ SIM Stations
□ Government Centre
— Road
-- River
— Area Boundary
🌫 Lake
Tribal Groups
▣ Govt. Sub-District Towns
Soddo Govt. Centre

WOLAITTA

MAP NUMBER 4.0

Showing Wolaitta Evangelists'
Home Sub-Districts

Created by:
E. Paul Balisky

Drawn by:
Debra Roberts

Basic geographic information from Ethiopia Mapping Agency 1978

functionary to predict the future or identify the root cause of a problem. The Amhara officials introduced a new element, the *afàrsata*, to determine the cause of community mishaps and to find out who committed a criminal act.[7] When a crime was committed in a certain locality, the entire community was forced into a fenced enclosure; no one was allowed to

7. See the well-written novel by Sahle Sellassie, *The Afersata* (Heinemann, 1970. *Däjazmach* Yigäzu is credited with first introducing the *afàrsata* to Wolaitta in 1924. Mälkamu Shanqo, "*Hulum Ades Honwal*," 11.

leave until the offender was identified. All those present were asked to give information about their whereabouts at the time of the crime and what they knew about the crime. This information was dutifully written down by a scribe. The Amhara would carefully weigh the written evidence of the *afärsata* proceedings and then pronounce the judgment. The illiterate in Wolaitta society would listen with awe to the written Amharic verdict as it was interpreted into their own language.[8]

Another means of impacting the Wolaitta through the written medium was through the *awaj* (proclamation) made at the market or at the government center. A government official would authoritatively read the *awaj* in Amharic, which in turn would be interpreted into Wolaitta sentence by sentence.[9]

Amharic, the vernacular language of the Orthodox Church and Haile Sellassie's government, has been a unifying as well as a dominating factor within Ethiopia.[10] Those residing in the South who were not conversant in *yänägus qwanqwa* (the language of the king) were denied government positions and participation in Ethiopia national life. It was for this reason that after 1941 Amharic literacy was a priority for those within the new churches movement.

It was the reading of the Bible within the confines of the Orthodox Church compound that impressed the Wolaitta who came to visit. The gospels and the psalms would be read or recited in the Ge'ez language.[11] What was significant for the Wolaitta, along with the ritual of worship, was that the northerners based their religion on a book—the Bible.[12] For those who followed the traditional religion of the South, credence in determining the future was placed in dreams, oracles of the *qalicha* or *sharechewa*, reading of the entrails of animals, and the tossing of pebbles on a pocketed

8. An Amharic proverb, *Yätaṣafä aywashäm* (that which is written tells no lies) enforced the concept of the integrity of writing.

9. Wändaro Däbäro went to Soddo town to hear a tax proclamation from *Däjazmach* Mäkonän in 1935. Personal information to EPB, December 12, 1988.

10. Trimingham, *Islam in Ethiopia*, 145 n. 2, and Shack, *Gurage*, 199.

11. Sergew H/Selassie and Belaynish Mikael write, "In principle the Mass is conducted in Ge'ez . . . however, the readings and certain portions of the liturgy are in the vernacular, Amharic." "Worship in the Ethiopian Orthodox Church," 67.

12. Ullendorff, *Ethiopia and the Bible*, 36–38, conjectures that the Old Testament was translated into Ge'ez from the Septuagint in the fifth or sixth centuries. In 1968 Alan Tippett worshipped in an Orthodox Church at Dembi Dolo. He reports, "The Bible was prominent. . . . Several passages were read by different officials and one of them carried the book about the congregation for whosoever would to kiss." *Peoples of Southwest Ethiopia*, 256.

board. The Ethiopian Orthodox Church displayed the Bible as a power-ful means in worship. But it remained a means for worship only to those within the Amhara community whose native language was Amharic and who felt comfortable with the Ge'ez church liturgy. For the most part, the Wolaitta remained only as "Gentiles," standing as observers in the outer precincts of the Church.

Menilek's northern colonizers must be credited with the technology and communications that were introduced to the South. The telegraph and postal systems meant that provincial administrators were in close communication with Addis Ababa and with one another.[13] The northern judicial system was put in place throughout the South and with it was an attempt to curb brigands and the illicit slave trade.[14] The *näftänyoch*, quartered on farmsteads throughout the fertile southern highlands, under the command of provincial governors, served as a volunteer army ready to quell intertribal fighting.[15] But colonizers, regardless of their color or country of descent, have left their negative impact on subjugated cultures. The Amhara were no exception.

Subsequent to the conquest of Wolaitta by Menilek's army[16] in 1894, about 500 *näftänyoch* were quartered throughout Wolaitta. The attitude of the subjugated Wolaitta to the northerners was varied. A long-time resident of Koysha district, *Ato* Zema, said, "The Amhara made slaves out of our children."[17] Wolaitta Bible teacher Markina Mäja indicated that during the occupation and prior to the return of Emperor Haile Sellassie to Ethiopia in 1941, only a few northerners were residing in Wolaitta.[18] But after 1941 the administrative positions of government were again in the hands of the northerners. And with this control by a small minority there was the temptation for exploitation and coercion.[19] However, there

13. Dr. Haile Giyorgis, former mayor of Addis Ababa, had relatives administrat-ing distant posts under Menilek. They reported daily to their sovereign by telephone. Personal information to EPB, September 15, 1993.

14. As mentioned in chapter 3, slavery within Ethiopia was not functionally curbed until the Italian occupation of 1936.

15. It was in 1919 that Ethiopia began to train and arm a national standing army with the assistance of Russian officers. In 1926 Belgian officers assisted, and in 1934 five Swedish officers served as drill sergeants. See Perham, *Government of Ethiopia*, 165–66.

16. Chiatti, "Divine Kingship in Wolaita," 334, estimated Menilek's army could have numbered up to 120,000.

17. *Ato* Zema, personal information to EPB, December 9, 1996.

18. Markina Mäja, personal information to EPB, March 1991.

19. Charles McLellan wrote, "These Northerners soon became 'important' people,

were provincial governors who were just, fair, and religious. *Däjazmach* Mäkonän, governor of Wolaitta from 1932 to 1937 attempted to curb thievery.[20] In the neighboring province of Sidamo, *Däjazmach* Balcha Abo Näfso was appointed governor three different times, terminating in 1927. Balcha was a religious man and had the *Sänkäsar* (Lives of the Saints) read to him every day in his court residence at Agäre Sälam.[21] Because of his pious nature and commitment to the Orthodox tradition, he built the Mädhané Aläm, Giyorgis, and Sellassie churches at Agäre Sälam. Balcha was also concerned about the spiritual development of the Amhara in his court. He disciplined those who were unruly and had regular teaching for servants, deacons, and priests. As was the pattern of the administrators representing the imperial government in the South, "He [Balcha] seems to have given less attention to the conversion to Christianity of the Sidamo in general."[22] The reason for this was that serving within the Orthodox Church were the secular clergy. Two or three priests, together with several deacons and cantors in a local church, were assigned to meet the religious needs of the northern settlers. It was not the prerogative of these secular clergy to evangelize the local population.[23] These religious functionaries were to look after the routine services of a local church. The secular clergy were identified with the *näftänya*. For this reason they retained the status quo. Historically, the effective structure for evangelism within Ethiopian Christianity had been the monasteries.[24] The monks retained a certain mobility and flexibility to itinerate from their established centers for evangelism or to establish new monastic centers, as Anoréwos and Filipos did at

members of a small ruling elite, whereas in the North, most would have remained peasants." "Reaction to Ethiopian Expansionism," 111.

20. Dana Mäja, personal information to EPB, September 8, 1987, said he was awarded the title *Danya* by *Däjazmach* Mäkonän and rewarded with a gun for capturing a notorious bandit.

21. Tsehai Berhane, "Life and Career," 176–77. The two sons-in-law of Haile Sellassie, *Däjazmach* Beyene, governor in Bulqi, and *Ras* Dasta Damtew, governor in Yirga Aläm, were judicious, kind, and helpful to the SIM missionaries. See Cotterell, *Born at Midnight*, 47, 48, 62, 63, and Fargher, *Origins of the New Churches Movement*, 40, 41.

22. Tsehai Berhane, "Life and Career," 176.

23. Taddesse Tamrat, *Church and State*, 112–14, 180. It was the monasteries such as Däbrä Libanos, Zäqwala, and Lake Zway that produced zealous evangelists who won converts from local southern populations in the fourteenth and fifteenth centuries. Rey acknowledges this about the clergy: "They do not go in for missionary work themselves, but are tolerant of other existing forms of religion in the country." "Abyssinia," 22 n. 27.

24. See Taddesse Tamrat, "A Short Note," and Shenk, "Ethiopian Orthodox Church's Understanding of Mission."

Lake Zway in the fifteenth century.[25] Except for the occasional wandering *bähitawé* (hermit) who preached repentance, very little overt evangelizing was done by the Orthodox Church until after 1950.[26]

The primary contact the secular clergy had with the indigenous population was in a landlord-tenant relationship. For example, each of the eight Orthodox churches in Wolaitta were deeded hundreds of hectares. The Wolaitta tenant farmers dispersed on these church lands were obligated to give a certain portion of their produce for the upkeep of the clergy.[27] The tenant farmers residing on church holdings were also perceived by the clergy as a source of free labor when the church roof or fence was in need of repair.[28]

Within the Ethiopian Orthodox Church exists a "three-fold hierarchical structure, namely, episcopate, presbyterate and diachonate."[29] The church officials within the episcopate are the patriarch, the archbishops, and the bishops. The *qésoch* (priests) serve within the presbyterate, and the diachonate consist of the deacons and the *däbtära,* who are not only professional singers but are well-taught in the "mysteries" of the Church.[30] Because of the rigid hierarchical structure of the Ethiopian Church, it was nearly impossible for a non-Amhara Southerner to aspire to a leadership position unless there was a radical change of ethnic identity, as described below.[31]

25. Taddesse Tamrat, *Church and State,* 189. According to Isichei, *History of Christianity in Africa,* 217, it was not until 1963 that the Ethiopian Orthodox Church established a centralized missionary organization.

26. According to the SIM missionaries stationed at Burji, Aläta Wändo, Dilla, Durami, Soddo and Hosanna, the Orthodox Church began baptizing local populations in 1950. It is not clear if this was done to counter the new churches' rapid growth. A similar phenomenon took place among the Anuak of Western Ethiopia. Charles Partee writes, "When a mission became successful, the Ethiopian Orthodox Church moved in, distributed a few religious trinkets, sprinkled some holy water, and declared the area closed [to missions]." *Adventure in Africa,* 451 n. 56.

27. McLellan confirms that within Darassa, "Priests of the Ethiopian Orthodox Church were allowed a maximum of thirty *gäbbar.* The lower ranking clergy would have less." "Reaction to Ethiopian Expansion," 142.

28. Mälkamu Shanqo, *"Hulum Ades Honwal,"* 29, expressed that when several of the Boloso tenant farmers refused to work on the Sellassie Church fence, they were punished by imprisonment.

29. Matthew, "Hierarchy," 60.

30. *Abba* Yohanis, student at the Dilla Bible School, indicated that most *däbtära* study with one able instructor for up to five years, "learning the mysteries of the Church." Personal information to EPB, September 1994.

31. Matthew gives the following Ethiopian Orthodox Church clerical statistics for 1970: 60,972 priests, 12,078 monks, 56,687 deacons, and 39,010 *däbtära.* "Hierarchy,"

*4.1 Ethiopian Orthodox Church priest reading his
well-used Ge'ez bible
(Lila W. Balisky, 1994)*

Orthodox churches in the South were usually unpretentious, unlike those in the North, and constructed on a prominent hill. . Trimingham notes: "On the highest point the church, which is simply a larger hut, will be seen standing within its own walled enclosure."[32] Some churches are ornate and up to thirty meters in diameter. *Qidus* Giyorgis, built in 1896 at Gadam, thirteen kilometers south of Bonga, has life-size murals depicting the deaths of the twelve apostles. After the 1894 conquest of Wolaitta, the following eight Orthodox churches claimed their founding from the time of Menilek: St. Mikael in Afama, St. Mary in Dubbo, Sellassie in Boloso, Qädist Mädahanit in Hanchiuchio, St. Mikael in Gära, Qädist Mähärät in Wandara, Qädist Maryam in Bodete, and St. Gabriel in Dälbo.[33] These Orthodox churches were no doubt an incentive to the new churches communities in Wolaitta to construct their own buildings subsequent to the 1941 overthrow of the Italians.[34]

61. The Orthodox Church statistics for 1995 were: 16,879 churches, 134,602 priests, and a combined total of 361,078 monks, deacons, and *däbtära*. "Religion and Faith in Ethiopia," 153.

32. Trimingham, *Islam in Ethiopia*, 12. See also Ullendorff's description of various styles of Orthodox churches in *Ethiopians*, 109.

33. Haberland, "Influence of the Christian Ethiopian Empire," 236, reports that there were only four Orthodox churches in Wolaitta built in the Menilek era.

34. In 1943 a prayer house twenty-five meters in diameter was built at Wanché, seventeen kilometers south of Soddo. Markina Meja recalls that two men could barely put their arms around the cedar center pole. It took three years for master builders Gigato, Anéga, Käbu, and Botcho to complete the construction. *Unbroken Covenant*, 31–32.

The new churches communities benefited from several contributions of the Orthodox Church, such as the Amharic Bible, a literate society, and church buildings. But there were practices of the Orthodox that caused continuous conflict; these were the sanctity given to the *tabot* (the covenant box) and the veneration of Mary. When a new Orthodox worship center is erected, it is the *tabot*, not the church building as such, that is sanctified by the priest. Ullendorff writes that the event at the *Ṭimqet* celebration during which the *tabot* is taken out, "accompanied by singing, dancing, beating of staffs or prayer-sticks, rattling of sistra, and sounding of other musical instruments remind[s] one most forcefully of the scene in 2 Samuel 6:5,15,16."[35] During the post-Italian Haile Sellassie era, when the Wolaitta evangelists did not give obeisance to the *tabot* as they passed by an Orthodox church, they were accused of insulting the state religion.[36] The accusation *ṣara Mariam* (haters of Mary), was made by the Orthodox functionaries against members of the new churches movement. Because the non-Orthodox Christians would not pray through the mediation of Mary, it was thought that they were against Mary.[37]

There was little incentive for a Wolaitta to become an adherent to Orthodox Christianity until after the Italian occupation. For those who became proselytes, this meant baptism, a change of name, the *matäb* tied around the neck, dressing like a Northerner, joining a *mahibär*, and speaking the Amharic language. In other words, the Wolaitta who became adherents to Northern Christianity changed their ethnic identity. As is evidenced in much of southern Ethiopia, and this has been the reality within Wolaitta, Orthodox Christianity "produced few converts with an irreversible commitment to Christianity."[38]

Ésa, a Prophet from Gämo

We now focus on a significant prophet within the traditional religion context of the South. Ésa *Lalé* (the one who releases to freedom)[39] was born

---

35. Ullendorff, *Ethiopians*,110.

36. Evangelist Sawl Salgédo was interned in the Bonga prison for twelve months, 1975–1976, for not doing obeisance. EPB, personal observation.

37. See Crummey, *Priests and Politicians*, 32. Gobat was unwilling to call Mary "the Mother of God."

38. Kaplan, *Monastic Holy Man*, 132.

39. Täṭämqä Yohanis Shondé, personal information, December 13, 1995, defined the word *lalé*, "to release from bondage to freedom."

c. 1880 in the district of Zara, Gämo *awraja*. His father was from the prestigious Gola Malla clan, not from the *sharechewa* or *qalicha* clans.[40] Oral information indicates that Ésa launched his popular ministry around 1920 within his home community of Zara, near Chäncha, from whence it rapidly spread to the Omotic-speaking people of Gämo, Qucha, Boroda, Gofa, and Wolaitta.[41] Ésa travelled with his assistant, Mera, on preaching excursions to various areas within southern Ethiopia.[42] Wolaitta elders Dana Mäja, Täntu Bädécho, and Täsäma Täntu confirmed that Ésa did not frequent Wolaitta very often—two or three times at most—but many Wolaitta went to hear him in his district of Zara in Gämo *awraja*.[43] There is evidence that Ésa's companion, Mera, travelled alone from his home base to bring Ésa's teaching to distant communities within the Omotic language group. Ésa was arrested at his Zara home by *Däjazmach* Habtä Giorgis, Gämo provincial governor of Chäncha, in 1924 and was escorted to Addis Ababa by several armed foot soldiers. When the Wolaitta were asked, "Why was Ésa arrested by the northern officials and marched off to Addis Ababa?" they answered, "Ésa prophesied that the Amhara would one day be driven from the South and the land once again be given back to us."[44] This may be the reason his Amhara accusers determined that he was a disturber of the peace. It was feared that his preaching might incite the local population to rise up against the Northerners. On the way to Addis Ababa, the soldiers with their prisoner Ésa stopped at the Gulgula market, sixteen kilometers south of Soddo, to rest and replenish their supplies. Dana Mäja, residing at Wanché near the Gulgula market, along with hundreds of other Wolaitta, went to hear Ésa. Dana Mäja recalled:

> I remember very clearly what Esa wore and what he looked like. He did not wear trousers, rather had a long white cotton cloth thrown over him similar to what the Gämo people wear. He was a

40. Täntu Bädécho, personal interview with EPB, December 1987.

41. Oral information from Mahé Choramo, Laliso Täntu, Dana Mäja, Tesfaye Tolé, and Markina Mäja. Lolamo Boké indicated that Ésa's teaching had reached as far as Kambatta.

42. See also Singleton, "Asa," 84, Cotterell, *Born at Midnight*, 114, and Isichei, *History of Christianity in Africa*, 215, for a brief account of Ésa's teaching and itineration.

43. Dana Mäja, Wändaro Däbäro, and Täsäma Täntu, personal interview with EPB, September 22, 1987.

44. Wolaitta oral history remembered by Earl Lewis and communicated to Raymond Davis, September 12, 1961. See also Raymond Davis's comment that "Ésa was arrested on political grounds and taken prisoner." *Fire on the Mountains*, 141.

tall man and had his hair cut short, it was not long and unkempt as the *qalicha* or *sharechewa* were prone to wear theirs.[45]

Not much more than this is known about Ésa *Lalé* in terms of biographical data. Michael Singleton noted in 1978 that written data about Ésa was both "scanty and slanted. Further research is imperative before the last remaining oral witnesses disappear."[46] Before a study is made of Ésa's teaching within the Ethiopian social context of the 1920s, a definition of a prophet and a brief survey of prophetism within the broader Ethiopian context will be made.

A seminal study on the rich textures of prophets and prophecies within East Africa is by D. M. Anderson and D. H. Johnson. They define a prophet as "a charismatic leader . . . free from family and social ties as well as economic interests. . . . He creates new obligations and brings about a radical reorientation of attitudes and values.[47]

It appears that a prophet is driven by two forces. First, there is the engine of crisis within a given society. The prophet has a message that shows the way into the future that will form a break with past tradition. One could say that these are the external forces that shape the prophet's message. And second, there is the inner spiritual force that impels the prophet, which could be called "divine inspiration."[48] The prophet is undergirded with a strong divine call to restore society back to health and well-being. The prophet sees clearly into the future as to what might be if there is renewal and revitalization of society.[49] The prophet functions in a different manner from the *qalicha*, who foretells the future by dreams, or from the solitary *sharechewa*, who under a trance reveals that which is hidden. The prophet functions openly and is in conversation with his society. He yields a certain authority in that he expresses cogently and with passion what

45. Dana Mäja, personal interview with EPB, September 8, 1987. (Dana Mäja, who appears several times in this chapter, was to become the leader of the Wolaitta *amanyoch* communities after 1946.) Wändaro Däbäro went to hear Ésa when the soldiers camped at the Humbo market several days before he arrived at Gulgula. Personal interview, 12 December 1988. For accounts of other Ethiopian prophets see also Crummey, "Shaikh Zakaryas," and Cotterell, *Born at Midnight*, 114–15.

46. Singleton, "Asa," 88. Singleton does not identify his sources of "written data."

47. Anderson and Johnson, *Revealing Prophets*, 11. For a study of prophetism within the African Christian tradition see Sundkler, *Bantu Prophets*, Shank, "Legacy of William Wade Harris," 170–76, and Wyatt MacGaffey, *Modern Kongo Prophets*.

48. This would be the same force that inspired the Old Testament prophets such as Isaiah, Ezekiel, Jeremiah, and Amos.

49. See Wallace, "Revitalization Movements."

the society feels and thinks about their present situation. These are the qualities that define a prophet—qualities that have been evident among Ethiopian prophets for centuries.

In the eighteenth century, near Gondar, a certain prophet had a large following from among both the peasants and religious leaders. This created a significant disturbance among the local population. This so-called "fake Christ" was eventually apprehended by the authorities and his movement quelled.[50]

Another prophet, *Shaikh* Zäkaryas (1848–1920), forsook Muslim beliefs and embraced Orthodox Christianity.[51] Donald Crummey describes Prophet *Shaikh* Zäkaryas of Soqotä, north of Lalibäla, accordingly:

> *Shaikh* Zäkaryas thus represents a classical type of prophet. Inspired by visions, gifted with supernatural powers, he boldly preached a message of conversion and repentance."[52]

Because of harassment from local Muslim followers, in 1905 *Shaikh* Zäkaryas made formal appeal to Emperor Menilek for a permission letter that would allow him to preach freely in Soqotä. An official document of permission was granted, and through *Shaikh* Zäkaryas's forceful preaching a crowd of around 10,000 were attracted to Christianity.[53]

In southern Ethiopia there were other prophets contemporary to Ésa. Abbaye was from Unfura, Kambatta. In 1939 he began calling his neighbors together and told them to forsake their ancestor worship and worship only Christ. He encouraged his listeners to put on clean clothes and come to hear him preach on Sundays. Because Abbaye's message was similar to that of the "Jesus people" in the Dubancho district of Hadiya, *Abba* Gole was sent for. When *Abba* Gole heard the preaching of Prophet Abbaye, he admonished Abbaye:

> What you taught previously was Satan's work. Now teach the truth. Pull down your old house. Build a new one. Have your

---

50. Bartnicki and Mantel-Niecko, "Religious Conflicts and People's Movements," 20.

51. According to Iwarrson, the Swedish Evangelical Mission saw in *Shaikh* Zäkaryas the possibility "for the reformation of the old Abyssinian Church, because all nominal Christians in the country are deeply impressed by this movement." "Moslem Mass Movement towards Christianity," 289.

52. Crummey, "Shaikh Zäkaryas," 66.

53. Lambie became interested in providing evangelical teachers for the *Shaikh* Zäkaryas movement in 1925. See Cotterell, "Dr. T. A. Lambie."

hair cut off. Drink water [not alcoholic *tej*], and eat your food with gladness."[54]

It was reported that when Abbaye would preach, he would hold up the palm of his hand and appear to be reading the Bible.[55] He claimed that the high god of Kambatta, *Magano*, communicated to him directly and, in faithful trust, he spoke the true words of *Magano* to the people.

Another prophet of the South was Chäläké from Gofa. At one time he was a practicing *sharechewa* with power over many other sorcerers. Prior to the Italian invasion of Ethiopia, Chäläké began to prophesy that men would fly and that the mountains would shake. This was fulfilled when the Italian planes flew over and dropped bombs on Wolaitta and Gofa in 1936. He also predicted that someone carrying a golden book would come by way of the river with a walking stick curved at the top and explain the meaning of the book. This was fulfilled in the early 1940s when Wolaitta evangelist Laliso sought out Chäläké while he was sitting under a *wanza* tree.[56] Chäläké was convinced that Laliso's message was indeed from *Tosa*. He became a powerful force in admonishing the *sharechewa* in Gofa to forsake their worship of the clan deities and *wuqabé* (ancestors) and worship only *Tosa*.

There were other prophets in more recent decades who called southern Ethiopian followers of primal religion to repentance. Evangelist Mahé Choramo recalls a certain Goda Kao who succeeded Ésa and toured the Qucha *wäräda* around 1935, calling people to repentance. Mahé does not think that Goda Kao had any direct affiliation with the Orthodox Church. Observing Sundays, he would preach the following message:

> Those who stop offering sacrifices to the ancestral spirits and believe only in God will be saved from judgment. People will fly in boxes in the sky. . . . God will descend from heaven holding a golden umbrella. He will judge the world. The dead will rise again.[57]

54. As cited in Cotterell, *Born at Midnight*, 114.

55. Prophet Abbaye may have been influenced by a local Orthodox church or by the pre-Italian evangelizing activity of the SIM or the Italian Roman Catholics near his district of Unfura, Kambatta.

56. Laliso Täntu, personal information to EPB, December 12, 1995. Documented in Davis, *Winds of God*, 53–61, and Cotterell, *Born at Midnight*, 115.

57. Mahé Choramo, "Philip," 21–22.

Goda Kao brought a challenging message of hope and expectation to the people of Qucha. This was not unlike the message of *Wäydo Goda Albé*, a man from near Humbo who foretold in 1930:

> A man and wife will read a golden book together. They will travel together from one village to another teaching from this book. The teaching from this book will be about salvation and judgment.[58]

Albé predicted that one day all Wolaitta, regardless of clans, would belong to one *mahibär* (an association of like-minded people) and would eat together around one table. The Amhara would disappear.

And more recently, in 1975, Wolaitta evangelists Sawl Salgédo and Arshé Dubé were invited by the renowned traditional religious functionary, Ibäda Goda, to teach and preach in Adiya Kaka, near Käfa, Bonga. He cooperated by providing a building for literacy instruction and housing for the evangelists.[59]

The Ethiopian prophets just mentioned attempted to serve their societies in their space and time. It is now possible to say something about the social and political forces that were shaping southern Ethiopian culture to produce the Prophet Ésa. Mention has already been made in chapter 2 about the Abyssinian imperial expansion to the South subsequent to 1890 and the ensuing burden this imposed upon indigenous cultures. Donald Donham has argued that the Omotic cultures at the end of the nineteenth century shared a "pattern of 'kingship.'"[60] These southern Ethiopian societies, the Käfa on the west, Wolaitta on the east, and the Bänna on the south had a common ritual language.

> The perpetuity of peoples, the fertility of their lands, and multiplication of their cattle and goats were said to depend on the vitalizing presence of divine kings.[61]

As the kingdoms in the South were subjugated by Menilek's army, the majority of the kings were either imprisoned and replaced by northern administrators or temporarily made vassal kings, as was the Wolaitta king

---

58. Laliso Täntu, as found in *"Bäwängél Amanyoch Andinät,"* 31.

59. Sawl Salgédo, *"Achir Yähiywäté Tarik,"* 76–79. Unfortunately the Marxist/Leninist Ethiopian Government incarcerated Ibäda Goda in Addis Ababa 1975. His final demise is unknown. Not all Wolaitta evangelists would concur that Ibäda Goda was a prophet in the same way that Ésa, Albé, and Chäläké were.

60. Donham, *Work and Power in Maale*, 38.

61. Ibid.

Ṯona. During this process, a significant alteration took place in the belief system of these Omotic peoples. The mythical concept of a "vitalizing presence of divine kings" was diminishing. This can be illustrated by what took place in Wolaitta after Ṯona was recalled to Addis Ababa in 1903 because of his insubordination to Menilek's government.[62] Robe, Ṯona's son, was allowed to return to Wolaitta as the newly appointed vassal king and perform ritual roles within Wolaitta society. When Robe's son, Desta, was appointed to succeed Robe in 1920, "It was clear to everyone in the [Wolaitta] elite that at this point, the *Ṯosa-Kawo* was no longer the immortal divine king, source of fertility and well-being of the kingdom."[63]

The Omotic societies of the South were in a state of religious disorientation. Because of unusual social change brought about by Amhara hegemony, the Southerners' primal belief systems were no longer functioning as before. And after 1906 the political instability was exacerbated because of Menilek's failing health.

Prior to Menilek's serious illness in 1906, various initiatives were taken to modernize old Abyssinia and bring about positive changes for her citizens.[64] After a prolonged illness, Menilek was dead by 1913. But during the following twenty years there was political and religious instability in Ethiopia.[65] From 1910 to 1916 *Lij* Iyasu, Menilek's grandson, was the tentative ruler of Ethiopia. Because of *Lij* Iyasu's Muslim affinities and inability to govern well, he was replaced by co-regents Zauditu, daughter of Menilek, and *Ras* Tefere Makonnen. The period from 1916 until 1928 was an exploitative period when northern *Ras*es situated in the South, without strong centralized control, became powerful and wealthy. Because of this, southern Ethiopia was impacted negatively in two ways. First, there was an increase in slavery.[66] Mention has already been made in chapter 2 of entire districts of Käfa being depopulated. All that remained behind were

---

62. According to Chiatti, "Politics of Divine Kingship," 339, Ṯona armed himself in response to neighboring chiefs' infringing on Wolaitta territory. Because of this, the Abyssinians accused him of insubordination and exiled him to Addis Ababa.

63. Chiatti, "Politics of Divine Kingship," 381.

64. See Marcus, *Life and Times of Menelik II*, where the French minister took an extensive trip to southern Ethiopia to investigate the country. He reported, "The government's authority is solidly established everywhere in these countries." 248.

65. Marcus, *Life and Times of Menelik II*, 268.

66. Pankhurst stated that the demand for Ethiopian slaves "led to extensive slave raiding, thus resulting in the breakdown of law and order and a considerable exodus of population in many areas." "Ethiopian Slave Trade," 221.

abandoned houses and overgrown fields.[67] Wolaitta was not free of slave raiders. A Capuchin priest in Wolaitta wrote in 1931:

> The capture of children is frequent. Two of our neighbors had seen the disappearance of two of their children. Others are sold by their close relatives. Terrible moral poverty, which can only disappear by changes in them, i.e. Faith.[68]

The second negative impact on the southern population was the implementation of the *gäbbar* (serf) system. Each *näftänya* (poor northern soldier turned landlord), controlled up to fifteen or twenty households residing on holdings he possessed. Higher officials would be granted larger holdings and, consequently, more *gäbbaroch*. Some governors were known to have hundreds of *gäbbaroch*.[69] The demands made upon the *gäbbar* were that he must turn over to the landlord a portion of his produce, whether grain or animals, and be available to grind grain, haul water, fetch firewood, and carry produce to market. At certain times the *gäbbar* was to provide hard cash in taxes to his landlord. If cash was not forthcoming, a child of the *gäbbar* was forcefully apprehended by the landlord and sold in a local market.[70] The *gäbbar* system introduced a new tyranny to the South. As one author wrote in understated terms, "The primary economic effect was a depression in the level of living for the peasantry."[71]

A cautious description of the moral poverty of the southern Ethiopian societies is found in the letters and reports of resident missionaries prior to the Italian occupation.[72] In 1928, several months after the initial SIM party arrived in Wolaitta, a farmer from a distant district said this to the missionaries: "We Wolamo are ignorant people and very wicked; we steal and kill and do so many bad things."[73]

---

67. Donald Donham, *Work and Power in Maale*, 51. Some estimated the population of Käfa had declined by 75 percent from 1895 to 1930.

68. Paschal de Luchon, *Journal*, June 1, 1931, as quoted in Chiatti, "Politics of Divine Kingship," 201.

69. Donham, *Work and Power in Maale*, 52.

70. *Ato* Zema, personal information to EPB, December 10, 1995.

71. Markakis, *Ethiopia*, 116.

72. Access to limited quotes from the letters and journals of R. P. Paschal de Luchon of the Capuchin Order, who was a resident priest in Wolaitta and Kambatta from 1930 to 1937, has been provided through Chiatti, "Politics of Divine Kingship." Paschal's diaries, letters, and reports are in the Archives of the Capuchin Order in Europe.

73. Duff, *Cords of Love*, 61.

A 1936 letter to friends and supporters from SIM missionaries Walter and Marcella Ohman reports:

> Eight years ago our pioneer party entered Wolamo. Here we found a very degraded people. . . . Indeed the Amharas (ruling class), told us that the Wolamos were cows and that they did not have souls and would never respond to the Gospel.[74]

Capuchin priest in Wolaitta, Paschal de Luchon, whose sympathy was also for the Wolaitta, describes the colonizers in a rather critical manner in his journal entry for June 1, 1931:

> The *näftänya* are only in the country temporarily. Their concern is not the improvement of the Country or of its tenants; no, they worry about only making more money by extortion. . . . They double the tax when they foresee a change.[75]

Paschal continues, "The Amhara view the Wolaita as slaves, thieves, liars, potters, and well-diggers."[76]

Wolaitta elder Tässama Tântu Borago recalls that there was much famine and poverty in the country after 1920. All the people were crying to *Tosa* because of the impending disaster. At this time they would go the *sharechewa* who worshipped the Maraqo deity. The clients were told to bring a black goat and some cash.[77]

Reports of the period prior to the Italian occupation indicate that fear of death and of malevolent spirits was on the increase.[78]

After *Tona* was recalled from Wolaitta, the indigenous court of elders no longer functioned. By 1920 the society had become demoralized. The Wolaitta lacked pride because much of their own societal structure had been replaced by that of the Northerners. Their primal religious system no longer functioned. All they could say was, "We are poor and miserable."[79]

---

74. Walter and Marcella Ohman, February 21, 1936, letter to prayer supporters. Apparently some Amhara landlords delighted in calling the Wolaita, *"Wey lam o o,"* meaning, "Oh, what cows you are!"

75. de Luchon, *Journal*, June 1, 1931, as quoted in Chiatti, "Politics of Divine Kingship," 202.

76. de Luchon, *Journal*, July, 27, 1935, as quoted in Chiatti, "Politics of Divine Kingship," 6.

77. Täsämä Tântu, personal information to EPB, September 22, 1988.

78. Eshetu Abate, "Origin and Growth of Evangelical Christianity in Wollayta," 3.

79. As found in Chiatti, "Politics of Divine Kingship," 340.

The malevolent aspects of the Omotic peoples' belief system were being exploited by the functionaries in their attempt to restore control and health to society. A *sharechewa* from the Donga district threatened to kill by his sorcery anyone who offended him. People became afraid of him because it was said he could manipulate the unseen world and bring death to members of households.[80]

As shown in chapter 3 the Omotic peoples of the South fear several malevolent spirits, which must be appeased. One of these is *gomé*. As an example, because Dana Mäja feared that the SIM nurse at Soddo might harm him with *gomé*, he carried several tobacco leaves in the folds of his coat for protection.[81] Another kind of power is *gormotiya*, a detrimental power activated by medicine or a specially prepared food. Markina Mäja and his father found *gormotiya*, meat wrapped in an *ensette* leaf, placed on the path next to their residence at Wanché by a jealous neighbor.[82] And then there is the fearful malevolent power *ṭälähéya*, the spirit of the crocodile who desires to ride a person as one rides a horse.[83] According to the Wolaitta, *ṭälähéya* is the most dangerous spirit by which one could be inflicted.[84]

It could well be that Prophet Ésa felt burdened for his compatriots. They were socially and economically harassed by the Northerners. And they were being exploited by their religious functionaries. His burden was translated into action. Whether he received his inspiration for his messages through divine dreams or through contact with the Orthodox Church is unknown.[85] He would gather his followers out in the fields and in market places. His message was direct. Eshetu Abate calls Ésa the John the Baptist of Wolaitta. He continues, "Whatever the effect of his preaching, he stirred up the consciousness of many people and left a lasting impression on their hearts."[86]

80. de Luchon, *Journal*, October 10, 1930, as quoted in Chiatti, "Politics of Divine Kingship," 80.

81. Dana Mäja, personal interview with EPB, December 1987.

82. Markina Mäja, *"Autobiography,"* 10.

83. Trimingham, *Islam in Ethiopia*, 259, says *ṭälähéya* is the spirit of the Omo River. The Wolaitta who believe that *ṭälähéya* is "riding" them are known to dash across the highway in front of a fast moving vehicle, anticipating that the spirit will be crushed. See Cotterell, *Born at Midnight*, 125.

84. Chiatti, "Politics of Divine Kingship," recorded that a young woman from the village of Borkoshe, said to be possessed by *ṭälähéya*, could hardly be restrained by four men.

85. Eshetu Abate, "Origin and Growth of Evangelical Christianity in Wollayta," 4.

86. Ibid., 4–5.

This "lasting impression" on the hearts and minds of Ésa's listeners can be divided into three components. First, the people were to worship the creator God, *Tosa,* and offer him "that which was sweet and expensive."[87] The head of a household, dressed in his best, was to take a pot of pure white honey early Sunday morning and have his family stand behind him in a field facing east. He would dip the fingers of both his hands into the honey, and as he flicked the honey into the sky, the father would say, "You are the creator of all, *Tosa,* have mercy upon us. We offer this which is the best we have to you."[88] This was done three times. The women were to pray to Mary asking mercy from her. The people were to turn away from the fixation on the power of *ṭälähéya* and worship only *Tosa.*[89] They were to destroy any objects of divination or magic they kept in their houses.

Earl Lewis, SIM missionary from 1929 to 1936, travelled extensively within Wolaitta. He interprets the function of Ésa as follows:

> He [Ésa] challenged the matter of Satan worship and taught that the people would worship only God, because there was a God that created the heavens and the earth and everything, and He alone was worthy of worship. So he began to denounce Satan worship, and in its place, he challenged the people to worship God. The form of offering their prayers seemed rather strange and interesting because on Sunday morning the head of the house would go out and dip his fingers in honey, and then flip the honey toward the heavens as he prayed to God instead of to Satan. Then this man taught them a kind of ten commandments that we have in the Word of God. There was a lot of interest in his message, and soon he had a great following.[90]

87. Mahé Choramo, "Philip," 21.

88. Markina Meja, *Unbroken Covenant,* 15. According to Donham, *Work and Power in Maale,* 42, the bee is significant in the mythology of divine kingship to the Maale, one of the Omotic societies located 150 kilometers south-southwest of Wolaitta. Alfred Roke, *Indigenous Church in Action,* 48, sites a Sidama functionary flicking the blood of a slaughtered animal to *Magano,* saying, "May it reach you." As found in Cotterell, *Born at Midnight,* 125.

89. Cotterell, *Born at Midnight,* 114. Ésa's plea to worship only *Tosa* and put away false gods is much like the ministry of Sampson Oppong of Ghana. See Haliburton, "Calling of a Prophet."

90. Earl Lewis, letter to Raymond Davis, September 12, 1961. Few SIM missionaries saw anything positive in primal religion or in prophets such as Ésa. This is the basic thesis of Kraemer, *Christian Message in a Non-Christian World.*

African church historian Elizabeth Isichei poses a pertinent question about Ésa and other prophets: "Do they represent an intellectual's response to a changed and enlarged world?"[91] The answer is affirmative. Ésa was able to bring a far distant _Tosa_ into the daily lives of the ordinary family.

This brings us to the second component of Ésa's teaching—an adaptation of rituals. Families were to worship together, with the head of the household acting as the intercessor. Previously the head of the family would offer oblations to the ancestor spirit at the center pole (*tusa*) of his house. Now, fathers were to pray to _Tosa_ and the mothers to *Mariam*. The ritual for family worship was to be carried out every Sunday morning. This seven-day sequence was no doubt borrowed from the Ethiopian Orthodox Church. Another ritual introduced by Ésa was fasting every Friday.[92] This practice may have been borrowed from the Ethiopian Church or from the few Muslims located in Chäncha.

The third component of Ésa's teaching that made a lasting impression was to foster better relationships one with another. Partially because of exploitation by the Northerners, ill-will, hate, and jealousy pervaded the Omotic societies. It appears that Ésa borrowed the Decalogue from the Ethiopian Orthodox Church.[93] He taught that all people were to live at peace with one another and not to create divisions among themselves. They were not to argue with their neighbor. They were not to create class distinctions among themselves. Humility was to overrule the tendency to clan pride. All must be careful to do good deeds. All people were to love their enemies. They were not to commit adultery nor to speak falsely.[94] The new component that Ésa emphasized was that true religion makes an ethical demand upon an individual and upon society. Religion not only makes demands upon people in their vertical relationship to _Tosa_, but the truly religious have moral obligations in their horizontal relationships.

For example, at the Gulgula market in 1924, Dana Mäja overheard this conversation between a client and Ésa:

91. Isichei, *History of Christianity in Africa*, 215.

92. Mahé Choramo, "Philip," 21, said that even children above two years of age were to fast from sunrise to sunset.

93. There is no evidence that Ésa was literate or developed skills to communicate in Amharic.

94. Mälkamu Shanqo, "*Hulum Ades Honwal*," 10, lists Ésa's teachings, five of which are directly from the Decalogue. This may be the author Mälkamu's extrapolation of what he thinks Ésa really taught.

A certain man asked Esa, "My house has been burned down. Tell me who did it." Esa replied, "Because you did such and such evil to that man in the first place, your house has been burned down."[95]

Ésa's arrest, trial and imprisonment are evidence enough to show that Ésa was a prophet of substantial influence in southern Ethiopia. He was not intent so much on overthrowing the existing government but rather on reforming and seeking to renew society and the structure of government.[96] Testimonies by living witnesses confirm his influence. Mahé Choramo of Qucha said, "The whole countryside responded to his message."[97] Mälkamu Shanqo wrote that Ésa's teaching was followed very closely by several clans in Boloso *wäräda*.[98] And Tesfaye Tole recorded that in 1942 the residents of Bonké *wäräda*, some thirty kilometers south of Chäncha, were followers of Ésa.[99]

From the evidence available, the majority of witnesses affirm that Ésa was both a pre-Christian prophet and a providential precursor of Christianity. Mahé Choramo was a lad of two when Ésa visited in Qucha in 1924. Mahé was told by his mother and neighbors that Ésa's message was, "Don't go to the diviners. Don't offer animal sacrifices to the ancestral spirits. Don't slaughter goats and sheep so that people can read future events by their intestines."[100] And Chäncha elder Tesfaye Tole recorded the following about how Ésa's teaching had initially penetrated Bonké *wäräda* in Gämo:

> In 1950 Wolaitta evangelist Gofilo Golo travelled to Bonké to preach the gospel. But for the district of Bonké this was not the first time they received preaching. For most of them this was the second time. The reason for this was that some years before a man by the name of Esa travelled around many districts [including Bonké] and taught the people not to worship the *qalicha*, stones, trees or any other objects.[101]

95. Dana Mäja, personal interview with EPB, December 1987.

96. Raymond Davis writes, unfortunately, that Ésa's movement "became involved in politics." *Fire on the Mountains*, 241.

97. Mahé Choramo, "Philip," 21.

98. Mälkamu Shanqo, "*Hulum Ades Honwal*," 10.

99. Tesfaye Tole, as quoted in KHC, "*Bäwängél Amanyoch Andinät*," 34.

100. Mahé Choramo, "Philip," 21.

101. Tesfaye Tole as quoted in KHC, "*Bäwängél Amanyoch Andinät*," 34.

Wolaitta evangelist Gofilo Golo, Chäncha elder Tesfaye Tole, and the *amanyoch* in Bonké acknowledged that Ésa was God's messenger. Earl Lewis also expressed what he understood about the prophetic ministry of Ésa:

> I firmly believe that somewhere in the time back before we arrived, God in this way perhaps, was preparing the way for the Wälamo to hear. I think that was one of the reasons why they were willing to listen to the Gospel.[102]

In 1985 a Wolaitta elder, Danél Ganébo, compiled a brief church history. He wrote that Ésa was "like God himself." He continued:

> Those who did not see him face to face longed to see him and those who saw him desired to live with him. Because of his teaching that spread throughout Wolaitta, the power of Satan and his honour was weakened. The way was prepared and a door was opened for Christ's Gospel. Today the Wolaitta Church points out that the prophet Esa functioned as the forerunner of our spiritual history.[103]

Singleton interprets Ésa's ministry as Hebraistic, that is, he was a forerunner of Christianity and prophetically appealed to the societies of Wolaitta, Gämo, Qucha, and Gofa to "rid itself of its rottenness."[104]

Ésa was a "John the Baptist" to the Omotic populations of southern Ethiopia. He expanded the limited cosmology of the Wolaitta so that entire families could freely and openly worship *Tosa*. Dana Mäja did just that in the 1920s. But after several years he reverted to worship of his clan *wuqabé* for spiritual power. He said, "No cows came out from the ground as Ésa promised. Because I needed power to overcome the possible dangers of *gomé* and *tälähéya* I again offered sacrifices to the Wojuwa clan *wuqabé*."[105]

It has been argued that the socio-political situation of southern Ethiopia in the early twentieth century was a contributing factor in shaping the prophet Ésa and his message. That he brought joy and a sense of relief to hundreds is incontestable. The focus of our study has been an

---

102. Earl Lewis, letter to Raymond Davis, September 12, 1961. In the same letter Lewis penned, "It seems as if He was working with the Wolamo long before the missionary ever went to that part of the country."

103. Danél Ganébo, "*Yäwolaitta Bétä Kristeyan Tarik*," 5.

104. Michael Singleton, "Asa," 84. For an expanded definition of "Hebraist," see Turner, "Typology."

105. Dana Mäja, personal interview with EPB, September 22, 1988.

attempt to understand the extent to which he was a "bridge" between the primal religion that was his heritage and the non-Orthodox Christianity to which he pointed. It could well be that what Moshoeshoe of Lesotho experienced about living in two worlds may have been true of Ésa of southern Ethiopia: "Though I am still only a pagan I am a Christian at heart."[106]

Could it be that the Omotic societies of southern Ethiopia paid Ésa his greatest tribute when they addressed him as Ésa '*Lalê* because he was a catalyst in "releasing" them from bondage and moving them towards spiritual freedom?

The SIM Evangelists in Wolaitta

In December 1927 the first party of nine SIM missionaries arrived in Addis Ababa. Dr. Tom Lambie, who led the party, was not new to Ethiopia, as he had served with the American United Presbyterian Mission in Sayo, Wallega, and subsequently in Addis Ababa since 1919.[107] Other veteran missionaries were Mr. and Mrs. George Rhoad, formerly with the Africa Inland Mission in Kenya, and Rev. and Mrs. C. J. Rasmussen, who had experience with the Danish Mission in Aden. New to the missionary enterprise were Glen Cain of Australia, Walter Ohman, and Clarence Duff of the United States.

When the missionaries arrived in Addis Ababa, they were temporarily housed in the Gulele section of the city.[108] Because of opposition from the hierarchy of the Ethiopian Orthodox Church and an unsettled political situation in Addis Ababa, the SIM party were delayed until March 7, 1928, before they were granted permission to make their way south. After four days of travel by mules and horses they stopped at Maraqo and stayed with an Armenian trader, who encouraged them to open a school for the local Gurage population. The missionary party continued to press on to their destination—Jimma. Rather than crossing the Gibe River, just south of Walqeti, the Ethiopian guides steered them through Hadiya country, planning to cross the Omo River to the West and trek through mountainous

106. Thompson, *Survival in Two Worlds*, 319.

107. For information about the beginnings of SIM in Ethiopia, see Lambie, *Boot and Saddle in Africa* and *A Doctor's Great Commission;* Quinton, *Ethiopia and the Evangel;* Forsberg, *Land beyond the Nile;* and Willmott, *Doors Were Opened.* A concise account of the SIM beginnings in Ethiopia is found in Cotterell, *Born at Midnight,* and a carefully documented account is given in Fargher, *Origins of the New Churches Movement.*

108. Cotterell, *Born at Midnight,* 22.

Kullo Konta to reach Jimma.[109] When they arrived in the town of Hosanna, Lambie discovered a former acquaintance and patient of his from Wallega, *Däjazmach* Mäshäsha, who was now serving as governor of the Kambatta/Hadiya district.[110] The missionaries were invited to begin a medical work in Hosanna.[111] While in Hosanna, Lambie was informed that another friend of his from Wallega, *Däjazmach* Yigäzu, was the governor of Wolaitta, based in Soddo, some 100 kilometers south of Hosanna. The missionaries were welcomed by Yigäzu to put down roots in Wolaitta, which they eventually did at Otona, on the northeast outskirts of Soddo town. The fourth location that the SIM party explored for potential evangelization was in the east, across the Rift Valley at Agär Sälam. Here Lambie found another Wallega acquaintance, *Däjazmach* Biru, who had recently displaced the former governor of Sidama, *Däjazmach* Balcha.[112] By January 1929, SIM missionaries were located, albeit rather tenuously, at Maraqo, Hosanna, Soddo, and Garabicho, thirty kilometers southwest of Agär Sälam.[113]

The written goals of the SIM missionaries regarding what they intended to accomplish in southern Ethiopia following their arrival in Wolaitta in 1928 appear rather vague. After Fargher carefully researched SIM primary sources pertaining to SIM involvement in Ethiopia from 1927 to 1938, he commented, "The convictions which SIM evangelists took with them from North America can be accumulated from what they did rather than from what they wrote."[114] This is reflected in a rather broad mission purpose statement drafted in June 1927 by Lambie:[115]

> We also recognize that we consider our call to the regions beyond and should bend every effort to go as far into the regions where Christ has never been preached . . .

109. Duff, *Cords of Love*, 31, where guide Biru Dubalä suggests to Duff that the missionary party will not likely have a reception among the Jimma Muslims, "but if we go to [Kullo Konta] country, people will be glad to receive us." See also Quinton, *Ethiopia and the Evangel*, 49, for a similar account.

110. Cotterell, *Born at Midnight*, 25.

111. See Bahru Zewde, *History of Modern Ethiopia*, 61, for a description of the islamization of Hadiya. The new churches movement expanded among the traditional religionists of Hadiya beginning in 1928.

112. See Tsehai Berhane, "Life and Career," 37–38.

113. The Sidama based SIM missionaries again moved location in August 1929 to the lower and warmer elevation of Homacho. See Cotterell, *Born at Midnight*, 35–36.

114. Fargher, "Origins of the New Churches Movement," 343.

115. Thomas A. Lambie five-page paper presented to Abyssinian Frontiers Mission board members, June 27, 1927, as found in Cotterell, *Born at Midnight*, 16–20.

In the same document Lambie enthusiastically writes, "The opportunity of these many tribes, millions of people, is so great as to be almost incapable of exaggeration."[116]

Earl Lewis, one of the SIM pioneers in Wolaitta, reflecting on the initial ten years of SIM in Ethiopia, writes, "We did not have too much of a plan. And yet as we look at it, God was leading and He caused things to come into our experiences."[117] It appears the SIM evangelists functioned in a rather pragmatic manner, allowing for flexibility and ingenuity as they carried out their evangelistic efforts within Wolaitta.

Fargher identifies three cardinal SIM convictions that undergirded the SIM evangelists in their missionary activities. These SIM convictions are presented in the following discussion because each proved to be a significant catalyst in the formation and growth of the believers' communities within Wolaitta. Their first conviction was that the Christian life began with conversion, and the conversion experience was brought about by preaching the basic facts of Jesus Christ's life, death, and resurrection. The reality of the conversion experience was measured by a visible profession of faith.[118]

The second conviction of the SIM evangelists was that a radical behavioral change in the lives of the converts was to be expected.[119] There was to be a change of practice in their refusal to eat raw meat at the *Mäsqäl* celebration. The Wolaitta believed that because this meat was offered to a local deity it should not be eaten by the *amanyoch*.[120] Because the ritual of circumcision involved various licentious activities, it was forbidden among the *amanyoch*. Drinking or the serving of alcoholic beverages of any kind was also prohibited.[121] The SIM missionaries also discouraged the baptizing of Wolaitta polygamists. The *amanyoch* were taught that anyone who had more than one wife was living in an adulterous relationship.[122] During the

116. As quoted in Cotterell, *Born at Midnight*, 20.

117. Earl Lewis, letter to Raymond Davis, September 12, 1961.

118. Fargher, *Origins of New Churches Movement*, 26–29.

119. Alfred Roke letter to the SIM New Zealand Council, January 10, 1933, indicated that because the converts at Homacho "were showing signs of the fruits of the Holy Ghost, four were baptized."

120. Tiṯämqä Yohannis Shondé, personal information to EPB, December 11, 1995.

121. Davis, *Fire on the Mountains*, 75–76, relates the story of Diasa's not serving beer at the erection of his house. The Wolaitta *amanyoch* were called the "water people" because of their refusal to drink at wedding and funeral celebrations.

122. Some SIM pre-occupation missionaries held a different view regarding baptizing polygamists. Of the first four Sidama *amanyoch* to be baptized at Homacho in 1932,

pre-baptismal teaching of the candidates, observation of their behavior and questioning of the candidates prior to their baptism were determining factors in ascertaining whether the *amanyoch* were truly separated from certain practices in their former lives and from allegiance to the clan deities.[123]

The third cardinal conviction was that the converts should form themselves into a Christian community, which we will designate the *amanyoch* community.[124] Fargher is careful to point out that these communities were independent of both the Ethiopian Orthodox Church and the SIM structure but were interdependent with one another. Immediately after the converts were baptized, they were then invited to take part in a communion service, which was administered by those who baptized them. After the *amanyoch* were baptized and took communion they were given full rights to become members of a local *amanyoch* community. After the first baptism in Wolaitta in 1933, the missionaries did not perform another baptism. The authority to baptize others rested upon the first elected elders, Desta, Diasa, and Godana.[125] It was now the responsibility of these elected elders to incorporate these new members into the *amanyoch* community.[126]

---

one was a polygamist. See Cotterell, *Born at Midnight*, 58. There is no evidence that polygamists were baptized in Wolaitta throughout the occupation. To date (1997), neither the Wolaitta church nor her evangelists baptize polygamists.

123. Fargher, *Origins of the New Churches Movement*, 29–31. The first baptismal candidates at Soddo desired to examine themselves because they knew they could not "fool one another and none of us can fool God." Davis, *Fire on the Mountains*, 70, 71. For the second and third generation of Wolaitta *amanyoch*, separation has tended to become obedience to rules and regulations.

124. Fargher, *Origins of New Churches Movement*, 32–33, and 49–58. Because the new believers called themselves "*amanyoch*" (believers), the new congregations that were formed will be designated "*amanyoch* communities." The *amanyoch* referred to the building in which they met for religious functions as their "*ṣälot bét*" (prayer-house), purposefully differentiating themselves from the Orthodox, who called their place of worship "*bét kristeyan*." After the SIM-related congregations officially formed themselves into a denomination called Kale Heywet Church in February 1971, they freely used the term "*bét kristeyan*" to identify both their congregation and their building.

125. Cotterell, *Born at Midnight*, 69.

126. Thomas Lambie was aware of the potential confrontation with the Orthodox Church if non-Orthodox churches were established in Ethiopia. Lambie wrote, "We are in only on sufferance and we are anxious to get into a dozen other places. To begin baptizing and organizing churches now, would certainly arouse the Abyssinian Church." Letter to Bingham, May 5, 1932. When Lambie and his colleagues drafted the *Principles and Practice* of the fledgling Abyssinian Frontiers Mission in 1927, their intention was clear. Their purpose for coming to Ethiopia was "the development of the Native Church on sound Scriptural lines." Lambie, papers; quoted in Cotterell, *Born at Midnight*, 16–20. Gustav Arén acknowledges that the decision of the Home Board of the Swedish

These three cardinal convictions of the SIM evangelists were like the three legs of a stool. All three convictions—conversion, radical behavioral change, and the formation of Christian communities—were essential components that were carefully presented by the SIM evangelists to the Wolaitta. We will now follow through the process of how the Wolaitta were able to accept and incorporate these three SIM religious convictions into their own belief system and, as it were, "own the stool and use it."

Conversion was not a new phenomenon to the Wolaitta. As referred to above, Ésa's teaching about repentance, the turning away from the use of the malevolent spirits such as the *gomé*, *ţälähéya*, and *gomatiya*, which brought harm upon their enemies, had reached Wolaitta around 1920. At that time many Wolaitta turned away from the use of magic to the worship of *Ţosa*.[127] Dana Mäja recounted that after he heard the teaching of Ésa, he forsook his former use of magic and, together with his family, began worshipping *Ţosa*. But Dana Mäja eventually reverted back to his former practices because, "I did not receive the cows that Ésa promised would come from the ground to all those who followed his teaching."[128]

As regards the process of conversion, the SIM evangelists offered the Wolaitta two additional components, absent in the teaching of Ésa. The first was the basic evangelical teaching about Jesus Christ. This teaching is best expressed in a song taught to Dana Mäja and his son Markina by *Ato Gunta* in 1936.

> Our Lord descended from heaven;
> He was born of Mary,
> To bring new life, he died on the cross for our sins;
> Defeating death, he rose from the dead;
> He ascended into heaven;
> He will come again and will take us to be with him.[129]

Evangelical Mission in 1893 and 1894 "persisted in pointing out that its [SEM] principal aim was evangelism and not the formation of congregations." *Evangelical Pioneers*, 331 n. 96. The SEM policy of attempting to revive the Ethiopian Orthodox Church continued until after the occupation. See Saeveras, *Church-Mission Relations in Ethiopia*, 24.

127. Mälkamu Shanqo notes that after the preaching of Ésa, "In all their places [the Wolaitta people] raised their hands to God and prayed." *"Hulum Ades Honwal,"* 9.

128. Dana Mäja, personal information to EPB, September 8, 1987.

129. Markina Meja, *Unbroken Covenant*, 20.

This song expresses the basics of the Christian faith as found in New Testament creeds.[130] Another early Wolaitta hymn, called *Dusai tuma* (My life, my living is now authentic) expresses the Wolaitta faith in Jesus.

> My life is true, my living is authentic in Jesus,
> Life is true, with whom is it true?
> It is authentic with Jesus.
> How do you know it is true?
> The Bible says so.
> The Good News of Jesus cleanses.
> Our hearts have become full of light.
> Worship in the mornings.
> How can I truly worship?
> By avoiding sin.
> Jesus will come the second time.
> When Jesus comes we will live in a bright house.
> Are there no unsolvable problems in this world?
> There are no problems.
> How are the problems solved?
> Through the Son of God, born for us, Jesus is His name.
> The Bible affirms it.
> God will reveal all this at the end.
> Praise be to God.[131]

This Wolaitta hymn expresses five basic teachings about Jesus. First, Jesus is true and authentic, unlike some of the Wolaitta clan deities who disappoint. Second, Jesus has the power to cleanse. There was much rottenness in Wolaitta society. Jesus has power above all ancestors to cleanse and bring healing. Third, Jesus is able to solve any problem. The Wolaitta lived in fear of the malevolent spirits that brought harm. Fourth, Jesus is the Son of God, born into this world for us. And fifth, Jesus will return to this earth, and the dead will rise to life again. This new teaching about Jesus brought hope to the Wolaitta.

The second component offered was the authoritative word of God. The SIM missionaries could be called "biblicists," in that they believed the Bible was *Tosa's* authoritative word. When they preached from it,[132] the hearers

---

130. 2 Timothy 2:3–13.

131. As sung by Gäfäto Jagiso, December 9, 1995. When Gäfäto became an *amanyä* in early 1937, this song was being sung among Wolaitta *amanyoch*.

132. When the SIM evangelists preached, they used the local Wolaitta language because none of them, prior to 1945, had facility in the Amharic language. "We feel it absolutely necessary for each missionary to learn the language in common use in the area to

were in no doubt that *Tosa*'s written word was indeed *Tosa*'s spoken word.[133] The Wolaitta perceived that the Bible contained a new authority. The one hundred and forty selected scriptures translated into the Wolaitta language and published by the Scripture Gift Mission in 1933 were compiled into a small booklet called *Tosay Yotes* (God has Spoken).[134] The name itself carried a ring of authority.[135] The Gospel of Mark translated into the Omotic Gofa language by Walter Ohman, stationed in Bulqi, Gofa, was published by the British and Foreign Bible Society, Addis Ababa, in 1934. These two booklets were significant for sustaining faith and teaching Christian truths in the vernacular to the Wolaitta *amanyoch*.[136] But it was the Amharic *Abba Rumi* Bible that proved to be the mainstay of the *amanyoch* communities until the Haile Sellassie Amharic Bible was printed in 1961.[137]

Two practical skills that the SIM missionaries offered to Wolaitta proved to be catalysts for change. One of these was the skill of reading and writing. The opportunity of southern societies to learn to read and write had been very limited until the advent of the modern missionary movement.[138] Prior to the post-war policies of Emperor Haile Sellassie, it appears that it was not to the advantage of the northern government officials nor the Orthodox clergy to teach literacy to the southern societies. Now, however, ordinary Wolaitta farmers were given the opportunity of

---

which he is assigned. . . . We felt it was necessary to do this so as to get the Gospel to the unevangelized tribes in as short a time as possible. We realize the impossibility of doing this through native interpreters." Letter from Lambie to Duff and Annan, February 21, 1929, as quoted in Fargher, *Origins of the New Churches Movement*, 90.

133. The missionaries chose not to use the Amharic *Egziabihir* for God but retained the Wolaitta name of their high God, *Tosa*.

134. The 140 verses were translated into the Wolaitta language by Earl Lewis and Biru Dubalä. Earl Lewis, letter to Raymond Davis, September 12, 1961.

135. Forsberg, *Land beyond the Nile*, 69.

136. Markina Meja, *Unbroken Covenant*, 29, relates how he taught literacy to others from these two booklets. Bengt Sundkler says, "In Africa, Protestantism is a book of religion." "Worship and Spirituality," 548. On November 1, 1935, Walter Ohman began translating the Gospel of John into the Wolaitta language. See Percy and Violet Roberts, letter to family, November 1, 1935. Eventually in 1943, 900 copies of John's Gospel printed in London were distributed in Wolaitta by Laurie Davison.

137. Ullendorff, *Ethiopia and the Bible*, 62–67. Fargher describes the *Abba* Rumi Bible as "a museum piece." "Its disjointed, choppy sentence structure stands in stark contrast to the flow of well written prose." *Origins of the New Churches Movement*, 169–70.

138. There is no indication that the evangelists and the clerics of the Solomonic period taught literacy in southern Ethiopia beyond the confines of the monasteries and their immediate families. See Taddesse Tamrat, *Church and State*, 157, 175, 181, 189, 202, and Shack, *Gurage*, 15–16.

learning a new skill. Several of the early *amanyoch* such as Toro, Wäldé, and Dästa, employed at the Otona mission station, learned how to read and write under the tutelage of the missionary wives.[139] Wändaro Däbäro began learning to read and write several weeks after his conversion in February 1933, walking the seventeen kilometers to Otona from his home in Humbo for his lessons.[140]

There are also examples of women learning how to read and write. In the past, Wolaitta men had said that it was not possible "to teach the women because they are only cows."[141] The SIM women attempted to teach some Wolaitta women at Otona from 1932 to 1937. When the Davisons returned to Wolaitta in 1945 they discovered that women in the Wolaitta countryside "had taught their children. The children had taught others."[142] The *amanyoch* in Wolaitta took advantage of this catalyst for change.[143]

Another skill the SIM missionaries taught the Wolaitta converts was preaching.[144] The missionaries themselves set the example of travelling about Wolaitta and preaching. Percy Roberts, resident doctor at Otona, and his wife, Vi, went out to the countryside on Sundays to preach.[145] The early *amanyoch* were taught the stories from the Bible on Saturday and on Sunday were sent out to designated areas to teach the same. Proclamation by religious practitioners was not entirely new in Wolaitta, as men such as Ésa and his assistant Mera had used this method.

There was a similarity in the moral content of the teaching of the SIM evangelists and that of Ésa. After repentance it was expected that there

139. Toro Dubusho, personal information to EPB, December 12, 1995. See also Davis, *Fire on the Mountains*, 70.

140. Percy and Vi Roberts letter to family, June 1, 1934, states, "His reading is coming slowly. He isn't what you would call brilliant."

141. Davison, "Re-entry of the SIM," 11.

142. Ibid.

143. Earl Lewis recognized the high symbolic power that literacy carried in Wolaitta. Some Wolaitta confided to Lewis that writing was "delving into the mysteries of witchcraft." Interview with Raymond Davis, January 21, 1961. From 1931 to 1937 SIM education at Maräqo (Gurage), Lambuda (Hadiya), Otona (Wolaitta), and Homacho (Sidama) was basically literacy classes directed towards new converts. The SIM pre-occupation education policy "was to teach converts to read their Bibles." Fargher, *Origins of the New Churches Movement*, 125.

144. Prophet Ésa and his assistant Mera preached and taught at markets and open fields. Dana Mäja, personal information to EPB, September 22, 1988.

145. Percy and Violet Roberts wrote, "We have been hurrying out on our animals right after Sunday School . . . holding services in the countryside." Letter to family, November 20, 1935.

would be a change in the behavior of the *amanyä*. The *amanyoch* focused on several changes of behavior that the SIM evangelists knew little about. The *amanyoch* decided, without advice from the missionaries, that adult circumcision,[146] eating of raw meat, and the practice of wailing and body mutilation at funerals were forbidden.[147] In addition, new converts were told to "offer a prayer of thanks to *Tosa* before meals."[148] The *amanyoch* were expected to keep the commands, based on the Decalogue, that Ésa had taught. The SIM evangelists expected that the *amanyoch* would have a quality of life that was different from their pre-conversion state.

The *amanyoch* community was a new entity in Wolaitta. To become part of this community the individual must first be converted. Then there was a period of time for teaching and nurturing the new believer. For the initial baptisms the SIM missionaries made the decision as to how long this process should take. Some *amanyoch* were delayed for more than two years.[149] For Wändaro it was ten months. After the missionaries left Soddo in 1937, the Wolaitta *amanyoch* made their own decisions as to who was ready for baptism. The span of time from conversion to baptism was usually six to twelve months, but in special cases the time was shortened.[150] Baptism, which was witnessed by the assembled *amanyoch* community as well as bystanders from the neighborhood, was a public affair performed in an open stream or river. Those who were to be baptized were examined by elders from the *amanyoch* community on Saturday evening.[151] The bap-

146. Percy and Violet Roberts wrote, "Now just what they do [at circumcision] we do not know but apparently all that goes along with it is just the work of Satan and the native believers that have been baptized say that it should be done away with." Letter to family, May 30, 1934.

147. See Davis, *Fire on the Mountains*, 70–73, which refers to the prohibition of circumcision of an *amanyä*.

148. Wändaro's advice to Dana Mäja after his conversion, as found in Markina Meja, *Unbroken Covenant*, 18. It is not clear from where Wändaro got his notion, "prayer of thanks to *Tosa* before meals." Was it from observing Earl and Pauline Lewis in their home at the SIM station at Otona?

149. Lambie delayed the first baptism at Homacho for nearly three years (December 1932), fearing repercussions from the Orthodox Church and eventually from Haile Sellassie. See Fargher, *Origins of the New Churches Movement*, 149–50.

150. Toro Dubusho baptized Gäfäto Jagiso three months after he believed, "because he understood more of the teachings of Jesus than I did." Toro Dubusho, personal information to EPB, December 10, 1995.

151. Percy and Violet Roberts wrote, "Ten sought baptism but the former baptized believers examined them and felt that only three were ready." Letter to parents, October 25, 1934,

tism was conducted by these same elders on Sunday. Immediately after the baptismal service, those who had been baptized were served the sacrament of the bread and wine. For the *amanyoch* communities in Wolaitta, the Eucharist consisted of small pieces of dough made from their staple food, *ensette*, and honey water. This eucharistic service incorporated the new *amanyoch* as full members into the broader *amanyoch* community.

The SIM evangelists were catalysts in establishing how the *amanyoch* community performed certain rites of passage, such as weddings and funerals. The first wedding of the Otona *amanyoch* community was arranged by Biru Dubalä. Godana and Bärame were to be married in what Vi Roberts described as, "the first Christian wedding in the Mission—that is in southern Ethiopia."[152] A marriage contract was written up and duly signed by bride and groom.

As for funerals, when baby David Lewis died at Soddo in 1932, Wolaitta neighbors and friends came to pay their respects to Earl and Pauline Lewis. This funeral was different from the former funerals in Wolaitta. Instead of wailing, jumping high and landing on the knees, and pricking the cheeks with thorns until they bled,[153] the Lewises told the mourners, "Don't weep. We are going to see our boy again."[154] This funeral of the missionaries' baby no doubt set a pattern within the *amanyoch* community for the hope there is even in death.

By 1937 the *amanyoch* communities were beginning to creatively incorporate the three SIM cardinal convictions as their own. Through their own initiative, the *amanyoch* were able to tell the story of Jesus and his power to their Wolaitta neighbors. Conversions took place. The new *amanyoch* were encouraged by teaching and example to accept a lifestyle different from that of their unconverted neighbors. Love, truthfulness, and morality were practiced. By April 1937, when the SIM missionaries departed from Wolaitta, there were forty-eight baptized *amanyoch*.[155] And these new *amanyoch* were eventually incorporated by baptism and the Eucharist into the *amanyoch* community.

---

152. Violet Roberts, *Soddo News*, 3rd ed., June 13, 1934.

153. For a vivid description of this phenomenon see Hooper, "The Wail of the Wolamo," 317–18.

154. Earl Lewis, letter to Raymond Davis, September 12, 1961.

155. Cotterell, *Born at Midnight*, 98; Davis, *Fire on the Mountains*, 107.

Italian Soldiers and Priests

We will now consider the contribution that Italian priests and soldiers made to the religious scene in Wolaitta.

Since the defeat of the Italian forces at the Battle of Adowa in 1896, Ethiopia had experienced a tenuous relationship with Italy. A Treaty of Peace and Friendship was signed in 1928 between Italy and Ethiopia, but the border clash at Walwal in December 1934 between the two nations was the pretext for Italy to invade Ethiopia in October 1935.[156] Ethiopian patriots in the North were unable to withstand the superior military power of the Italians. It was the Italian air force and their use of mustard gas that decimated the Ethiopian troops. In May 1936 the Italians entered Addis Ababa without resistance.[157]

When the Italian military invaded Ethiopia in 1935, an unhindered opportunity for the Roman Catholic Church to expand their missionary force within Ethiopia was presented. Cardinal Tisserant reported from Rome in *Gazetta del Popolo*, October 22, 1937:

> A group of missionaries of The Sacred Heart of Verona left Italy for work in Abyssinia in October; the advance guard of a large army of Italian missionaries which will follow.[158]

As stated previously in this chapter, Catholic missionary, Paschal de Luchon, under the auspices of the Capuchin Order, arrived in Wolaitta in 1930. He initiated schools and evangelistic work at Lalla, twenty kilometers northeast of Soddo; Dubbo, on the outskirts of Areka; and Afama, along the banks of the Omo River, some thirty kilometers west of Areka. Because of Paschal de Luchon's French connection, the Italians asked him to leave in 1937, and his varied ministries were taken over by Italian priests. The Italian missions in Wolaitta, such as the Capuchin Order, aggressively challenged the authority of the *sharechewa*. From 1937 to 1941 a conflict ensued between the *sharechewa* and the Catholic missionaries.

> Father Gervasio Scoffon is reported as having shaved thirty magicians; he went with his boys from his school to different areas and, having broken into the palisades of those people, took them by force and cut their hair with scissors. As a result, he was re-

---

156. Bahru Zewde, *History of Modern Ethiopia*, 153.

157. Ibid., 159, states that the Italians had 300 airplanes for their northern front and 100 for the southern front. The total Ethiopian air force consisted of eleven airplanes.

158. As quoted in Paton and Underhill, "Survey," 100.

garded as a most powerful man because, without being harmed, he destroyed the power of his competitors.[159]

No doubt this imposition of another religious belief system upon the Wolaitta traditional religious practitioners could only take place because of the control the Italian colonizers exerted over the local population.

The traditional religious functionaries were not the only suppressed religious group in Wolaitta during the occupation. The new churches movement also experienced harsh treatment from Italian soldiers. Playfair, Roke, and Couser visited Soddo in 1943. After talking to Wolaitta leaders, Playfair wrote:

> When the Italians realized that the church was making progress in spite of the persecution they arrested fifty leaders, who were taken to prison under police escort, where each of them was given up to one hundred lashes and one poor man, who lives to tell the story, received four hundred.[160]

Within Wolaitta, from 1937 to 1941, each district was patrolled by the *banda*, a group of Wolaitta militia who were under the command of the Italians.[161] This control by the Italians may be one of the reasons for the rapid growth of the Catholic community during this period.[162] By 1940 it was reported that the Wolaitta Catholic community grew to 20,000

---

159. Chiatti, "Politics of Divine Kingship," 93. Angelo Del Boca records the official stance of the Italians after the attack on Graziani's life, February 19, 1937. The following telegram attempts to justify the liquidation of all "soothsayers" throughout Ethiopia: "After the attempt on my life on February 19, I learned through departmental channels and police headquarters that the greatest menace to public order came from soothsayers, traditional story tellers, and witchdoctors. . . . As I was convinced it was essential to root out this unhealthy and dangerous element, I gave orders that all soothsayers, story tellers and witch doctors in the forest city to be rounded up and shot." As quoted in *Ethiopian War*, 224, n. 28.

160. Playfair, *Trials and Triumphs in Ethiopia*, 26. There was similar Italian resistance to the believers at Dembi Dolo in 1937. Gidada Salon reported, "About a month later [after the missionary left] the Italians came and they took over the mission compound and our church building." *Other Side of Darkness*, 32. According to Debela Birru, "History of the Evangelical Bethel, 1919 to 1947," 203–5, the Italians in Dembi Dolo and Sayo (western Ethiopia) allowed a certain amount of religious freedom to the evangelicals.

161. Wändaro Däbäro, personal interview with EPB, December 12, 1988.

162. Markina Mäja stated, "The Catholic Church spread very rapidly during the Italian occupation. It was easy to become one of their followers. When a Wolaitta converted to Catholicism, a string was tied around the convert's neck similar to the Orthodox *mateb* practice. But after the defeat of the Italians in 1941, many of the Catholic members joined the Wolaitta 'Jesus people.'" Personal interview with EPB, April 9, 1991.

members.[163] But the Catholic communicants dropped off significantly after the Italian military and priests were evicted in 1941. It appears that the Italian mission work in Wolaitta was rather ephemeral during their brief stay from 1937 to 1941.

The Italian presence in the South did bring about some positive change. The heavy hand of the Abyssinians was removed from the local populations as the Italian administration was installed. For example, in 1972 a Maale elder confided in Donham, while he was researching in the area: "When the Italians came we became people again. We got back our lives."[164] The Abyssinian slave trade with the Arab countries was terminated during this period.

The Italian presence in Wolaitta allowed the Wolaitta people to continue on their religious pilgrimage. The local Amhara landlords lost their political and social control. Most of them left Wolaitta and joined other patriots to engage in battle against the Italians. This indirectly assisted the Wolaitta *amanyoch* communities in developing their own identity during the initial formative stages of the new churches movement.

Conclusion

The Ethiopian Orthodox Church presented an option for religious change to the Wolaitta. But the fact that the Orthodox Church accompanied the intrusion of the northern colonizers was an impediment to its acceptance by the indigenous population of Wolaitta. The eight pre-occupation Orthodox Churches located within the environs of Wolaitta functioned for the benefit of the Amhara. Only those who were willing to abdicate their Wolaitta culture and adopt the language and culture of the northern settlers were welcomed into the fold of the Orthodox. A small minority were willing and able to do this prior to the Italian occupation.

Prophet Ésa proved to be an effective catalyst for change among the Wolaitta. Both the Catholic and Protestant missionaries who succeeded him benefited from this precursor. Unfortunately, it was the Orthodox religious and political leaders who eventually silenced him. Ésa played a unique role not only in that he encouraged the Wolaitta to worship their high God,

---

163. Trimingham, *Islam in Ethiopia*, 29 n. 2, quoting from *Annali dell' Africa Italiana*, iii (1940), 713–20. This number appears rather large for Wolaitta. According to Mikre-Sellassie G/Ammanuel, "Church and Missions in Ethiopia," 357, by 1941, the Roman Catholic Church claimed their total membership within Ethiopia was 75,537.

164. Donham, *Work and Power in Maale*, 62.

Tosa, but he also introduced a new ethical dimension into their primal religion. This was a new factor within the Wolaitta primal religion.

The contribution of the SIM missionaries was the Scripture in the language of the Wolaitta and the announcing of the Good News of Jesus. The expatriate evangelists' demands for behavioral change may have been a deterrent for some to join the new churches movement. But it appears that, prior to the occupation, the SIM objective of establishing several self-perpetuating *amanyoch* communities within Wolaitta was attained.

The Catholic Church expansion within Wolaitta was enhanced by the hegemony of the Italian colonialists. Positive factors such as a sympathetic political climate, sufficient clerical teachers, and an openness to religious change all contributed to this. It is easy to imagine that Wolaitta may well have been a Catholic stronghold if the Italian presence had been sustained. This, however, was not to be the case. For a few years after the occupation, Wolaitta was allowed freedom to pursue her own religious pilgrimage. The majority retained their commitment to and practice of primal religion. A small evangelistic core espoused allegiance to Jesus. Through their preaching and teaching, and by example of their changed lives, they became the initiators of the new churches movement. The following chapter will describe this new face of the Wolaitta Christian community.

5

The Evangelists' Religious Community

Beliefs, Structure, and Practice

> Experience shows that when a church grows . . . .
> by the witness of one to one, by the testimony of
> the Christian family to its non-Christian relatives,
> by the service of the unpaid evangelists, by the
> personal witness of those who have been set on fire
> by the love of Christ—the church is true to its own
> nature, manifests its being as the body of Christ,
> and so grows from strength to strength.[1]

Introduction

THE EMERGENCE AND GROWTH of the *amanyoch* community within
Wolaitta during the years 1937–1975 provides the theme for the following
chapter.[2] In 1937 a significant dynamic for religious choice presented itself
with the exodus from Wolaitta of the Amhara political structure and the
forced removal of the SIM missionaries due to the Italian occupation. The
initial years of the Italian Occupation proved to be a time of respite for the
Wolaitta from the demands of the Amhara landlords. For ten months prior
to their eviction, the Italians viewed the Wolaitta *amanyoch* communities
as a political movement that must be suppressed. After the eviction of the
Italians, from 1941 to 1945, the Wolaitta *amanyoch* communities again

---

1. Neill, *Salvation Tomorrow*, 55.

2. The Amharic word *amanyoch* indicates "those who believe," as distinct from the
adherents of the Orthodox Church, who call themselves *kristeyan*. *Amanyoch* is what
the Wolaitta believers called themselves when requesting official permission from the
Ethiopian government. See appendix 3 for a copy of the *Bäwängél Amanyoch Andinät
Mahibär* permission, which was granted by the Ethiopian Ministry of Interior Public
Security Department on Säné 28, 1955 EC.

experienced freedom to evangelize, baptize, and construct their *sälot bé-toch*. When the SIM missionaries returned to Wolaitta in 1945, their role within the *amanyoch* communities was different from what it had been in 1937. They were no longer needed as "conductors of the orchestra." In the new Wolaitta *amanyoch* communities, they found "a new conception of life and of God, new forms of association in worship, and a new notion of the rights of persons."[3] The missionaries were welcomed back as teachers in the academic and Bible schools as well as to serve the physical needs of Wolaitta in the Soddo hospital.

The growing self identity of the Wolaitta *amanyoch* communities was shaped by various outward circumstances. It was from within this new community that the values and belief systems of the future evangelists were nurtured and molded. As the *amanyoch* grew in maturity they consciously developed their own structures and institutions, several of which were able to support Wolaitta evangelists beyond their own borders.

Opportunity for Religious Choice (1937–1940)

When the SIM missionaries left Wolaitta on April 17, 1937, there were forty-eight baptized *amanyoch*.[4] Until January 1938, when the SIM missionaries were posted to Sudan, reports from Wolaitta continued to reach them in Addis Ababa of an additional 152 baptisms, which brought the total up to 200.[5]

The Italian army's occupation of Addis Ababa in May 1936 presaged their eventual control of Ethiopia. During the previous year, Ethiopian governors from the South had been summoned with their soldiers to fight the encroaching Italian military, but by May 1936 defeated armies were retreating from the northern battlefield to their home areas. On May 16, 1936, Violet Roberts recorded in her diary, "*Däjazmach* Wäldä Mariam arrived from Addis Ababa with his men bound for Gämo. They looted

---

3. Wilson, "To Whom Do They Pray?" 693.

4. For detailed accounts of the April 17, 1937, departure from Soddo see Forsberg, *Land beyond the Nile*, 97–99; Roberts, "Soddo Diary"; and Lass-Westphal, "Protestant Missions," 96–97.

5. Walter and Marcella Ohman, letter to prayer partners, November 5, 1937, enumerates three additional baptisms in Wolaitta since April 17, 1937, stating that seven, sixteen, and fourteen were baptized. The locations of these baptisms within Wolaitta are not indicated. A postscript to the January 1938 letter to prayer partners says, "Another believer has just arrived in Addis Ababa with the news that the total number of baptized believers has now reached almost two hundred."

and burned [houses] all the way down."[6] From the letters and diaries of
the SIM missionaries located at Soddo, May 1936 to April 1937, we ascertain the turbulence and uncertainty within Wolaitta.[7] Because of the
breakdown of law and order, there were inter-tribal skirmishes in the districts north of Wolaitta between the Maräqo, Hadiya, and Amhara.[8] It was
only through the skillful negotiations of *Däjazmach* Mäkonän, governor
of Wolaitta, that there was a measure of peace between the Wolaitta and
Amhara.[9] Prior to the Italians' peacefully occupying Soddo on January 27,
1937, the majority of Amhara fled Wolaitta[10] to return to their former
homeland in central Ethiopia.[11] After over forty years of Amhara occupation, Wolaitta was about to welcome a new oppressor.[12]

On April 17, 1937, ten years after their arrival, SIM personnel left
Soddo for Addis Ababa by Italian trucks and airplane.[13] They had stayed as
long as possible. Baptized *amanyoch*[14] were congregating at four different

6. Roberts, "Soddo Diary," May 16, 1936.

7. See Davis diary entries of 29 April to 27 November 1936 in Raymond Davis,
Fire on the Mountains, pp. 89–97; Malcolm and Enid Forsberg, letter to family, March
29, 1937; Myrtle E. Mitchell, letter to prayer partners, October 5, 1936; and Roberts,
"Soddo Diary," May 15 ,1936, to April 17, 1937, regarding unrest in southern Ethiopia.

8. Roberts, "Soddo Diary," May 20 and July 5, 1936.

9. Roberts states, "Heard rumours today that Wolamo would fight the Amhara
sometime." Ibid., June 29, 1936.

10. Roberts wrote, "If Amhara have to flee, Wolamo will not plunder and will let
them go to their country in peace." Ibid., December 9, 1936. See also January 6, 1937:
"Many fleeing. Hardly any Amhara around nearby hillside. . . . Saw them going with all
their goods."

11. Ibid., January 8, 1937.

12. Marcus, *Life and Times of Menelik II*, 257, makes reference to Shoan *näftänyoch*
being assassinated by Wolaitta Patriots. Roberts writes, "Wolamo would welcome Italians
or anyone else who could give them a good government and not take all they have in *gura*
[taxes]." "Soddo Diary," August 31, 1937.

13. Davis, *Fire on the Mountains*, 106. Reference is made to nineteen missionaries
and seven children leaving Soddo April 17, 1937, on the Italian truck convoy. Malcolm
and Enid Forsberg flew from Soddo to Addis Ababa on an Italian Air Force plane.
Forsberg, *Land beyond the Nile*, 99.

14. On December 10, 1933, the first ten Wolaitta *amanyoch* were baptized at the
Otona SIM station. For a list of their names see Markina Meja, *Unbroken Covenant*, 222;
Cotterell, *Born at Midnight*, 69; Davis, *Fire on the Mountains*, 75. On August 1, 1935, an-
other seven were baptized at Bosa Qacha by Birru Dubalä and an assistant from the first
group that were baptized. See Percy and Violet Roberts, letter to family, July 25, 1935,
and Davis, *Fire on the Mountains*, 107. The third baptism was conducted in Humbo on
March 7, 1937, where fifteen were baptized. See Walter and Marcella Ohman, letter to
Jean Trout, March 7, 1937, and Dana Mäja, personal interview with EPB, September 22,

locations: near Birru Dubalä's house at Bosa Qacha, at Wändaro Däbäro's residence at Humbo, at *Ato* Gunta's near the Gulgula market, and at Toro Dubusho's residence at Gärära in Koysha district.[15]

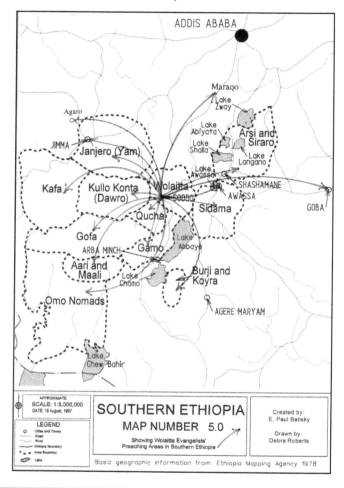

ADDIS ABABA

Maraqo
Lake Zway
Agaro
Lake Abiyata
Arsi and Siraro
JIMMA
Lake Shalla
Janjero (Yam)
Lake Langano
Lake Awassa
Kafa
Kullo Konta (Dawro)
Wolaitta SODDO
SHASHAMANE
AWASSA
GOBA
Sidama
Qucha
Gofa
Lake Abboya
ARBA MINCH
Gamo
Aari and Maali
Lake Chamo
Burji and Koyra
Omo Nomads
AGERE MARYAM
Lake Chew-Bahir

APPROXIMATE
SCALE: 1:3,000,000
DATE: 18 August, 1997

LEGEND
Cities and Towns
Road
River
Ethiopia Boundary
Area Boundary
Lake

SOUTHERN ETHIOPIA
MAP NUMBER 5.0

Showing Wolaitta Evangelists'
Preaching Areas in Southern Ethiopia

Created by:
E. Paul Balisky

Drawn by:
Debra Roberts

Basic geographic information from Ethiopia Mapping Agency 1978

1988. Ohman, letter to prayer partners, April 5, 1937, indicates that the fourth baptism was conducted on April 4, 1937, when eleven were baptized, and it was anticipated that on April 11 five more would be baptized at Koysha. When the SIM missionaries left Soddo on April 17, 1937, there were forty-eight baptized Wolaitta believers.

15. Earl Lewis, who remained at the SIM Furi Leprosarium (present-day Zänäbä Wärk Hospital, Addis Ababa) until his departure from Ethiopia on August 8, 1937, was visited by thirty-six Wolaitta *amanyoch*. Lewis writes, "Many of them thought that when the Italians came in that the Roman Empire was being restored and they expected the Lord to come again any time. . . . During those six weeks they were with us we went through the [Book of] Revelation again." Letter to Raymond Davis, September 12, 1961.

Subsequent to April 1937, the two major catalysts for religious change—the Amhara Orthodox, which included the majority of the Amhara *näftänyoch* population, and the SIM missionaries—were no longer present in Wolaitta. We have no specific evidence regarding the number of Ethiopian Orthodox Church adherents who remained within Wolaitta during the Italian occupation. The eight Orthodox Churches located throughout Wolaitta continued functioning throughout the Italian occupation.[16]

It appears that when the Italians took control of Wolaitta in 1937 they had a definite policy to appease and to gain the respect of the Ethiopian Orthodox Church. For example, generous financial aid was given to rebuild the monastery at Däbra Libanos.[17] The Italians encouraged various Ethiopian Orthodox Church calendar celebrations in areas where the Italians were firmly in control, but "where the Church supported the Patriots it was subject to terrorism."[18] It appears that tolerance was their policy towards the Ethiopian State Church. When the Italians removed the SIM missionaries from Wolaitta in April 1937 and took possession of the Otona station, it no doubt seemed to the Italians that the small Protestant movement was for all practical purposes snuffed out.[19] On the other hand, in Wälläga (western Ethiopia) the new churches movement was given official permission by the Italian authorities to meet in four centers.[20]

After April 1937 there were several religious options available to the Wolaitta. First, they could remain within the dominant religious tradition of Wolaitta—primal religion. As was discussed in chapter 3, for the past decade there had been evidence of movement within the Wolaitta primal

16. It is not likely that the remaining adherents of the Orthodox Church in Wolaitta would have numbered over several hundred. The secular clergy and their families would have remained in Wolaitta. Birru Dubalä was cautioned by an Orthodox priest residing in Soddo not to expose himself to the Italian authorities in 1940. Eshetu Abate, "Birru," 8.

17. "It was part of the Italian policy to respect the religion of its subjects and preserve their traditional customs so the new life of the church (EOC) could find its expressions in feasts." Shenk, "Italian Attempt to Reconcile the Ethiopian Orthodox Church," 126.

18. Ibid., 133. This was subsequent to the 1936 Italian retaliatory action, when over one hundred monks were slaughtered at Dabrä Libanos.

19. The Roman Catholic view of the church, including the importance of ordained clergy and a building in which to worship, would lead them to this conclusion.

20. Debela Birru, "History of the Evangelical Church Bethel," 182. This permission to meet openly may have come about through the intervention and influence of Duncan Henry, who was residing in Addis Ababa at the time. After the attempted assassination of Graziani on February 19, 1937, active measures were taken by the Italians to have all non-Italian missionaries leave Ethiopia. See Lass-Westphal, "Protestant Missions," 98.

religion. External events were affecting Wolaitta culture and forcing new interpretations of religious forms and practices. There was, consequently, an openness to experiment with new religious practices. Second, the Wolaitta might have chosen Islam, but that would have been unlikely, as in 1937 there were few Muslims in Wolaitta aside from a few traders who resided in Soddo town.[21] One could say that the Muslim faith was not a serious option for the Wolaitta.

The third option was to become an adherent of the Ethiopian Orthodox Church. As discussed in chapter 2, one of the stated purposes of Menilek II when he marched his army against Wolaitta in 1894 had been to Christianize the pagan Wolaitta Kingdom.[22] However, there is no evidence of an expansion of Orthodox Christianity among the Wolaitta during the Italian occupation. There are several possible reasons for this. Possibly Orthodoxy was rejected because it was the religion of their former oppressor. Another reason may have been that the cultural requirements and demands upon the Wolaitta to become Orthodox neophytes were too stringent. Also, during the occupation the Orthodox Church did not have the clerical resources to evangelize Wolaitta.[23]

A fourth option available to the Wolaitta was to accept the religion of the Italian colonizers. It is significant that in 1940 the Italians reported 20,000 Roman Catholic adherents in Wolaitta, the fruit of the Italian Capuchin Order.[24] Previously, in 1930, French-Canadian Paschal du Luchon of the Capuchin Order had established friendly relationships with *Kowna* (ruler) Dästa, son of Tona, and implemented a successful mission at Dalbo.[25]

21. Trimingham, writing in 1952, states that, "Islam is rare among the Sidama [meaning non-Oromo and non-Amhara] and is only professed by four tribes of the Eastern Sidama—Tämbaro, Alaba, Bosha, and Hadiya." *Islam in Ethiopia*, 182.

22. Refer to chapter 2 of this thesis.

23. Taddesse Tamrat, *Church and State*, 108–14, states that it was the monks who primarily did the evangelizing, not the secular clergy. There is no evidence that there were "evangelizing monks" active within Wolaitta in 1937.

24. *Annali dell' Africa Italiana, iii* (1940), 713–20, as quoted in Trimingham, *Islam in Ethiopia*, 29 n. 2. Trimingham comments that the figure is probably exaggerated. Mikre-Sellassie G/Ammanuel, "Church and Missions in Ethiopia," 357, comments that by 1941 the Roman Catholic Church had gained 75,537 new members throughout Ethiopia. Birru Dubalä assisted the Capuchins in changing the Ethiopic orthography of the Wolaitta Gospel of John to the Latin script. See Lily Davison, letter to Eric and Sylvia Horn, July 5, 1942.

25. See Chiatti, "Politics of Divine Kingship," 80. In 1937 French-Canadian Paschal was replaced by Italians of the Capuchin Order.

And the fifth option of religious choice for the Wolaitta was to accept what a small core of Wolaitta *amanyoch* were teaching, preaching, and practicing. These *amanyoch* were the progeny of the SIM missionaries. For the missionaries, the Bible was accepted as the external sign of their belief system. The basis for instruction, both in the pre-baptismal classes and for the baptized *amanyoch,* was the Bible. Before the missionaries left Wolaitta in 1937, the Bible was used as their authority when they preached in the countryside under the shade of trees and in market places. Instead of carrying the cross, as did the Orthodox clergy, the *amanyoch* went out from village to village carrying their Wolaitta Scripture portions or their Amharic Bibles.

It seems that there were at least three factors that made the teaching of the new *amanyoch* attractive to the Wolaitta. First, the power of Christ to conquer all the forces of the spirit world was crucial to the Wolaitta. *Ayana,* or power, was a critical element in the Wolaitta traditional belief system, as described in chapter 3. Acquiring *ayana,* which in turn would be used to control the malevolent forces of sickness, disease, and death, was the quest for many in Wolaitta. They sought protection from the debilitating effects of *gomé* and *ṭälähéya.* Because Christ had power over death and adverse powers, the Wolaitta were willing to give him their allegiance.[26] Accepting the Jesus story gave them peace and freedom from fear.[27] The power of Christ superseded the power of any of the clan deities and gave them the legitimate *ayana.*

Second, the *amanyoch* belief system was based on the authority of a book—the Bible. In the past, the Wolaitta had been prepared to receive authentic messages from the *sharechewa* or *qalicha.* Later the authority of the written page was impressed upon the Wolaitta by the Amhara written documents in court proceedings or by the *afarsata.*

26. See Okorocha, "Salvation in Igbo Religious Experience." His thesis is a carefully presented argument that Christ is conqueror over all powers within the Igbo Christian worldview. "Igbo conversion to Christianity was the search for an alternative source of salvation in the face of the apparent failure of the native gods and in view of the new socio-economic order." Ibid., 328. Okorocha's published thesis is *The Meaning of Religious Conversion in Africa,* Aldershot, UK: Avebury, 1987.

27. Interviews with leaders of the Wolaitta *amanyoch* indicated that their chief motive for accepting Jesus was to have freedom from fear. See Fargher, *Origins of the New Churches Movement,* 28 n. 2, where reference is made to Ethiopian "fear-culture." Markina Mäja admits, "We lived with fear." Markina Meja, *Unbroken Covenant,* 15. Colossians 1:20 refers to Christ's reconciling all things to himself by his death, "making peace through His blood."

Third, prayer as practiced among the *amanyoch* made it possible for all to participate both privately and corporately. Prayer was not new to the Wolaitta because their traditional religious functionaries prayed and received predictive messages through ecstatic trances. But the prayers of the *amanyoch* were directed to *Tosa* through Jesus, who was their intermediary. This factor was a new element in the prayers of the *amanyoch*. We will now observe what actually happened in the lives of four Wolaitta who became leaders within the *amanyoch* community.

Conversion of Four Wolaitta "Founding Fathers"

Birru Dubalä was born in 1899 in Dawro/Bobe, Kullo Konta. His father died before Birru was born, so according to Ethiopia custom, the father's brother inherited the wife. Because Birru was not wanted by his step-father, orders were given to a servant to bury the child soon after his birth. A relative intervened, and Birru's life was spared. In retrospect, Birru compared his life with that of Moses. It was because of this experience that Birru felt from an early age that God had a special task for him in life.[28]

When Birru was eleven years of age he was taken from Käfa province to Gondar with soldiers and a number of "domestic slaves when *Ras* Wäldä Giyorgis of Käfa was made "supreme commander of northern Ethiopia."[29] Birru later made his way back from Gondar to Addis Ababa with some Orthodox priests. At seventeen years of age, Birru was recruited with others from Addis Ababa to join a military campaign against *Lij* Iyasu's father, *Ras* Michael, at Sagale, on the Sandafa plains, about eighty kilometers north of Addis Ababa.[30] After his experience in the military, in 1918 Birru temporarily enrolled in "Doctor" Cederqvist's English School, located at what is now the Mekane Yesus Church at Amist Kilo, Addis Ababa.[31] It was at the English School that he was taught the gospel. Because of lack of finances, Birru dropped out of school and worked as a day laborer. In early February 1928, he was hired by the SIM missionaries to serve as a guide to the South. Birru, with his knowledge of English and the countryside, was of real value to this missionary party, as only the Lambies had previous experience in Ethiopia.

28. Eshetu Abate, "Birru," 1. Birru believes he was saved from infanticide, "even as Moses was."

29. Marcus, *Life and Times of Menelik II*, 246–47.

30. Eshetu Abate, "Birru," 2. See also Marcus, *Life and Times of Menelik II*,280.

31. Arén, *Evangelical Pioneers in Ethiopia*, 437 n. 349, indicates that there were fifty students enrolled from 1916 to 1918 under the tutelage of Ole Eriksson.

5.1 Three of the four Wolaitta Kale Heywet Church "Founding Fathers," Birru Dubalä (on left), Wändaro Däbäro (centre), and on the right, Dana Mäja Mädaro (Füssle, SIM Int'l Archives, 1961).

In a letter from Addis Ababa dated February 27, 1928, Clarence Duff gives a description of Birru:

> Some of the men we are hiring for the trip I am sure must be true Christians. Some are very eager to have us and go with us to take the Light to their own lands—Wolamo, Kullo, etc. . . . I was much impressed and encouraged last night by the earnestness of one man whose name is Biru. He came to our tent to get a New Testament in English, and got started telling me about his country Wolamo [Kullo Konta]. . . . He believes God brought him here, and I think so too.[32]

Birru proved to be an invaluable assistant to the SIM pioneers as guide, translator and preacher. Because of assigned mission responsibilities elsewhere, Birru was not always in attendance at the *amanyoch* meetings, such as the pre-baptismal teaching.[33] Earl Lewis, one of the SIM pioneers in Wolaitta confirmed that Birru "professed to believe before he ever came here."[34] He was regarded by the missionaries as one of the more mature believers, but the missionaries were hesitant to recognize Birru's Orthodox baptism. At the December 10, 1933, Otona baptism, Birru wanted to be a good example to the other *amanyoch*.

32. Duff, *Cords of Love*, 31.

33. From March to June of 1931, Birru Dubalä guided the George Rhoad party from Addis Ababa through Jimma, Kullo Konta, and Bulqi to Soddo. See Rhoad, "Wayside Jottings," (being a Personal account of the Second Advance Towards the Frontiers on the Southwesterly Route through Jimma Province, March to June, 1931). Shortly after the December 10, 1933, baptism, Birru, together with Dästa and his wife, was sent to Bulqi to guard the SIM station. SIM Ethiopia, Field Council Minutes.

34. Earl Lewis, personal interview with Raymond Davis, January 1961, 16.

The people said we do not know [how] to enter the water. They said, "We won't be baptized unless *Ato* Birru our teacher [is] be baptized." The missionary told me the case [situation] saying, "Why don't you show them by being baptized?" Though I was already a Christian and baptized, though by the hands of the Orthodox, I said, "Alright," and was baptized by the hands of the missionaries.[35]

From this brief biographical account it can be ascertained that Birru's conversion to Christianity was a process. The Orthodox priests in Gondar no doubt played a significant role in this process because Birru valued his Orthodox baptism. Bible studies at the Swedish Evangelical Mission's "English School" in Addis Ababa would have strengthened his Christian commitment. It appears that because his life displayed the qualities of a genuine *amanyä*, the SIM missionaries baptized him by immersion along with nine others in December 1933.[36]

Another of the founding fathers of the Wolaitta *amanyoch* communities was Wändaro Däbäro. He was born ca. 1906 in the district of Humbo, some twenty kilometers south of Soddo. He followed the occupation of his father as a tenant farmer and a weaver.[37] As a boy he had a keen interest in matters of religion. From 1915 to 1920 he attempted to practice the teaching of the prophet Ésa Lalé of Gämo.[38] Ésa's message to the people of Gämo, Gofa, Qucha, Boroda, and Wolaitta was that they were to leave the worship of Satan and to worship the true God and to live in peace and harmony with one another. As Wändaro understood it, Ésa predicted that all tribal groups in the South would eventually have freedom from the oppression of the Amhara. God would give them joy instead of the sorrow they were experiencing. The Wolaitta were told to curse the influential Wolaitta *qalicha* named Wayachayé and to ask God for mercy.[39] As a lad, Wändaro witnessed the Amhara soldiers marching Ésa through the Humbo mar-

35. Eshetu Abate, "Birru," 5. See also Davis, *Fire on the Mountains*, 73, and Cotterell, *Born at Midnight*, 69.

36. Earl Lewis and Walter Ohman baptized the ten *amanyoch* by immersion at the SIM Otona station. Cotterell, *Born at Midnight*, 69. Dästa, one of the ten baptized at Otona, was another Wolaitta who spent several years in Addis Ababa prior to 1927. The Ohmans wrote to their prayer partners on November 5, 1937, "Desita . . . has now backslidden."

37. Eshetu Abate, "Origin and Growth of Evangelical Christianity," 16.

38. Wändaro's father was a practicing *qalicha* in the Humbo area. See Davis, *Fire on the Mountains*, 58.

39. Wändaro Däbäro, personal interview with EPB, September 10, 1987.

ket when he was in transit from Gämo to be imprisoned in Addis Ababa according to the orders of the Ethiopian government. Impressed upon Wändaro's mind was the message of Ésa, "Forsake the worship of trees and sacrificing of animals to Satan."[40] Thus Wändaro began the process of leaving the gods of his fathers.

Injustice was never far away from Wändaro. One day when he returned to his village at Humbo, he discovered that his plowing ox had been taken by *Fetawrare* Dogeso, the Amhara landlord, and was yoked to another ox plowing the landlord's corn field. Wändaro was concerned lest his only ox be slaughtered or sold elsewhere. In this distraught state of mind he pressed charges against his landlord in the local Humbo court, but there was no justice. "I was only crying to *Tosa*, not knowing to do anything else."[41]

A new governor, *Däjazmach* Mäkonän was appointed to Wolaitta in about 1932.[42] News was travelling from market place to market place that a new directive had come from Haile Sellassie that would ease all taxes and lessen the forced contribution of farm produce.[43] *Däjazmach* Mäkonän was responsible for the upholding of justice in every court of Wolaitta. Wändaro heard this amazing news from *Abba* Choramo, and it was confirmed by *Fetawrare* Bäqälä, both residing in Humbo. All citizens were told to go to *Däjazmach* Mäkonän's compound in Soddo to hear the details of this new directive. Because this sounded like "good news" to Wändaro, he rushed off to hear for himself whatever this might be. But only disappointment awaited him. When he arrived at the Amhara garrison of *Däjazmach* Mäkonän in Soddo, he found no one around. The crowd had already heard the pronouncement and dispersed. Dejected, Wändaro returned home with no rest or peace of heart.

In desperation Wändaro went for help to the mission at Otona. When he saw the white faces of the missionaries he said to himself, "Among these

40. Täsäma Täntu and Dana Mäja transcribed interview with EPB, Wolaitta KHC center at Anka, September 7, 1987 (EPB personal collection, 4:119).

41. Eshetu Abate, "Origin and Growth," 16.

42. *Däjazmach* Mäkonän, a kindly aristocrat, retained his Wolaitta governorship until the Italians commandeered Soddo in January 1937. Walter Ohman acknowledged Mäkonän's concern and kindness: "The Governor has been very good to us, even sending us a very fat ox when he heard that we were selling clothing to buy necessities." Letter to Thomas Lambie, August 11, 1936, 2.

43. Since the time Wolaitta had been subjugated by Menilek II, the area had been known as the *mädäbét* (breadbasket) for the royal court in Addis Ababa. See also Tsehai Berhane, "Life and Career of *Däjazmach* Balcha Aba Näfso," 177.

people God is surely dwelling." Canadians Percy and Violet Roberts, who had arrived in Wolaitta several months before, report this incident, which took place in mid-March 1933:

> A few weeks ago a man came in from Humbo, a mountain to the south of us about 6 hours. He asked to be told something about Jesus Christ. He went back to his people and the next week on Sunday he brought another man. They were both converted and have since been testifying to their people. Last Sunday they came in a body of 20 or more to the service.[44]

The message of salvation through Jesus Christ was what Wändaro had been prepared to hear. Earl Lewis recalls that his sermon that day was about the "Lamb of God that takes away the sin of the world." Lewis was cognizant of Wolaitta traditional religion and that "they knew quite a bit about blood sacrifices."[45] After attending three consecutive meetings Wändaro stood up and said, "Now I have heard the message three times. I believe. I accept Christ as my Saviour."[46] He reported to others that the message was "like honey to my stomach."[47]

That event was a turning point in Wändaro's life. Nearly fifty-five years later Wändaro could recall:

> I began to tell others about Jesus in my community of Humbo. My message, as I went from house to house was, "Those who believe and are baptized will be saved. He who refuses, will be thrown into the lake of fire. God will judge." I preached this message to all because Christ commanded in his Gospels that we were to go to all and preach.[48]

There is evidence that Wändaro began preaching in the local Humbo market soon after he heard the gospel. SIM nurse Ruth Bray, stationed in Chäncha, some three days' travel south of Soddo, reported that during the preaching hour in their newly opened clinic someone stood up and said, "I have heard all that before. I was up in Humbo and they were all talking about it there."[49]

44. Roberts, letter to family, March 23, 1933, 1.

45. Selma Bergsten and Earl Lewis, personal interview with Raymond Davis, December 16, 1961, 32.

46. Wändaro Däbäro, personal interview with EPB, September 22, 1988.

47. Eshetu Abate, "Origin and Growth," 16.

48. Wändaro Däbäro, personal interview with EPB, September 22, 1988.

49. As quoted in Percy and Violet Roberts, letter to family, March 23, 1933, 2.

After reporting to SIM director Lambie that over 100 had been attending Sunday meetings at the Otona station, Lewis wrote on April 6, 1933:

> About 30 men have been coming regularly from Humbo South of us. They became interested because of the testimony of one man who has been coming here for about six months. He says he believes and has been witnessing in the neighborhood where he lives with the result that these 30 men have been coming here for the past three Sundays. They all beg that we come out to their village and have a week's meetings with them so that their wives and children may hear.[50]

Percy and Violet Roberts, reporting on the Sunday morning services at Otona, nicknamed Wändaro, "Humbo Bill" in letters to their family. Their September 1933 letter reports:

> Of course you remember Humbo Bill, well he comes as regular as ever and brings a great crowd with him each Sunday. People say that the road to Soddu on Sunday is like the road to the Saturday market, meaning that there is just as great a crowd coming to service as go to the market and that means something.[51]

Wändaro's conversion had begun before the SIM missionaries reached Wolaitta, for the Prophet Ésa Lalé had had a profound influence on Wändaro's religious pilgrimage. At this point in his life, Wändaro continued to experience injustice from his landlord, even though he had forsaken the gods of his ancestors. In desperation he walked from Humbo to the SIM station at Otona to hear what the missionaries were preaching. The message of Jesus must have answered his religious quest. Within a month of hearing the gospel, he began to preach this same message to others in his home district of Humbo. Seven months later Wändaro was baptized at Otona.

Toro Dubusho, from Koysha, began working for the SIM missionaries around 1932. The SIM missionaries began to doubt his conversion in 1936 when he married a second wife.[52] But Toro confessed to this moral lapse and returned the second wife to her father. Two months before the Italians evicted the SIM missionaries from Wolaitta, Toro returned to his

---

50. Earl Lewis, letter to Thomas Lambie, April 6, 1933. There appears to be an error as to the date of this letter. According to the Roberts's diary and their personal correspondence of April 6, 1933, the Lewis letter should have been dated May 30, 1933.

51. Percy and Violet Roberts, letter to family, September 15, 1933, 6.

52. Davis, *Fire on the Mountains*, 100.

home district of Koysha. In his new home, constructed at Gärära, Koysha, he began preaching to his neighbors. In mid-February 1937 *Kowna* (son of royalty) Gäfäto took refuge from a rain storm in Toro's house. It was at that time that Gäfäto heard the gospel of Jesus from Toro. Two weeks later Gäfäto was back at Toro's to ask questions and to hear the good news more clearly. Gäfäto recalls that he preached his first sermon three weeks after he first heard about Jesus from Toro. After his neighbor's house had burned to the ground, Gäfäto told the gathered crowd, "If you do not believe, you will face the punishment of hell which will be hotter than this fire you have just witnessed."[53] Several of these neighbors joined Gäfäto as they attended pre-baptismal classes at Toro's house. On April 5, 1937, Gäfäto and his wife plus three others were baptized by Toro at Koysha.[54] Birru Dubalä rebuked Toro for moving too quickly on baptizing Gäfäto and the four other Koysha converts. Toro's reply was, "You do not need to wait any longer for him [Gäfäto]. He knows Jesus. He really believes."[55] When Gäfäto was asked the reason for his immediate conversion he replied that he longed for deliverance from the oppression of the Amhara landlords and freedom from the demands of the *sharechewa*. He said that everything that Toro taught him from the Wolaitta selected texts, *Tosay Yotes*,[56] was authentic.[57] Gäfäto's conversion is another example of a Wolaitta who made a reasoned decision. Various factors within Wolaitta convinced Gäfäto that doom and judgment were imminent. It appears that his motive for conversion was escape from this impending judgment.

53. Gäfäto Jagiso, personal interview with EPB, December 9, 1995.

54. Walter and Marcella Ohman, letter to prayer partners, April 5, 1937. Elders of the Wolaitta *amanyoch* community at Otona, Dayésa, and Godana assisted Toro in examining the five candidates.

55. Davis, *Fire on the Mountains*, 105. Nearly sixty years later Toro confirmed why he baptized Gäfäto soon after his conversion: "He was stronger in faith than me. I also had elders approve of his faith in Jesus." Toro Dubusho, personal interview with EPB, December 11, 1995.

56. There has been confusion in the past as to whether this translation was initially in the Wolaitta or Gofa language. Markina Mäja, personal information to EPB, August 18, 1997, insists that it was in the Wolaitta language. See Fargher, *Origins of the New Churches Movement*, 173 n. 137, who insists that *Tosay Yotes* was a Gofa translation.

57. Gäfäto Jagiso, personal interview, December 9, 1995. It is puzzling why Gäfäto made reference to Amhara oppression. Most Amharas had vacated Wolaitta by the end of 1936.

5.2 Toro Dubusho, another of the 'Founding Fathers' of the Wolaitta KHC being interviewed by researcher Tiṯämäqä Yohanis Shondé (Lila W. Balisky, 1995)

The final example of conversion within Wolaitta is that of Dana Mäja, born ca. 1907 in the Wanché Mortato area, fifteen kilometers southeast of Soddo. By young adulthood he had become relatively wealthy through the purchasing and selling of slaves.[58] Since the subjugation of Wolaitta by Menelik II in 1894, slave raiding had been a lucrative business for able bodied risk takers. Families would be preyed upon at night; the fathers would often be killed so that wives, children, and young people could easily be captured.[59] But by the mid-twenties, slave raiding, by then officially outlawed, was only carried on as a clandestine activity by a few bandits. Consequently, Dana Mäja became concerned for his own reputation.[60] As

58. KHC, "*Qalä Hiywät Bétä Kristeyan Bäsilsa Hulät Amätat,*" 48. Dana Mäja was involved in slave-trading at a Sidama market. "I bought a lady who was 8 months pregnant for 8 Maria Teréza and was able to sell her at the Dolo market [Sidama] for 60 Maria Teréza." Dana Mäja's son, Markina, underplays his father's role as a slave trader. Markina Mäja, personal information to EPB, January 4, 1983.

59. Prior to his conversion in March 1937, Dana Mäja attended a baptism. One of the young ladies being baptized fled across the stream when she spotted Dana Mäja, her former owner, from whom she had escaped several years before. Dana Mäja Madäro, personal interview with EPB, Wolaitta KHC center at Anka, September 8, 1987. At the KHC Kuriftu celebration held in 1990 *Abba* Gole, long-time leader of the Kambatta/Hadiya *mahibär*, and Dana Mäja bantered as to who owned the most slaves in former days; the crowd clapped when Dana Mäja related that *Abba* Golé himself was captured by the Wolaitta!

60. These stringent measures taken against other slave traders served as a deterrent to Dana Mäja, former owner of one hundred slaves.

a young man, Mäja was awarded the distinguished title of *danya* (judge or arbitrator) by the Wolaitta governor *Däjazmach* Yigäzu because he had killed a brigand with his spear.[61] He was perceived as an upholder of truth and integrity by his community.[62]

By 1920 Ésa's teaching had made a strong impact throughout Wolaitta,[63] and Dana Mäja left the worship of his father's *wuqabé* for a limited time to practice what Ésa taught. He destroyed all objects in his house that had to do with traditional religion, such as his pipe, tobacco, and various holy objects used in sacrificing to his *wuqabé*.[64] The anticipated results, however, were not forthcoming. There was no reprieve from the harshness of the Amhara oppression. In addition, the personal benefits he sought never did materialize. "The cows which I was promised would come out from the earth never did, so I returned back to Satan worship."[65]

In 1935 while Dana Mäja and his oldest son Märkina were travelling home they came upon a group of people listening to a small fiery preacher outside *Ato* Agädo's home. They were invited to stay and listen. The preacher was Wändaro. His message:

> The Lord Jesus is going to come back to this world. When he comes he will take all those who believe in him to heaven. But those who do not believe he will cast into the lake of fire. Therefore, all of you who do not believe in the Lord Jesus but worship and make sacrifices to Satan, you will be thrown into the lake of fire along with Satan. Believe today.[66]

Then he sang this song to them:

> When the sheep hear the voice of Jesus Christ
> They follow Him.
> He runs after the sheep that remain behind

61. Markina Meja, *Unbroken Covenant*, 14.

62. Ibid. Markina Mäja, the son, relates, "My father told me that before he became a Christian he had done all sorts of sins." Ibid.

63. According to Täntu Bädacho, Esa was not from the *qalicha* or *ṭänqway* clans, rather he was from the Golamalla. Täntu Bädécho, personal interview with EPB, October 21, 1988.

64. Dana Mäja and Täsäma Täntu, personal interview with EPB, September 22, 1988.

65. Ibid.

66. Markina Meja, *Unbroken Covenant*, 16. See also Laurie Davison's description of the Italian war machine encounter in "The Re-entry of the SIM to Ethiopia," May 1, 1961, transcribed tape, 24, as referenced in Davis, *Fire on the Mountains*, 18–19.

And rescues them.
Oh God, make them reach out to you;
Make them to see
And in seeing, may they give praise to you.[67]

The dreaded Italian war machines arrived in Wolaitta in December 1936 with the sight and sounds of low-flying airplanes, wide-eyed Italians whose appearance was as frightening as wild horses, and bursting hand grenades, sure signs of an impending judgment.[68] Some months later, in desperation and with a burden of guilt and fear of impending judgment, Dana Mäja and his son, Markina, walked the forty-five minutes from Wanché to Galdabo to see pastor Lolamo Boké. When Dana Mäja arrived at Lolamo's house, he discovered, to his disappointment, that Lolamo had gone to a church meeting. Lolamo's wife hesitated to give Dana Mäja specific directions because Dana Mäja had gained a reputation as a powerful man, still being known as a slave trader. As he was retracing his steps to his house he met Lolamo, preacher Wändaro, and Gunta. The men were reluctant to invite him to the baptism, but Lolamo convinced his friends by saying, "Our Lord did not turn away from the one sheep after the ninety and nine were safe in the fence. Why should we refuse this man just because we are fearful?"[69]

After observing the baptism of about fifteen people in a small stream, Dana Mäja was told to wait outside the house.[70] Lolamo and the others went inside to celebrate the Lord's Supper with the newly baptized *amanyoch*. Dana Mäja became very angry at having to wait outside in the hot sun. He perceived himself as a respectable man of the community, impressively dressed in coat and jodhpurs with a wide cloth wrapped around his waist. Ordinary Wolaitta citizens wore the common *hadiya*, a woven garment. As a visitor to this community he expected to be treated with respect. When the sweat began to pour down his face because of the hot sun, he decided to get up, mount his mule and make his way over to his sister's house which was nearby. However, when he tried to get up, somehow his

67. Markina Meja, *Unbroken Covenant*, 17.

68. Dana Mäja and Täsäma Täntu, personal interview with EPB, September 22, 1988. A picture of the steaming hot springs at Lake Abbaya also conjured up God's judgment in Dana Mäja's mind. Violet Roberts records in her diary that the first Italian planes flew over Wolaitta on December 5, 1936.

69. As quoted by Selma Bergsten, personal interview with Charles Anderson, 62.

70. The date of this baptism was March 7, 1937, according to Walter and Marcella Ohman, letter to Jean Trout, March 7, 1937.

legs would not work and he felt glued to the ground.[71] Finally Lolamo came out and asked Dana Mäja if he really wanted to believe. Upon being ushered into the house, father and son were asked by Wändaro to raise their hands and repeat after him:

> I have denied Satan.
> I have accepted Jesus.
> I believe that Jesus died for my sins.
> I will not worship Satan again.
> I will follow Jesus.[72]

Markina recalls that Wändaro advised them to throw all cultic objects out of their house when they returned home.[73] Father and son gathered up the water pipe, tobacco, all the clothes of the brigand Dana Mäja had killed with his spear, and some old keepsakes passed down from one generation to another—objects that were supposed to give *ayana* to the household. All these objects used in traditional religion were discarded over a cliff.

Wändaro also taught them how to pray to Jesus.

> When you eat, when you work, and even when you sit down to plan something, first pray. When you get to the end of your prayers, say, "We plead in Jesus name." As you bow down, shut your eyes, and pray. At the end say, "Amen."[74]

Unusual changes came about in Dana Mäja's personal and family life. Before they ate their first meal at home, father and son bowed their heads and gave thanks for the food according to the instructions they had received from Wändaro. When they completed their ritual with a loud "Amen" they noticed that the mother, Biramé, and smaller children were laughing at them. The mother asked them, "Why are you doing such strange things now?"[75]

Because members of the family saw such a change in Dana Mäja's behavior, they knew something significant had happened to him. Previously

---

71. Dana Mäja, personal interview with EPB, September 7, 1987.

72. Markina Meja, *Unbroken Covenant*, 18.

73. In the 1920s Ésa's message to Wolaitta was, "Throw away all things that have to do with Satan worship. Get rid of your pipes and tobacco from your homes. Stop your arguments with other men." Dana Mäja and Täsäma Täntu, personal interview with EPB, September 22, 1988.

74. Dana Mäja and Täsäma Täntu, personal interview with EPB, September 22, 1988.

75. Markina Mäja, personal interview with EPB, April 9, 1991.

he would get very angry and say harsh things. Now he was kind. It was not long before his wife, Biramé, believed. The family began to enjoy singing together after their evening meal, for joy marked their conversion. "We felt very happy. Everything seemed new now in our house!"[76] They would sometimes go to great efforts to learn new songs. Markina recalls one of these occasions:

> In order to learn a new song, we went to *Ato* Gunta's house. After learning the song, we started home, singing it as we went. After nearly reaching home, to our dismay we discovered that we had forgotten one line of the song. So we decided to return to *Ato* Gunta's house which was over one hour away. When my father, my brother Yigäzu and I arrived there we were told that *Ato* Gunta was asleep. We said, "Because we forgot the song he taught us, we have come all the way back. Please, ask him to get up and sing the song just once for us and then he can go back to sleep." His wife woke *Ato* Gunta from his sleep and he sang for us again.[77]

This is the new song they sang as they walked home in the dark.

> Our Lord descended from heaven;
> He was born of Mary;
> To save us he died on the cross for our sins;
> Defeating death, he rose from the dead;
> He ascended to heaven;
> He will come again
> and take us to Him.[78]

Dana Mäja now had a new orientation to life. Instead of spending time and money at the Soddo courthouse accusing and being accused by others, he became a person of peace and gained a reputation as a reconciler in the community. He, who once raided houses at night and snatched children and later sold them in the Gulgula market, now began to take in orphan children and assist widows.[79]

The message the new *amanyoch* preached was repentance. Soon after Wändaro Däbäro believed, he began preaching in his local market of

76. Ibid.

77. Markina Meja, *Unbroken Covenant*, 20.

78. Markina Mäja, personal interview, April 9, 1991.

79. Ibid. Märkina Mäja recalls the section of the Gulgula market partitioned off for the sale of slaves. Dana Mäja said, "Because I received the Lord I now coordinated the caring for the needy and the poor by bringing them to my house." KHC, "*Yäqalä Hiywät Bétä Kristeyan Tarek*," 49.

Humbo. His message was repentance, based on the text from Mark 16:16: "Whoever believes and is baptized will be saved, and whoever does not believe will be condemned."[80] This message of repentance by the evangelists would recall to the minds of the Wolaitta Prophet Ésa's plea for repentance. Prophet Ésa called the people of the South to turn away from their magic and from placing the curse of *ṭälähéya* upon their enemies. Rather, they were to turn to God as individuals and as families and offer their sacrifice of pure honey. They were then to give evidence of their changed attitude by a change in their behavior, which was to keep the Ten Commandments.[81] The preaching of the *amanyoch* went beyond Ésa's message of repentance. This is best explained by examining the formula repeated by those who declared a desire to repent.

The evangelists would ask the repentant to stand before the group and raise both their hands to God.[82] Markina Mäja recalls that when he and his father repented, Wändaro asked them to respond affirmatively, with both hands held high, to the following questions:[83]

> Have you decided to follow Jesus?
>
> Do you renounce Satan?
>
> Will you deny Jesus during persecution even if it means death?
>
> Will you leave former practices such as offering sacrifices to Satan, fornication, lying, and stealing?

Three significant things were transacted in this process of conversion:[84] First, it was an individual choice of will. Standing individually or

80. Wändaro Däbäro, personal interview with EPB, September 22, 1988.

81. Mälkamu Shanqo, "*Hulum Ades Honwal,*" 10, lists five of the Ten Commandments and adds the New Testament injunction, "love your neighbor."

82. Some have indicated that this practice of raising one's hands originated when the Wolaitta were asked to pledge their allegiance to the Italian flag sometime after January 1937. Evidence indicates that Prophet Esa asked those who were repentant to lift both hands to God in penitent prayer and say, "*Tosa* be merciful to me." Dana Mäja, personal information to EPB, September 22, 1988. Also, in 1937 when Dana Mäja and his son, Markina, confessed their allegiance to Jesus, they raised their hands to God. See Markina Meja, *Unbroken Covenant,* 18.

83. Markina Meja, *Unbroken Covenant,* 23.

84. "The people of Igboland rushed to the church because they saw within the church the source of power that was so needed—this was their *mana.*" Okorocha, "Salvation in Igbo Religious Experience," 328. In the Wolaitta situation they were searching for *ayana,* the power that would enable them to achieve. Horton, "African Conversion," postulates that conversion is often prompted by an expanded universe. This may be one of the keys

corporately before the group, each person made a verbal profession. Second, there was a denunciation of Satan and allegiance was given to Jesus.[85] And third, there was an expected behavioral change in the life of the convert. He was to turn away from offering sacrifices to the clan deities and to forsake illicit sex, lying, stealing, and disruptive practices in the community.[86]

We now move to a discussion of how the heralding or proclamation of basic beliefs of the *amanyoch* was significant in Wolaitta. Proclamation provided an open opportunity for the people to choose. From 1933 until they vacated Wolaitta in April 1937, the missionaries were actively involved in preaching or proclaiming the Jesus story at the Otona clinic, through Bible teaching in Soddo town, and in trekking to the Wolaitta districts.[87] After the initial baptism of ten adults on December 10, 1933, the new *amanyoch* began preaching at markets,[88] at funerals,[89] and at community work projects.[90] The response was minimal. It was after the Italians secured themselves in Wolaitta in January 1937 that there was a significant response to the preaching of the evangelists.[91] Birru Dubalä, Wändaro Däbäro in Humbo, *Ato* Gunta near Gulgula market, Dayésa in Soré, and Toro Dubusho in Koysha were energetically preaching. It was while Toro was preaching under a tree at Gärära, Koysha, that Gäfäto Jagiso heard the message of judgment.[92]

---

for understanding the phenomenon of conversion. But for the Wolaitta, other considerations such as achieving power, gaining freedom from fear, and gaining self-respect and dignity were all factors that prompted their turning to Christ. For a description of various conversion experiences, see Anderssen, *Churches at the Grass-Roots*, 125–30.

85. It is difficult to ascertain exactly what the Wolaitta mean by the term "Satan." The Amhara in southern Ethiopia use the word "Satan" rather broadly to mean a negative force or circumstance or object that impedes one in life. As was noted in chapter 3, the cosmology of southern Ethiopia had been affected by the Christian North.

86. Rules and regulations soon became prevalent among the Wolaitta *amanyoch*, and former practices such as drinking alcohol, eating raw meat, circumcision, fasting, beating one's wife, etc., were forbidden. See Mälkamu Shanqo, "*Hulum Ades Honwal*," 18, for additional prohibited practices for the *amanyoch*, including "work" on Sundays.

87. See Percy and Violet Roberts, letters to family, March 23, 1933, July 6, 1934, August 23, 1935, November 8, 1935; and Davis, *Fire on the Mountains*, 38–44.

88. Markina Meja, *Unbroken Covenant*, 22–23.

89. Percy and Violet Roberts, letter to parents, July 6, 1934, August 23, 1935.

90. See Davis, *Fire on the Mountains*, 60–64.

91. Davis, Ohman, and Lewis went to Koysha on April 4, 1937, to witness the baptism of eleven *amanyoch*. Walter and Marcella Ohman, letter to prayer partners, April 5, 1937.

92. Gäfäto Jagiso, personal interview, December 10, 1995.

Growth of the *Amanyoch* Communities from Five Centers
(1937–1940)

Humbo

Wändaro Däbäro, from the Humbo district, invited his neighbors to hear the missionaries preach at the SIM station at Otona in March 1933. Soon about twenty people were frequently walking the four hours from Humbo north to Otona to hear teaching and preaching about Jesus.[93] Wändaro himself began to preach the good news at the Humbo (Täbäla) market by the end of March. Migrant workers carried the gospel message from Humbo to the cotton plantations along the shore of Lake Abbaya in 1937. Several men from Chäncha heard the Jesus story from these Humbo *amanyoch*.[94] On March 7, 1937, the leaders of the Humbo *amanyoch* community, Wändaro and Lolamo,[95] baptized fifteen new believers. This was the third baptism conducted in Wolaitta.[96]

It appears that the gospel message spread into much of the Humbo district through Wändaro and other *amanyoch*. Laliso Täntu was from a village two hours southwest of Täbäla. Laliso heard unusual prophecies from his neighbor *Wäidé Goda* Albé that troubled him. Eventually, members of Laliso's family urged him to visit Wändaro at Täbäla. Laliso found Wändaro, where he heard various Wolaitta texts from *Tosay Yotes*, such as Acts 16:31 and Isaiah 46:13. Laliso readily accepted Wändaro's teaching and became an evangelist within the Humbo district for several years before he began preaching in distant places such as Boroda, Gämo, and Gofa. Because the Humbo *amanyoch* were growing in numbers, a local Humbo official, *Fetawrari* Dogeso from the prestigious Tegré clan, made a determined effort to thwart the growth of this movement. Wändaro was ridiculed as being "merely an uneducated Wolamo."[97] In 1938 when Wändaro was preaching in the Humbo market, Dogeso sent a group of ruffians to beat Wändaro. As sticks were flying, Wändaro's tiny wife attempted to rescue him. Dogeso shouted to his henchmen, "Strike and beat

---

93. Percy and Violet Roberts, letter to family, March 23, 1933.

94. KHC, "*Bäwängél Amanyoch Andinät,*" 21–38.

95. Lolamo Boké, a Wolaitta born near the Kambatta border, once traded in slaves. See Eshetu Abate, "Origin and Growth," 16–17. Lolamo heard the Gospel while in prison from Dästa, one of the original ten baptized on December 10, 1933.

96. Walter Ohman letter to Jean Trout, March 7, 1937; Markina Mäja, "Autobiography," 2–3.

97. Wändaro Däbäro, personal interview with EPB, September 22, 1988.

this dog's wife as well!"[98] To which she retorted, "Today I might be the wife of what you call a dog. But tomorrow I hope to be the bride of Christ." False charges were made that Wändaro had predicted Haile Sellassie would return to Ethiopia with the help of the British and Wändaro's American friends.[99] The Humbo *amanyoch* experienced a setback as their leader was incarcerated in the Soddo prison for several months.

Bosa Qacha

From 1933 to 1937 the small group of Wolaitta *amanyoch* were meeting for teaching and fellowship at the Otona SIM station. Plans were in progress by the Otona missionaries to build a chapel from dried mud bricks at the mission station for the growing number of *amanyoch*.[100] This was discouraged by the December 1–6, 1933 SIM Field Council meetings held at Otona, where it was decided that "churches should be built by believers themselves."[101]

In April 1937 Birru Dubalä was elected as the leader of the Wolaitta *amanyoch* who were meeting on the Otona mission compound.[102] Times were rather uncertain for Birru after the SIM missionaries left Soddo on April 17, 1937, riding out on the Italian "camios."[103] Prior to their leaving, Birru had been assigned by the missionaries the responsibility of guarding the SIM Otona compound. After the Italian military arrived in Soddo in January and the missionaries departed from Otona in April 1937, Birru continued on as a guard at Otona and eventually was employed by the Italians who moved onto the Otona premises. It is not clear how long Birru remained under the employ of the Italians. But Wändaro and other leaders were disturbed:

98. Ibid.

99. Selma Bergsten and Earl Lewis, personal interview with Raymond Davis, December 16, 1961.

100. Percy and Violet Roberts, letters to family, November 10 and 23, 1933, indicate that the missionaries were assisting the *amanyoch* build a chapel from dried mud bricks, 22 x 42 feet. See also Davis, *Fire on the Mountains*, 57.

101. As quoted in Cotterell, *Born at Midnight*, 73. The pre-Italian SIM missionaries were ardent followers of Roland Allen's indigenous church principles as found in *Spontaneous Expansion of the Church* and *Missionary Methods*. For confirmation see Forsberg, *Land beyond the Nile*, 63.

102. Eshetu Abate, "Origin and Growth," 22; Davis, *Fire on the Mountains*, 107.

103. Roberts, "Soddo Diary," April 17, 1937.

We held baptisms at regular times and when we would make
an appointment with Birru to assist, he would never be able to
make it because of his job responsibilities with the Italians. So
we just went ahead and conducted baptisms on our own. Later
he left his work with the Italians and we did the work of the
Gospel together.[104]

Birru was encouraged by Dayésa Darge and other Christians to purchase a piece of farm land some four kilometers south of Otona in the district of Bosa Qacha. Dayésa also arranged his marriage to a young Wolaitta
lady.[105] The *amanyoch* saw in Birru a potential teacher and leader of the
nascent Wolaitta *amanyoch* of only forty-eight baptized believers. Even
though his family roots were in Kullo Konta, Birru's spiritual family was
in Wolaitta. The Otona *amanyoch* began to gather at Birru's new location
at Bosa Qacha (Kokaté) for worship, teaching, and fellowship. By January
6, 1938, forty-five of the *amanyoch* "had a happy Christmas together, all
meeting together at Birru's house."[106] By April 1938 a *ṣälot bét* was built
near Birru's residence to serve the *amanyoch* in the vicinity of Otona and
Soddo.[107] About one year after the departure of the SIM personnel from
Otona, Birru, with other Wolaitta *amanyoch* such as Wändaro Däbäro,
Dayésa Darge, Godana, Lolamo Boké, brothers Jaldo and Sälando Sägaro,
Agébo Aläta, Dana Mäja, and Toro Dubusho, began an intensive itinerant
ministry throughout Wolaitta, teaching and baptizing. We have no evidence that other *ṣälot bétoch* were established from the outreach of Birru in
the immediate Bosa Qacha district during 1938 and 1939.

Koysha

Toro Dubusho, former SIM employee, was the evangelistic impetus in
the Koysha district. By April 1937 there were sixteen baptized *amanyoch*
meeting together in the Gärära *ṣälot bét* newly erected beside Toro's grass-
roofed residence.[108] Toro's first convert, Gäfáto Jagiso, soon organized the

104. Wändaro Däbäro, personal interview with EPB, September 20, 1988, (EPB
personal collection, 4:248).

105. She was a candidate in the initial baptismal class of 1933. She and about thirteen others were deferred to the next baptism, which took place in July 1935.

106. Arébo from Wolaitta, personal letter, as quoted in Walter and Marcella Ohman,
letter to prayer partners, February 5, 1938.

107. Markina Meja, *Unbroken Covenant*, 27, writes that Birru's prayer house at Bosa
Qacha was destroyed by the Italians in late 1939.

108. Toro Dubusho, personal interview with EPB, December 11, 1955.

amanyoch of the Sadoyé area to erect a <u>s</u>*älot bét* next to his own house.[109] We have no evidence that <u>s</u>*älot bétoch* other than these two were built in the Koysha area until after the occupation. Before their incarceration in 1939, both Toro and Gäfäto recall that about two hundred *amanyoch* were regularly attending the Sunday meetings in their two <u>s</u>*älot bétoch*.

Wanché

In April 1937 the *amanyoch* in the Gulgula area worshipped at Gunta Gugalé's house in the sub-district of Kotte. By 1938 a small <u>s</u>*älot bét* was constructed next to Gunta's residence, but after a few months it was destroyed by the *banda* sent by the Italians.[110] The *amanyoch* were invited to worship at Shanqo Abet's residence. Rumors were spread throughout the Gulgula district that if *amanyoch* were meeting together in anyone's residence, the Italians would destroy it. Shanqo refused to allow the *amanyoch* to meet in his home.[111] It was then that Dana Mäja said, "Take my house. Just build me and my family a small hut."[112] Eventually the Wanché <u>s</u>*älot bét* became the inspiration for nearly a dozen other <u>s</u>*älot bétoch* in the Gulgula district.

Dana Mäja was able to attract effective teachers and preachers to Wanché. Two brothers, Irasho and Godaté <u>Ch</u>äbo, whose home was near Soddo, began their ministry at Wanché in 1938. Both men were well versed in Amharic. Irasho was the teacher and Godaté was the preacher/pastor. Without asking any remuneration for their duties they served the Wanché *amanyoch* for over one year.[113]

Markina Mäja recalls various programs that were initiated at the Wanché <u>s</u>*älot bét*. For example, one Sunday about seventy of the *amanyoch* were being sent out two by two from Wanché to evangelize throughout the Gulgula and Humbo districts. Whenever they would find a small crowd gathered they would preach, pray, and sing. All seventy returned to Wanché that evening and related their experiences to those who had

---

109. Gäfäto Jagiso, personal interview with EPB, December 10, 1995.

110. Markina Meja, *Unbroken Covenant*, 29.

111. Ibid.

112. Ibid.

113. Preacher Godaté appeared to be somewhat of a mystic. One day he went into seclusion in a cave on Humbo Mountain. After fasting and praying for more than a month he returned to Wanché, where he related his visions and experiences. He died shortly after this experience. Markina Mäja, peronsal interview with EPB, April 17, 1987.

remained behind to pray and prepare coffee. It was through this manner of evangelism that eleven other *ṣälot bétoch* were established in the Gulgula district.[114] Another program that was conducted by the Wanché *amanyoch* was a literacy school. About eighty adolescent boys and girls studied under the instruction of Irasho C̱häbo and Markina Mäja. The students were taught how to read and write Amharic as well as basic Bible texts in the Wolaitta language. An additional new program from Wanché was evangelism beyond the Gulgula district. After the occupation, men and women from Wanché went outside the borders of Wolaitta as evangelists. Balcha Bala went to Gämu; Mäna Ako and Bunaro Sumago went to Arsi; Omoché Ukulo and his wife Baloté Aymalo went to Gofa; Amoné Aba with her husband from Humbo went to Gofa; and Faränjé Buré and her husband from Koysha went to Gofa.[115] The Wanché *ṣälot bét* was a model of innovative programs for other *amanyoch* in Wolaitta to follow.

Soré and Other Districts in Wolaitta

When the missionaries left Wolaitta in 1937, they encouraged their employees to return to their home districts. Dayésa Darge was from Soré. He became an effective evangelist in his home district of Soré, beginning from 1937. Dayésa's religious pilgrimage was varied. His parents were followers of traditional religion. When he was around thirty years of age he heard Prophet Ésa from Gämo. He attempted to follow the teaching of Ésa but was not satisfied. Dayésa was a deacon in the Ethiopian Orthodox Church before he began working for the SIM missionaries at Otona in 1933 as a night guard. "He was a man who did not want to miss anything. He wanted to be sure."[116] He was a fluent speaker of Amharic when he arrived at Otona and soon learned to read the Amharic Bible. Dayésa gained a reputation for preaching the gospel at funerals, not only in Soré, but in other districts as well. He was fearless in challenging the *sharechewa* of his district.[117] It was from the Soré district that evangelists were sent to the

---

114. Markina Meja, *Unbroken Covenant*, 22–23.

115. Markina Mäja, personal interview with EPB, April 16, 1987.

116. Selma Bergsten and Earl Lewis, personal interview with Raymond Davis, December 16, 1961. See also *Fire on the Mountains*, 60, where Davis mentions that Dayésa may have also been a follower of Islam for a short time. Dayésa was one of the initial ten baptized December 10, 1933.

117. See account of Dayésa's challenging Gocha Goda in Davis, *Fire on the Mountains*, 63–68.

Kindo and Boloso districts after the occupation.[118] This was largely due to the effective teaching and initiative of Dayésa Darge.

Preacher Godaté C̲h̲äbo took leave of absence from the Wanché *s̲älot bét* in 1939 and evangelized in the Duguna district.[119] It appears that a pattern of itinerant evangelism by the *amanyoch* began to develop throughout Wolaitta by 1938 and 1939. Godaté's brother, Irasho, and young Markina travelled to C̲h̲iraqé to evangelize.[120] Birru Dubalä was off baptizing some thirty *amanyoch* near the Omo River in the Soré district.[121] And Lolamo Boké, now residing near Gulgula but whose family roots were in Kambatta, was preaching in the Admancho district, which bordered on Kambatta. Others such as Wändaro, Toro, and C̲h̲äramo Gäläso were travelling extensively in Wolaitta, teaching and baptizing the new converts.[122]

Italian Opposition (1940–1941)

Until 1939 the Italians, who made Soddo one of their southern Ethiopia centers, took little notice of the growing Wolaitta *amanyoch* community. But after the impressive 1939 parade and display of military might in Soddo town,[123] the foreign invaders made a proclamation: "The one who gathers and preaches to the people in the [domains] kingdom of Italy, beware."[124] Ethiopian Patriots Adeno Bora, *Däjazmach* Arega, and others made mountainous Kullo Konta one of their strongholds. This prompted the Italian forces to take military action against the inhabitants of Kullo Konta. Hundreds of families were dislocated.[125] Harsh measures were meted out to any Patriot collaborators. During the succeeding months the *amanyoch* continued their public preaching in the market places and at funerals, and the number of *s̲älot bétoch* were expanding. Reports of this growing counter-culture movement came to the attention of the Italians through the Wolaitta local officials called c̲h̲iqa shum and the *whuduga*.

118. Soré evangelists, C̲h̲ondo Wola and Mara, preached in Boloso for more than ten years. Mälkamu Shanqo, *"Hulum Ades Honwal,"* 15, 34. Dayésa continued as a Soré leader well into 1950. See also Markina Mäja, personal interview with EPB, April 18, 1987.

119. Markina Mäja, personal interview with EPB, March 6, 1987.

120. Markina Meja, *Unbroken Covenant*, 22. Irasho and Markina evangelized Buge, Sessa, Abéta, Konte Wéga, and Ada in the C̲h̲iraqé district.

121. Eshetu Abate, "Birru," 5.

122. Wändaro Däbäro, personal interview with EPB, September 22, 1988.

123. Cotterell, *Born at Midnight*, 112.

124. Eshetu Abate, "Birru," 5.

125. Cotterell, *Born at Midnight*, 116–17.

The *amanyoch* were looked upon with disfavor by their neighbors.[126] First, they challenged the funeral customs. Instead of wailing, striking their cheeks and breasts with a thorn branch to cause bleeding, and jumping high in the air and landing on their knees, the *amanyoch* would say, *Ṭosi dandayiso* (May God uphold you). And at the funerals they would ask permission to preach about the power of Christ over death and the resurrection of the body, and then they would lead the entire group in an antiphonal song. Second, they were accused of disturbing the equilibrium of Wolaitta society by challenging the power and authority of the *sharechewa* and *ṭänqway* and no longer sacrificing to the clan deities.[127] Third, the *amanyoch* prayed for the return of their former SIM teachers and the safe return of their sovereign, Haile Sellasie.[128] And fourth, the *amanyoch* were accused of disregarding the hierarchical status of the many clans within Wolaitta. They allowed the lowest clans from among the artisans, such as the *faqi* (tanners), *fuga* (potters), and the *bariya* (slaves), to eat together in one *mahibär* or association. Followers of traditional religion thought that the clan deities would become angry and the general well being of the Wolaitta society would be upset.[129]

During the Italian occupation, the fifty to sixty functioning *ṣälot bétoch* were destroyed.[130] By August 1940 nearly all leaders of local district *ṣälot bétoch* were arrested by the local *whuduga* and marched to Soddo, where they were first interrogated by an Italian official.[131] When these leaders refused to salute the Italian flag and show their allegiance to Mussolini, this was interpreted as a flagrant anti-Italian stance deserving of severe beat-

126. See Eshetu Abate, "Origin and Growth," 33–35, for additional reasons for persecution of the Wolaitta *amanyoch*.

127. Dayésa Dargé challenged the power of the *tänqway* in his home district of Soré. See Davis, *Fire on the Mountains*, 60–66.

128. In Donald Crummey's review of *Fire on the Mountains*, he correctly notes that David did not explore the political dimension of this new Christian movement. There is no evidence that the Wolaitta *amanyoch* collaborated in any manner with the Patriots in resisting the Italian oppressors. The *amanyoch* and the Wolaitta Patriots such as Bogalä Walälu and others had this in common: they shared prison cells and food brought by other *amanyoch*. Gäfäto Jagiso, personal interview with EPB, December 10, 1995.

129. Mälkamu Shanqo, "*Hulum Ades Honwal,*" 18–19.

130. Dana Mäja, personal information to EPB, September 8, 1987.

131. Toro Dubusho and Gäfäto Jagiso indicated a total of about fifty-five who were incarcerated in the Soddo prison. Lolamo Boké insisted that the numbers were up to seventy-six. Personal information to EPB, December 22, 1988.

ing.[132] The Italians did not personally inflict the beatings with the hippo-hide whips on the imprisoned *amanyoch*, rather they delegated this to the *askari*, the majority of whom were non-Wolaitta.[133] An extreme instance of Italian cruelty to the *amanyoch* prisoners was when soldiers jumped on the backs of several prisoners.[134] Nor were all leaders imprisoned. Dana Mäja had developed a friendly relationship with his local *whuduga* so was not imprisoned.[135] Although there was cruelty to those imprisoned, the extent of the harshness appears to have been exaggerated somewhat by sympathetic missionaries.[136]

The resistance against the new churches movement had the positive effect of developing a self identity among the *amanyoch*. As was customary within Ethiopia, the families of the imprisoned were responsible for bring-ing food and blankets. When the church fathers were incarcerated in the Soddo prison, *amanyoch* from the Wolaitta districts such as Bosa Qacha, Humbo, Wanché, Koysha, Soré, Dubancho, Chäraqé, and Duguna orga-nized themselves to bring food on certain days of the week.[137] The attack by the Italian military against the new churches movement had the effect of uniting the *amanyoch* and bringing an inner cohesion among them.[138] The heroic stories of their leaders' resistance to the threat of the authorities

132. Lolamo Boké, transcribed interview with EPB, December 22, 1987.

133. Wändaro Däbäro called them *banda*. Personal information to EPB, September 22, 1988.

134. The Italian soldiers jumped on the backs of Wändaro and Lolamo with their hob-nailed army boots.

135. Gäfäto Jagiso stated that Dana Mäja's status as "Big Man" was also a factor. Personal information, December 10, 1995. Laliso's father, not one of the *amanyoch*, pro-tected Laliso from the local *whuduga* (local officials relating to the Italians). Laliso Täntu, personal information, December 13, 1995. Ebamé Amdo, wife of Birru Dubalä, was the only woman *amanyä* imprisoned. Eshetu Abate, "Origin and Growth," 37.

136. Selma Bergsten and Earl Lewis, personal interview with Raymond Davis, December 16, 1961, where there appears to be an over-emphasis on the punishment meted out to the *amanyoch*. Apparently only two *amanyoch*, *Ato* Alämbo and Sälando Sägaro, died in prison. See Markina Meja, *Unbroken Covenant*, 26, and Eshetu Abate, "Origin and Growth," 24. Davis, *Fire on the Mountains*, 115 notes that three died.

137. Markina Meja, *Unbroken Covenant*, 26; Gäfäto Jagiso, personal interview with EPB, December 11, 1995; and Toro Dubusho, personal information to EPB, December 12, 1995.

138. M. Louise Pirouet affirms this position: "There is evidence from a number of different areas that Christianity took root better where this conflict is clear, and involved converts making a decided and costly stand as innovators than in areas where the issue was never dealt with." *Black Evangelists*, 164

and the ensuing punishment were told and retold among the *amanyoch*. A theology of suffering was developed through a song that became popular. Toro from Koysha, a gifted singer, composed this song while in prison:

> If we have little trouble here, we will have little reward there.
>   We will reign.
> Why should we not suffer a little while here and now.
>   We shall reign.
> We will reign with him through all eternity.
>   We will reign.[139]

This song embodies a theology of suffering that will eventually be rewarded. It is significant that the leaders of the Wolaitta *amanyoch* shared their suffering together in one locality. Gäfäto Jagiso and Toru Dubushu recall that the detained *amanyoch* leaders in the Soddo prison were treated humanely after their initial beating. They were allowed Scripture portions and several Bibles. Their Christianity was expanded from legalistically following prescribed rules and regulations about circumcision, not eating raw meat at the *mäsqäl* celebration, and forsaking horse racing at weddings and funerals, to that of becoming identified with Christ and his suffering on the cross.[140]

One night in 1941, Wändaro Däbäro had a dream that the gospel would spread throughout Wolaitta like a fire sweeping down Damota Mountain. When he left his prison cell the next morning to relieve himself, he saw lightening flash across the sky, and then tongues of flames began to burn on Damot Mountain. For Wändaro, this was a sign from *Tosa* that the seventy *amanyoch*[141] would be released from prison to return to their home areas to rekindle the flame.[142]

139. As found in Davis, *Fire on the Mountains*, 136. It appears that this song has elements of escapism from the harsh realities of this present life. For several accounts of churches under persecution, see Latourette, *History of the Expansion of Christianity*, 135–56.

140. Gäfäto Jagiso recalls that Soddo prison official Léga (Yäṣahai Abat) was very kind and "made our time in prison bearable." Personal interview with EPB, December 10, 1995.

141. Lolamo Boké, personal interview with EPB, December 22, 1987, claims that there were seventy-six *amanyoch* incarcerated in the Soddo prison for ten months.

142. Marqos Hébäna, personal interview with EPB, February 12, 1997. This event has taken on a mythological dimension among the Wolaitta *amanyoch*.

Several weeks later on May 22, 1941, Italian generals Liberati and Bacarri, based in Soddo, surrendered to the English and Patriot forces.[143] The Soddo prison doors were flung open for the release of all political prisoners. The *amanyoch* leaders displayed the scars on their backs to authenticate their suffering.[144] They related how *Ṯosa* had cared for them while they were in prison. They also shared about the oneness and fellowship they had experienced. This unity among the leadership was retained after their release.

But beyond this unity was the fact that a mythology had been created by the leaders of the Wolaitta *amanyoch*. The fire of the gospel ignited within Wolaitta would spread throughout the land. They perceived that an alternative model of Christianity was now a Christian movement with its center deeply rooted within Wolaitta.

Freedom to Grow and Expand (1941–1945)

The Case of Boloso District

Boloso district has been selected to portray how evangelism was carried on within Wolaitta during the immediate post-Italian era. The following discussion sets forward the basic thesis that the pattern of evangelism the evangelists employed within Wolaitta was that which they later found operational beyond their geographic borders.

Boloso is one of the sixteen sub-districts of Wolaitta located in the northwest of Wolaitta *awraja*, bordering the Omo River. Prior to the Occupation (1937–1941), the peasants of Boloso had little freedom and few personal rights. They were forced to work two days per week for their Amhara landowners; one day for the *balabatoch* and one day for the *qalicha* or *sharechewa*. The illiterate peasants were often cheated by officials who falsified tax receipts and demanded extra tax payment. If taxes were not paid on time the officials would write a letter to a higher official, sent by the hand of the illiterate peasant. Imprisonment awaited the offender until his family paid all arrears. No schools were available for children in Boloso before 1941, so the best that parents could do for their offspring was to feed and clothe them and teach them to dance, hunt, accuse and defend themselves in court, and perform domestic tasks around the farmsteads.[145]

143. Thompson, *Liberation*, 178.

144. For a description of their suffering see Davis, *Fire on the Mountains*, 133–35.

145. Mälkamu Shanqo, "*Hulum Ades Honwal*," 5–6.

Boloso researcher and writer Mälkamu Shanqo describes the prevailing attitude towards women at that time:

> Women were not treated with respect or honour. They were seldom given an opportunity to speak or discuss family matters. They were encouraged to dress in a less than beautiful manner because of their husbands' potential jealousy. It was generally thought that women were unable to learn to read. When a girl was born into a family, there was usually great sorrow.[146]

The teaching of the Prophet Ésa Lalé had reached the people of Boloso some twenty years before 1941. Many from the Boloso district made Ésa Lalé their ancestor to whom they offered prayers.[147] The followers of Ésa Lalé fasted every Wednesday and Friday from dawn to dusk, and on Sunday they worshipped _Tosa_, the creator of heaven and earth, by flicking honey with their forefingers and thumb into the sky. Prayers of confession were made with their hands held high. The women prayed to Mary, asking for mercy and forgiveness. Mälkamu Shanqo was told by a revered Boloso elder named Dana Adayé that Ésa had taught them to obey these commandments:[148]

1. Do not lie or bear false witness.
2. Do not steal.
3. Do not commit adultery.
4. Do not worship any other gods.
5. Do not kill.
6. Love each other.

We see here that five of the Ten Commandments are listed, and the sixth command is from the teaching of Jesus—no doubt an addition by a recent _amanyä_. Ésa's teaching made a lasting impact on the people of Boloso.[149] They were in the process of putting away their clan deities and worshipping _Tosa_.

146. Ibid., 6.

147. Esa Lalé rebuked the Omotic people of the south for worshipping their ancestor spirits as well as clan deities. See Earl Lewis letter to Raymond Davis, September 12, 1961, and Dana Mäja, personal interview, September 22, 1988.

148. Mälkamu Shanqo, _"Hulum Ades Honwal,"_ 9–11.

149. Dana Mäja and Wändaro Däbäro, personal interview with EPB, September 22, 1988, indicate that Esa's assistant, Mera, not Esa himself, itinerated within Gämo, Gofa, Qucha, and Wolaitta.

It was into this cultural and religious milieu within Boloso that the evangelists from surrounding districts came in 1941. Among them came Borsamo Boké, who was from Soré. He was the first leader of the Boloso *amanyoch* association and was instrumental in establishing many churches. It was said of him, "He was a man of fervent prayer, strong faith, spiritual ministry, and without blemish in his life."[150] Chondo Wola was another evangelist from Soré. Chondo was a short man, hard of hearing because of a blow inflicted on the side of his head by an Italian gun. He was effective in establishing fifteen *sälot bétoch* in the Boloso district.[151] The three Gädébo brothers, Danya, Maya, and Molta from Koysha, made a significant contribution in the Adela, Gämo, Zäba, and Mätala *sälot bétoch* in Boloso by teaching literacy and Bible texts. Amanta Soso was from the neighboring district of Damot Fulasa, and his contribution to the Boloso new churches movement was preaching at Homba and Hombecho. He had a gift for training leaders, who later represented Boloso at the association of *amanyoch* who met at Otona, Soddo Zuriya.[152] Within five years a corps of local Boloso leaders were trained sufficiently in literacy and basic Bible truths so that they could preach, teach, baptize, administer communion, and incorporate the Boloso *amanyoch* into disciplined communities that had the capabilities of expanding and replicating themselves.[153]

The *amanyoch* throughout the entire *awraja* of Wolaitta would assist one another by celebrating baptisms, weddings, and funerals together. This association became a supportive mechanism for the *amanyoch*. This fact impressed the unbelievers, who then realized that the new church movement encompassed the entire Wolaitta *awraja* and was larger than what was visible within the Boloso district. Slowly those who were not *amanyoch* were impressed by the love and concern displayed by the evangelists from neighboring districts such as Soré, Koysha, Damot Zuriya, Damot Fulasa, and Humbo. And at special events like a baptism, a wedding, or a funeral,

150. Mälkamu Shanqo, "*Hulum Ades Honwal*," 12.

151. Sawl Salgédo, "*Achir Yähiwäté Tarek*," 11, attributes his own skills in evangelism to the training received from Chondo.

152. Mälkamu Shanqo, "*Hulum Ades Honwal*," 16–17.

153. The goal of mission, according to Alfred G. Roke, "was to so guide and instruct those who would push out to the frontiers of their tribe and perhaps beyond to complete the task of evangelism." *Indigenous Church in Action*, 47. The following is a list of Boloso *amanyoch* leaders from 1941 to 1974: Borsamo Boké, Misébo Amaché, Mata Kayro, Taso Mijiré, Taltamo Hanjälo, Asha Alämbo, Mijire Moleso, Lächubo Däntägo, Däbäb Tänto, Samuél Hébäna, Kasa Gafäro, Génsa Kuké, Däsaläny Därächo, Märäqo Haläbo, and Goshu Také, as listed in Mälkamu Shanqo, "*Hulum Ades Honwal*," 13.

leaders of stature among the Wolaitta *amanyoch* such as Birru Dubalä, Wändaro Däbäro, Toro Dubusho, Dayésa Darge, *Ato* Godana and Dana Mäja were invited to attend. One of the songs that expressed the joy of the Boloso *amanyoch* was:

> The old thoughts have been taken away.
> A new heart has been given.
> We have travelled over to the domain of Jesus.[154]

This briefly describes how the Boloso district within Wolaitta was being evangelized during the period of relative freedom from 1941 to 1945. We will now look at the development of the larger *amanyoch* community within the Wolaitta *awraja* during the same time frame.

The Wolaitta Amanyoch Community, 1941–1945

When SIM left Wolaitta on April 17, 1937, there were forty-eight baptized *amanyoch* meeting in the homes of leaders Birru Dubalä at Bosa Qacha, Wändaro Däbäro at Humbo, Toro Dubusho at Gärära, Dayésa Darge at Soré, and Gunta Gugale at Kottie. In August 1941, former SIM missionary Laurie Davison returned to Addis Ababa with the British Army to repatriate Ethiopian soldiers to their home areas. In November 1941 two leaders, Säbäro and Shäguté, from the Kambatta/Hadiya *amanyoch* arrived in Addis Ababa bringing the following report, as recorded by Davison:

> They say it took them fifteen days to see all the churches and all the Christian work that is going on there. They report sixty-seven churches in all and some holding over a hundred people and needing from five to seven lanterns to light them at night. They say that whereas once it was hard to find any believers . . . people are coming from Maraqo (Another very hostile tribe) and from Gofa, to learn of spiritual things from Biru, the leader of the Walamo work. They stay from ten to fifteen days sometimes, and then return with hearts aglow.[155]

One year later, July 1942, Birru Dubalä arrived in Addis Ababa together with several Wolaitta *amanyoch*. The Davisons were now able to get a first-hand account of the Wolaitta movement:

> I cannot hope to tell you all Biru told us of the work. He has three other Wolamo Christians here with him, and they bear out

154. Mälkamu Shanqo, "*Hulum Ades Honwal*," 22.
155. Laurie Davison, "News from Ethiopia."

all he says, and even add to it. There is no doubt that Biru has done a wonderful work—and he has certainly grown old in the Lord's work. He spends all his time walking around the province, telling the Gospel and teaching the young Christians. He does not baptize any under one year's instruction in the things of the Lord, but even then, one day he baptized five hundred. He has leaders in all the different sections of the province. They say that when we left there were only about ten Christians who stood by the Lord, but now there are ten thousand![156]

We must now place the Wolaitta new church movement in the broader context of Emperor Haile Sellassie's regaining his throne in Addis Ababa on May 5, 1941, and the defeat and routing of the Italians. The Ethiopian Patriots, with the assistance of the British military and forces from Kenya, Sudan, West Africa, and South Africa, demobilized and captured the Italian troops. On May 22, 1941, with a minimum of resistance, the town of Soddo surrendered with more than 4,000 Italian officers and soldiers taken as prisoners of war.[157]

At the local Wolaitta level, all political and religious prisoners were released when the Italian military structure collapsed. Beginning in May 1941, the new churches movement was afforded another opportunity to operate in relative freedom until 1945, when the former Amhara landlords were again entrenched in Wolaitta.[158]

In July 1943, Guy Playfair, SIM general director, along with Alf Roke and Norm Couser, former SIM missionaries to Ethiopia, were granted permission to visit Soddo. It was now more than seven years since SIM had left Soddo. The verbal reports brought to the Davisons in Addis Ababa

---

156. Lily and Laurie Davison, letter to Eric and Sylvia Horn, July 5, 1942. Fargher's modest estimate of 5,000 *amanyoch* adherents in Wolaitta in August/September 1941 is reasonable. See Fargher, *Origins of the New Churches Movement*, 226.

157. Thompson, *Liberation*, 178. Markina Mäja recalls observing hundreds of Italian soldiers imprisoned inside the barbed wire fence situated at the Soddo airport. Some of the soldiers were bartering their jackets and shirts for food. Personal information to EPB, March 15, 1987.

158. It appears that some in the new churches movement in Wolaitta and Kambatta/Hadiya were experiencing certain restrictions from Amhara petty officials soon after the Italians were evicted from Ethiopia in 1941. While residing in Addis Ababa the Davisons reported regarding Shäguté from Kambatta/Hadiya, "At last he has got his signed paper authorizing him to hold meetings and preach the gospel, so he will soon be going back to Kambatta." Lily and Laurie Davison letter to Eric and Sylvia Horn, July 5, 1942. See also Laurie Davison, "News from Ethiopia," where reference is made to Säbäro and Shäguté requesting the Ethiopian officials in Addis Ababa for permission to hold religious meetings.

from southern *amanyoch* could now be verified. Playfair wrote this account of what he observed in Wolaitta:

> It is decidedly not a youth movement; but is touching every age. In one congregation of three hundred we counted twenty grey or white-headed men, probably all of them grandfathers. The large majority seem to be men and women of twenty-five years of age and upwards.[159]

After a two-week stay in Wolaitta, Playfair reported enthusiastically, "The Good News has penetrated into every part of the tribe until almost one-third of it is Christian. Three hundred Walamo churches cover a wide area."[160] A reasonable estimate of *ṣälot bétoch* in Wolaitta for 1943 would be just over one hundred. When Walter and Marcella Ohman arrived in Soddo in July 1945 they estimated that there were 150 *ṣälot bétoch* in Wolaitta.[161] In December 1946 the Ohmans report, "There are two hundred and seven churches in Walamo today, all in fellowship."[162]

With the growth of local *ṣälot bétoch* in Wolaitta, there was a growing need to develop a culturally appropriate structure for coordination. The Wolaitta *amanyoch* borrowed the concept of the *mahibär* from the Ethiopian Orthodox Church but transformed the function to meet their needs. The word *mahibär* is a Ge'ez word and in Amharic parlance denotes a social feasting club, usually a small group of men or women (probably not mixed) meeting together on a Sunday or church holiday under the name of an Ethiopian saint, an angel, or an Eastern saint.[163] In the Ethiopian Orthodox Church, those belonging to an intimate association one with another describe themselves as "eating or drinking from the same *mahibär*."[164] In the new churches movement, a single congregational

159. Playfair, *Trials and Triumphs in Ethiopia*, 30–31.

160. Ibid., 30. In the SIM publication *Ethiopia is Stretching out Her Hands to God*, appears a balanced summary of Playfair's 1943 Ethiopia reports: "There is now a total of 155 churches with an estimated following of between fifteen and twenty thousand." p. 13. This figure would combine together the Wolaitta and Hadiya/Kambatta churches.

161. Walter and Marcella Ohman, letter to Raymond Davis, February 15, 1961.

162. Walter and Marcella Ohman, letter to prayer partners, December 31, 1946. The Ohman letter to prayer partners, December 15, 1950, says that 1,793 were baptized in Wolaitta during 1950, and their February 16, 1953, letter records 4,921 for 1952. There is no reason to doubt these figures.

163. Tsehai Berhane, "Political and Military Traditions," 56.

164. Ibid., 59. Walker, *Abyssinian at Home*, 121–29, describes the function of *mahibär* in Shewa province in the 1920s. Between twelve and thirty compatible men would agree to meet on the feast-day of a saint to eat and drink together. An Orthodox priest

meeting on Sunday was called the *Yäihud sibsäba* (the Sunday meeting), not a *mahibär*. A *mahibär* meeting of the *amanyoch* would transact various business matters dealing with the life and well being of members within the *sälot bétoch*. Agenda items such as discipline of members, marriage irregularities, charity for the needy, the collection of funds for evangelists' salaries, and feeding of *amanyoch* in prison were cared for. In Wolaitta there are two levels of *mahibär* meetings. One level is when several *sälot bétoch* gather together for fellowship and prayer. Another level is when representatives of a district representing from thirty to forty *sälot bétoch* meet together on a monthly basis. This meeting is called the *kifle mahibär*. But when delegates from the entire *awraja* of Wolaitta meet together for their monthly gathering at Otona, this gathering is called the *tärapéza*.[165] Since 1991 the term *mahibär* has been used less frequently among the Wolaitta *amanyoch*.

The spiritual development among the Wolaitta *amanyoch* can be assessed in their songs. The following song is christological in theme and originated around 1940, when the Wolaitta *amanyoch* were incarcerated in the Soddo prison.

> He loves me
> His goodness is abundant to me
> He was sent by God the Father
> He descended from the heavens
> He came down to earth
> He took upon himself our flesh
> He was born of Mary
> During the reign of Pilate
> His body was broken
> He shed his own blood
> He died on the cross
> He was victorious over death
> On the third day
> He rose from the tomb
> He ascended to heaven

---

was invited to bless the gathering. This "in-group" was rather exclusive and functioned as a volunteer association of Christians. Michael Singleton, "Ethiopia Tikdem," 291–309, contains a fascinating description of a Roman Catholic *mahibär* functioning outside of Bonga, Käfa.

165. In Wolaitta the monthly meeting of all representatives from the sixteen districts, called *tärapéza*, meaning "meeting around the table," probably originated soon after the exodus of the SIM missionaries in 1937. See Davison's report of a functioning *täräpéza* in 1945, as found in Cotterell, *Born at Midnight*, 103.

My guarantor will return
To whom is he a guarantor?
To all the *amanyoch*
He is the guarantor
How did he become our guarantor?
By being victorious over death
He healed us from all our diseases
He removed all our difficulties
In the house of God
He is now at the right hand of his Father
In order to give us eternal life
He is the guarantor.[166]

The following three songs[167] were popular in 1941, following the eviction of the Italians:

The Country Blessed of God,

Walamo the Flower Like Galilee.

There Is Jesus' Teaching Place.

Oh, Children Come to the Teaching Place.

Men, Come to the Teaching Place.

Everyone Come to the Teaching Place.

The above song expresses a strong ethos of Wolaitta's being blessed and becoming the center of teaching and learning in the new churches movement. The teaching is about Jesus, and everyone is invited to come and learn at the "teaching place."

The next song is a strong affirmation that the future life for all *amanyoch* will be in heaven.

There is a heaven.
The beloved servants are in heaven.
What shall we do? What shall we do?
We earthly servants, what shall we do?
I am here. I am here.
I am on earth.
I shall be in heaven
It is also true. It is also true . . .
The medicine is Jesus—it is also true.

166. A collection of nearly fifty early Wolaitta hymns, compiled by Lily Davison, Selma Bergsten, Markina Mäja, and others, is in my possession.

167. As found in Laurie Davison, "News from Ethiopia."

A Christian woman whose husband and three sons were killed by Italian soldiers composed the following song. Instead of weeping loudly and mutilating her body, as was customary at a Wolaitta funeral, she sang:

> Understand men. Understand men.
> Our home is that which is in heaven.
> Our Father is he who is in heaven.
> Our children are those who are in heaven.

In other early songs of the church, topics include: Jesus born of Mary, his death on the cross, his resurrection, and his ascension to his Father, his second coming, his wonderful miracles, salvation through Christ, security in Christ regardless of circumstances, hell and everlasting punishment for those who reject God, the significance of the word of God; benefits received as Christians, praise and worship to Jesus, encouragement to be strong in faith.

Most of these songs, responding to attacks upon the faith and life-style of the *amanyoch*, were composed during adversity. There is a focus on heaven, where there are no perverse people and no evil and where there will be fair judgment against the enemies of God. These songs emphasize a faith dimension, but little is mentioned about loving one's neighbor as oneself. This practical dimension of their faith may have been practiced but not put to song.

The Quest for Maturity and Expansion, 1945–1975

SIM missionaries Guy Playfair, Alf Roke, and Norm Couser visited Wolaitta July 3–10, 1943.[168] Playfair observed, "This Church is alive. It is Spirit filled. Its witnesses are out to save the lost, to make God's saving grace known."[169] It was another two years before SIM missionaries were granted official permission to reside again in Wolaitta.[170] In March 1945 the Wolaitta *amanyoch* welcomed Laurie and Lily Davison. The Davisons were able to see firsthand the functioning of the Wolaitta *ṣälot bétoch*. They

168. For accounts of this visit to Wolaitta, see Playfair, *Trials and Triumphs*; Guy Playfair, letter to Eric Horn, August 10, 1943; Davis, *Fire on the Mountains*, 113–15; and Guy Playfair, report to Whitaker, October 2, 1943.

169. Guy Playfair, report to Whitaker, October 2, 1943, 3.

170. The 1944 Ethiopia *Missions Decree* delineated areas as "open" or "closed" to mission agencies. The "open" areas were those where the Ethiopian Orthodox Church was not predominant. For example, Balé, Arsi, Sidamo, Käfa, and Gämo Gofa provinces were declared "open" by the "Memorandum in Regard to Missionary Work in Ethiopia." In areas designated "closed," the Orthodox Church has been firmly established for centuries.

noted that the *awraja* was divided into fifteen districts, with one ruling elder responsible for each district. These fifteen elders, called *hospun dana* in Wolaitta, initially met in a different district every full moon.[171] For each local *ṣälot bét*, four elders were appointed. Matters of discipline, teaching, performing the sacraments, and preaching were carried on by the *tärapéza* elders. Davison noted:

> Evangelism in Wolamo and even in the neighboring provinces, at least to the south, should be left in the hands of the native evangelists, while we concentrate all our energies upon a teaching ministry for the immediate future.[172]

When the Ohmans, Beatrice Barnard, and Selma Bergsten arrived in Soddo in July 1945, they began, in rented quarters, to teach informally both men and women from all fifteen districts. Such was the enthusiasm for learning that each month, from August 1945 to October 1946, they had an average of 1,200 coming to learn.[173] In November 1947 the missionaries were able to move back to their former station at Otona. In April 1947 the Otona Bible School opened with over eighty in attendance. Each of the students paid a 3.00 birr fee for books and writing materials. In August 1947 ninety-five registered for the second semester. The goal of the Bible school was not only to train preachers and teachers for the local churches, but that "some should be called of God to become missionaries to tribes beyond which still sit in darkness."[174] By 1965 the Bible school at Otona could not cope with all the students, so the leaders of the districts suggested that lower level Bible schools be established in each of the eight districts.[175] These training centers provided a strong impetus to Wolaitta evangelism and to the health of the Wolaitta *ṣälot bétoch*.

The first spiritual life conference to be held among the new churches movement in southern Ethiopia was at Otona in November 1947.[176] The

171. After 1950 the *tärapéza* began to meet at Otona.

172. L. A. Davison, "Notes on the Situation in Wolamo," May 1945, 3. Nineteenth century Catholic missionary Bishop Justin de Jacobis was of a similar mind: "Indigenous priests could suffice to renew the face of Abyssinia without it being necessary to have lots of European missionaries." As found in Donald Crummey, *Priests and Politicians*, 82.

173. Walter Ohman letter to Raymond Davis, February 15, 1961, 5.

174. Walter and Marcella Ohman, letter to prayer partners, August 18, 1947.

175. Markina Meja, *Unbroken Covenant*, 85. By 1972 these district Bible schools had expanded to sixteen Wolaitta districts.

176. Walter and Marcella Ohman, letter to prayer partners, January 27, 1948. These conferences were usually four days in duration—Wednesday through Sunday.

Ohmans reported that 2,500 attended during the week, "But on Sunday the crowd swelled to over 4,000."[177] Markina Mäja suggests that the purposes of the spiritual life conference were to renew the spiritual life of the Christians; to challenge couples for missionary work outside Wolaitta; to select and appoint the evangelists to their various locations; to strengthen the love and unity among the Wolaitta *amanyoch*; and to allow people to give offerings, tithes, and pledges for the work of evangelism.[178]

At the 1949 conference, the offerings totaled 341.00 birr. This was divided among the twenty-seven evangelists serving in Qucha, Gofa, Gämo, Kullo Konta, Arsi, and Sidamo. At the 1950 conference the amount was more than doubled—828.00 birr.[179] In 1951 the two speakers, Guy Playfair and Martha Moenick, had just come from the Kambatta conference where the people had given generously in cash and pledges. The Wolaitta *amanyoch* were challenged by the generosity of the Kambatta and gave a total of 5,200.00 birr.[180] The conferences had a strong missionary emphasis. Not only would the Wolaitta evangelists return to renew fellowship with their extended families and friends at conference time, but evangelists would sometimes bring recent converts from their missionary outposts.[181]

Within the SIM hospital at Otona a Dresser Training Program was launched in 1946. The first group of trainees selected were from each of the fifteen districts in Wolaitta. After two years of training, these fifteen men established small dispensaries in their home districts. These dispensaries proved to be invaluable in providing a substitute for the Wolaitta who were accustomed to go the *sharechewa* or *qalicha* for their physical illness.[182] Dozens of young men and women within the new churches movement of southern Ethiopia received training at the SIM Dresser Training

177. From 1991 to the present, the average annual attendance at the Wolaitta conference convened at the Anka KHC center has been around 35,000.

178. Markina Meja, *Unbroken Covenant*, 169. As a weakness of the conference, Markina listed "too many choirs who took much time." See Eshetu Abate, "Origin and Growth," 45, for his positive assessment of the Wolaitta conferences.

179. Walter and Marcella Ohman, letter to prayer partners, December 15, 1950.

180. Walter Ohman, letter to Raymond Davis, February 15, 1961, 2. The tithes and offerings at succeeding conferences have averaged 1.00 birr for each person attending.

181. For example, a special attraction at the 1974 conference was the attendance of two Bänna converts, Girisho and Garsu, from the nomadic Bänna ethnic group of South Omo. See Markina Meja, *Unbroken Covenant*, 168.

182. Nathan Barlow, personal interview with EPB, June 6, 1997.

Program, and these medical specialists provided support to the Wolaitta evangelists.

Finally, reference must be made to the training of women in Wolaitta. Mention has been made of Selma Bergsten and Beatrice Bernard teaching women in rented quarters in Soddo town for fourteen months beginning in August 1945. By January 1947 Selma Bergsten began an itinerant teaching program among eight district centers throughout Wolaitta.[183] The course of study included: literacy, Bible study and memorizing verses, and a variety of skills such as knitting, embroidery, food preparation, household management, growing of vegetables, and earning funds for the support of evangelists.[184] This informal training program, which continued for some twenty years, nurtured and equipped a group of young women, most of whom became wives for the pioneer Wolaitta evangelists. Baloté Aymalo, herself trained in this program, recalls that several of these young women volunteered for missionary activity at the 1952 spiritual life conference. Wolaitta leaders Dana Mäja, Wändaro Däbäro, Gäfäto Jagiso, and Lolamo Boké matched these young ladies with male volunteers.[185] Markina Mäja comments about the training of women in their local church setting:

> The fruit of this service is still shining today because all the students of Miss Bersgten did their job faithfully wherever they went for the Gospel work with their husbands.[186]

The following is a short list of those who went as evangelists with their husbands to the following places: Baloté Aymalo to Gofa, Faränje Buria to Silté, Amoné Aba to Gofa, Mägdalawit to Gofa, Aster to Silté, Laréba Känka to Sidama, Bulälé to Sidama, Era to Burji, Mokonä to Arsi, Ganä to Sidama, Birhane Chälalo to Gofa, Anjule Cholo to Gofa, Lafame Langano to Gofa, Falahé Midoré to Gofa, Dorane Gämbéra to Bale Goba, Dakité Bochole to Bale Goba, and Badalä Amacho to Gofa. Without the commitment, skills, and spiritual resourcefulness of these able wives, the evangelistic outreach of the Wolaitta *amanyoch* would have been less than successful.

183. Walter Ohman, letter to Raymond Davis, February 15, 1961, 6. Ohman recalls that before the trainees could be enrolled, they had to be engaged to be married.

184. This information was gathered from Baloté Aymalo, personal interview with EPB, December 26, 1987.

185. Ibid., 12.

186. Markina Meja, *Unbroken Covenant*, 82–83. A full account of the noble Wolaitta women remains to be written. See Davis, *Fire on the Mountains*, 196–230, for the account of five Wolaitta women evangelists.

Conclusion

In this chapter there has been an attempt to describe some of the qualities of the growth and development of the Wolaitta *amanyoch*. We have seen that conversion for the Wolaitta was a pilgrimage from their primal religion to Christianity. Disruptive social and political changes within greater Ethiopia and specifically within Wolaitta from 1936 to 1945 produced a climate of freedom juxtaposed alongside Italian oppression. Those who made a deliberate, reasoned choice to join the *amanyoch* communities attained freedom from fear, a sense of dignity, and unity among themselves. They experienced a new power in Jesus that superseded the *ayana* that their primal religion depended on. In the absence of the missionaries, the *amanyoch* relied on corporate prayers, their Wolaitta Scriptures, and their few Amharic Bibles. The *amanyoch* were innovators in creating a new community within Wolaitta. They organized their own leadership, constructed their own churches, provided among themselves the sacraments of baptism and communion for the *amanyoch*, and went about evangelizing Wolaitta and neighboring tribal groups.

There are lingering questions that demand further investigation: What provided the motivating factor for growth and expansion of the Wolaitta movement? Why did the salvationist message of the Wolaitta preachers have a strong appeal? And how did the message of impending judgment furnish the incentive for many Wolaitta to believe? It is evident that the strength of the Wolaitta *amanyoch* movement was that the gospel was fully able to meet the needs and aspirations of the Wolaitta in their own context when the missionary was absent.[187]

---

187. See Pirouet, *Black Evangelists*, 189, where she faults the missionaries for "not being able to meet the Teso on their own grounds," and Cotterell, *Born at Midnight*, 168, for the positive effect of the "isolation of the church in the formative years [from SIM missionaries]."

6

The Wolaitta Evangelists' Outreach to Gämo, Qucha, Gofa, and Kullo Konta (Dawro)

"It would seem that southern peoples [of Ethiopia]—
suddenly aware that northern domination was not inevitable—
began to reassemble and recreate their religious lives."[1]

Introduction

IN CHAPTER 5 WE discussed the emergence of the *amanyoch* communities within Wolaitta. We observed that the Italian intrusion into and expulsion from southern Ethiopia had a bearing on the expansion and development of these communities. By May 1941 the seventy-five Wolaitta *ṣälot bétoch* were able once again to meet together in freedom. Worship centers that had been destroyed by the Italian *banda* were rebuilt and the seventy *amanyoch* leaders, recently released from prison, were again functioning as spiritual guides and catalysts in each of the *ṣälot bétoch*. We also observed in the previous chapter that the *amanyoch* were given an opportunity to develop their own identity during the ten-month period of harassment by the Italians. Men like Birru Dubalä, Wändaro Däbäro, Lolamo Boké, Toro Dubusho, and others had been willing to sacrifice their lives for their religious commitments. On the national level, by May 1941 the Wolaitta received news from returning soldiers that Emperor Haile Selassie had been restored to his throne in Addis Ababa. This gave the *amanyoch* a sense of stability and well-being. Even though the task of evangelizing Wolaitta was incomplete, there were those within the Wolaitta *amanyoch* community who began to travel out beyond the geographic confines of Wolaitta to preach. On their own initiative, the Wolaitta desired to tell the Jesus story

1. Donham, "Old Abyssinia," 46.

to those of similar language, culture, and religious background over the next mountain range.

Beyond the confines of Wolaitta, the evangelists continued the preaching and teaching tradition of the SIM evangelists. It was the preaching of the Wolaitta evangelists, armed only with their Bibles, that effected the conversion of people from the geographic areas of Gämo, Qucha, Gofa, and Kullo Konta, who were within the Omotic language group.[2] Although there were slight linguistic variations between Wolaitta and these four ethnic groups, the similarity of a common culture and their shared primal religion were an advantage to the evangelists.

This chapter will describe the endeavors of the Wolaitta evangelists to preach and organize *amanyoch* communities that related to one another in the wider Omotic area of southern Ethiopia. An attempt will be made to portray the context of the theatre in which the evangelists operated, to describe their activities, and finally to assess the performance of the evangelists.

Gämo

Gämo region lies immediately south of Wolaitta and west of Lake Abbaye (see map 6.1). The population of the area in 1940 was around 90,000, the majority of people being involved in subsistence farming on land above 1,800 meters altitude. Some chose to farm the fertile lowlands, located immediately west of Lake Abbaye as well as along the fertile Maaze River basin, living with the hazards of malaria and other diseases prevalent in lower altitudes. Prior to 1965 the administrative center of Gämo alternated between Chäncha and Gidole.[3] Within Gämo the following sub-groups take their name from the localities in which they reside: Dorze, Ocholo, Boroda, Bonké, Bälta, Algudé, Marta, Gäräsé, Kämba, and Maaze.[4] These ethnic groups are able to communicate with each other at local markets through the medium of Gämo, an Omotic language.

In 1933, SIM located at Balé Shasha, near Chäncha town, and established a clinic. But there was little response to the teaching and preaching of the two resident single missionaries who attempted to reach the residents of Chäncha and the nearby Dorze village.[5] Several Gämo residents

2. See Adams, "Tagmatic Analysis of the Wolaitta Language," 28–31.

3. In 1965 the provincial capital of Gämo Gofa was shifted to Arba Minch.

4. Cerulli, *Peoples of South-West Ethiopia*, 98.

5. See Cotterell, *Born at Midnight*, 66, where Selma Bergsten reported, "It all seemed fruitless." Apparently the Dorze women ran away when the missionaries came

remember Walter Ohman's travelling from Bulqi in 1935 and preaching at the C̲h̲äncha market.[6] There were no lasting results from the SIM pre-Italian outreach in Gämo. It was the efforts of the Wolaitta evangelists who succeeded the SIM missionaries that made a lasting impact on three Gämo districts, to which we will now turn.

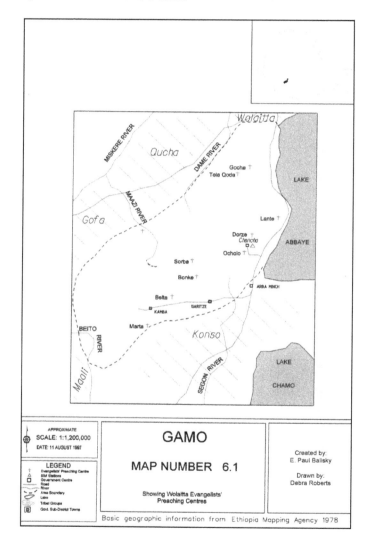

APPROXIMATE SCALE: 1:1,200,000
DATE: 11 AUGUST 1997

GAMO

MAP NUMBER 6.1

Showing Wolaitta Evangelists' Preaching Centres

Created by:
E. Paul Balisky

Drawn by:
Debra Roberts

LEGEND
† Evangelists' Preaching Centre
△ SIM Stations
□ Government Centre
Road
River
Area Boundary
Lake
Tribal Groups
Govt. Sub-District Towns

Basic geographic information from Ethiopia Mapping Agency 1978

---

near. In 1934 the O. J. Kirks joined single missionaries Selma Bergsten and Ruth Bray at C̲h̲äncha.

6. KHC, *"Bäwängél Amanyoch Andinät,"* 22. See also Cotterell, *Born at Midnight*, 114.

Preaching of the Gospel to the Ocholo

Because of tribal warfare with the Guji near the <u>Ch</u>amo and Abbaye lakes around 1860, the Ocholo were driven to their rock fortress near the town of <u>Ch</u>äncha.[7] But the Ocholo retained their farmlands in the fertile lowland plains near Lake Abbaye, some three hours' descent from their Ocholo defense, cultivating corn, cotton, and a variety of fruits. Some of the Ocholo also became day-laborers on the cotton plantations bordering Lake Abbaye that were being developed by private entrepreneurs in the 1930s. Around 1937, Ocholo resident Gémbo Sägamo[8] was working on the Abbaye cotton plantation, near the village of Lanté. There he was befriended by Hirboro and Farängé Buré, two Wolaitta *amanyoch* from Humbo, who were also day laborers in the cotton fields. They told Gémbo the Jesus story. He recalled that he had heard this message preached at the Ocholo market several years before by Ohman, the SIM missionary from Bulqi. Gémbo invited the two Wolaitta cotton workers to his highland village of Ocholo so that they might tell the same story to his family and neighbors. Hirboro and Faränjé left their cotton-picking employment and temporarily moved in with the Gémbo family. During Hirboro and Faränjé's stay of several days at Ocholo, Gémbo and five others said they understood the message and desired to follow this new teaching. When the two Wolaitta *amanyoch* returned to their homes in Humbo, their intention was to continue their contact with Gémbo at Ocholo. But because of unsettled conditions brought about by the Italian invasion of the South, contact was not sustained between the Humbo and Ocholo *amanyoch*. It appears that the initial impact of the gospel upon the Ocholo was ephemeral. Tesfaye Tole, present church leader, says of the first six Ocholo *amanyoch*, "In actuality, there was very little difference in the manner of life style and orientation to cultural practices between the *amanyoch* and the others living in the Ocholo village."[9]

In 1939 the Italians staged a military parade in Soddo to display their might to the Wolaitta and Gämo Gofa residents.[10] All able-bodied men

---

7. Abéles, "La guerre vue d'Ochollo (Éthiopie méridionale)." By 1955 the Ocholo settlement, contained within three hectares, had grown to 5,000, according to Ed and Edna Ratzliff, *Letters from the Uttermost Parts of the Earth*, 206.

8. For an expanded account of the story of Gémbo Sägamo, see Davis, *Winds of God*, 15–31.

9. KHC, "*Bäwängél Amanyoch Andinät,*" 22.

10. Cotterell, *Born at Midnight*, 112–13.

from these two regions were obligated to attend. As Gémbo and five of the Ocholo who had previously heard the gospel were passing through Humbo on their way to Soddo, they inquired about their former acquaintances, Hirboro and Faränjé. Gémbo and his friends were led to Hirboro's residence. Hirboro summoned his *amanyoch* neighbors. Then throughout the night Hirboro and the Humbo *amanyoch* taught the Ocholo visitors from the Scriptures and answered many of their questions about sacrificing to the ancestor spirits, the consequences of violating prohibitions (called *gomé*),[11] and the power of prayer through the name of Jesus. In 1943 Hirboro again decided to go to Ocholo, and taking with him several Humbo *amanyoch*, he travelled to visit Gémbo and the other *amanyoch*.[12] Soon after this, the first *ṣälot bét* was constructed at Zaza Ocholo, next door to Gémbo's house. It was not long before the Ocholo community began to insult and ostracize the *amanyoch* because various ones from different social strata were socializing and eating together in the Zaza *ṣälot bét*. It was thought that this kind of behavior was breaking long held prohibitions. The *fuga* (the potters), the *faqi* (tanners), and the *bariya* (slave) clans were singing, learning, and even eating together with the upper strata of Gämo clans, such as the Gämo Malla, in Gémbo's new *ṣälot bét*. Because the *amanyoch* were violating long-held traditions of the Ocholo, the community believed that the deities and the ancestor spirits would become angry. The Ocholo community leaders accused the *amanyoch* and brought them to the Chäncha government officials. As a result, twelve *amanyoch* were imprisoned in chains and iron shackles for three years. Two died from excessive beating and exposure while imprisoned in Chäncha.[13] There is no record of any Wolaitta evangelist's being incarcerated with the Ocholo *amanyoch* at this time, but regardless of the opposition, Wolaitta evangelists Hirboro, Laliso Täntu, Wogaso Walila, and Jara Bakalo continued to make occasional visits to the growing group of Ocholo *amanyoch*.[14]

Probably the most severe persecution against any of the *amanyoch* in southern Ethiopia occurred in Ocholo in May 1951. Edna Ratzliff writes from Chäncha:

11. *Gomé* is thought to be a malevolent spirit that resides in certain objects or places.

12. KHC, "*Bäwängél Amanyoch Andinät*," 23.

13. Ibid.

14. Laliso Täntu, personal information to EPB, December 13, 1995, and Yosef Menna, "*Yätinsaéw Näṣibiraq*," 199.

> It seems that all hell has broken loose. Our compound has be-
> come a refuge for over a hundred Ocholo who have been forced
> to flee their homes. They were given a choice, either deny the
> faith or get out. Some did deny the faith and signed their finger-
> prints to a paper to prove it. . . . The raiders wanted Ato Gimbo
> and several of the other church leaders but they were warned in
> time and got away. . . . The raiders and looters have cut down the
> crops and the banana trees [*ensette*] on the land of the Christians,
> drove them from their homes and stole all their property, their
> cattle—everything. . . .The only safe place was here. . . . I've cried
> so much these days. I feel like the Psalmist who said, "Tears have
> been my meat day and night." One feels so desperate. . . . We've
> prayed and prayed but so far there is no change.[15]

The Ocholo *amanyoch* remained at the SIM C̲h̲äncha station for over
one year. Several had been badly bruised by being stoned and clubbed.
Gémbo Sägamo and Tolcha fled to Wolaitta for advice from their friends.
They were assisted by the Wolaitta *amanyoch mahibär* and SIM to take
their plea to the Addis Ababa government officials. Swift justice was meted out by the Addis Ababa officials. The offenders were arrested and the
amanyoch compensated for their loss.[16]

Preaching of the Gospel in the Bonké and Sorba Districts

In 1950 Gopilo Golo and Biramo, accompanied by Gämo *amanyä* Gémbo
Sägamo, travelled from Wolaitta to Ocholo. Gopilo continued his journey
another day southwest to the Bonké district and made Kächa his preaching center. Gopilo read from the Gospels that Jesus would return to the
earth to judge the living and the dead and those who believed would be
saved but those who refused would suffer a terrible punishment forever.
When his listeners heard this they said,

> This is the second time we have heard this kind of preaching.
> Over thirty years ago a man living near C̲h̲äncha came preach-
> ing and told us not to worship trees, stones, or any *qalicha* or
> any kind of idol. He taught us to go outside our houses both at

15. Ratzliff, *Letters*, 117. See Cotterell, *Born at Midnight*, 149–50 for a description
of the same event. See also Abéles, "La guerre vue d'Ochollo," 455–70, for a description
of how the Ocholo have defended themselves for several generations along Lake Abbaye
as well as up in their mountain fortress near C̲h̲äncha.

16. Cotterell mentions that "government action was swift. Fifty of the plunderers
were arrested, and a total of some four thousand dollars was awarded to the church as
compensation." *Born at Midnight*, 150.

morning and night and pray to God for mercy and to repent of our sins and to fast on certain days of the week. Now, many years have passed since we first heard this kind of teaching and because no one has taught us since, we have returned to our former ways of worshipping.[17]

After hearing Gopilo tell the Jesus story, entire families, including the elders, said they would forsake their clan deities and believe in Jesus. For the past decade the Bonké residents had been disturbed by spirits. Israél Goda recalls being awakened each morning while his father spoke audibly with a spirit.[18] These conversations brought fear to the households because new prohibitions of what the family could or could not do were imposed. The people of the Gämo highlands believe misfortunes are caused by the breach of rules and regulations, which number in the hundreds, called *gomé*. These prohibitions touch all aspects of Gämo life: economy, social behavior, family life, agricultural practices, and religion.[19] From the Kächa centre, between 1950 and 1954, the number of *amanyoch* grew rapidly and the following eight *sälot bétoch* were erected in the Bonké district: Wosantu, Däla, Käylé, Sayté, Bul'o, Kuto, Haringa, and Därba.[20]

Moga Goda Guna was an influential *tänqway* in the Bonké district. His decision to leave his former profession and to convert to the religion of the *amanyoch* was prompted by a crisis in his family. When his wife was in labor, it appeared that both mother and child would succumb to death. In desperation, *Moga Goda* Guna made an oath to *Sosa*. If his wife and child survived, he would become an *amanyä*. His wife rallied and gave birth to a healthy boy. His conversion brought the wrath of the Bonké *balabat* upon him. Fearing for his life, *Moga Goda* Guna fled from Bonké and took shelter with the Chäncha *amanyoch* for a time.[21]

Another area that was impacted by the preaching of Gopilo was Sorba, located about four hours northwest of Bonké. In 1957 a certain *näftänya* residing in Sorba was disturbed that many of the *chisänyoch* residing on his *gult* land were becoming *amanyoch*. Evangelist Gopilo was confronted in

---

17. As reported to Tesfaye Tole by the Bonké *amanyoch* in KHC, "*Yäqalä Hiywät Bétä Kristeyan Tarik*," 34.

18. Israél Goda, personal information to EPB, March 1987.

19. See Olmstead, "Agricultural Land and Social Stratification," 232, about some of these prohibitions. From 1986 to 1989, while stationed in Kamba, Gämo, I observed the debilitating *gomé* phenomena amongst the Gämo.

20. Cotterell, *Born at Midnight*, 115.

21. KHC, "*Bäwängél Amanyoch Andinät*," 34–35.

the Sorba market with these words of warning by the *näftänya*, "Why have you come here to teach these illiterate people? Do you not realize that if this continues they will not obey me in the future? You better watch out."[22] When Gopilo responded that it was not a crime to teach literacy to those who wanted to learn and that there was freedom of religion in Ethiopia, the *näftänya* and his cohorts began beating Gopilo with their walking canes and clubs. Gopilo soon lost consciousness and was left for dead. The *näftänya* ordered some of his men to tie a rope around Gopilo's feet and dragged him off to the market dung heap. The Sorba *amanyoch* came to his rescue, and after two weeks of medical treatment, Gopilo recovered and was back teaching and preaching in the Sorba district.

Preaching in the Boroda District

The Boroda district is located in the northern section of Gämo, bordering on the southern edge of Humbo. Two Humbo evangelists, Laliso Tãntu and Jara Bakalo, made an exploratory trip to Boroda in 1942. Laliso quoted Mark 16:15–16 to people in markets, in their homes, wherever he and Jara stayed overnight, and to travelers along the road: "Go into all the world and preach the good news to all creation. Whoever believes and is baptized will be saved, but whoever does not believe will be condemned." All listened politely. When the two evangelists were returning home from their preaching tour of several weeks, bandits attacked them and stole their clothing and Bibles.[23]

This minor hardship did not deter Laliso from returning to Boroda to preach, this time taking along with him Balcha Bala. In 1942 they were preaching and teaching in Téla Kodo district to a small group of recent converts. Evangelists Laliso and Balcha were arrested and imprisoned for three months along with eight of the Boroda *amanyoch*. The Boroda *amanyoch* and the two evangelists suffered from cold and lack of food at Télo Kodo, located at an altitude of more than 3,000 meters. Few *amanyoch* in Boroda at that time were willing to risk bringing them food and blankets, except for one *amanyä* by the name of Moga. Every seven days he supplied the prisoners with *ensette* filled with eggs and butter. When the eight Boroda *amanyoch* were released from the Téla Kodo prison, Laliso and Balcha were informed that their crime was serious. The evangelists were escorted to the

22. Gopilo Golo to Tesfaye Tole in KHC, "*Bäwängél Amanyoch Andinät,*" 35.

23. Laliso Tãntu, personal information to EPB, December 13, 1995. At the very place Laliso and Jara were robbed, the Dengélé *sälot bét* was erected.

provincial prison at <u>Ch</u>äncha to await trial. It was there they served a one year prison sentence together with twelve Ocholo *amanyoch*.[24]

A lasting contribution of Laliso Täntu and the other evangelists in Gämo was in assisting the Gämo *amanyoch* to establish their own *mahibär*. The following seven *s̱älot bétoch* in Gämo joined together and formed the Gämo *mahibär* in 1946: Ochollo Zaza, <u>Ch</u>äbo, Zärdo, Digida, Dedané, Shomära Zegeya, Boroda Gocho.[25] As the *amanyoch* met together as a *mahibär* to pray, sing, and study the Bible at regular intervals, the unity among the seven *s̱älot bétoch* was strengthened.

6.1 *Evangelist Ombolé Odiro served in* Tämbaro, Kullo Konta, Bali Goba Aäri, Käfa, *and Awassa (Kay Bascom, 1994)*

From the Wolaitta evangelists' operations in Gämo one can make several observations. The evangelists remained in Gämo only for a limited time. They preached, taught, baptized the *amanyoch* and then withdrew.[26] A second observation is that those who exercised power in Gämo resisted the evangelists' message and presence because this new movement threatened their authority and control in the area. Reports of the growth of the *amanyoch* in Wolaitta would have reached the government officials, the

24. Laliso Täntu, as quoted in KHC, "*Bäwängél Amanyoch Andinät,*" 33.

25. KHC, "*Bäwängél Amanyoch Andinät,*" 33.

26. For a similar deployment of evangelists, see Brant, *In the Wake of Martyrs*, 136–38. Three Kambatta/Hadiya evangelists arrived in Gédéo in 1951, twelve in 1953. These Kambatta and Hadiya evangelists were withdrawn from Gédéo in 1956 and leadership of the *mahibär* handed over to the Gédéo who were trained in the Dilla Bible School.

näftänyoch, and Orthodox clergy in the Gämo administrative center of Chäncha.[27] A third observation is that because of the ostracism and imprisonment the Gämo *amanyoch* experienced, they were drawn together in unity and love.

Quᶜha

Background

Geographically, Quᶜha is bordered by three rivers: Gogara on the east, Maazi to the west, and the Omo River to the north (see map 6.2). Around 1870 Quᶜha[28] separated from Wolaitta and became a small separate kingdom, its borders delineated by rivers and mountain ranges. The Ethiopian government structure of Quᶜha related to the provincial capital of Chäncha. After the subjugation of Wolaitta by Emperor Menilek in 1894, northern *näftänyoch* began occupying not only Wolaitta but the sub-provinces of Quᶜha, Gämo, and Gofa.[29] And where the *näftänyoch* located, Orthodox churches were established. In 1940 there were Orthodox Churches serving the needs of the northern *näftänyoch*[30] in four different centers in Quᶜha: Mikaél and Yäsus Churches in Dälbo, Maryam and Gäbriél in Bola, and Mädihin Aläm in the Géréra area.[31] It was not until after 1955 that there was any evidence of the Orthodox Church becoming pro-active in spreading Christianity among the indigenous Quᶜha population.[32]

---

27. *Ato* Mäkonän, descendant of a Wolaitta *näftänya,* remarked to me that when his family returned to Wolaitta in 1942, "All of Wolaitta had become missionary." *Ato* Mäkonän, personal information to EPB, January 10, 1994.

28. Quᶜha has been administered alternatively from the provincial capital of Gämo Gofa, located in Chäncha and from the *awraja* center at Bulqi.

29. Markakis writes, "The northerners were granted land as a reward for military service and on condition of continued service." *Ethiopia,* 11.

30. George Rhoad makes mention of overnighting at Bola, the Quᶜha administrative center on May 25, 1931. He referred to "the old soldiery [*näftänyoch*] who are so conservative and so opposed to the entering of the light that is certain to alter the mode of living to themselves as well as to the people over whom they have had such peculiar control." "Roadside Jottings," 41.

31. Bassa Däa, "*Yätämärätä Tiwild,*" 21–22.

32. Mahé Choramo, "Philip," 43.

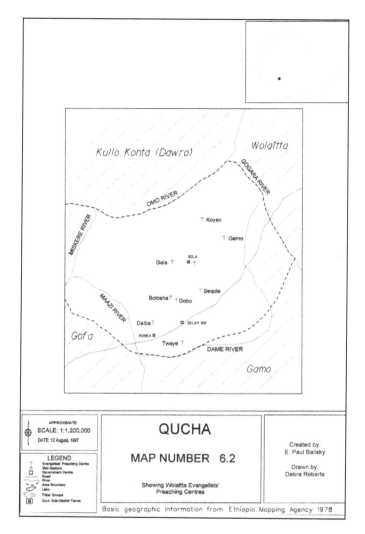

In 1931 George Rhoad, while trekking from Jimma to Soddo, Wolaitta, anticipated the day Ethiopian evangelists would preach in Qucha province:

> Here as everywhere else we will need to believe God for a native agency that can, without the encumbrance of camp equipment and so forth, freely move in and out amongst the people and live on such foods as make up their daily fare. One rejoices that all this section of country can be reached through the Walamo language, and that Walamo teachers and those won for Christ at

any point can be used throughout this whole area most readily and successfully.[33]

It was ten years after Rhoad made this prophetic statement that the Wolaitta evangelists began penetrating Qucha. By 1941, the Wolaitta *amanyoch*, residing in the southwestern districts of Koysha, Ofa, and Humbo, took the responsibility of evangelizing Qucha. The Wolaitta *amanyoch* perceived Qucha as an extension of their own country because of a common language, culture, and clans.[34]

Evangelistic Preaching in Qucha prior to the Wolaitta Evangelists

In 1933 Walter Ohman, located at the SIM station at Koybe, Gofa, trekked to Bola in Qucha. As was his custom, Ohman preached in the Bola market. Qucha resident Yaya Argäbo heard the message and was impressed by what he heard. There is no indication that Yaya had subsequent discussions regarding religious matters with Ohman. According to Qucha historian Basa Däa, "It appears that Ato Yaya Argäbo was truly converted back in 1933 because at that time he began to pray fervently."[35]

In 1941, soon after the Italians were defeated in southern Ethiopia, Bilaté Shashogo, a resident of Dälbo Qucha, visited his relatives in Humbo, Wolaitta. While at Humbo he heard the new teaching about Jesus from Wändaro Däbäro, was converted, and worshipped for a time with other *amanyoch* at Humbo. After several weeks, he returned to Dälbo Qucha, eager to tell his family and neighbors about this new faith. After several months, Bilaté returned to Wolaitta and recruited evangelist *Washa Goda* Wadébo to assist him in preaching and teaching.[36]

This was Bilaté and Wadébo's message as they itinerated around Qucha. "There is only one who can give life after death and deliver you from fear. This is Jesus Christ. Those who trust in him will live forever. Those who reject him will be judged by him."[37] To become a believer in the Qucha context would mean forsaking adherence to the intricate set of taboos (called *gomé*) the people were attempting to follow. For example, the first fruits of a field must be offered to the elder brother before anyone

33. Rhoad, "Roadside Jottings," 38.

34. The Qucha *amanyoch* were structurally incorporated into the Wolaitta *amanyoch* communities until 1962.

35. Bassa Däa, "*Yätämärätä Tiwild*," 23.

36. Ibid.

37. Ibid.

else could eat some of the produce. Another taboo was that a stranger must not be allowed to watch a mother breastfeed her child. The people of Qucha had become weary of these burdens. One of the first to believe was Ashäbo Adéto, a neighbor of Bilaté's from Qolé. After several months, thirteen others believed. Wadébo encouraged this nucleus of *amanyoch* to build their own grass-roof *ṣälot bét*, similar to the one he had been worshipping in back in Humbo. This they did, making the *ṣälot bét* at Qolé the first to be erected in Qucha.[38] It not only served as a Sunday prayer house but as a literacy center. About a dozen young men, after working in their fields, would arrive in the evening carrying a load of firewood, bread, a cotton blanket, and literacy books. Under the tutelage of evangelist Wadébo, these young Qucha men struggled to learn the Amharic alphabet and vocabulary by the light of their wood fire and, when exhausted in body and mind, would stretch out and sleep.[39]

Didana Dilbato, a resident of Koysha, Wolaitta, travelled to Qucha in 1941 to visit his relatives in the Bolosha district, some five hours' walk southeast of Qolé. Didana had become a believer through the preaching of Toro Dubusho and had begun worshipping in the Gärära *ṣälot bét* in Koysha, Wolaitta. While visiting his relatives at Bolosha, Didana explained how he had found that Jesus Christ gave him peace from the fear of death. He told them that many in Wolaitta were believing in Jesus, forsaking the worship of their clan deities, and that now people from different clans were forming *amanyoch* communities. Before Didana returned to Koysha, several households stood with hands held high and made their profession of faith. They repeated the believer's creed that Didana knew well from his own conversion in the Gärära *ṣälot bét*.[40] Because of the conversion of several people some distance from Qolé, Bilaté Shashogo and Ashäbo Adéto invited evangelist Didana to become a permanent evangelist in Qucha, with special responsibilities for shepherding the new *amanyoch* at Bolosha. He consented and moved his wife, Asoté Sirina, and children to Qucha. While preaching and teaching, Didana and several Bolosha *amanyoch* were arrested and imprisoned at the provincial capital, Chäncha, in 1946. The Bolosha *ṣälot bét* was burned to the ground. Didana was severely beaten in the Chäncha prison; after being released six months later, he never fully regained his health.[41] One of the Wolaitta hymns that sustained wife

38. Abraham Alämbo, personal information to EPB, December 1991.
39. Mahé Choramo, "Philip," 30.
40. As stated in chapter 5. "I believe in Jesus Christ. I have denied Satan," etc.
41. Asoté Sirina, personal interview with EPB, December 9, 1995.

Asoté's faith during Didana's imprisonment was *Dusaytuma* (My life, my living, is it authentic?).[42]

While Didana was imprisoned in Chäncha, three other Wolaitta evangelists, Hardedu Hantiyé, Gäfäto Gäbré, and Géta Halala, arrived at Bolosha to assist in teaching, preaching, and encouraging the recently converted *amanyoch*. These three evangelists were able to assist in rebuilding the destroyed Bolosha *salot bét*.

When Didana returned to Quçha from the Chäncha prison in 1950, he established his second *salot bét* at Fula and served there as pastor and literacy teacher for about twenty years. In 1966 he was elected to serve as one of the Quçha representatives to the annual national meeting of the *Amanyoch Andinät* (Fellowship of Believers).

In 1944, the third Quçha *salot bét* was established at Säqolo, located about six hours' walk from Bolosha, by evangelists Gizaw Adamo, Färacho Chalalo, and Gäfäto Gäbré.

The fourth *s älot bét*, located about three hours northeast of Säqolé, was established in 1945 at Gemo by a young Quçha convert by the name of Mahé Choramo. He was assisted occasionally by Didana Dilbato and other Wolaitta evangelists. About thirty worshippers would attend each of the *salot bétoch* now established at Bolé, Bolosha, Säqolé, and Gemo.

For various reasons, the main factor being persecution, there was limited growth in numbers of *salot bétoch* after 1945. In 1959 the same four were reported, but by 1963 the number had increased to nineteen.[43] Increased freedom in Quçha, a connecting road from Soddo, an elementary school in Selam Bir, and additional Wolaitta evangelists were some of the factors that contributed to the increase of the Quçha *salot bétoch*.

Because Mahé became an evangelist of some significance in southern Ethiopia and, although a convert from Quçha, was accepted and supported by the Wolaitta *mahibär*, we will give a short sketch of his formative years in Quçha.

Short Biography of Mahé Choramo

Mahé Choramo was born in 1922 in the village of Gébo, Quçha.[44] When he was about ten years of age, his father died. As he assisted his mother in

42. Words to *Dusaytuma* are quoted in chapter 4.

43. Dick and Vida McLellan, letter to friends, June 1, 1963.

44. The information for this biographical section was obtained from, Mahé Choramo, "Philip," 18–28, and personal information to EPB, December 1995.

providing food from their small plot of land, she would advise him, "Do not use the name of *Tosa* to curse other people or an animal." On Sunday his mother would dress Mahé, his two sisters, and his brother in clean clothes and they would offer prayers to *Tosa*. Mahé never understood why his mother feared and worshipped *Tosa* as she did. She herself was born in Wolaitta and her relatives may have been members of the *amanyoch* communities. Or she may have been a follower of the teaching of Ésa, the prophet from Gämo, who was reported to have visited Qucha around 1923 or 1924.

About 1932 Mahé's mother died and he was left with the responsibility of caring for his older sister, who had recently been divorced, as well as a younger brother, Danél. At the funeral of his mother, when the entire community was mourning, he was despondent and wished he himself would die. He asked himself, "If a person dies will he live again?"[45] In the Gébo community, a man by the name of *Goda* Ka'o, would gather people together on Sunday and would talk about such things as the dead coming back to life again. Mahé recalls that *Goda* Ka'o related:

> Those who stop offering sacrifices to the ancestral spirits and believe only in God will be saved from judgment. In the future people will fly in boxes through the sky. The big forest located in Boroda will be hewn down and become arable land.[46]

Mahé wanted to know more, so he questioned *Goda* Ka'o. He was told that *Tosa* will come down to the earth holding a large golden umbrella and will judge all men.

Not only the question of death but many other matters troubled Mahé. He argued and fought with his brother and sister. At the market at Bola and at the *wäräda* administrative center he observed people fighting and accusing one another. He asked himself, "Why is there no peace?"[47]

Around 1942 Wolaitta evangelist Bonja Albé, together with Qucha *amanyä* Bilaté Shashogo, visited Mahé at his home. Bilaté and Bonja took time to answer the questions that troubled Mahé. They translated various

45. Mahé Choramo, "Philip," 22.

46. Ibid. This prophecy was not unlike that given by a contemporary prophet, *Wäidé Goda* Albé Acha from Humbo. At that time much of Boroda, located adjacent to Lake Abbaya, was forested.

47. Bassa Däa, "*Yätämäräṭä Tiwild*," 28–29, explains the hierarchical structure of the Qucha clans, indicating that intermarriage between the Gämo Malla and the Dogalla clans is strictly forbidden.

Amharic Bible texts into Wolaitta so Mahé could understand. The texts from the Bible about everlasting life to those who believe and judgment to those who refuse were words of truth for Mahé. To confirm that he was sincere and desired to believe, Bonja and Bilaté asked Mahé to raise both his hands and repeat after them:

> I deny Satan.
> I will follow Jesus Christ.
> I was a sinner before.
> Forgive me.
> I believe in the Lord Jesus Christ who gave his life for me.

When Mahé asked the evangelists about rules and regulations he should now begin to observe as a follower of this new religion, they gave him this advice:

> Pray before each meal, saying, "I am a sinner; please forgive me. Bless and make this food holy to me. I pray this in the name of Jesus Christ, Amen." The Lord will bless this food to you.[48]

About six months later, Mahé joined evangelist Bilaté for three days as he preached and taught. Mahé learned important lessons from the life of Bilaté. Mahé wanted to hear over and over again the story of Jesus: his life, death, and resurrection, his promise to come again to raise the dead and judge the wicked. This gave Mahé a strong incentive to preach to others. But his next challenge was to learn to read and write in Amharic. He had a strong desire to preach from the Amharic Bible because he believed in its power. It was evangelist Bonja who gave him his first literacy lessons. After a few lessons, Mahé purchased an Amharic Bible and an Amharic alphabet book and essentially taught himself.[49] It was after he mastered reading and writing that he began preaching certain texts from his Amharic Bible in the Gämu subdistrict and eventually established a *sälot bét* there. He also organized *amanyoch* in two other nearby areas called Gobo and Gela. By 1952 Mahé desired to preach further afield, and he looked over the Qucha mountain ranges towards Gofa. But before he could leave for Gofa, Mahé and three other evangelists were arrested for disturbing the peace and were detained in the Bola police station. *Däjazmach* Tesfaye, governor of Gämo

---

48. Mahé Choramo, "Philip," 26. The prayer appears very similar to the prayer suggested to Dana Mäja and his son Markina by Wändaro Däbäro in 1936.

49. Ibid., 30.

Gofa region, based in Chäncha, arrived in Bola for government business. While in Bola he enquired about the incarcerated evangelists. Their accusers stated that the evangelists were a threat to the peace and "were destroying the Christianity of Ethiopia."[50] The *Däjazmach* commanded that the four prisoners be brought to him with the goods they had in hand when they were arrested. The four stood before the governor with their Bibles and walking sticks. The *Däjazmach* asked the Bola government officials in an angry voice, "Is this all they had in their hands?" A Bola policeman replied that these *säbakeyoch* (preachers) were going around the countryside "attempting to destroy the religion of the fathers. They have brought a new religion that does not belong to our fathers."[51] Mahé was allowed to make a full defense before the *Däjazmach* as to his conversion and what he was teaching his neighbors and friends. *Däjazmach* Tesfaye returned the evangelists' Bibles and personal effects to them and released them, saying, "They have done nothing against the law. They should not have been detained."

Mahé's roots were in Qucha, but because he joined the Wolaitta evangelists in their outreach in both Qucha and Gofa, in 1955 he was incorporated into the Wolaitta *mahibär* and began receiving the evangelists' monthly stipend.[52]

Those who have known Mahé Choramo have the highest regard for him. One who has travelled with him on evangelistic trips said this of him:

> I would say that our closest dealings were with Mahé, and feel that he stands near the top, if not at the top of an ideal evangelist. Time and again he would tell of his love for the people. . . . He was happiest when he had a Bible in his hand and was sharing in a hut or under a tree or along the paths. . . . [53]

Resistance and Persecution in Qucha

The Wolaitta evangelists and the *amanyoch* in Qucha experienced opposition from three different sources. Influential *näftänyoch* usually resented the evangelists' intrusion into "their territory." Local religious functionaries, the *qalicha* and *tänqway* group, also opposed the evangelists, as did the

50. Ibid., 46.

51. Ibid., 46–47.

52. Eyob Ololo, born in Kullo Konta, was also eventually incorporated as an evangelist into the Wolaitta *mahibär*. Personal interview with EPB, July 7, 1988.

53. Merle Dye, letter to EPB, June 5, 1991.

clergy of the Orthodox Church. The clergy claimed they had been in the South first and had an obligation to be the guardians of Christianity and defend the integrity of Ethiopian culture from foreign influences.

By 1942 the Amhara *näftänyoch* had returned to Quᶜha and taken up their former landholdings. They viewed the *amanyoch* as a threat to their own authority and control. The *amanyoch* gathered together in each others' homes. In 1952 Quᶜha believer and teacher of the *amanyoch* Ashäbo Adéto crossed the mountain range to Wolaitta to attend meetings. This disturbed the local Amhara authorities because it appeared that the *amanyoch* who were also *chisänyoch* were posing a threat to obedience and to loyalty.[54] Because the *amanyoch* met together to sing, pray, and learn from the Bible, it appeared that they were organizing an alternative community. It was for this reason that the *amanyoch* were arrested. When placed on trial in the courts, they would boldly declare their allegiance to Jesus Christ. Because their loyalty was first to Christ, they were falsely charged of disloyalty to Emperor Haile Selassie, who was again ruling Ethiopia from Addis Ababa.

In 1953, when the opposition became intense against the Quᶜha *amanyoch*, some fled to Wolaitta for safety and remained there. It was over a year before the *sälot bétoch* at Qolé, Bolosha, Siqolé, and Gemo were rebuilt.[55]

In 1943 Bilaté Shashogo and a recent Quᶜha convert, Ashäbo Adéto, were arrested and sentenced by the Bola officials. After three months of detention in the Bola police station, they were transferred to the *awraja* centre prison in Chäncha, where they were incarcerated for twelve additional months. Their case was then transferred to the high court in Addis Ababa. Because Bilaté Shashogo was sickly, the Chäncha governor *Däjazmach* Zäwdé, in a gesture of compassion, recommended that Bilaté be tried in the Chäncha provincial court in order to forego the arduous trip to Addis Ababa. Bilaté refused, stating, "I, together with Ashäbo Adéto, have been

---

54. Bassa Däa, "*Yätämärätä Tiwild*," 24. See McClellan, "Reaction to Ethiopian Expansionism," 203, for a carefully researched account of a southern Ethiopia society being dominated by the northern Amhara administration subsequent to the imperial expansion of Menilek II. McClellan states that in the rich coffee-producing area of Darasa, northerners were members of a small ruling elite and became "clearly patronizing and exploitative . . . of Darasa." Ibid., 279.

55. Abraham Alämbo, personal information to EPB, December 25, 1991.

accused falsely because of our religious beliefs and together we will stand trial in Addis Ababa."[56]

In 1944 Bilaté Shashogo and Ashäbo Adéto, together with forty-nine criminals, were escorted from Chäncha to Addis Ababa under the escort of twenty soldiers. After trekking the 140 kilometers to Alaba, they were placed on a truck and transported to Addis Ababa. On April 25, 1944, Bilaté Shashogo succumbed to sickness and died in the Addis Ababa Kärchäle prison.[57]

Qucha believer Ashäbo Adéto stood trial on May 22, 1944, and was sentenced to forty lashes and one year imprisonment. When released from prison in May 1945, he carried the sad report of evangelist Bilaté Shashogo's death to his family and friends in Qucha and Wolaitta.[58]

Sometime in 1945 the Ethiopian Orthodox Church issued a decree, proclaimed in the Qucha markets, that all Qucha inhabitants were to be baptized and become full members of the Orthodox Church. Qucha government official *Ato* Gäbrä Giyorgis, based in Bolain, in cooperation with the clergy of the Orthodox Church attempted to convert all traditional religionists in Qucha to the Orthodox faith. Those who refused baptism were fined one Ethiopian birr.[59] Because several *amanyoch* families were *chisänyoch* residing on Orthodox Church *gult* property, they were charged excessive taxes.[60] This precipitated further persecution against the *amanyoch,* who refused to accept Orthodox baptism, affirming that they were already baptized Christians. The *amanyoch* were accused of being *sara Mariam* (against the Virgin Mary), and sixty-four were imprisoned in the local Bola *wäräda* prison for four months. The prisoners' personal effects were plundered and their cattle stolen.[61]

In 1951 *Fetawrare* Sälo Sébano, the Amhara official in Qucha who was responsible for controlling the peace and collecting taxes, arrested Wolaitta evangelists Wada Damana, Shanka Tada, Gagébo Mäna, and

---

56. Bassa Däa, "*Yätämäräță Tiwild,*" 24. Injustice against the Darasa (who now call themselves "Gédeo") by the Amhara landowners is described in Brant, *In the Wake of Martyrs,* 220–24.

57. Ibid., 25.

58. The account of how Ashäbo was assisted in Addis Ababa by Selma Bergsten and Lionel Gurney in 1945 is recorded in Bassa Däa, "*Yätämäräță Tiwild,*" 26.

59. In Burji a similar imposition was placed on the local population, as recorded by Theresa Fellows, "Burji Log Book" October 23, 1951.

60. Bassa Däa, "*Yätämäräță Tiwild,*" 22.

61. Ibid., 26.

Ganamo Dokilé, along with several Quc̱ha *amanyoch*.[62] The accusation against them was that they were changing the religion of the country and were *ṣara Mariam*. When one of the Quc̱ha prisoners asked *Fetawrare Ṣälo* for an official letter stating that it was an offense against the laws of Ethiopia to believe in Jesus and to tell others about him, this was refused.[63] The four evangelists and the Quc̱ha *amanyoch* were imprisoned for three months in the crowded quarters of the Bola *wäräda* police station.

In 1953 the Ethiopian Orthodox Church accused the Wolaitta evangelists and the Quc̱ha *amanyoch* of proselytism. Six Quc̱ha *amanyoch* were imprisoned. Near the Koyso *ṣälot bét* two Quc̱ha *amanyoch* were killed by ruffians incited by Orthodox clergy.[64] In 1960 the source of antagonism against the Quc̱ha *amanyoch* was from those who controlled the land—the *balabatoch* and the *c̱hiqa shumoch*. Sixty members of the Koyso *ṣälot bét* were imprisoned at Bola *wäräda* for three months and subsequent to that were transferred to the prison at the Bulqi administrative centre. The Quc̱ha administrator, *Fetawrare Ṣälo Sébano*, was adhering to a long held Ethiopian tradition that only Orthodox Christianity was valid and that foreign religion was divisive to a united Ethiopia.[65]

The Methods the Evangelists Used in Quc̱ha

The following methods made the evangelists effective in Quc̱ha: First, they effectively communicated the gospel in homes, in marketplaces, at funerals, and to travelers along the road. The evangelists also did many good deeds of kindness for the Quc̱ha people, such as assisting to clothe the destitute, helping widows and those who were disadvantaged, and looking after orphans. Second, the evangelists established literacy centers at the *ṣälot bétoch* and taught the young men in the evenings. Some of these literacy centers eventually grew into elementary schools. Third, the evangelists willingly suffered hardship, beatings, and imprisonment along with the Quc̱ha *amanyoch*. And fourth, the evangelists taught the *amanyoch* how to live as a new community showing love, respect, and care to one another. To those

---

62. Ibid., 27.

63. Mahé C̱horamo, "Philip," 42.

64. Bassa Däa, "*Yätämäräṭä Tiwild*," 28.

65. Sven Rubenson reports that Tewodros was reluctant to "allow Catholic missionaries in his kingdom, since all his subjects ought to have the same faith." *Survival of Ethiopian Independence*, 176. See also John Markakis's statement that Menilek's unifying policy of the South was to make Orthodox "Christianity the official religion of the state." *Ethiopia*, 68.

who were imprisoned, the Qucha *amanyoch* brought food and blankets. They assisted one another in setting up cooperative work programs, such as building and repairing one another's' houses.[66]

Qucha *mahibär* leader Bassa Däa has noted the following positive changes in Qucha: First, the antagonism between the various clans, such as the *bariya* (slaves), the *fuga* (potters), the *faqi* (tanners), and others within Qucha, has diminished. Now they are practicing the truth of God's word that all men and women are created in the image of God and are all equal.[67] Second, they now follow wholesome hygiene and dietary practices. They keep their bodies clean, wash their clothes, eat wholesome food, and take malaria medicine. And third, they have become literate and no longer walk in darkness but in the light of the knowledge of the Bible. It is for these reasons that the Qucha *amanyoch* give thanks to the thirty-nine Wolaitta evangelists who served faithfully for limited periods of time from 1941 to 1963 in Qucha.[68]

Qucha provided a theater for the Wolaitta *amanyoch* to direct their outreach beyond their own geographic borders. It was the Wolaitta *mahibär* leaders, such as Toro Dubusho and Gäfäto Jagiso from Koysha and Wändaro Däbäro from Humbo, who cooperated together in order that the evangelistic outreach to Qucha be sustained and expanded. These men within Wolaitta felt a responsibility to recruit, to pray for, to encourage, and to provide with resources the Wolaitta evangelists who went to Qucha. The Wolaitta *mahibär* leadership began developing another purpose for meeting each month for their *tärapéza*. They were developing a concern for those beyond the Wolaitta geographic borders. And this new evangelistic enterprise began to demand much of their time, energy, and resources.

Another new factor that the Wolaitta *mahibär* dealt with was its own relationship with the Qucha *amanyoch*. In the formative years of expansion into Qucha in the early 1940s, the Wolaitta *mahibär* viewed the Qucha *amanyoch* as part of Wolaitta and not as a distinct *mahibär*. It was not until 1962 that Qucha became an independent entity, by mutual agreement between Wolaitta and Qucha. This was a positive step. In 1963 the Qucha Bible School was begun at Tuza (later transferred to Sälam Bir), with eighteen students and two Qucha instructors.[69] Qucha leadership

66. Bassa Däa, "*Yätämäräṭä Tiwild,*" 32.

67. Ibid., 41.

68. Ibid., 34.

69. Bassa Däa, personal interview with EPB, May 9, 1997.

could now be educated within the context of their own *s̱älot bétoch*. The Wolaitta *mahibär* was willing to assist Quc̱ha to become an independent sister *mahibär*, with responsibilities to evangelize beyond her borders.

Gofa

Introduction

Before rehearsing the story of the Wolaitta evangelists' operations within Gofa, a brief summary of the pioneer work of SIM in Gofa (see map 6.3) is in order. In May 1931 Walter and Marcella Ohman and Laurie Davison transferred from Soddo, Wolaitta, to Koybe, Gofa.[70] SIM was invited by Emperor Haile Selassie to provide a medical clinic and elementary school in this remote area of Gämo Gofa. *Däjazmach* Bäyänä Märid, late husband to Princess Roman-Wärq and son-in-law to Haile Sellassie, was governor of the province. With the assistance of *Däjazmach* Bäyänä Märid, a site was selected at Koybe, about five kilometers west of Bulqi, where there was ample spring water, and a land contract was duly signed.[71]

While the Ohmans were residing in Koybe, in January 1932, they observed the Orthodox Church celebration of *Ṯimqat*, a commemoration of the baptism of Jesus. As the *tabot* (Ark of the Covenant) were transported from the three Gofa Orthodox Churches—Mariam, Mädahin Aläm, and Mikaél—to a central tent by the river where the celebration was to take place, Ohman was told by his Gofa friends that "*Sosa* was in each box."[72] Ohman went on to say that the Orthodox Church was held in great respect throughout the South and that "I do not believe a single Amhara (ruling class) can be found who is not an adherent."[73]

---

70. Walter and Marcella Ohman, letter to Prayer Partners, May 6, 1931.

71. See Rhoad's report that *Däjazmach* Bäyänä Märid begged Rhoad "to accept a gift of money for all the many expenses I had been put to in coming to his province." "Wayside Jottings," 35.

72. Walter and Marcella Ohman, letter to Prayer Partners, January 28, 1932. It appears that the Gofa perceived that the various Amhara clan deities resided in the box called the *tabot*.

73. Ibid.

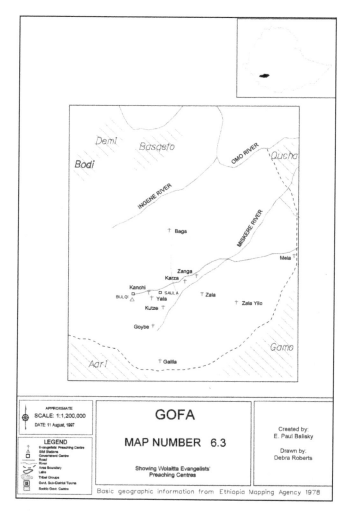

The Ohmans were allowed freedom to itinerate and preach through-out Gofa province. But they wrote critically of the Amhara exploitation of the southern Ethiopian population.

> In many ways the Amhara are like parasites. . . . The people are either slaves or serfs to the Amhara. Even today slavery exists. The slave, however, as a rule is better off than the serf. . . . The serf, however, must give much of his time, produce, etc., to his over-lord, while the overlord owes him nothing.[74]

74. Ibid.

But regardless of the exploitation the Ohmans observed in Gofa, they attempted to retain amiable relationships with officials at Bulqi and with the forward-looking Gofa provincial governor, *Däjazmach* Bäyänä Märid, who granted them residence permission.[75] They also recognized their obligation to provide medical and educational service to the Gofa population.

After the Ohmans established their grass-roofed buildings at Koybe, they began to travel extensively throughout the Gofa countryside, preaching to individuals as well as to crowds on the edge of the markets: "We can reach in one day what it would otherwise take us months to reach."[76] But regardless of their enthusiasm to preach to large Gofa market crowds, when they withdrew in 1936 the Ohmans and other SIM missionaries left only four baptized *amanyoch* in Koybe—Sämburu, Säka, Sänkura, and Däfarsha Dägäro.[77] From 1937 until 1942, because there were no evangelists in Gofa to assist them in their Christian faith, most of these *amanyoch*, except Däfarsha, reverted to their former traditional religion.

The important role Walter Ohman played in Gofa was very similar to that of the Gämo prophet Ésa, who preceded Ohman by ten years.[78] Both men travelled throughout the highlands of Gofa preaching repentance and warning of a coming judgment. Both men, one from America, the other from the neighboring area of Gämo, were forerunners to more than seventy Wolaitta evangelists who would travel over the Gofa mountains from 1942 to 1975, preaching the Jesus story.

Pioneer Activity of the Wolaitta Evangelists in Gofa

In 1947 Mahé Choramo, together with his brother Danél and three other evangelists, traveled to Zänga through the Zala lowlands. In the same year, Yohanis Darota and Boltana Borécho, both from the Ofa district of

75. See Fyfe, "Race, Empire and Decolonization," for an insightful discussion about how whites utilized "the white uniform" in retaining power and authority in much of Africa. Similarly, SIM missionaries in Ethiopia were also shown preferential treatment because of their color. The Wolaitta evangelists were not afforded this privilege. (Fyfe's paper was also published in *Rethinking African History*, edited by Simon McGrath et al. Edinburgh: Centre of African Studies, University of Edinburgh, 1997.)

76. Walter and Marcella Ohman, letter to prayer partners, October 7, 1932.

77. Davis, *Winds of God*, 57–58. See also Forsberg, *Land beyond the Nile*, 74–77, regarding Aari believer Dafarsha in Gofa.

78. Not all pre-occupation SIM personnel acknowledged anything positive or of a preparatory nature in the preaching of Prophet Ésa. Lewis did; Ohman did not. See Cotterell, *Born at Midnight*, 114.

Wolaitta, arrived at Karza in Gofa. Through the preaching of these two evangelists, a former *näftänya*, Alämu Dänäbu, was converted.[79] Alämu's conversion was cause for alarm among the Amhara in the administrative center at Bulqi. The other Gofa *näftänyoch* were not favorably impressed with the spread of the "Jesus teaching" from Wolaitta and the changes that were beginning to take place in Gofa society. As a consequence of the Wolaitta evangelists' preaching, Yohanis Darota was arrested and imprisoned in Bulqi for nine months. His imprisonment meant that the *amanyoch* at Karza had no one to assist and coordinate the worship and teaching at the newly constructed *ṣälot bét*. This was a setback for the *amanyoch* at the first *ṣälot bét* in Gofa.

By 1948 Yohanis Darota was back at Karza, and with the assistance of Laliso Täntu, Mahé C̱horamo and one or two other Wolaitta evangelists, the Karza *ṣälot bét* was significantly expanded with new converts. Five of these were baptized by the evangelists.

The Wolaitta evangelists used Karza as a center in 1949 and fanned out to other areas of Gofa. Mahé C̱horamo located at Bäga and Laliso at Goybe, the former SIM station, where thirty-three were baptized. Jara Bakalo went to Silbé, where eleven were soon baptized, and Boltana Borécho was assigned to Zänga, where fifteen were baptized.[80] By 1949 other preaching centers were established from these four recently founded *ṣälot bétoch*. The evangelists began teaching Amharic literacy to the nuclei of converts at each center, as there were no other options for learning available. The pattern of teaching the new converts was similar to how Mahé had learned to read and write Amharic back in Qucha. When the men would return to their houses in the evening, after working their fields during the day, they would gather together their writing material, their cotton shawls, a bundle of firewood, and some corn bread and pursue their studies with the evangelist long into the evening. Because they were learning a new language, the process took discipline and commitment. Some, finding the program too demanding, dropped out. Other able young Gofa men soon surpassed their teachers. The opportunity to become part of "greater

---

79. Mahé C̱horamo, "Philip," 52. Alämu asked Mahé, "Are you Mr. Ohman's man?" Alämu heard Ohman preach fifteen years before at Koybe. See also Walter and Marcella Ohman, letter to Prayer Helpers, June 20, 1933, where they tell the story of another Amhara, *Qanyazmach* Täsäma, who was converted. See also Cotterell, *Born at Midnight*, 144.

80. KHC, "*Bäwängél Amanyoch Andinät*," 13. See also Walter and Marcella Ohman, letter to prayer partners, February 27, 1950.

Ethiopia" gave the young men incentive to learn. They wanted to be able to converse in the national language of Ethiopia in the markets and at the government centers. Unfortunately the literacy program of the evangelists was limited to young men. It would be another two decades before the Gofa *amanyoch* communities would launch their own elementary schools in many of the Gofa districts that offered all children and young people, regardless of sex, the opportunity to learn.

By 1950, the evangelists' forces were again expanded, with Amanta Soso serving at Kanchi, Libabo Wabilo at Yalä, Ayällä Alito at Qota, Atangé Adaré at Zala Yilu, Titämqä Yohanis Banta at Wuba Hayla, and Laliso Täntu at Zako Deda.[81] At each of these places the evangelists carefully taught a select group of *amanyoch* for baptism and made preparations for *şälot bétoch* to be erected. This meant that at each location at least seven baptized heads of households would be actively participating in the *amanyoch* community.[82] The baptizing of the Gofa *amanyoch* was done by the mature Wolaitta evangelists such as Yohanis Darota and Laliso Täntu. Both these men were respected leaders among the Wolaitta *amanyoch* prior to ministry in Gofa. In most instances the Wolaitta evangelists encouraged the appointment of Gofa elders in these nascent *amanyoch* communities, but the evangelists themselves retained a leadership function because "The Gofa *amanyoch* were not yet ready."[83]

An example of consistent ministry in a local *şälot bét* was evangelist Amanta Sosa who, together with his wife Mägdalawit, served at Kanchi. During Amanta's eight years serving as a teacher and pastor, the Kanchi *şälot bét* became a strong church that sent her own Gofa evangelists and preachers to other areas of Gofa.[84] As a husband and wife team, they served the Kanchi *şälot bét* with compassion. They took several orphans into their home and assisted the needy with food and shelter. Amanta was known to have healed many by his prayers.[85]

In January 1951 nine Wolaitta evangelists assigned to Gofa met together with leaders from the Gofa *amanyoch* for a planning and coordination session at the Kanchi *şälot bét*.[86] They were concerned about the

---

81. KHC, *"Bäwängél Amanyoch Andinät,"* 12.

82. The first baptism in Wolaitta of eight men and two wives may have set a pattern for the minimum number within a *şälot bét*.

83. Laliso Täntu, personal information to EPB, December 13, 1995.

84. Dick McLellan, transcribed tape to Raymond Davis, 1978.

85. Dalsha Dana Sigo, taped interview with Hizkél Zäkarius, Bulqi, April 16, 1962.

86. KHC, *"Bäwängél Amanyoch Andinät,"* 13. Their names are not listed.

future expansion and growth of *amanyoch* communities both within and beyond the mountain ranges of Gofa. After several days of discussion, they decided that the Aari, the Gofa, the Wuba, and the Zala districts should each be organized into their own district *mahibär* or association of *ṣälot bé-toch*. Karza was to be the central meeting place for the delegates from each of these areas to gather for their monthly prayer and business session at each full moon. The evangelists called this monthly meeting of discussion around a table *ṭärapéza*, just as it was referred to back in Wolaitta. It was at the Kanchi meeting that the evangelists and the Gofa *amanyoch* reached a consensus that Wolaitta evangelist Laliso Täntu be elected as the first president of the Gofa association of *ṣälot bétoch*, called a *mahibär*.[87] At that time the group realized that no one among the Gofa *amanyoch* was capable of assuming leadership of the expanding Gofa *ṣälot bétoch*.[88] Shortly after this re-structuring, adversity once again came against the *amanyoch*. This time Laliso Täntu and a number of Gofa *amanyoch* were imprisoned in Bulqi. The Gofa *mahibär* designated Yohanis Darota to act as their temporary leader during Laliso's imprisonment. Because the persecution persisted in Gofa, seven of the nine evangelists with their families returned to the safe haven of Wolaitta.

By 1952 Laliso Täntu and the fifteen Gofa *amanyoch* had been released from prison. When they returned to their own districts and their own local *ṣälot bétoch*, they discovered that many new *amanyoch* were being added and distant districts were asking for teachers. Evangelist Laliso Täntu trekked to Wolaitta in order to invite the former seven evangelists to return to Gofa and to enlist additional evangelists. Laliso was successful in recruiting fourteen evangelist families through the Wolaitta *ṭärapéza* for the Gofa outreach.[89] By the efforts of these additional evangelists, the *amanyoch* movement spread to the majority of the Gofa districts. These evangelists were involved in preaching and teaching about Jesus at roadsides, at funerals, in markets, and in small preaching houses erected on the land of recently converted *amanyoch*. During the evenings the evangelists would gather the young men together and teach them the Amharic alphabet so they could read the Amharic Bible. Teaching literacy was a

87. Laliso Täntu, personal information to EPB, December 13, 1995, and KHC, "*Bäwängél Amanyoch Andinät*," 13.

88. Dalsha Dana Sigo respectfully referred to Laliso as, "My father." Taped interview with Hizkél Zäkarius, April, 16, 1992.

89. Laliso Tantu, personal information to EPB, December 13, 1995. He could not recall all their names. See appendix 2 for a list of Wolaitta evangelists who served in Gofa.

challenging task, as most of the Wolaitta evangelists were only semi-literate themselves.

By 1954 the elders of the Wolaitta *mahibär* were encouraged by the results of the evangelism in Gofa, yet they had reservations about the leadership role the Wolaitta evangelists were assuming over the Gofa *amanyoch*. Wolaitta elders Gimja Gärba and Shäla Jije were sent by the Wolaitta *t̲ärapéza* to Gofa to observe the development of the Gofa *amanyoch*. They were also commissioned to see to it that the leadership of the Gofa *amanyoch mahibär* was in the hands of Gofa elders. The Wolaitta elders recognized the distinct role of their evangelists in the formation of the Gofa *mahibär* and acknowledged their success. But by their own experience within Wolaitta they understood that the ongoing administrative function of the Gofa *mahibär* must be the responsibility of the Gofa elders. After six months of discussion and instruction, the Gofa and surrounding district *amanyoch* selected their own elders with the qualifications of "Ability to govern well and to be men of strong faith."[90] The following leaders were selected: from Gofa, Dälbo Delä; from Zala, Bäyänä Ankuté; and from the Aari district, Sät̲äyé Shara and Zidä C̱ẖodo. Wolaitta evangelists Laliso Täntu and Yohanis Darota served as advisors to the Gofa elders when their monthly *mahibär* was convened.[91] The election of officers for the Gofa *amanyoch* took place at the Kuste ṣ̱alot bét in 1955.

From 1957 to 1958 additional Wolaitta evangelists, together with their families, were sent to Gofa. The new factor within Gofa was that the Gofa *mahibär* assigned one or more of their own evangelists to work closely with a Wolaitta evangelist. In this way, Gofa men were taught how to evangelize and gain skills in preaching and teaching, and the addition of workers meant that unreached Gofa villages were evangelized.

Karza ṣ̱alot bét experienced another "first" in 1958. The first Gofa five-day spiritual life conference was organized by the Wolaitta evangelists and held there with Markina Mäja, secretary of the Wolaitta *mahibär*, invited to be the Bible teacher. It was reported that more than four hundred Gofa *amanyoch* attended. The *amanyoch* who were scattered throughout the Gofa mountains had the opportunity to sing, pray, and study the Bible

---

90. KHC, "*Bäwängél Amanyoch Andinät*," 13.

91. Laliso Täntu admitted, "This business of being the leader meant that they gave me too much honour. It was not good for me or for the Gofa *amanyoch*." Personal information to EPB, December 13, 1995.

together. Elders of Gofa *ṣälot bétoch*, mothers with babies, young men and women together experienced fellowship and unity at Karza.[92]

By 1958 the contribution of the Wolaitta evangelists within Gofa was substantial. Ratzliff reported from Soddo, "Now there are thousands of believers living in the mountains and the plains below. . . . The Christians are clamoring for teaching, the countryside for medicine."[93] In April 1958, Don Gray travelled from Bako to Bulqi, attempting to finalize SIM permission papers with Bulqi government officials. He was told by Gofa *amanyoch* at Koybe that there were twenty-five *ṣälot bétoch* in the Gofa region, established by Wolaitta and Gofa evangelists.[94]

In March 1959, Dick and Vida McLellan arrived in Bulqi to launch the elementary school and medical clinic. These SIM personnel cooperated closely with the Gofa *mahibär* and Wolaitta evangelists in all phases of their outreach and nurture. By the end of 1959, the thirty-five Wolaitta evangelists and representatives from the forty-nine *ṣälot bétoch* met at the Bulqi station for a planning, restructuring, and Bible teaching meeting. There were now eight hundred baptized *amanyoch* in Gofa, with over 920 *amanyoch* in baptismal classes.[95]

Short Biography of Evangelist Laliso Täntu

Laliso was born in a village about five kilometers south of Humbo. At the age of thirteen or fourteen he began to ask such questions as, "Why am I here?" "What is the purpose of life?" and, "What happens to me when I die?" Residing near Humbo, but originally from Gofa, *Wäidé Goda* Albé Acha was a wise man who had the ability to predict the future. All in the community respected him because what he predicted came to pass. Laliso recalls that one day *Wäidé Goda* Albé made this pronouncement: "The white *färänjoch*, the black *shanqäloch* and the *qay* (red) Wolaitta will all one day eat together in one *mahibär*.[96] This seemed unbelievable to Laliso because at that time various Wolaitta clans would have no dealings with one another, let alone eat with those from other races.

92. Dalsha Dana Sigo, taped interview with Hizkél Zäkarius, Bulqi, April 16, 1992.

93. Edna and Ed Ratzliff, *Letters*, 312. See also Willmott, *Doors were Opened*, 97.

94. Fargher et al, "New Churches' Movement in the Hammer-Bako Area," 30.

95. In 1960 Don and Christine Gray visited Ayällä Alito's preaching point southwest of Bulqi. They heard of triumphs and frustrations the evangelists had experienced and were impressed with the evangelists' determination and "vision which motivated them to reach out to lost people." Ibid., 37–38.

96. Laliso Täntu, personal information to EPB, December 13, 1995.

While Laliso was pondering this hard-to-believe prediction with some vexation, his aunt, Chaché Jemem, advised him to go to Humbo town and seek out evangelist Wändaro Däbäro. Laliso went the next day to the house of Wändaro, who read various verses to him from the Wolaitta *Tosay Yotes*. Laliso recalls hearing about "believing in the Lord Jesus Christ," from Acts 16:31, and, from Isaiah 45:22, "Return to me and you will be saved."[97]

Soon after his conversion, Laliso attached himself to Wändaro's assistant, Wanna, who taught him the basics of the Amharic alphabet and other reading skills for about six months. Laliso then sold his jacket and purchased the Gospel of Mark written in the Gofa language. After he mastered this book, Laliso went to Soddo and purchased an Amharic Bible from an Orthodox priest for the price of a two-year-old heifer.

Laliso's father was a follower of the Wolaitta traditional religion and was upset that his son, still residing with him, had begun practicing a different religion. Every morning Laliso would pray to *Tosa*, asking that the sins of the family would be forgiven. Angered by such prayers, Laliso's father asked, "How do you know my sin? What sin have I done?" He then threatened to punish Laliso unless he left this new religion. For a time Laliso experienced cruel punishment at the hands of his father, but eventually relatives interceded on Laliso's behalf and the father relented.[98]

From 1937 to 1939 Laliso assisted Wändaro as he preached in several districts of Wolaitta. Soon Laliso ventured into Gämo province, Boroda district, with a friend, Shanka Boroda. Laliso followed the example of his spiritual father, Wändaro, in his own preaching. Wherever people were gathered, at a marketplace, a funeral, or a house-building enterprise, Laliso and his assistant would take out their Bibles from their carrying cases and, holding them high, would quiet the crowd by shouting, "Listen, listen." They would then tell the Jesus story.

On most occasions the common people would listen with respect and attentiveness and the evangelists would be invited to their homes. Difficulties came from two sources: the first was from ruffians or highway robbers, who would overpower them and steal their clothing, Bible, and other books. Very seldom did they lose cash, because they carried little on them. The second source of irritation was incarceration by government officials. Throughout Laliso's forty years of evangelistic service he was imprisoned eleven times, with sentences ranging from two months to five

97. Ibid.
98. Ibid.

years.[99] While imprisoned he suffered from hunger, cold, infestations of lice, bedbugs, and rats, crowded and cramped sleeping conditions, and several severe beatings. When Laliso was halted and questioned at road blocks by customs officials or police as to where and why he was travelling, he would reply, "I am going over that mountain range to look for my lost brother."[100]

Evangelist Laliso made several noteworthy contributions to the Gofa *amanyoch* communities. First, he is acknowledged as the father of the Gofa *amanyoch*. Gofa elder Dalsha Dana Sigo said, "He is my father in the faith. He is an outstanding person. He preached and taught very well."[101] Several Gofa *amanyoch* households have named their children "Laliso." The second contribution that Laliso made was in the area of administration. Through his efforts the scattered Gofa *ṣälot bétoch* were organized into a functioning *mahibär*. Even though he was elected by the Gofa *amanyoch* as their first president, he gladly relinquished this position some five years later when the Gofa elected their own leader.

The third contribution Laliso made while serving in Gofa was introducing the "golden book" to a well-known *ṭänqway* called Chäläqé. Before 1930 Chäläqé had prophesied that men would fly in airplanes, that the mountains would shake, and that someone would bring him a golden book by way of the river while he was sitting under his wänza tree. This messenger would come carrying a cane with a crooked handle. In 1951 Laliso arrived at Chäläqé's house. When Laliso opened his satchel and produced the four-page wordless book, with the last page the color of gold, Chäläqé exclaimed, "My ancestor spirit told me years ago that a golden book would come to me while I would be sitting under this very tree."[102] The conversion of *Ṭänqway* Chäläqé caused not a few other primal religion functionaries in Gofa to accept the message of the evangelists.

Laliso served as an evangelist in Gofa in various capacities for fifteen years. When asked what hardships and temptations he faced, he enumerated the following: losing hope while suffering in prison, getting over-involved in farming or trading in salt, considering invitations to join the

99. Dick and Vida McLellan, letter to prayer partners, June 1, 1963.

100. Davis, *Winds of God*, 54.

101. Dalsha Dana Sigo, taped interview with Hizkél Zäkarius, Bulqi, April 16, 1992.

102. Davis, *Winds of God*, 60. See also Cotterell, *Born at Midnight*, 115. This account was verified by Laliso Täntu, personal information, December 13, 1995. Laliso, well over eighty-five years of age in December, continued to serve as an elected officer of the Wolaitta *ṭärapéza*.

Seventh-Day Adventists at a much higher salary, and relishing the honor and prestige given to Wolaitta evangelists by the Gofa *amanyoch*.[103] Laliso overcame these various temptations. The Gofa *amanyoch* proudly refer to him as "the father of our Gofa *mahibär*."

Short Biography of Baloté Aymalo, a Woman Evangelist

Baloté Aymalo was born in 1917 in Koysha *wäräda* and was converted in 1944 through the songs her father sang while performing chores around his farmstead. Aymalo was one of many *amanyoch* attending Toro Dubosho's *sälot bét* at Gärära, Koysha. Baloté attended the literacy classes that Toro was teaching several afternoons a week at the Gärära *sälot bét*.

In 1946 Selma Bergsten, with pre-Italian experience in the South,[104] began discussions with the Wolaitta *mahibär* elders about a special teaching program for young Wolaitta women. Baloté, along with twenty other young women from Wolaitta *sälot bétoch*, was selected for this initial two-month learning program convened at the Wanché *sälot bét* in 1947. After this first course at Wanché, the twenty-one ladies returned to their local districts to begin teaching what they had learned. Baloté returned to Gärära, Koysha. In 1950 Baloté and other trainees assisted in organizing

6.2 Evangelist Baloté Aymalo continued her ministry in Gofa for another 10 years after her evangelist husband, Omoché Ukulo, died in 1955 (Kay Bascom, 1994)

103. Laliso Täntu, personal information to EPB, December 13, 1995.

104. Sudan Interior Mission Daily Prayer Calendar, 1933–1937.

the Wolaitta women's *mahibär*. Their function was to provide teaching, fellowship, and the collecting of funds for the evangelists. Through Bible conferences at Otona and the Wolaitta districts, a number of women volunteered for evangelism outside of Wolaitta.[105]

In 1954 Baloté, her husband, Amoché, and their son, Dästa, travelled by donkey to Yala, Gofa, to begin evangelistic work. They opened a literacy school, and Baloté taught handcrafts to the young ladies. Within a year a *şälot bét* was erected by the recent converts. In January 1955 Amoché went to Wolaitta for the annual Bible conference and before returning to Gofa made a business trip to Yirga Aläm in Sidamo Province. While crossing the Bilaté River, Amoché was murdered by Arsi bandits. When a messenger from her home church in Koysha brought Baloté the news of Amoché's death, she now had to make a choice whether to remain in Gofa or to return to Wolaitta. Her decision was, "I have been called of God not by man. I am going to stay."[106] Baloté and her son remained in Gofa for seven years, teaching children and women literacy, handcrafts, and Bible texts in designated *şälot bétoch* for up to two months in each.[107] She had no home of her own but was dependent on the hospitality of the wives of the other evangelists and Gofa *amanyoch* as she itinerated throughout Zalla district. In 1962 Baloté returned to Wolaitta when the *ţärapéza* elders assigned her to assist in coordinating the women's ministry within the Wolaitta *mahibär*. Baloté's faithful years of service in Gofa have been recognized by the Wolaitta *mahibär*. Many in Gofa continue to rise up and call her blessed.

Harassment of the Evangelists in Gofa

From 1958 to 1961 the Gofa *amanyoch* communities and the Wolaitta evangelists experienced undue harassment. During this period, 114 *amanyoch* were incarcerated. Two of the *amanyoch*, Kulé C̲h̲äräqa and Anjä Adamo, died in prison from beatings and exposure.[108] There is evidence that officials encouraged ruffians and people of ill-will to plunder the possessions of

105. Baloté Aymalo estimates that forty-seven of the women trained through the Bergsten program served as evangelists with their husbands beyond Wolaitta. Personal interview with EPB, Soddo, December 26, 1987.

106. Ibid. Also recorded in Selma Bergsten, personal interview with Charles Anderson, January 1961. The Baloté story is also found in Davis, *Fire on the Mountains*, 196–206.

107. Baloté Aymalo, transcribed tape, 26 December 1987, listed thirty-two Gofa *şälot bétoch* at which she taught.

108. KHC, "*Bäwängél Amanyoch Andinät*," 14.

the *amanyoch*. As a result, cattle, coffee, grain, and clothing were taken by force from the *amanyoch* residing near Bulqi. There were severe beatings.[109] The officials attempted to forbid food and blankets from being brought to the prison. During the day the prisoners were forced to do hard labor, and at night they were crowded into a building with few provisions.

In December 1958, the Ratzliffs and Dick McLellan travelled from Soddo to Bulqi in order to finalize the SIM land contract prior to opening the elementary school and clinic. Edna Ratzliff wrote:

> Saturday when we had been up at the governor's [*Fetawrare Kibret Zamanuel*] our hearts had been torn as we saw a group of our Christians, chained but carrying heavy loads, working in the yard under the supervision of an officer who kept shouting at them and lashing them when it suited his purposes. We heard, from the Christians, that one was an evangelist [Wolaitta] who had been put in under trumped-up charges.[110]

Chief of police for Gofa Province, *Shaläqa* Bäqälä <u>Ch</u>oofa, made no apology to the missionaries for the detained *amanyoch*, stating that the charges against them were legitimate.[111]

While evangelist Déngo Sana was serving his nine-month sentence in the Bulqi prison, he received word from the Galila district that his wife was very ill. Under police escort, Déngo was allowed to travel the two days to Galila, only to find his wife dead. He dug her grave on the rocky hillside and later related, "I was all alone burying my wife and Jesus came to me. He came and stood with me and I was not alone."[112] Several months later, while still in prison, he received word that two of his three sons had died of malnutrition and disease. Again he returned to his home under escort to perform another family burial.

During this time of extensive persecution in Gofa, the Wolaitta elders, together with other *amanyoch mahibär* in Kambatta, Hadiya, Gämo,

---

109. Ratzliff tells how he and Ohman transported an evangelist from the Bulqi prison to the Soddo hospital for medical treatment in January 1958 because "he had been badly trampled." *Letters*, 277.

110. Ibid., 315. The name of the evangelist is unknown.

111. Dick McLellan stated that the Gämo Gofa and Sidamo government officials were called to meetings in Sidamo about every six months. When they returned it was inevitable that action was taken against the *amanyoch* for a limited time. Personal information to EPB, March 1996.

112. As related by Dick McLellan, transcribed tape, 1978, for Raymond Davis prior to publication of *Winds of God*.

Burji, Ari, Gédéo, and Sidama, were making a unified plea to Emperor Haile Selassie for recognition and freedom to practice their own kind of Christianity.[113] It was the evangelists who were the catalysts in prompting each sending *mahibär* to persist in gaining religious recognition from the Ethiopian government (see appendix 3). Wolaitta evangelist Gagébo Mäna from Ofa became proficient at composing letters to various levels of Gofa government offices and pleading for fair and just treatment of the imprisoned evangelists and Gofa *amanyoch*.[114] Gofa was one *awraja* in southern Ethiopia where the Wolaitta evangelists conducted an ongoing discussion and polemic for over fifteen years with government officials about the nature of freedom, justice, and peace. In courtrooms, prisons, and police stations they quoted verses from their Bibles to the effect that, without disobeying the laws of their country or edicts of their king, they would not be disobedient to their higher authority, Jesus Christ, who commanded them to "go into all the world."[115]

Evangelists Functioning as Clerics and Administrators in Gofa

When the Wolaitta evangelists pioneered the outreach to Gofa in 1943, their goal was to preach the gospel so that men and women would be converted, *amanyoch* taught and baptized, and *şälot bétoch* established. They were pragmatists and went to Gofa with the understanding that the methods employed in Wolaitta could be successfully used in Gofa. In Wolaitta, the *amanyoch* communities were in constant dialogue with practitioners of primal religion, not with those within the Orthodox Church.

In Gofa two unanticipated new factors faced the evangelists. The first was a concerted opposition from government officials, encouraged by the

---

113. Markina Meja, *Unbroken Covenant,* 155, records that in 1960 eighty *amanyoch* from Wolaitta presented their petition in person to Haile Sellassie at the Royal Palace in Addis Ababa. The Ethiopian Evangelical Church Mekane Yesus was granted official Ethiopian government recognition in 1959. See Saevaräs, *Church-Mission Relations in Ethiopia,* appendix 1, 165–79. It was on December 22, 1966, that the Fellowship of Evangelical Believers finally received their official permission. See Ishätu Gäbré, "*Yäwängél Amanyoch Andinät,*" 25.

114. Dalsho Dana Sigo, interview with Hizkél Zäkarius, Bulqi, April 16, 1992.

115. Yohanis Darota, interview with Hizkél Zäkarius, Karza, Gofa, April 14, 1992. Yohanis related that in 1955, when Chama Tumato was interrogated by a Bulqi magistrate about why he came to Gofa, Chama responded, "Mr. Ohman sent me to Gofa to preach the Word of God." Because the other evangelists were disappointed in Chama's statement in the court that Mr. Ohman, rather than God, had sent him, he was ordered back to Wolaitta for discipline after his release from prison.

Orthodox clergy. This created a certain vulnerability for the inexperienced Gofa *amanyoch* and caused the evangelists to be over-protective. The second factor was a result of the first. Little did the evangelists realize that it would take some fifteen years before a viable Gofa *mahibär* with the vitality to stand on its own would be formed. In Wolaitta the development of *s̱älot bétoch* and a *mahibär* was much faster. Because we have already discussed persecution among the Gofa *amanyoch*, this section will deal with the second factor, which was the changing role of the evangelist to that of clergyman and administrator.

In 1951 the evangelists recognized the need for structuring the *s̱älot bétoch* into a functioning *mahibär*. Their goal was to assist each *s̱älot bét* in becoming part of a larger movement within Gofa. This was a positive move, but as we saw earlier, no Gofa person was willing or able to assume the leadership role for the *mahibär*. Evangelists Laliso Täntu and Yohanis Darota (whichever one was not in prison) served as the Gofa *mahibär* president, whose role was to coordinate the Gofa *mahibär* baptisms, settle local church disputes, and encourage the *amanyoch*. And at the local *s̱älot bét* level, the evangelists took on the mantle of resident clergyman. At this harassing period of time within Gofa, the *amanyoch* appreciated the protective umbrella provided by the evangelists, and the evangelists in turn were honored and rewarded in providing this kind of assistance. Most of the Wolaitta evangelists suffered insults and imprisonment together with the Gofa *amanyoch* and so felt a oneness and unity with them. The evangelists sacrificed their evangelistic role in order to preserve and protect the existing *amanyoch*.

In 1959 the permission for SIM to take up residence in Bulqi was finally granted after nine years of negotiating.[116] The SIM presence in Bulqi brought certain changes for the evangelists and the Gofa *mahibär*. First, SIM attempted to recover the role of evangelism for the Wolaitta evangelists. Second, in 1961 the church leaders, together with the evangelists, were called together for a time of repentance and prayer. The Gofa *amanyoch* determined to support financially each of their own *s̱älot bétoch* and the *mahibär* from their offerings and tithes.[117] There was evidence of a spiritual

---

116. On April 27, 1950, Walter Ohman and the Barlows drove to Bulqi to present SIM's application and choose the mission site, as stated in Walter and Marcella Ohman, letter to prayer partners, August 18, 1950. On March 19, 1959, Edna Ratzliff wrote, "Bulki station which the mission tried to re-open for eight years is now a fact." Ratzliff, *Letters*, 323.

117. KHC, "*Bäwängél Amanyoch Andinät*," 14.

awakening among the *amanyoch* and an eagerness in various places of Gofa to hear the gospel. The third change was that in 1962 a Bible school was launched in Bulqi. This SIM training center provided the possibility of developing Gofa *amanyoch* for *ṣalot bétoch* and *mahibär* leadership.[118]

Olav Saeveräs has presented a strong case for mission/church integration in his *On Church-Mission Relations in Ethiopia 1944–1969*. His thinking was influenced by the writing of Bishop Stephen Neill, who maintained:

> It is my profoundest conviction that the moment a group of Christians land on the shores of an island in which the Gospel has never been preached, their first business is to meet together, and say solemnly, "We are the Church in X," or if they so prefer it, "We are the Church of Jesus Christ in X." There may not be a single national in the group; that makes no difference. Those who have come have taken possession of the whole land in the name of Christ. . . . When any of the nationals believe, they will find already in existence a living Church of their own land.[119]

The Wolaitta evangelists were basically operating within a paradigm of integration between the evangelists and the *amanyoch* communities that were emerging in Gofa. The Wolaitta *ṭärapéza* was aware of this when they sent elders Gimja Gärba and Shäla Jije to Gofa in 1954 to ensure that the Gofa *mahibär* was functioning under Gofa leadership, not that of the evangelists. The Wolaitta elders were committed to the concept that the Gofa *amanyoch* must provide the leadership for the Gofa *mahibär* from the very beginning.[120] Even though the Gofa *mahibär* elected their own leaders in 1954, for all practical purposes the authority over the *ṣalot bétoch* and the Gofa *mahibär* was still under the aegis of the Wolaitta evangelists.

Ed Jones arrived in Bulqi in 1964, determined "to help the local churches become independent of the control of the Wolaitta, some of

---

118. Bruce Adams letter to EPB, May 16, 1991. In 1963 there were twenty-five students enrolled in the Bible school, according to Dick and Vida McLellan, letter to friends, March 1, 1963.

119. Stephen Neill, *Creative Tension*, 91, as quoted in Saeveräs, *Church Mission Relations in Ethiopia*, 114.

120. See Bosch, *Believing in the Future*, 29, where the European concept of mission is "Christendom"—that "the church might wrest 'territory' from the world and incorporate this into the church." The Wolaitta elders did not perceive the Gofa *mahibär* as an extension of Wolaitta "territory," even if some of the Wolaitta itinerant preachers did.

whom had set themselves up as little kings."[121] The issue was complicated because among the Gofa *amanyoch* there was, "conflict of loyalties—evangelists versus local [Gofa] elders—which has brought serious division in the Church."[122] Jones further comments, "The evangelists had a very comfortable, entrenched situation, and many of them had forgotten their calling."[123] Jones was unable to appreciate that the evangelists supplemented their meager stipend by farming in Gofa, for there was clothing to buy for school-age children and the entertaining of many guests that fell to the lot of the evangelists.

Within the next two years, the more than thirty Wolaitta evangelists in Gofa were recalled and reassigned elsewhere, except for two who chose to stay and become permanent residents. For Gofa, the era of depending on external evangelists had come to an end. The decision to remove the Wolaitta evangelists proved correct. By 1966, the number of *sälot bétoch* had doubled to ninety-five. The Gofa *mahibär* continues to respect, with great sincerity, the Wolaitta men and women who brought the gospel to them.[124]

Kullo Konta

Background

Kullo Konta (see map 6.4) is located northwest of Wolaitta, on the west side of the Omo River. The Kullo Konta claim superiority over the Wolaitta because they say they were the first people. According to the Kullo Konta mythology, they gave birth to the Omotic-speaking Wolaitta through the Malla clans, who eventually established themselves in the mountain fortress of Kindo, Wolaitta.[125]

---

121. Ed Jones letter to EPB, August 16, 1991. Not all evangelists were so entrenched. Ratzliff reports that Mahé Choramo "left the church he had been used of God to establish and sought another 'virgin' field." *Letters,* 368.

122. Ed Jones, letter to prayer partners, December 1964.

123. Ed Jones, letter to EPB, August 16, 1991.

124. Hizkél Zäkarius, personal information to EPB, April 1992.

125. The Wolaitta deny this, stating that their ancestors were from Käfa Gomära, Damota, or Tegré.

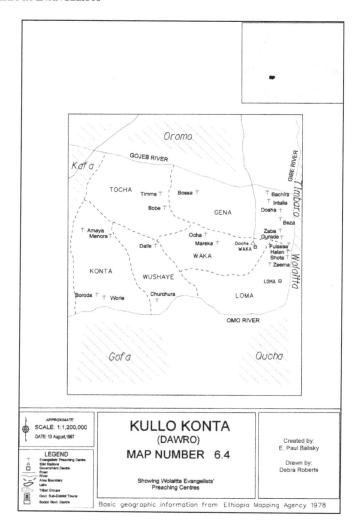

Before the Oromo invasions of the sixteenth century, the Däwaro inhabited the area presently occupied by the Arsi. This area would have been south of the Awash River, east of the Silṭi Guragé and north of Lake Awassa.[126] From 1562 to 1570 the Oromo pushed into Däwaro territory,[127] with the result that the Däwaro chose to flee to the mountain strongholds of Kambatta/Hadiya and Kullo Konta to escape the ensuing devastation of

126. Trimingham, *Islam in Ethiopia*, 67.
127. Ibid., 93–94.

war and famine.[128] It was to Kullo Konta where the majority fled, taking their name with them.[129] To the present, the Wolaitta refer to Kullo Konta as "Dawro,"[130] and a significant number of Dawro, who are a prestige clan, reside in the mountain strongholds of Kullo Konta.[131] In the eighteenth century a small kingdom was established in Kullo Konta. When the military forces of Menilek attacked the area from Jimma in 1891, Kullo Konta ruler *Kawo* Kanta fled south to the mountainous area of Kuyilee and held out for some six months.[132] It was after his capture and baptism that he took the Christian name Haile Ṣiyon (Strength of Zion).[133]

6.3 The rewarding fruit of the Wolaitta evangelists, a multiple baptism in Kullo Konta (Jean King, 1996)

128. See map in Merid W/Aregay, "Southern Ethiopia and the Christian Kingdom," 155, which traces the movements of the Oromo into Dawaro, Fatigar, and Ifat territory during the time of King Galawdewos, ca. 1555.

129. See Cerulli, *Peoples of South-West Ethiopia*, 85, 97, and Beckingham and Huntingford, *Some Records of Ethiopia*, lxvi, lxvii. These authors affirm the migration of the Däwaro.

130. In 1996 the name of Kullo Konta was officially altered to Dawro Konta.

131. Dr. Mulatu Baffa, former general secretary of the KHC, related that his clan in Kambatta were descendants of the Däwaro. Personal information to EPB, April 10, 1997.

132. Cerulli, *Peoples of South-West Ethiopia*, 86, confirms that Kullo Konta was ruled by kings, the last of whom was *Kawo* Kanta, who was defeated by Menilek's troops in 1892.

133. Gershon Dilbato, personal information to EPB, July 11, 1997.

It is uncertain to what extent the Däwaro were practicing Christians when they migrated to the secure mountain area of Kullo Konta in the sixteenth and seventeenth centuries. Braukamper suggests that Orthodox Christianity has been practiced for centuries by the Däwaro in this rugged area.[134] It is from post-Menilek times that the five functioning Orthodox churches in the *wäräda* centers of Tocha, Amaya Konta, Gäna Bassa, Wushay, and Loma, as well as the two Orthodox churches in the *awraja* center of Waka, were established. Beyond the confines of these government administrative centers, the rural Kullo Konta population practice primal religion. The Dawro clans, residing in the central highlands of Kullo Konta, made only a limited response to the preaching of the evangelists and pioneer SIM missionary Bob King during the 1950s and 1960s.[135]

From 1950 to 1975, several dozen *balabatoch* controlled the rugged mountain terrain of Kullo Konta, 100 by 150 kilometers in area. These *balabatoch* lived in a non-combative relationship with one another but exploited the *chisänyoch* who were under their jurisdiction. The Kullo Konta settlements of Boroda and Manora in the southwestern lowlands experienced occasional plundering of their cattle and personal effects by the Podi nomads of the South.[136]

Evangelist Sawl Salgédo has listed eighty-one different clans within Kullo Konta. Of these eighty-one clans, thirty-six are also in found in Wolaitta.[137] The Kullo Konta who reside on the immediate west bank of the Omo River are called "Goqa" (the people) and have a strong affinity to the Wolaitta.

Kullo Konta Refugees to Ṯämbaro

At the outset of the Italian occupation of southwestern Ethiopia in 1937, Amhara Patriots from Wolaitta, Gämo Gofa, and Käfa, led by Adeno Bora, utilized the inaccessible fortress mountains of Kullo Konta as their stronghold. From there the Patriots conducted clandestine military operations against the Italian intruders. In 1940 a contingent of Italian soldiers

---

134. Braukamper, "Correlation of Oral Tradition and Historical Records," 47.

135. Gershon Dilbato, personal information to EPB, July 11, 1997. Gershon, a former resident of Kullo Konta, recalls that Bob and Jean King and Wolaitta evangelists spent from 1950 to 1960 preaching and teaching with very limited results in Dawro area.

136. Bill Watson, stationed at Doché, provided food and blankets to several hundred Manora refugees in 1975.

137. Sawl Salgédo, *Birhan Anṣäbäräqä*, 4–5.

left Jimma and crossed the Gojeb River with the intent of flushing out these subversive Patriots and driving them east across the Omo River into the control of waiting Italian forces located at Tämbaro (see map 6.4). The Amhara Patriots eluded the Italians, but hundreds of Kullo Konta families, fearing the bombs, the burning of their houses, and the shelling inflicted on their villages, fled east across the Omo River and took up temporary residence at Tämbaro, which borders Kambatta and Hadiya.

In 1941 leaders such as Birru Dubalä, Wändaro Däbäro, and Dana Mäja of the Wolaitta *mahibär* heard from the Hadiya *amanyoch* about the dislocated Omotic speaking Kullo Konta families now residing in Tämbaro.[138] Wolaitta sent two of their evangelists from the Damot Wédé district, Ombolé Odiro and Godana Gutolo, to the Kullo Konta refugees in Tämbaro.[139] These two evangelists found the displaced Kullo Konta people responsive to the Christian message. Their former worship of their clan deities was no longer effective. About 1946 the dislocated Kullo Konta, many of them now converted and active participants in the *amanyoch* community, re-crossed the Omo River. Rather than returning to their former homesteads in central Kullo Konta, they took up residence on the western banks of the Omo River. *Ato* Aldada Atébo, a Tämbaro man and one of the first converts of the evangelists, moved with the returning Kullo Konta people and became an apprentice to the Wolaitta evangelists. Additional evangelist reinforcements, Mäja Mädéro and Madalcho Gésamo, came from Wolaitta. Soon after the refugees returned to Kullo Konta, other *amanyoch* communities were established. By 1947 there were four *sälot bétoch*, and by 1948 the number had increased to eight.[140] Converted Kullo Konta returnees played a significant role in the life of the Kullo Konta *amanyoch* communities for several decades. These included Dilbato Oyato and *Ato* Hatiso from the Intäla *sälot bét*, *yäEyob abbat*, *Ato* Zema from the Ocha *sälot bét*, Tona Jägo from the Dosha *sälot bét*, and *Ato* Bebeso from the Bäza *sälot bét*.[141]

In 1951 there was a new turn of events for the future of evangelism in Kullo Konta. That year Wolaitta evangelists Ombolé Odiro, Madalcho Gésamo, Aldada Atébo[142] (now the leader of the Kullo Konta *amanyoch*),

138. Yosef Menna, "*Yätinsaéw Näsibiraq*," 224.

139. Cotterell, *Born at Midnight*, 118.

140. Ibid., 119.

141. Gershon Dilbato, personal interview with EPB, July 11, 1997.

142. Aldada Atébo was an able Amharic speaker because of his previous association with an Amhara family in Tämbaro.

and several Kullo Konta *amanyoch* attended the Wolaitta conference at Soddo. While at the conference these men approached Walter Ohman and Homer Wilson about the possibility of SIM's launching a station somewhere within Kullo Konta. With SIM approval, Ohman and Wilson authorized the Wolaitta evangelists and the several leaders of the Kullo Konta church to begin negotiating a land agreement near the Waka government center. The Wolaitta evangelists befriended a prominent land owner named *Danya* Dale Daymo. He was willing to sign a twenty-year lease with SIM for a plot of his land at Doché located near Waka. In June 1952 Walter Ohman finalized the land contract, and by November SIM missionaries Bob and Jean King had begun building a school, clinic, and residences at Doché.

Birru Dubalä's Initiative in Kullo Konta

We have seen in the previous chapter that shortly after Birru Dubalä was converted in Addis Ababa at Cederqvist's "English School," his intention was to bring the gospel to his people in Kullo Konta.[143] After Birru assisted in guiding the first SIM party to Wolaitta in 1928, it was three years before he was able to take missionaries to visit his home in Dawro Bobe, Kullo Konta. In April 1931, while Birru was escorting an SIM party from Jimma to Soddo via Bulqi, he realized his lifelong ambition and brought "his teachers" to his home country.[144] But SIM did not have the resources to launch an outreach into Kullo Konta at that time.

In 1935 Birru Dubalä went on an extensive trek through Kullo Konta with Earl Lewis. This may have been another attempt by Birru to encourage SIM to extend an outreach to Kullo Konta. On this trip of several weeks' duration, they visited two communities in Loma *wäräda*: Koysha and Qäné. Their preaching met with little response. Yosef Menna interviewed several from the Qäné community some forty-three years later and wrote, "The people in Kullo Konta did not believe because this preaching was a new thing to them."[145]

But Birru Dubalä was not to be deterred. In 1947 he organized an evangelistic tour into Kullo Konta, taking along with him Anjaja Kurka, Mäläbo, and Agaga, all men from the Bosa Qacha community, located near Soddo. They went to Tocha *wäräda*, to Bobe, Birru's own birthplace.

143. Duff, *Cords of Love*, 31.
144. Rhoad, "Wayside Jottings," 17.
145. Yosef Menna, *"Yätinsaéw Näṣibiraq,"* 223.

But because Birru's initial desire had been to bring missionaries to his Kullo Konta homeland, in 1945 he eventually developed a liaison with his former friends within the Swedish Mission *Bibeltrogna Vänner.*[146] Through them Birru was able to establish a school and a Lutheran Church outreach center at Bobe.

Wolaitta and SIM Partnership in Kullo Konta

After SIM located at Doché in 1952, six additional Wolaitta evangelists worked in partnership with SIM in outreach and witness. Tumébo Tala was effective in his ministry at the Intalla *ṣälot bét.* Chondo Wola, Dumicho Durésa, Pawlos Lugo, Asha Alänbo, and Eyob Ololo alternated in their evangelism between the Bäza, Dosha, Ocha, and Hal'ane *ṣälot bétoch.*[147] Eyob Ololo was effective as an evangelist as he used his gift of healing. At the Dosha *ṣälot bét* Eyob prayed in the name of the Father, Son, and Holy Spirit for a sick girl by the name of Batame Darota. She was healed and was strong enough to go to the local market the following day. Through this unusual sign, many of the local people left their worship of the ancestor spirits and began to attend the Dosha *ṣälot bét.*[148]

In 1958 the Wolaitta church recalled the six evangelist families because it appeared to the Wolaitta *mahibär* that the evangelists were dominating the Kullo Konta *amanyoch* communities. Even though the Kullo Konta *amanyoch* were supporting six of their own evangelists, Ruth McCoughtry, SIM school teacher/director at Doché, was concerned about the decision. She wrote, "There is still the crying need for leadership in the churches now."[149] McCoughtry also questioned whether the resources of the Kullo Konta *amanyoch* were adequate to evangelize the vast population scattered throughout the mountains and Omo River lowlands of Kullo Konta. By March 1959 the Wolaitta elders had reconsidered the withdrawal of their evangelists and were making preparations to redeploy another contingent to Kullo Konta.[150] By 1972 there were twenty-six long-term Wolaitta

146. Walter Ohman, letter to Alfred Roke, February 9, 1945.

147. Eyob Ololo, personal interview with EPB, July 7, 1988. Eyob was born in Kullo Konta but grew up in Kendo Angäla, Boloso. In 1955 he married Dästa Bafé, wife of drowned evangelist Dumicho Durésa.

148. Ibid.

149. Ruth McCoughtry, letter to prayer partners, November 18, 1958.

150. In other areas, such as Sidama, Burji, and Koyra, after eight to ten years the new *amanyoch* communities were sufficiently taught and organized so that the Wolaitta evangelists were deployed elsewhere. Gershon Dilbato thinks it may have been Bob King who

evangelists assigned to Kullo Konta. Dick McLellan commented, "Their zealousness in getting out the Gospel and their love of the Saviour is a constant rebuke and challenge to us."[151] In 1975 there were 105 *şälot bétoch* functioning in Kullo Konta.[152]

6.4 Evangelist Mäja Adélo served in Kullo Konta, Qucha, Burji, Koyra, Aäri, Käfa and Bänna (Lila W. Balisky, 1972)

Little attempt was made by the SIM members within Kullo Konta or by the evangelists' sending agency in Wolaitta to ensure that the evangelists serving within Kullo Konta met together regularly. Travel over formidable terrain no doubt was the deterring factor. The Kullo Konta returnees from Ṯämbaro started well as functioning *amanyoch* communities along the Omo River. But this religious movement did not retain its momentum because it was not incorporated into the overall plans for evangelism spearheaded from the SIM station located at Doché. It seems that the factors of distance, rugged terrain, and rivers limited the communication

influenced the Wolaitta leadership to prematurely withdraw their evangelists. Personal information to EPB, July 11, 1997.

151. Dick and Vida McLellan, letter to prayer partners, September 1972.

152. Dick McLellan, letter to EPB, April 22, 1991.

between the Wolaitta evangelists and SIM missionaries. This problem was somewhat alleviated when the Missionary Aviation Fellowship (MAF) established a route to Doché in 1965 and to three other locations within Kullo Konta in 1973.

Resistance and Hardships Experienced in Kullo Konta

The Wolaitta evangelists and the Kullo Konta *amanyoch* experienced hardship, ostracism, and abuse from the traditional religious functionaries and local officials of Kullo Konta. These officials attempted to thwart the development of the nascent *amanyoch* communities with threats and accusations. Eventually, in 1955, evangelist Ombolé Odiro, leader Aldada Aṭébo, and three Kullo Konta *amanyoch*, Hatasa, Molesa, and Baldada, were imprisoned. Ombolé and Aldada were detained in the Waka administrative center prison for six months. The Kullo Konta men were incarcerated at the provincial capital, Jimma, for one year. Kullo Konta *amanyä* Hatasa died of malnutrition and exposure in the Jimma prison. The Kullo Konta accusers were *Rasha* Abiché Alälo, from Bosa *wäräda*, and *Däjazmach* Abäbä Awrares, chief administrator of Kullo Konta *awraja*. The Kullo Konta *amanyoch* had no legal recourse to which they could appeal except to the emperor, Haile Selassie. But at that time, within the Kullo Konta *amanyoch*, there was no one with Amharic ability except Aldada Aṭébo, who was himself detained in the Waka prison.[153]

Evangelist Wanna Dägalo experienced a confrontation with the government authorities located in Bossa Gäna. While he was teaching in the Hangala *ṣälot bét*, soldiers came and arrested him. While marching to the Bossa police station, they passed by evangelist Choramo Cholo's house. Wanna asked permission from his escort to stop and pray with his fellow evangelist. This request was granted. When they arrived at the Bossa government center, Wanna was interrogated by the officials. After he explained that he was a preacher from Wolaitta and that he taught literacy in various places in the countryside, an argument erupted among the officials. Some said Wanna was a disturber of the Kullo Konta society. Others argued that he was making a contribution to the local population. Wanna was released that same evening. One of the officials said to Wanna, "You have an advocate that we cannot defeat."[154]

---

153. Yosef Menna, "*Yätinsaéw Näṣibiraq,*" 226.
154. Wanna Dägalo, personal interview with EPB, July 7, 1988.

In 1967 Bob and Jean King reported that many of the Kullo Konta *sälot bétoch* lacked able leaders who could "shepherd and teach them."[155] Consequently, there was dissension and strife among the *amanyoch*, and some reverted to their traditional religion.

In 1970 a new generation of nine Wolaitta evangelists, with their families, were located in Konta Koysha. The local population, living in isolation from greater Ethiopia, were followers of traditional religion. Their social structure had remained unchanged for generations. Some of the evangelists involved in this outreach were: Indriyas Täntu, Héliso Kuké, Harkéso Halé, Ingäshaw Recho, and Samuél Sälasé. The difficulties they faced included mountainous terrain, muddy roads, and animals such as buffaloes, lions, and elephants in the forest.[156]

Gus and Lois Kayser wrote from Waka in 1971:

> Many new churches have been planted but they are without trained pastors to lead them. Many of them cannot read the Word of God for themselves. . . . There are harassments to no end, but the work is rolling along. Last year we started full-time Bible School in the Quonset huts."[157]

The evangelists and the SIM missionaries experienced various difficulties in Kullo Konta. But through their efforts an alternative community was established in Kullo Konta, a community where unity, trust, and love were nurtured and a community where there was worship of the true God through his Son, Jesus.

Wolaitta Evangelists in Kullo Konta—an Assessment

During the years 1942–1975, Wolaitta made the investment of sending more than ninety-one evangelists to Kullo Konta.[158] Between 1942 and 1970 there were about eight Wolaitta evangelists resident within Kullo Konta at any one time. After 1970 this number increased to twenty-five or twenty-six. Of the four Omotic groups that we have discussed in this chapter, the Kullo Konta are most similar to the Wolaitta in language and culture, yet there was the least response among them to the Christian

155. Bob and Jean King, letter to prayer partners, September 28, 1967.

156. Yosef Menna, "*Yätinsaéw Näṣibiraq*," 233–34.

157. Gus and Lois Kayser, letter to friends, July 24, 1971.

158. This number does not include the 175 short-term rainy season evangelists who served in Kullo Konta in 1969, 1970, and 1971. See appendix 2, the list of Wolaitta evangelists who served outside of geographic Wolaitta for at least two years.

message. One cannot say that the methodology of the evangelists was significantly different in any of the four geographic areas discussed in this chapter. However, one is tempted to offer the conclusion that the primal religion of the Kullo Konta had altered little in the past century. On the other hand, the small group of Kullo Konta refugees in Ṭämbaro, once dislocated and under stress, were responsive to religious change after 1940. It would seem that the isolation fostered by the formidable mountainous terrain, the Gojeb and the Omo rivers, the lack of roads, and the scarcity of opportunities for the education of children,[159] all contributed to the conservative cultural and religious belief system of the Kullo Konta. Also, there has been no evidence that the message of Prophet Ésa Lalé had reached Kullo Konta. Modernity and change from the outside had not impacted the Kullo Konta as it had the other Omotic groups.

Another reason for the slow response to the message of the evangelists was the geographic expanse of Kullo Konta. The isolated communities had little communication with each other. There were limited weekly markets functioning in this vast area. The Ethiopian government built an elementary school in Waka in 1950, and SIM established another at Doché in 1952, with Ruth McCoughtry as the school director.[160] But able students made their way either to government high schools in Jimma or in Soddo, and very few were willing to return to the isolation of Kullo Konta, where government job opportunities were limited. In the expansion of "greater Ethiopia" from 1895 to 1975, Kullo Konta did not develop into a single cohesive ethnic group with a strong self identity. Somehow the degree of incorporation into "greater Ethiopia" by a given southern ethnic group appears to be an indicator of that group's willingness to be flexible in religious pilgrimage.

Perhaps the single greatest factor in the Kullo Konta lack of receptivity to religious change was that they were unaware of the teaching of Ésa. To date I have no evidence that his teaching penetrated Kullo Konta. They had not been challenged to put away their clan deities. Their focus on lesser deities made *Ṭosa* seem distant and unrelated to their needs. Their concept of a creator God who is to be feared and worshipped was deficient.

---

159. Between 1970 and 1975 the Ethiopian School Building Unit constructed permanent elementary schools in the *wärräda* centers of Tocha, Gäna Bassa, Amaya Konta, Wushay, and Loma.

160. Shepley, "SIM Stations in Ethiopia."

By 1975, after many years of sacrificial service in Kullo Konta, nearly all of the Wolaitta evangelists were recalled to Wolaitta.[161] Without doubt, Wolaitta sent the largest contingent of her evangelists to this area. The harvest reaped was not commensurate with the substantial commitment in finance and manpower.

Conclusion

When the Wolaitta evangelists began itinerating beyond their geographical borders to tell the Jesus story, they were motivated by the command they read in their Bibles: "Go to all the world." As members of *amanyoch* communities, they were motivated by what they themselves had experienced within Wolaitta. They were free from the fear of death. They were at peace with their neighbors. They were treated with honor and dignity within the *amanyoch* community. These were the realized ideals within their own lives and society that propelled them from one mountain range to another.

Several significant things took place within the Wolaitta *mahibär* because of the evangelists' activities outside Wolaitta. First, it caused the sending *mahibär* to retain a serving attitude. Every month thousands of birr were collected from the Wolaitta *sälot bétoch* and sent to the evangelists for their monthly stipend.[162] Second, the evangelists made an indirect contribution to their sending *mahibär* by their example of dedication and obedience to their calling. Third, because of the imprisonment of the evangelists in neighboring areas, the Wolaitta *mahibär* and other *mahibäroch* serving in partnership with SIM were forced to obtain official recognition from Addis Ababa authorities for their existence. The *Bäwängél Amanyoch Andinät Mahibär* became an official Ethiopian organization in 1964. And fourth, the Wolaitta *mahibär* had to establish relationships with the new *amanyoch* communities that came into being through the work of

161. Some Wolaitta evangelists such as Danél Madalcho, Kasa Koyra, and Yaiqob Chunfuré chose to remain in Kullo Konta and sever their dependency upon Wolaitta. If they had taken a Kullo Konta wife, the pull to remain in Kullo Konta was rather strong. Some had developed their farmsteads into self-supporting ventures that promised security for their old age. A recent report from evangelist Sawl Salgédo, located in Kullo Konta, states that many former adherents to primal religion are now confessing that "Jesus is Lord." Sawl Salgédo, letter to EPB, July 4, 1997.

162. From 1946 to 1965 the average monthly stipend was 10.00 Ethiopian birr. From 1965 to 1975 it was increased to 30.00 birr. In 1975 the annual Wolaitta contribution for evangelism was 39,000.00 birr. Markina Mäja, personal information to EPB, March 1991.

the evangelists. The Wolaitta *mahibär* treated each of these new entities as a sister *mahibär*, allowing them full membership within the *Andinät*. Wolaitta also expected each established *mahibär* in Gämo, Qucha, Gofa, and Kullo Konta to begin sending out its own evangelists.

In retrospect, it appears that the success of the Wolaitta evangelists among their Omotic speaking neighbors can be attributed to several factors. First, the groups shared similarities in language and culture. Second, the evangelists were reaping where prophets such as Ésa had sown. Except in Kullo Konta, Ésa's message of repentance was still echoing across the mountains of Gämo, Qucha, and Gofa. Finally, these areas, being contiguous to Wolaitta, were accessible by foot. We will see in the following two chapters that, with the assistance of an expatriate evangelistic agency, the Wolaitta evangelists were enabled to penetrate differing cultures at some distance from Wolaitta. We will attempt to determine whether this abated their efforts or provided new opportunities for the evangelists to express their religious innovation.

7

The Evangelists' Outreach to Arsi, Sidama, Burji/Koyra, Aari, and Käfa

A neat separation between missionaries and the
African mission agents is an artificial construction.
From the beginning there existed a real link and
actual cooperation, although not without ambivalence.[1]

Introduction

IN CHAPTER 6 WE observed that the Wolaitta evangelists themselves took
the initiative in evangelizing the Omotic peoples of Gämo, Qucha, Gofa,
and Kullo Konta (Dawro). This chapter will show that the Wolaitta evangelists functioned in a partnership relationship with SIM as they attempted
to evangelize the Arsi, Sidama, Burji/Koyra, and Käfa. After 1944 the missionaries were granted government permission to open schools and medical
work among the Arsi (from a base in Shashämänä, later to be transferred
to Kuyära), the Sidama (at Aläta Wändo), the Burji and Koyra, the Aari (at
Bako), and the Käfa (at Bonga). Post-occupation southern Ethiopia once
again came under the hegemony of the Amhara. To government officials
and to the clerics of the Orthodox Church, it appeared that the Wolaitta
evangelists were agents of SIM. Because the evangelists functioned in
partnership with the missionaries, the evangelists were insulted and called
yämisiyon bucholoch (the puppy dogs of the mission). The goals of the evangelists and SIM were similar, therefore, it was natural for a partnership to
develop between them. SIM recognized that their evangelistic goals could
most satisfactorily be accomplished by the evangelists. In areas distant from
Wolaitta, the evangelists were dependent on the missionaries for the transfer of their salaries, schooling for their children, for medical treatment, and

---

1. Verstraelen-Gilhuis, *New Look at Christianity in Africa*, 93.

in some cases for transportation. The 1944 Ethiopian government policy, defining Amharic as the official language, further limited the expatriates from communicating in local dialects. Most evangelists were adept at learning and evangelizing in local dialects. There was no official policy that restricted Ethiopians from preaching in local dialects.

Those evangelists who went to the Omotic-speaking peoples experienced various kinds of harassment and isolation. They walked and lived in rugged mountain terrain. The challenges that faced the evangelists on the eastern section of the Rift Valley were of a more subtle nature. There was sometimes the temptation of higher salaries offered by other mission organizations. And in Arsi, there was the added temptation to become like other Wolaitta compatriots who acquired fertile land and became settlers.

On occasions the partnership between the evangelists and SIM was strained. At some of the SIM centers located among the non-Omotic language groups, the expatriate missionary dominated the evangelists. The evangelists, on the other hand, sometimes made unrealistic demands upon the resident missionaries. But through their joint efforts, they have left a proud legacy in southern Ethiopia of hundreds of *ṣälot bétoch*, where songs of praise to God are sung, Bible teaching is carried on, and *amanyoch* care for one another in love and respect.

Arsi

Background

In the middle of the sixteenth century, the Oromo left their homelands in southeastern Ethiopia, crossed the Galana River, and for several decades spilled over the central highlands of Ethiopia.[2] Bähäré, an Orthodox priest residing in Gämo during the Oromo migration, wrote about the movements of the two large clans of the Oromo, the Baraytuma and the Boran, who eventually occupied three-quarters of Ethiopia.[3] According to Merid Wolde Aregay, the Oromo travelled north from the southern regions of Bale, through the Rift Valley, and began fanning west after crossing the Awash River.[4] At present there are seven major families of Oromo residing in Ethiopia: Borana, Guji, Arsi, Harar, Tuluma, Yeju, and Matcha.[5] This

2. Bähäré, "Galla," 603–4. Bähäré, an Orthodox clergyman residing in Gämo, was an eye witness to the Oromo expansion.

3. Ibid., 604.

4. Merid W/Aregay, "Southern Ethiopia and the Christian Kingdom," 306–7.

5. Bartels, *Oromo Religion*, 378.

section will discuss the attempt of the Wolaitta, together with the SIM, to evangelize the Arsi Oromo (see map 7.1).

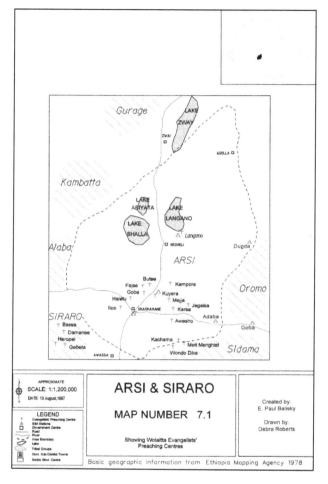

The Arsi retained their nomadic manner of life after they migrated to the Rift Valley lake district south of the Awash river. But since the 1936 Italian occupation, technology and modernity have encroached upon their life style. For example, the hydroelectric scheme on the Awash River meant that thousands of hectares of grazing land were flooded when the Qoqa Dam was created. Subsequent to that, the Wonji Sugar Factory and sugarcane scheme, lower on the Awash River, usurped another large tract of grazing land. Italian lumber entrepreneurs were allowed generous forest concessions at Jagésa, near Shashämänä. The two-thousand hectare Sisal

State Farm north of Awassa again impinged on their grazing territory. The Ministry of Agriculture fenced more than five-thousand hectares of choice grazing land immediately south of Zway for the purpose of grazing a select herd of Boran cattle. Unlike the Omotic and Sidamo peoples of the South who were colonized by Menilek's *näftänyoch*, the Arsi were largely bypassed because of the insecurity of living among them. As an alternative, in order to penetrate into Arsiland, the Haile Sellassie government allowed large land concessions to several organizations, including: CADU, a mechanized state farm; SIM Southern Leprosy Colony,[6] for agricultural and developmental schemes; and the Seventh Day Adventist College at Kuyära.[7] Several hundred Tigrai Patriots, called the *Simih Tiru Hamasän*, were resettled north of Shashämänä town in 1948. A continual source of irritation for the Arsi herdsmen near Shashämänä was the migration of Wolaitta and Kambatta settlers onto fertile Arsi grazing land. Occasional border clashes over land rights erupted in the Siraro district.

It was after the Italian occupation that the Arsi began converting to the Muslim faith.[8] When the Wolaitta evangelists arrived in Arsiland in 1947, many of the Arsi claimed to be Muslim, even though their former traditional religion was very much a part of their nomadic culture. In 1932 Cerulli reported, "All the Arusi tribes living east of the Chilalo between the Awash River and the source of the Wabi River are pagan."[9] Characteristic features of traditional religion in Arsi are the annual pilgrimages to sacred mountains, the veneration of sacred enclosures around hot springs, and retaining the name of their creator God as *Waqa*.[10] Orthodox Christianity has not made any significant inroads into Arsi culture.[11]

6. Shepley, "SIM Stations in Ethiopia," 3.

7. Mulatu Baffa, personal interview with EPB, April 10, 1997.

8. Trimingham states, "A large proportion of the Arusi are emphatic that their religion is Islam, but observance goes little beyond the observance of Ramadan in a faint way and the avoidance of eating meat killed by a non-Muslim." *Islam in Ethiopia*, 208.

9. Cerulli, "Le Popolazioni del Bacino Superiore dello Uabi," 141, as found in Trimingham, *Islam in Ethiopia*, 208.

10. See Bartels, *Oromo Religion*, 89–107, regarding the Oromo importance of retaining the name *Waqa*. According to Trimingham, *Islam in Ethiopia*, 240, the annual Arsi pilgrimage to Sheik Hussein in Bale province originated within their primal religion. See also Mohammed Hassen, *Oromo of Ethiopia*, 155–56.

11. Hector Blackhurst states that the Arsi were forcefully brought into the Amhara state by Menilek's army and have remained essentially untouched by Amhara culture. "Their attitude to the Amhara state is at best, ambivalent and they have adopted Islam." "Ethnicity in Southern Ethiopia," 55.

Evangelists and SIM Locate in Shashämänä

The pioneers of Arsi evangelism were SIM missionaries Albert and Evelyn Brant, Eva Alberda, and Mary Haney and Wolaitta evangelists Täntu Debana and Dodo Gémbéro.[12] They arrived in Shashämänä town in April of 1947 and lived in tents and rented local quarters for over one year while they opened a school and clinic. Täntu, Dodo, and Albert Brant trekked to Siraro and other places throughout the Rift Valley lake district with Arsi interpreter Gäbrä Wäldé.[13] The men did not feel safe as they trekked through dense acacia forests and tall grass because of the danger of attack from wild animals and *shifta*.[14] The initiative for Siraro evangelism continued both from Wolaitta and Kambatta, as there were settlers from both these areas living in close proximity to the Arsi. The evangelistic attempt from Shashämänä was weakened after sixteen months, when the SIM staff were transferred elsewhere[15] and one of the evangelists returned to Wolaitta for compatibility reasons.[16] Through this initial venture, the Wolaitta *mahibär* was made aware of the possibility and obligation of preaching the gospel to their former enemies, the Arsi.[17] Even though border scrimmages and full-scale war had been going on between the Wolaitta and Arsi for over a century,[18] the Wolaitta were committed to a joint venture with SIM to evangelize the Arsi.

Southern Leprosy Colony at Kuyära: A New Base for Arsi Evangelism

In 1949 SIM received permission and a land grant of over two hundred hectares from the Ethiopian Ministry of Health to open the Southern

12. Brant, *In the Wake of Martyrs*, 58–78. See also KHC, "*Bäwängél Amanyoch Andinät*," 64.

13. Alan Neal, letter to EPB, July 5, 1991.

14. Alan Neal, "Arsee Story," 63. SIM missionaries Tom Devers and Cliff Mitchell, along with twenty Amhara, were killed by Arsi bandits near Siraro in May 1936. Cotterell, *Born at Midnight*, 85–86.

15. Brant describes this sudden change of assignment of 1948: "We had not considered the possibility of being plucked up by the roots so early." *In the Wake of Martyrs*, 77.

16. Alan Neal, letter to EPB, July 5, 1991.

17. Wolaitta enmity against the Arsi goes back many generations, according to Wolaitta oral history. Duguna Oda and Hajeso Toshé, personal interview with EPB, November 1–2, 1988. Neighboring tribes look upon the Arsi as "feckless, untrustworthy, milk-drinking layabouts," as quoted in Blackhurst, "Ethnicity in Southern Ethiopia," 60.

18. Tsehai Berhane, "The Question of Damot and Walamo," 44, where reference is made to Wolaitta King Ogato's digging defensive ditches to restrain Arsi attacks.

Leprosy Colony at Kuyära, seven kilometers north of Shashämänä. Alan Neal was assigned to Arsi evangelism, and the Wolaitta *mahibär* responded on their part by sending the following evangelists to Arsi from 1949 to 1950: Tanga Dedo and Muné to Shashämänä, Mäna Ako and Bunaro Sumago to Kémpéro, Hadaro Hantuka to Butee, Täntu Debana and Gamo Gabeso to Awasho, Oida Odire to Halélu, Mola Urqé, followed by Bäza Bakalo, to Goba, Labéna Bonja to Iloo. And to the Siraro district— two brothers, Gälaso and Gänébo Gaga.[19] Galoré Guradé moved onto the SIM compound at Kuyära because his family were initially fearful of living among the Arsi.

In the Siraro district the response to the gospel was from among the Wolaitta and Kambatta population, not the Arsi.[20] By 1950 the *amanyoch* had constructed *ṣälot bétoch* at Heropé, Dämané, and Bassa. By 1960 Heropé and Gäbäta were in communion with the Arsi *mahibär*, but Dämané and Bassa *ṣälot bétoch* joined the Kambatta *mahibär*. And ten years later, in 1970, Awarcasa was added to Heropé and Gäbäta *ṣälot bétoch*.[21] Apparently there were volunteer evangelists from the Wolaitta Duguna district assisting for a limited time in the Siraro not reporting to either the Wolaitta *mahibär* or to SIM in Kuyära.

The first baptism was conducted at Goba[22] on June 25, 1950. Wolaitta *mahibär* leaders Biru Dubalä, *Ato* Jaldo, and C̱äramo Gäläso officiated. Three people were baptized: Dälu Fega, a former Muslim teacher, Shuba, and his wife. With a loud voice and raised hand, Dälu testified, "I was once a teacher of Islam, but I now believe in Jesus Christ, the Son of God, who died on the cross for my sins, and who rose again."[23]

Prior to his Christian conversion, Dälu struggled about leaving the faith of his fathers, Islam. He pondered his creed and practice:

> I believe in one *Waq* and Alah is his name. My religion is better than all other religions. We do not eat any kind of meat unless it has been slaughtered according to our laws. As a true Muslim, I pray to Mecca after I have washed in clean water.[24]

19. Alan Neal, letter to EPB, November 8, 1991.

20. Neal comments, "The Siraro churches could not be regarded as Arsee." Ibid.

21. Alan Neal, personal information to EPB, November 8, 1991.

22. An enclave of Wolaitta reside at Goba, some three kilometers northwest of Shashämänä.

23. Neal, "Arsee Story," 33. See also KHC, "History of the Kale Heywet Church," 64.

24. As quoted in Neal, "Arsee Story," 33.

He was accustomed to adhering to rules and regulations. The *amanyoch* community's rules forbidding drinking, adultery, stealing, and lying would have been relatively easy for him to observe. But for Dälu to forsake the social cohesion of the Muslim brotherhood was not easy. The Wolaitta evangelists and the few other Arsi *amanyoch* offered him a new community for fellowship but little promise of financial security. There may have been some benefits for him at the SIM medical center at Kuyära.

Several decades later an Arsi described this first baptism thus: "At that time, to witness the baptism of an Arsi was marvelous and wonderful."[25] Wolaitta leader Biru Dubalä encouraged the Arsi *amanyoch* to organize themselves into a *şälot bét*. This they did in 1949, with Galoré Guradé and Labéna Bonja serving as advisors, along with SIM missionary Alan Neal.

In early 1950 the SIM assisted the twelve or thirteen evangelists in Arsi by providing them with literacy material and with small hand-wind phonograph players. Several of these literacy centers became primary schools, with the teachers being young Arsi lads who had completed at least the sixth grade at the SIM elementary school at Kuyära. The evangelists, together with the Arsi *mahibär*, assisted in coordinating these schools, as they were another means of teaching the Jesus story to a younger generation of Arsi.

Soon after the evangelists arrived in Arsi they began a monthly Friday meeting when the "moon became bright" for discussion, prayer, and Bible reading. As Arsi church leaders were appointed, these monthly meetings developed into the Arsi *mahibär* meeting. From 1952 to 1957 Bill Wallace, who replaced Alan Neal, participated in these all-night gatherings, where the evangelists exercised a dominant role.[26]

> It was in their prayers where I felt the heart throb of the evangelists. They prayed specifically, meaningfully, often emotionally for their Arsi contacts. When Galoré, Labéna, Mäna and Bunaro prayed for the salvation of their neighbors, it was always by name and included a description of the evangelistic communication problems they faced. And their fervent prayers for new or stumbling believers sometimes included tears as they pled with God.[27]

25. As quoted in KHC, "*Bäwängél Amanyoch Andinät,*" 64. Alan Neal, letter to EPB, July 5, 1991, indicates that of the three baptized, only Dalu was Arsi. Shuba and his wife were Wolaitta settlers.

26. Bill Wallace, letter to EPB, October 29, 1996, called the Wolaitta evangelists "pastors."

27. Bill Wallace, letter to EPB, December 6, 1991.

As Bunaro Sumago and Mäna Ako were preaching and teaching at Kémpéro, five kilometers northeast of Kuyära, they were asked to assist in a reconciliation mission between warring tribes. Because of intertribal warfare between the Arsi and the Sidama, *Däjazmach* Asraté Kassa, governor of Arsi, based in Asella, requested SIM to assist. Alan Neal and the evangelists responded by assigning Bunaro and Mäna to the Arsi section of Wändo Dika, an area where there had been loss of life because of tribal clashes. This outpost at Wändo Dika proved unmanageable for the evangelists because of uncontrolled warfare between the Sidama and the Arsi. Insurmountable problems such as malaria, lack of fluency in the Oromo language, and lack of communication with their families and co-workers residing near Kuyära forced the evangelists to abandon the reconciliation project. Mäna returned to Kémpéro, where he continues to serve as the pastor.[28] Bunaro assisted in the evangelistic ministry at the SIM Kuyära hospital, clinic, and leprosy village.[29]

Several Evangelists' Stories

Several of the evangelists who went to Arsi were experienced leaders in the Wolaitta *mahibär.* Brief biographies of three of them follow.

Chäramo Gäläso

Chäramo arrived in Arsi soon after the Neals located at Shashämänä in 1949. Laurie Davison, one of the SIM missionaries of the pre-Italian period, knew Chäramo had facility in the Oromo language and arranged to have Chäramo assist Alan Neal as a translator in the second phase of the Arsi outreach.[30]

Chäramo was one of the ten original Wolaitta to be baptized at Soddo in 1933 and eventually served on the Wolaitta *tärapéza.*[31] When younger evangelists attempted to witness to the Arsi at Faji, an area some twenty kilometers east of Kuyära, very few were interested in listening. But when Chäramo began to speak, the *jarsa,* or old Arsi elders, became curious and drew near.

28. As of August 1997 Mäna continues to serve the Kémpéro congregation as pastor. This gives evidence of his identification with the Arsi because most non-Arsi were evicted from Arsiland during the 1974–1991 *dergue* years.

29. Alan Neal, letter to EPB, July 5, 1991.

30. Neal, "Arsee Story," 20. See also Cotterell, *Born at Midnight,* 122.

31. Davis, *Fire on the Mountains,* 73.

> He talked the Gospel to these who had never heard before. The old men . . . came and heard it gladly from the gray-haired elder <u>Ch</u>oramo. Many long evenings were spent around the fire talking about the reality of Christ and his power over all spirits. <u>Ch</u>oramo was one with them and his testimony had authenticity to it.[32]

Because he had recently arrived from Australia, Alan Neal was struggling with certain aspects of the Arsi culture, as was <u>Ch</u>äramo, who commented:

> At first this smell went against me, but God's work is sweet, and God gave me a love for those people; so I just went from hut to hut, and village to village, and now their huts smell differently."[33]

<u>Ch</u>äramo remained in Arsi for two years. When he returned to Wolaitta he was elected to a leadership position in the *mahibär*. From that position he provided encouragement and support for the ongoing evangelistic thrust in Arsi.

LABÉNA BONJA

Labéna left a good and prosperous life as a farmer in Wolaitta. From 1936 to 1941 he was greatly influenced by his neighbor, Israel, who was a devout follower of Roman Catholicism. During the post-Italian period, when it was unpopular to be a Roman Catholic in Wolaitta, and because he observed that the *amanyoch* were growing very rapidly, Labéna became an *amanyä*, was baptized, and became a member of one of the *ṣälot bétoch* in Damot Galé.[34]

Unlike most young men in Wolaitta, he was fluent in Amharic because during his youth he had lived near an Amhara enclave in the Damot Galé district. But he did not master reading and writing Amharic until he was an adult.

When Labéna arrived as an evangelist in Arsi, he was encouraged to build his house and settle his family amongst the Arsi and not on the secure, expansive SIM compound at Kuyära, as did others of the evangelists. Labéna was able to make contact with an Arsi man from Iloo who was sympathetic to the new teaching of the evangelists. This Iloo man invited Labéna to his area, about eight kilometers west of Shashämänä, near the

32. Neal, "Arsee Story," 21.

33. As quoted in Marcella and Walter Ohman, letter to prayer partners, February 27, 1950.

34. Neal, "Arsee Story," 46.

Alaba road, and offered him a plot of land on which to build his house and farm on a rental basis. Soon Labéna was joined by Dästa Amato. The practice of working in pairs was encouraged by their sending *mahibär*. When the men went out on evangelistic treks, their wives and children would have companionship. Labéna and his wife soon mastered the Arsi language and culture. Labéna's wife was known in Arsi as "a mother in Israel."[35] Their Arsi landlord, his two wives, and his children accepted the Jesus story, as did others in the area. Soon a *sälot bét* was built next to Labéna's residence at Iloo, and literacy classes were offered for the children.[36] Labéna adapted well to life in Arsi and was an industrious farmer, "slightly more prosperous [than most evangelists]."[37] Before 1955 the evangelists were concerned about their safety residing among the Arsi. But Labéna and his family "lived securely among the Arsee for many years."[38]

GALORÉ GURADÉ

Galoré was a trader pedaling his wares from one market to another in Wolaitta from 1937 to 1941. He heard the good news from a fellow trader and became an *amanyä* in 1941.[39]

> It became apparent to me that there was power in this new message I heard, for the people who believed were changed and became different inside. Death was a very fearful thing to me but the believers spoke of a life beyond the grave with hope.[40]

After going as an evangelist to Arsi, Galoré suffered a heart ailment that eventually confined him to his residence. This was a setback for him because he enjoyed getting out with people and attending various *mahibär* functions. Eventually he saved enough money to buy a mule so he could once again visit the various *sälot bétoch* and carry on his work as before.[41] Although he lived on the SIM Leprosy Colony compound, Galoré would saddle his mule and travel out to encourage the *amanyoch* by teaching literacy and by preaching, aided by a hand-crank gramophone with records in

35. Bill Wallace, letter to EPB, September 15, 1996.
36. Neal, "Arsee Story," 47.
37. Bill Wallace, letter to EPB, December 6, 1991.
38. Ibid.
39. Ibid.
40. As quoted in Neal, "Arsee Story," 55.
41. Neal, "Arsee Story," 56.

Oromifa.[42] Bésha, an Arsi Muslim woman, became an *amanyä* in February 1953 through Galoré's preaching. Her conversion to Christianity was a process. The Galoré family were buying milk from her for several months. It was when her child accidentally fell into the cooking fire and was fatally burned that Bésha considered seriously the message of hope in Jesus that Galoré had been teaching.[43]

7.1 Evangelist Galoré Guradé served in Arsi for 20 years (Bill Wallace, 1953)

Around 1955, when Galoré was attending the monthly Arsi *mahibär* meeting about twenty kilometers from Kuyära, his mule wandered off. Search as they did for two days, the mule was not to be found. The men attending the *mahibär* gave up all hope. But not Ha'da Safai, a poor illiterate Arsi woman dressed only in cowhides. This was her prayer:

> O *Waqa*, *Abba* Galoré is a good man. He left his home in Wolaitta to tell us about the Good News of Jesus. He needs his mule. O *Waqa*, will you please find his animal for him?[44]

On the third day after Galoré's mule had been missing, a Bible class held in the *ṣälot bét* was suddenly interrupted with a shout: "There is Ha'da Safai with *Abba* Galoré's mule!" When asked how she found the mule,

---

42. Bill Wallace, letter to John Davenport, January 1, 1953.

43. Bill Wallace, letter to John Davenport, March 25, 1953.

44. Neal, "Arsee Story," 57.

she replied, "I prayed to *Waqa* this morning and he answered my prayer. When I went outside my house, the mule was standing right there."[45]

7.2 Evangelist Mäna Ako, long-term evangelist in Arsi, seated in front row middle with Arsi congregation (Bill Wallace, 1974)

Tensions and Ambiguities for the Evangelists

The Wolaitta outreach to Arsi involved the Wolaitta evangelists in tensions and ambiguities. Except for one or two missionaries assigned to evangelism, the majority of the SIM staff at Kuyära were involved in one of the larger non-government institutions in southern Ethiopia from 1952 to 1977. Indirectly, SIM sent a message to the Wolaitta evangelists that evangelism could best be done through the means of a large institution.[46] SIM staff assigned evangelists Bunaro Sumago and Galoré Guradé to assist them in telling the Jesus story in the hospital wards, the leprosy village, and the out-patient clinic. Rather than retain their pilgrim role among the Arsi, these evangelists became settlers on the SIM premises, following the example of the expatriate staff who served those who came to them.

Another tension confronting the evangelists was that the Wolaitta settlers who were farming around Shashämänä were more responsive to

45. Ibid., 57–58.

46. Some of the thirteen SIM medical, agricultural, and educational staff at the Southern Leprosy Colony experienced their own ambivalence regarding their missionary calling. SIM administrator Mel Donald reported that SIM appointees to Kuyära evidenced "seeming reluctance . . . to really become involved in the missionary task there." Report to SIM Ethiopia Council, November 1962. Some from the SIM staff may have felt that Arsi evangelism was done vicariously through the Wolaitta evangelists.

the gospel than were the Arsi. The majority of *amanyoch* in the Iloo *ṣälot bét* were of Wolaitta extraction. Because the Arsi nomads had lost their grazing land to Wolaitta settlers, the Arsi were reluctant to listen to the message of the Wolaitta evangelists. The evangelists found they were alienated from the very ones they had come to tell about Jesus. The conversion of the Muslim Arsi to Christianity was a process.[47] First, there was the initial building of friendship. Secondly, the evangelists established some fifteen literacy and district elementary schools, scattered from Shashämänä to Nägäle.[48] Finally, there were conversions among the Arsi, mainly among the aspiring young men. Many of these drifted to urban centers beyond Arsi for further education or to find employment. But the Arsi *mahibär* continued to grow. In 1972 Alan Neal reported that there were twenty-five preaching places where Sunday services were held and of these, less than one-half could be regarded as organized *ṣälot bétoch*. Neal said this about the limited response among the Muslim Arsi: "People who believe may face persecution from members of their families."[49]

The Arsi *amanyoch* girls of marriageable age were caught in the exchange system of marriage practiced among the Arsi clans. One family would give a girl to a young man of another family if that family, in turn, offered a girl as a wife for one of their men. This practice made it rather difficult to establish strong Arsi Christian homes.[50]

The teaching of the Wolaitta *mahibär* against polygamy proved to be another obstacle to Arsi polygamists' becoming *amanyoch*. The Wolaitta *mahibär* practice is that a polygamist convert must put away all wives except the first before he is allowed to be baptized. According to Arsi *mahibär* leader Buli Kimeeso, the majority of Arsi families are polygamous. To his knowledge, no Arsi polygamist has been baptized and become a

47. J.S. Trimingham describes three stages of conversion from primal religion to Islam. "The first stage is preparatory, the infiltration of elements of Islamic culture into animist life. The second stage is conversion, characterized more by a break with the old order than the adoption of the new. The third is the gradual process by which Islam changes the life of the community." *Influence of Islam Upon Africa* (London, 1980), 43, as found in Hassen, *Oromo of Ethiopia*, 154.

48. Kurkura Waffa, World Vision project officer in Ansokia, Wollo, first heard the gospel from evangelist Mäna Ako at the Kémpéro elementary school operated by the Arsi *mahibär*. Kurkura Waffa, personal information to EPB, April 6, 1997.

49. Alan Neal, "Lecture to SIM Language School Students," January 3, 1972.

50. The Wallaces reported that a recently baptized Arsi bride was abducted from her new home. The reason given was that the groom had not paid the full bride price. Bill Wallace, letter to John Davenport, June 9, 1953.

member of the *amanyoch* community.[51] Under no circumstance does the Arsi culture condone a man's returning one of his wives to her family.

The Wolaitta evangelists experienced their own personal struggles. Evangelist Oida Odire's young wife succumbed to the cultural pressure of Arsi women and "they circumsized her after the birth of her second child."[52] The Wolaitta *amanyoch* disallowed circumcision for males and genital mutilation for women, so she was disciplined by the Wolaitta evangelists for several months. Because of low salaries, the evangelists' children had little money for food and clothes while they attended elementary school at Kuyära. Several of them found work cutting grass and planting out coffee trees for the missionaries. And in 1955, five of the Wolaitta evangelist force in Arsi temporarily joined the Seventh Day Adventists for higher salaries.[53] There was also the tension of evangelizing together with several Kambatta/Hadiya evangelists who received higher salaries and who came from a slightly different church tradition.[54]

Wolaitta Evangelists in Arsi—Some Concluding Observations

The evangelists made positive spiritual, social, and economic contributions in Arsi. Through the efforts of forty-one evangelists, over half of whom served for twenty-five years or more, the Arsi *mahibär* developed into thirty *sälot bétoch* with a membership of over 1,500 by 1975.[55] Through the encouragement and example of the SIM agricultural project at Kuyära, the Wolaitta evangelists used good farming practices to supplement their meager salaries from their small plots rented from Arsi farmers. They built rat-proof granaries on stilts, kept chickens, planted corn, fertilized their crops with manure, and planted coffee and eucalyptus trees. These farming

---

51. Buli Kimeeso, personal interview with EPB, June 5, 1997.

52. Bill Wallace, letter to prayer partners, March 3, 1954.

53. Bill Wallace, letter to prayer partners, May 8, 1955. The Wolaitta evangelists' monthly stipend was 10.00 birr (US$4.50); the Seventh Day Adventists paid 20.00 birr.

54. By 1985 there were six evangelists from Kambatta/Hadiya in Arsi. KHC, "*Bäwängél Amanyoch Andinät*," 69.

55. Ibid. The results of the two Wolaitta evangelists assigned to assist in evangelism at the SIM station at Dugda were less than successful. The Wolaitta re-assigned them elsewhere in 1970. SIM withdrew their personnel in 1975, after twenty-three years of attempting to convert the Arsi. To date, there is no KHC in Dugda. Shepley, "SIM Stations in Ethiopia," 2. From 1952 to 1975, about eighteen Kambatta/Hadiya evangelists were involved in Arsi evangelism.

practices in turn were taught to the semi-nomadic Arsi so they could live fuller lives and tithe their produce as well.[56]

7.3 Pioneer SIM missionary to Wolaitta, Walter Ohman, conferring with Wolaitta evangelists serving in Arsi
(Bill Wallace, 1957)

It is difficult to assess the contribution the SIM station at Kuyära made to the effectiveness of the evangelists. Alan Neal and Bill Wallace spent many days trekking in Arsi with the evangelists. The support that the educational and medical programs offered the evangelists and their families ensured a certain stability. Without this infrastructure of the SIM at Kuyära, the success of the evangelists would have been limited.

Several evangelists chose to settle in Arsi rather than return to Wolaitta when they were recalled. Hadaro Hantuka continues to make a valuable contribution to the Shashämänä town *şälot bét*.[57] Mäna Ako and his family have integrated into the Arsi community at the Qémporé *şälot bét*, where he serves as a pastor. And Bäza Bakalo continues to be involved with a *şälot bét* on the outskirts of Shashämänä town.[58]

We conclude the assessment of the Wolaitta evangelists' performance in Arsi by quoting Bill Wallace, who together with his wife, Iris, served with these evangelists in Arsi from 1953 to 1957 and returned for a visit in 1974.

56. Bill Wallace, letter to John Davenport, October 7, 1956.

57. Amdé Yesus Musa, personal information to EPB, April 21, 1997.

58. Bäza Bakalo, personal information to EPB, July 26, 1992.

> As the Wolaitta evangelists walked in our whole area they literally "gossiped the Gospel" to the Arsi and others. Their standard of living certainly was no higher than their neighbours . . . These families put up with linguistic and cultural isolation.[59]

Through their sacrifice and commitment, there are now <u>*sälot bétoch*</u> within Arsi that are supporting their own evangelists who are preaching and teaching the good news.

Sidama

Sidama Background

The Sidama[60] are contained within an area south of Arsi, north of Gédéo, east of Wolaitta, and west of the Jäm Jäm (see map 7.2). Like other Ethiopian highlanders they are of the *ensette* culture. In 1950 the Sidama population was approximately 100,000.

According to Sidama mythology, early in the sixteenth century the two founding brothers of northern lineage, Bushé and Maldea, settled between the Abbaye and Awassa lakes. The language of the Sidama is classified as part of the eastern Cushitic language stock associated with the Hadiya, Kambatta, Alaba, Burji, Tämbaro, and Gédéo.[61] There are about forty-six clans within the Sidama equally divided between the two founding fathers, Bushé and Maldea.

Sometime after the 1891 imperial expansion of the Menilek army into Sidamo province, *Däjazmach* Balcha Abo Näfso replaced *Däjazmach* Lulsägäd as governor of well-resourced Sidamo.[62] Balcha was known for his piety and loyalty to the Ethiopian Orthodox Church, and this was expressed in his construction of churches: the Kidanä Mihirät Church at

---

59. Bill Wallace, letter to EPB, September 15, 1996. Wallace conducted one-month teaching sessions annually for the evangelists at the SIM station at Shashämänä and later at Kuyära. Iris Wallace, letter to John Davenport, October 1, 1952.

60. The term "Sidama" is used by the people to identify themselves as a distinct ethnic group. "Sidamo" usually refers to the larger region consisting of the Sidama and other ethnic groups such as the Hadiya, Kambatta, and Alaba. See Shack, *Gurage*, 4 n. 5, 6 n. 11, for further clarification.

61. Hamer, "Sidamo Generational Class Cycles," 50. See also Cotterell, *Born at Midnight*, 109, for a chart showing percentages of common vocabulary among these Cushitic language groups.

62. Tsehai Berhane, "Life and Career of *Däjazmach* Balcha Aba Näfso," 180. He was governor of Sidama three different times from 1896 to 1928, at which time he was replaced by *Däjazmach* Biru.

Abära, and Mädahané Aläm, Giorgis, and Holy Trinity churches at his administrative center, Agärä Sälam.[63] But even though he was a religious enthusiast and attempted to promote education among the *näftänyoch* of Sidamo through the Orthodox Church schools, he made no attempt to convert the local Sidama population.[64] *Däjazmach* Balcha was replaced by *Däjazmach* Biru as governor of Sidamo in early 1928.[65]

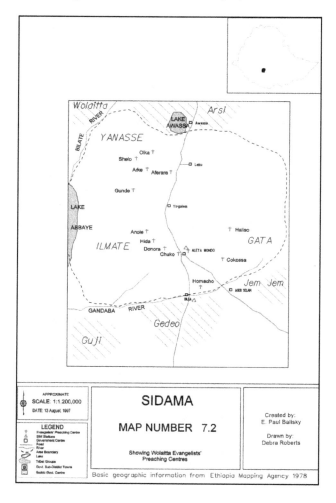

63. Ibid., 176.
64. Ibid., 183.
65. Bahru Zewde, *History of Modern Ethiopia*, 133.

In 1928 SIM missionaries took up residence in Sidama, initially in the highlands at Garbicho, then six months later at Homacho. By 1934 Glen Cain, competent in the Sidama language, translated Mark's gospel into Sidaminya. The first SIM baptism in southern Ethiopia took place December 25, 1932, at Homacho, when four converts, Twesa, Seda, Barkeso, and Otisa were baptized.[66] There were subsequent baptisms at Homacho. On October 9, 1933, Cain and Roke's assistant, Shamana, was one of three to be baptized. Because of various external factors in Sidama, only two of the baptized believers survived intertribal warfare, epidemics, and famine during the Italian occupation.[67]

Sidama Primal Religion

Anthropologist John Hamer, in his field research among the Sidama from 1964 to 1965 and in 1973, has described a pantheon of deities, ranking from the creator God *Mägano* to the departed ancestors and, finally, to the spirit beings that inhabit the streams, forests, and certain practitioners. According to Sidama mythology, *Mägano* quarreled with the people and returned to the sky. He can only be reached now through the departed ancestors. The ancestors communicate with the living through dreams. Because the departed ancestors have now attained *haloli* (the true way of life), they desire to communicate this to the living on earth. The departed elders are said to offer advice through dreams regarding truthfulness and justice in the complex situations in which the living find themselves. The dead communicate concepts that enhance faithfulness, generosity, and the avoidance of jealousy. The living who are attempting to pursue *haloli* in

66. Alfred Roke, letter to EPB, March 31, 1993, confirmed by author on June 21, 1992, visit to Homacho. Ralph Hooper graphically describes the opposition that these four candidates experienced from their families in Rice and Hooper, *Ethiopia*, 20–25. See also Thomas A. Lambie, letter to Eric and Sylvia Horn, January 21, 1933. The protests of the relatives to the first baptism could well have been fear of the *shatana* spirits who were thought to dwell in the rivers and streams. See Hamer and Hamer, "Spirit Possession," 394.

67. Cotterell, *Born at Midnight*, 121, identifies the two as Gänamé and Wärära. Johnny Bakke was misinformed when he wrote, "All baptized members of the Sidamo church had disappeared during the war." *Christian Ministry*, 129 n. 25. According to the assessment of Albert Brant, the Sidama *amanyoch* did not multiply because "they compromised with unscriptural practices of the EOC." *In the Wake of Martyrs*, 81. Guy W. Playfair, *Trials and Triumphs in Ethiopia*, 34, mentions that it was a combination of several calamities—intertribal wars after the Italians were defeated and a typhus epidemic in 1940, followed by devastating famine—that took the lives of thousands of Sidama.

their lives can expect to receive communications from the ancestors. Spirit beings, the lowest ranking of the deities, are those who possess people and are considered to be less powerful. The Sidama call these possession spirits *shaṯana* who, in effect, are tricksters and fickle liars.[68] These *shaṯana* are the demanding spirits that cause disruption to a community by demanding extravagant food and expensive jewelry, like gold necklaces. The possession spirits sometimes create fear in the community.

The Sidama religious practitioners were controlled by an influential *qalicha* called Sheffo. Whenever he would make an appearance all people would fall to the ground and do obeisance to him, saying, "There is no god like Sheffo's." The inhabitants of the Yanasse district would build small worship houses next to their residences and offer their worship of song and dance in rhythm to the beating of their drums. They would offer their *wuqabé* sacrifices such as bulls, oxen, sheep, heifers, and cows, as well as animals with special markings. The blood of the sacrifices would be sprinkled on the faces of all members of the household, from the oldest to the babies, and the blood was not allowed to be washed off.[69] The Sidama also add some butter mixed with incense and anoint their bodies and clothing, believing that a special blessing is inherent in this potion.

A Sidama man counted it a show of manhood if he killed another man. If he was unable to produce the genitals of a man he had slain, he would be mocked by the local women and his eligibility for marriage would be in question.

At the death of a man, the mourning would usually last for four days. In preparation for the mourning, the men would comb their hair and make it stand out in all directions. The women would anoint their hair with butter. An expansive level plain would be chosen for the gathering of the mourners. A large tree was cut down, and after all the bark was stripped from the trunk and branches, it would be left to dry out. This was a symbolic act of identification with the deceased. If the departed warrior had killed several enemies, the mourners would cover their faces and bodies with red earth. They would then dance before the body of the deceased, calling out the names of those killed by the departed warrior.

---

68. See Hamer, *Humane Development*, chap. 10, "Belief, Rituals and Authority."

69. See Roke, *Indigenous Church in Action*, 48–50, where the primal religious practice of cleansing is described. Families would be made to pass through an opening of boughs while the blood of a sacrificed white ox was sprinkled on each member of the clan. The blood was not allowed to be washed off their bodies.

When a woman died, they would erect a small effigy of the one who had died. A clay pot would be used for her body and ensette leaves for her arms. This imitation mummy would then be dressed with the clothes of the deceased. Wolaitta evangelist Sorsa Sumamo expressed his sorrow for those who lived in fear of the unknown beyond the grave.[70]

SIM Returns to Sidama

In 1946 Alfred Roke and the Delmar Stevens re-opened the former SIM station at Homacho. A year later it was decided to move the SIM operation to Aläta Wändo, the government administrative center of south Sidama, where a school and clinic were opened. Wolaitta evangelists Shonga Sadébo[71] and Lolamo Ébéro[72] assisted Roke and Stevens in establishing contact with the few pre-Italian Sidama *amanyoch* and initiating evangelistic outreach into the Aläta district. In 1949 a Sidama *ṣälot bét* was re-opened at Homacho, with other new centers soon to follow in the same year at Hida and Anole. The first post-Italian baptism was conducted at Gunde in 1950, in spite of mounting opposition.[73]

An Account of Two Sidama Men

In 1948 Gabiso Doyamo was residing with his father, who was possessed by a spirit the local people called *shaṭana*. The father became ill, and the spirit ordered a dapple grey heifer to be purchased from the local market and offered as a sacrifice to the spirit. Gabiso carefully followed through with the instructions and presented the slaughtered meat the next morning. His father informed him that his spirit would not receive the offering because a dog had nibbled at some of the slaughtered meat the night before. That meat was discarded, and Gabiso proceeded to the market to purchase another cut of choice meat. After this requirement was fulfilled, the spirit was still not satisfied. Through the father the spirit instructed Gabiso to return to the market and purchase white sorghum, grind it into flour, prepare a porridge, and serve it with butter. Gabiso obediently did

70. Sorsa Sumamo, personal interview with EPB, April 30, 1987.

71. Cotterell, *Born at Midnight*, 121, was misinformed when he spelled Shonga's name "Shanka."

72. This is the same Lolamo who was the Sidama/Wolaitta interpreter for the Playfair deliberations in Wolaitta in July 1943. Roke interpreted Lolamo's Sidaminya into English for Playfair and Playfair's English into Sidaminya for Lolamo to relate to the Wolaitta.

73. Cotterell, *Born at Midnight*, 121.

all this. His father's spirit again did not approve of the offering. After all this effort to appease the spirit, Gabiso's father died.

In Sidama it is customary for the oldest son to inherit the spirit(s) of his father.[74] It is believed that the spirit(s) are sent by *Mägano*, the sky God. In their study of spirit possession among the Sidama, John and Irene Hamer concluded that possession was not always welcome because of accompanying illness of the one possessed. It was thought the reason for the illness was the dissatisfaction of the spirit. The spirit would usually be satisfied by receiving an offering of food.[75]

Gabiso was possessed by his father's spirit and became the *qalicha* for the local district against his will. Soon after this event, he heard that there was an evangelist in the area. Gabiso relates:

> I understood that the new teaching of the Wolaitta evangelist had power to overcome the spirit within me that was disturbing me. I went to the evangelist who explained who Jesus was and his power over all spirits. When I put my faith in Jesus I had freedom from the *shatana* spirit.[76]

Gabiso was asked, "When you were a *qalicha* how did you know that the spirit which possessed you was not true?" He responded:

> I knew this was all from the father of lies because this spirit would say that he could make the poor become rich, cause the barren to become pregnant and give birth, heal the sick if proper sacrifices like sheep and chicken were sacrificed and their blood shed. I saw no positive results.[77]

Soon after he became one of the *amanyoch*, he joined himself to evangelist Shonga Sadébo on a preaching tour to the Sidama districts of Yanasse and to Gata.[78] From 1968 to 1971 Gabiso Doyamo attended the Aläta Wändo Bible School operated by SIM. He has been a faithful elder in his local church and has been a Sidama *mahibär* elder sitting on the monthly *shungo* meetings since 1955. He is a Sidamo elder who displays

---

74. According to the Hamers, spirit possession is generally transferred from parent to oldest child at the death of the parent. See Hamer and Hamer, "Spirit Possession," 395.

75. Ibid., 398.

76. As quoted in KHC, "*Bäwängél Amanyoch Andinät*," 61.

77. Ibid.

78. Gabiso Doyamo, personal information to EPB, February 1992.

the genuine qualities of *haloli*—the true way of life exhibiting faithfulness and generosity.

Before Gabiso Gämbura became one of the *amanyoch* in 1949, he too was possessed by a *shaṭana* spirit. In order to rid himself of this disturbing spirit, he went to a well-known *qalicha*, who advised him to sacrifice a red heifer or an unblemished sheep at the *qalicha's* house. Because this did not alleviate the problem, he returned to the *qalicha*, who then told him to buy some special jewelry inlaid with a rare stone, hang it around his neck, and present it to the *qalicha* at a certain date. He was warned that if he did not fulfil this demand, he would face death. Gabiso travelled to five markets searching in vain for this rare piece of jewelry. He finally returned home empty handed and uncertain of what to do. While Gabiso was away, Wolaitta evangelist Shonga Sadébo arrived in his district of Hida and began preaching. Gabiso was told by his mother that something wonderful had happened to the family when he was away. She told him that if he would believe the message of the evangelist, he would no longer be disturbed by the *shaṭana* spirit. Gabiso sought out the evangelist and heard the message of Jesus and his power over all spirits. After he understood this message about Jesus, he believed and renounced his allegiance to the troubling spirit.

But a new problem confronted Gabiso and his family, for their neighbors and extended family began to mock them. They were censured for not wholeheartedly participating in such time-honored practices as funerals, circumcision rites, and offering of sacrifices to appease the ancestor spirits. During a period of about two years the Gabiso family was ostracized and maligned. But during this time they were not afflicted with any sickness or death. On the other hand, those who despised the *amanyoch* suffered internal strife, sickness, and death. Through this experience, others in the community began asking the visiting evangelist, Shonga, and the recent convert, Gabiso, about the meaning of their beliefs in Jesus. Through this manner of open discussion, many others became *amanyoch* in the Hida district.[79]

Wolaitta Evangelists in Sidama

Shonga Sadébo, from the Oforé district, was sent to Sidama in 1947 by the Wolaitta *mahibär*. He was told his monthly stipend would be 10.00 EB. He was an itinerant preacher and made his initial impact in the Aläta

79. KHC, *"Bäwängél Amanyoch Andinät,"* 60–61.

district (see map 7.2). Shonga, a gifted communicator, addressed the Sidama who were disturbed by the *shaṭana* spirits with a simple but powerful message. "Believe in Jesus," he said, "He has conquered death and the *shaṭana* spirits. Repent of your past sins and leave off your loyalty to the spirits and the worship of your false gods. Pray to *Mägano* who is able to help you. Believe in Jesus."[80]

In 1949, through the effective preaching of Shonga, *ṣälot bétoch* were opened at Hida, Anole, and Gunde in the Ilmäté district. The first baptism of the Sidama *amanyoch* after the Italian occupation was conducted at Hida in July 1950.[81]

Shonga then travelled east to the Gaṭa district to preach.[82] Because there was little response in the Gaṭa district at this initial evangelistic attempt, no *amanyoch* were baptized nor was a *ṣälot bét* established.

After the Hida baptism in July 1950, the government officials attempted to intimidate the Sidama *amanyoch*. Thirteen were imprisoned in Yirga Aläm, the provincial center. Shonga escaped arrest, subsequently making his way to Addis Ababa, where he presented the Sidama *amanyoch* case to government authorities.[83] Shonga was aware of the April 1945 visit of Emperor Haile Sellassie to Soddo and the release from prison of two women *amanyoch*.[84] After some weeks, Shonga returned and presented an official letter from Addis Ababa to the Yirga Aläm authorities, which stated

80. Ibid., 61.

81. Mamo Bälätä, "*YäSidama Qalä Hiywät*," 2, makes mention of 195 baptized in the Gidabo River near Hida. *Ato* Mamo's number of those baptized is rather high.

82. Shonga was accompanied by Gabiso Doyamo.

83. Atara Gämädä, personal information to EPB, November 1988. The Gédéo *amanyoch* were granted official permission to teach literacy by the Ministry of Education in 1951. See also Mahé Choramo, "Philip," 1, for the account of an attempt by evangelist Mahé Choramo and *Ato* Alämu to get similar permission from officialdom in Addis Ababa in 1950. Emmanuel Abraham recalls that in 1947 there was mounting opposition by the Ethiopian Orthodox Church against his serving as Director General of the Ethiopia Ministry of Education. In 1947 he was relieved of this important post after serving only three years. "My being non-Orthodox was one of the main reasons for accusation." *Reminiscences of My Life*, 64.

84. Laurie Davison states that when Haile Sellassie visited Soddo, Wolaitta, in 1945, "He took the opportunity of making a public statement to all of the hundreds of people gathered around [in Soddo] to the effect the there was now to be religious freedom throughout his land." Letter to Raymond Davis, May 1, 1961. The phrase "*Agarachin yägara inje, haymanotachin yägil*" ("Religion is of a private matter but anything to do with the country is of public concern") is said to have been coined by Haile Sellassie at Soddo. On September 22, 1945, this saying of Haile Sellassie's was recorded in *The Ethiopian Herald*.

that there was religious freedom in the country and that the *amanyoch* could meet in their *ṣälot bétoch* to worship as well as to learn to read and write. This news alarmed the leaders of traditional religion as well the Orthodox clergy. Because there were attempts made to harm him, Shonga returned temporarily to his home area in Oforé, Wolaitta. Markina Mäja, who was hired by the Norwegian Lutheran Mission as a school teacher in 1950, said of Shonga, "He was a gifted evangelist and did a wonderful work in Sidama."[85] In 1953 Shonga accepted an invitation to assist the Norwegian Lutheran Mission in their Sidama evangelism.[86]

In 1951, together with Sorsa Sumamo, Shonga assisted in establishing the Arfé and Anolä *ṣälot bétoch* in Yanasse.

Sorsa Sumamo was born in Wolaitta *awraja,* Duguna district, in 1925. His father's clan honored the *Kitosa* spirit, and his mother and three other wives of his father worshipped *Mariam* and the clan spirits *Awlijano, Awlachäw, Hazulo,* and *Bajo.*

Sorsa's stepmother functioned as a *ṭänqway.* Her clan spirit was *Awlachäw,* through whom she made demands upon Sorsa's father, neighbors, and clients, saying, "Unless you bring me a certain number of heifers to feed *Awlachäw,* I will cause your death."[87] In this manner she caused fear in the home and throughout the neighborhood and district. Sorsa's family worshipped the spirit of his father's clan, *Kitosa,* whom they believed was the powerful sky god. At the annual *Mäsqäl* celebration, the family would offer *Kitosa* special offerings.

About 1936 Sorsa's stepmother developed an ulcer on her leg and went for treatment to the SIM clinic located at Otona. It was rumored in the Duguna district that the *färänjoch* had "powerful medicine." While receiving treatment for her ulcer at the clinic, she heard the gospel preached both by the SIM missionaries and clinic evangelists.

85. Markina Mäja, personal information to EPB, April 9, 1991. Delmar Stevens acknowledges that Shonga was a determined and forceful character, as evidenced by his confronting Ohman for withholding Shonga's monthly Wolaitta stipend. The matter was eventually settled in an Addis Ababa court. Delmar Stevens, letter to EPB, June 1990.

86. When the Norwegian Lutheran Mission arrived in Ethiopia in 1948 they cooperated with the SIM in recruiting evangelists from Kambatta, Hadiya, and Wolaitta *mahibäroch.* See Bakke, *Christian Ministry,* 171, where reference is made to Markina Mäja's ordination by the Lutherans in 1955. See also Markina Meja, *Unbroken Covenant,* 43–50, for his account of Kambatta/Hadiya and Wolaitta evangelists working for the Norwegian Lutheran Mission from 1950 to 1960, and Cotterell, *Born at Midnight,* 136–37.

87. Sorsa Sumamo, personal interview with EPB, April 30, 1987.

When she returned home, the neighbor ladies came over for news about the *färänjoch* at Otona and to see if her ulcer was on the mend. It was a cold morning, so Sorsa, a lad of about eleven, was warming himself beside the fire. He heard his stepmother relate the story of Jesus. She told of how Jesus had been born of the virgin Mary and, after he had reached manhood, died on a cross for the sins of all people of the world. She told how his hands and feet were pierced through with big nails when he was nailed to the cross. Sorsa heard his stepmother describe how a soldier's spear pierced Jesus's side, causing blood and water to pour out. This story penetrated the mind of young Sorsa. In his desire to hear more he searched out an evangelist who had recently come to the Duguna district. Several months later Sorsa believed and invited the evangelist to his home to explain this wonderful news of Jesus to his family. His entire family eventually believed in Jesus.

Around 1938 or 1939 Sorsa was taught to read and write by the son of the same evangelist who had told them about Jesus. When the Otona Bible School was opened on April 1, 1947, Sorsa was able to attend.[88] He served as an evangelist in the Duguna district from 1947 to 1950 then unofficially joined the Wolaitta evangelists in Arsi for one year. Because he was unsuccessful in gaining any converts among the Arsi people, he returned to Wolaitta and was assigned to the Yanasse area of Sidama in January 1951.

When Sorsa began his ministry in Yanasse in 1951 there was very little response to the message he preached. In 1953, just when a small nucleus of *amanyoch* was forming, the son of the district administrator falsely accused evangelist Sorsa and some of the recent *amanyoch,* saying, "These people are teaching that farmers are not to plow their fields. They are commanding their *amanyoch* not to pasture their animals with the non-*amanyoch*, and are forbidding traders to go about their trading."[89] Evangelist Sorsa and the *amanyoch* were judged guilty and imprisoned in the Läku *wäräda* prison in Yanasse district. While they were in the Läku prison, the other prisoners instigated a prison riot, in which Sorsa and his *amanyoch* friends were badly bruised and mutilated. All the prisoners were then put into iron stocks and their clothes taken from them, except their undershorts and a thin cloak. After nine days they were summoned to the provincial center, Yirga Aläm, for judgment. When asked by the judge to

88. Walter and Marcella Ohman, letter to prayer partners, August 18, 1947, state that seventy-nine students enrolled for the three-month Bible school.

89. Sorsa Sumamo, personal interview with EPB, April 30, 1987.

7.4 *Evangelist Sorsa Sumamo, long-term evangelist in Sidama, chatting with Sidama Bible School teacher Alemu Dämboyé (Lila W. Balisky, 2002)*

explain the reason for their arrest and imprisonment, Sorsa and his friends replied that they had done nothing against the laws of the land except preach the gospel and teach some of the Sidama the rudiments of reading and writing. Because the judge doubted that Sorsa was literate himself, he handed Sorsa a Bible and asked him to read a certain text in Amharic. This Sorsa did fluently. He was then asked where he learned to read and write.[90] Sorsa answered that he had studied both at the Soddo Bible School in Wolaitta and at the Aläta Wändo Bible School.[91] The judge, holding up a gramophone player, asked, "And what is this?" Sorsa replied, "A machine that tells Gospel stories." He was told to turn it on so all in the court could hear. Sorsa hand-cranked the gramophone as it played the account of Jesus's trial and how Barabbas was set free but Jesus was crucified. Those in the court began saying among themselves, "This is true, this is true." The chief judge pronounced Sorsa and the Sidama *amanyoch* innocent and signed their release papers. Sorsa and the *amanyoch* returned to their homes in the Yanasse district, where Sorsa resumed his preaching at Afarara.

In 1960 Sorsa was imprisoned again with evangelist Éqaso Eybéro. There were several charges against them. They were accused of coming

90. It was unusual for a non-Amhara to be literate prior to 1945. Emmanuel Abraham indicates that when he was responsible for the Ministry of Education, many government schools were built in the provinces, beginning in 1946. It was "young people who flocked to the schools in large numbers." *Reminiscences of My Life*, 63.

91. Sorsa Sumamo and other Wolaitta evangelists were offered rainy season Bible courses at the SIM station at Aläta Wändo in 1955 and 1956. Sorsa was enrolled in the Aläta Wändo Bible School from 1969 to 1971.

as spies from a different country, Wolaitta, and disturbing the peace. Furthermore, they were charged for teaching the Sidama people that the *tabot* found in each Ethiopian Orthodox church was nothing but a piece of wood. Lastly, they were accused of giving away Ethiopian secrets to the mission *färänjoch*, whose chief purpose for entering Ethiopia was to possess the land just as the Italians had. It was rumored that the *färänjoch* had a secret agenda to evict the Amhara people from the South.[92] With these charges against them, the evangelists were sentenced to nine months and nine days.

While they were serving their prison sentence in the provincial center of Yirga Aläm, a strong wind blew off the roof. Many prisoners were crushed under the fallen timbers and some died. None of the Christians were harmed, however, and they restrained other prisoners from escaping. Through this experience many prisoners believed and an *amanyoch* community was established in the prison.

By 1959 the Sidama *mahibär* had grown to eighty-eight *sälot bétoch* with effective leaders in place. In partnership with the SIM missionaries at Aläta Wändo, eight district elementary schools were now functioning.[93] Because of the maturity and stability of the Sidama *amanyoch,* the Wolaitta *mahibär* decided to redeploy their evangelists elsewhere. Two evangelists, Sorsa Sumamo and Alaro Gutolo, decided to remain in the Yanasse district as pastor/evangelists. In so doing, they both recognized that their monthly stipend of 15.00 birr from Wolaitta would terminate and that they would forfeit passing on their Wolaitta heritage and culture to their own children.

Aldabo Anshébo was born in the Damot Wédé district in 1930. He first went to Kullo Konta as an evangelist in 1951, together with six other Wolaitta evangelists. He was recalled and sent to Yanasse in 1952. From 1952 to 1953 the Wolaitta *mahibär* attempted to send some ninety supported evangelists to various unreached peoples of southern Ethiopia.

---

92. The Michele uprising of the Gédéo against the Amhara had just occurred some sixty kilometers to the south. For an account of this peasant uprising against the Amhara and the SIM implications, see McClellan, "Reaction to Ethiopian Expansionism." Emmanuel Abraham, a retired official of the EECMY, presents the Orthodox clergy perspective: "The Church came to the firm conviction that, in the interests of self-preservation, there was no alternative to the policy of denying access to Ethiopia of any kind of Christian doctrine which is contrary to her own beliefs and doctrine. It thus became impossible for her to look with favour at any kind of Christian organization." *Reminiscences of My Life,* 250.

93. Harry Atkins, personal information to EPB, April 15, 1992.

Leader of the Wolaitta *mahibär* Dana Mäja had a keen interest in the spiritual needs of the Sidama region and so directed evangelists to that area.[94]

When Aldabo arrived in the Yanasse area in 1952 he found the women wearing skins of animals made very supple by frequent application of butter. This garment was very durable and made it convenient to fix a baby on the mother's back under the folds of leather. The men wore a heavy cotton blanket, a *buluko*, thrown over their shoulders.

In the Olka sub-district of Yanasse, the *wuqabé* of the local residents was *Wäshibo*, to whom they would dance and beat their drums at night. When Aldabo and other evangelists began preaching in Afarara, the Sidama intensified their worship to the *Wäshibo bayra* spirit.

Evangelist Aldabo discovered that an effective place to communicate the gospel in Yanasse was at funerals. He and his colleagues would find hundreds of mourners gathered in one large open area, wailing and performing ritual dances. After getting the attention of the mourners, the evangelist Aldabo would preach in Amharic, with Bible in hand and a local Sidama person as interpreter. After the mourning period was over, there would be those who indicated that they wanted to hear more from the evangelists. It was in this manner that *amanyoch* were added to the Yanasse *mahibär*. Aldabo recalls that there were Kambatta evangelists assisting the Wolaitta in the Sidama outreach, as well other Wolaitta evangelists hired by the Norwegian Lutheran Mission.[95]

During the evangelists' time in Sidama, the SIM missionaries conducted various kinds of seminars for them at Aläta Wändo. These were initiated during the time of Delmar Stevens (1946–1952) and continued while George Middleton was at Aläta Wändo (1953–1958). George Middleton assisted the evangelists by transporting them in his small truck from Aläta Wändo to Yanasse. Some evangelists who studied with Aldabo were Sadébo Gundé, Sawl Salgédo, Taso Hébäna, Fanta Iltamo, Sorsa Sumamo, Toro Gadimo, and Sidama evangelist Gabiso Doyamo.

Aldabo remained in Sidama until 1959, at which time he returned to his home district of Damot Wédé and became a pastor of a local *sälot bét* and was elected to serve on the Wolaitta *tärapéza*.

94. Markina Mäja, personal interview with EPB, March 16, 1991. Dana Mäja was inclined to send Wolaitta evangelists to Sidama because of his son Markina's involvement in Sidama evangelism.

95. Confirmed by Markina Meja, *Unbroken Covenant*, 51. Markina Mäja played a significant role in the establishment of the EECMY in Sidama from 1948 to 1957. Ibid., 14–28. See also Bakke, *Christian Ministry*, 171.

The Sidama *mahibär* leaders recognize the following Wolaitta evangelists as performing a significant role in Sidama: Alaro Gutolo, Aldabo Anshébo, Ayälä Toru, Éqaso Eybéro, Fanta Iltamo, Sorsa Sumamo, Shonga Sadébo, Sadébo Gundé, Ṯaso Hébäna, Toro Gadimo, Täntu Mandoyé. There were also ten other evangelists who had secondary roles in Sidama.[96]

In 1975 the literacy of Sidama, with a population of 1.5 million, was around 20 percent—one of the highest in southern Ethiopia. The New Testament was translated into the Sidama language in 1985.[97]

An Assessment of the Wolaitta Evangelists in Sidama

One of the pioneer SIM evangelists to southern Ethiopia, Alf Roke, after nurturing the Sidama *amanyoch*, stated in 1938:

> Our object was to teach the Gospel principles and precepts and let the native church work these out in their own experience and according to the dictates of a conscience quickened by the Word of God.[98]

The Wolaitta evangelists to Sidama did teach and preach the gospel principles according to the word of God. When they arrived in Sidama in 1947, there were only a few pre-Italian *amanyoch* still alive. The Wolaitta evangelists to Sidama, such as Shonga, Tanga, and Täntu, provided a new biblical impetus for the Sidama *amanyoch*. Their preaching found a response chiefly among the primal religionists. They taught the new *amanyoch*, and when there was an evident change in their behavior and firm allegiance to Jesus Christ, the evangelists baptized them. These *amanyoch* were then incorporated into newly formed *ṣälot bétoch*, where the Sidama were appointed to take leadership.

The Wolaitta evangelists to Sidama were effective in several ways. First, they quickly learned the Sidama language and culture and engaged in intense dialogue with the primal religionists. The post-Italian SIM missionaries were at a disadvantage compared with their pre-Italian SIM forbears. They were limited to the national language of Ethiopia—Amharic. And unlike Roke and Cain, few, if any, of the post-war missionaries knew much about the Sidama primal belief systems.[99] Second, the fifteen or

96. Aklilu Lalégo, personal information to EPB, December 25, 1991.

97. Mary Breeze, letter and SIL information to EPB, March 15, 1996.

98. Roke, *Indigenous Church in Action*, 31.

99. It appears from their writing that both Roke and Cain understood the Sidama religious worldview. See Roke, *An Indigenous Church in Action*, 37–50.

more Wolaitta evangelists effectively trekked throughout the Sidama region, preaching in marketplaces and at funerals. The message of the gospel was heard throughout the region, and the Sidama responded. And third, the majority of the Wolaitta evangelists withdrew at an appropriate time— after the Aläta Wändo Bible School was functioning. Sidama leaders were given an opportunity to be trained to serve their own congregations.[100]

But there were new factors that the evangelists faced in Sidama. First, they discovered that several of their compatriots were employed by the Norwegian Lutheran Mission at a higher stipend than they were receiving. Then there was the fact that eventually two competing *mahibäroch* were being developed; one relating to Wolaitta and the SIM and the other relating to the Norwegian Lutheran Mission. The evangelists attempted to honor comity agreements made by the two mission organizations, but the Sidama *amanyoch* from both *mahibäroch* felt no obligation to follow these manmade regulations. In some cases the evangelists acted as peace-makers between the two Sidama *amanyoch* communities, who sometimes quarreled with one another. And at times the Wolaitta evangelists themselves felt circumscribed by the comity agreement of the two expatriate mission groups. But the Sidama *amanyoch* believed that their commission from Christ was not limited geographically. With freedom to preach to all, they took the opportunity to embody Roke's injunction that "the root, the stem and fruit must all be native if we are to have truly indigenous churches."[101]

Burji/Koyra

Background

When Glen Cain and Albert Brant arrived in Burji to finalize the land contract[102] for the future SIM station in November 1948, they were, "disappointed to find it such a small village with so few people."[103] In 1899 the Burji population[104] was estimated around 200,000, but it was depopulated in the 1920s when slave-raiding by northern Ethiopians became a lucra-

100. From 1969 to 1975 the attendance at the Aläta Wändo Bible School averaged 250 *mahibär* and *şälot bét* leaders annually. The author taught in this Bible school from 1969 to 1971.

101. Roke, *Indigenous Church in Action*, 54.

102. The Ethiopian Ministry of Education and the Ministry of Health granted SIM permission to establish an elementary school and clinic at Burji on April 5, 1947. Burji File, SIM Archives.

103. Brant, *In the Wake of Martyrs*, 85.

104. Vannutelli's 1899 estimate, as found in Cerulli, *Peoples of Southwest Ethiopia*, 53.

tive substitute for cash previously obtained by the sale of ivory.[105] By 1950 there were about 30,000 Burji residing in Ethiopia and some 8,000 across the border in Kenya. The present Burji population in Ethiopia is estimated at 55,000.[106] The Koyra ethnic group, located in the Amaro mountains, north of the Burji, numbered around 20,000 in 1930 and by 1975 had grown to 65,000.[107]

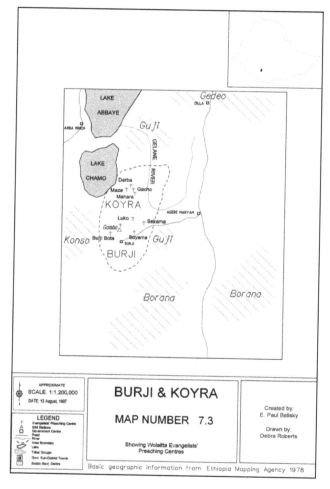

105. See Garretson, "Vicious Cycles," 217, where reference is made to departing Maji governors raiding for slaves and produce. Similar slave raiding was taking place further south among the Burji people.

106. Mary Breeze, letter to EPB, March 15, 1996.

107. Awäqä Amazé, "Silä Koré," estimates the population of the Koyra at about 80,000 in 1991.

Linguistically Burji is placed in the Cushitic family, the Sidama language group, whereas the Koyra is classified as an Omotic language.[108]

According to Koyra oral history,[109] the Koyra forebears arrived in the mountains of Amaro in the fifteenth century during the time of 'Amdé Seyon's expansion into southern Ethiopia and settled in the mountain strongholds of Amaro, displacing the local population of Burji and other residents.[110] Within a generation of this settlement, Orthodox evangelists from Mänz came to Amaro to Christianize these Amhara settlers.[111] It was then that churches such as Mädihin Aläm were built at Gärba. It is estimated that over fifty clans comprise the Koyra, the Wäjuwa clan being found in both Koyra and Wolaitta.[112]

During *Däjazmach* Balcha's governorship of Sidamo province from 1896 to 1928, *näftänyoch* were allowed to settle among the Burji and the Koyra populations.[113] Burdensome taxes and workloads were imposed on the farmers, and they were obliged to perform many duties for the *näftänyoch,* such as carrying timbers to build new residences, plowing, sowing, weeding and harvesting the fields, grinding grain by hand on stones, and carrying some of the produce by hand as far away as the government center at Agär Mariam.[114] The majority of the four hundred näftänyoch remained among the Burji and the Koyra during the Italian occupation and continued to exploit the local population when the SIM missionaries and Wolaitta evangelists arrived in Burji in the 1950s.

108. See Adams, "Tagmemic Analysis of the Wolaitta Language," 28–29; Fleming, "Omotic Overview"; Cotterell, *Born at Midnight*, 108–9.

109. Koyra writer Awäqä Amzayé recommends that the name Koyra, which refers to only one district, be changed to Koré, which he thinks is more representative. The name change from Amaro to Koyra is presently under debate by the Koyra.

110. The settlement of northerners in Koyra would have been similar to that which took place among the Haräri, Argobba, and Gafat, referred to by Taddesse Tamrat, *Church and State*, 41.

111. Haberland, "Influence of the Christian Ethiopian Empire," 237–38, makes mention of Amaro-Koyra claiming Amhara or Tigrai descent as well as a long history of Orthodox Christianity.

112. Wolaitta *mahibär* leader, Dana Mäja, is from the Koyra Wäjuwa clan. He recalls that his grandfather migrated from Koyra to Wolaitta in pre-Menilek times.

113. See Tsehai Berhane, "Life and Career of *Däjazmach* Balcha Aba Näfso," 180–85.

114. Awäqä Amazé, *"Silä Koré,"* 19–20.

SIM Arrival in Burji

On April 5, 1950, Alex and Theresia Fellows and Marge Langford arrived at Gämbo (Burji area) with building equipment and supplies loaded on eighteen camels. While Alex Fellows proceeded with the erection of the mission residences, school, and clinic, the women began preaching to their nearby neighbors.[115] The missionaries soon realized that by themselves they were ineffective in their attempts at evangelism. Even though the missionaries had been enrolled at the Amharic language school at Sire for several months, they found communicating in Amharic to the Burji through an interpreter less than ideal. In June they contacted Wolaitta requesting evangelists.[116] During the next six months, before the evangelists arrived, the missionaries continued their visitation and preaching in and around the station of Gämbo and northwest into the Amaro mountains to the Koyra population residing at Suluko and Luko. This itinerating was significant for Alex Fellows, in that he discovered the Koyra people belonged to a different language group from that of the Burji. He determined that the Gämbo center must be able to reach both the Burji and the Koyra people.[117]

Arrival of the Wolaitta Evangelists

Gänébo Gaga and Kusa Gatiso arrived in Burji on January 4, 1951, after a ten day trek overland from Wolaitta.[118] As was customary for the evangelists on their first visit to a new area, they left their wives and children in Wolaitta and came with only their Bibles, a shawl, and their walking sticks. Marge Langford recalls their arrival "as a red letter day. We had our first communion service, prayer together, etc., and tears of joy were shed."[119] There was no housing available for the two evangelists at the SIM Gämbo center so they found lodging with Burji neighbors. Famine had ravished the land in 1950. When evangelists Gänébo Gaga and Kusa Gatiso went on preaching expeditions, they carried corn with them, cook-

---

115. Marge Langford, letter to EPB, June 20, 1991.

116. Marge Langford, letter to EPB, June 20, 1991.

117. Alex and Theresia Fellows, personal information to EPB, April 2, 1997.

118. In 1951 bus service from Shashämänä to Dilla was limited and transport trucks from Shashämänä to Agär Mariam were infrequent.

119. Marge Langford, letter to EPB, June 20, 1991.

ing it at the place they were staying. They were careful not to impose on the local population.[120]

The first Burji convert was Säqo.[121] The evangelists continued to travel and preach throughout the Burji district. Kusa began spending more time among the highland Koyra because he discovered that the Koyra language was Omotic and nearly comprehensible by a Wolaitta speaker. By June 1951 he was sufficiently conversant to preach in the Koyra language. The Koyra gladly heard him tell the Jesus story. With passion and tears Kusa urged the listeners to repent from their misdirected worship and sinful ways and believe in Jesus, who said he was the way to God.[122] While preaching publicly near the Koyra administrative centre of Kéli, Kusa was arrested and imprisoned. Alex Fellows travelled two days from Gämbo by mule to present the Kéli officials an Addis Ababa Ministry of Education letter stating that SIM was authorized to teach literacy throughout the Koyra and Burji districts. On the basis of that letter, Kusa was released.

By October 1951 the Orthodox clergy in Burji, Därba, and Kéli had become aggressive in their own evangelistic outreach and baptized sixty Burji converts,[123] fixing the *matäb* around the neck of each new adherent.[124] To provide an incentive for non-Orthodox Burji residents to be baptized, a one birr tax was imposed upon each non-conforming household. Those who refused to pay were imprisoned. And one year later, on October 7, 1952, the Burji chief government official restricted the missionaries to preaching only on the Gämbo station.[125] This restriction applied only to the expatriates who were residing at the Gämbo center, not to the evangelists who had built little houses for themselves in the districts of Burji and Koyra. By March 1952, the evangelists were increased to four: Ganébo Gaga, Albazo Adaré, Mäja Adélo, and Indrias Gobäna, Ganébo's son-in-law. After one year of preaching in Burji/Koyra, Kusa Gatiso returned to Wolaitta because his wife refused to join him.[126]

120. Ibid.

121. Burji Log Book, January 21, 1951.

122. Marge Langford relates that Kusa was known as "the preacher who wept." Letter to EPB, June 20, 1991.

123. Burji Log Book, October 23, 1951.

124. Burji Durro recalls that his family was marched up to the Orthodox church at Shecha for baptism and the *matäb* tied around each of their necks. Personal information to EPB, January 27, 1997.

125. Burji Log Book, October 7, 1952.

126. Ibid., March 29, 1952. The Wolaitta *mahibär* discouraged evangelists from serving on a permanent basis in distant places without their wives.

On May 12, 1952, a Bible school was launched at the SIM station at Gämbo. Twenty-eight Burji and Koyra young men were enrolled, with the missionaries doing most of the teaching. It was the conviction of both the expatriate and Ethiopian evangelists that the future of the Burji and Koyra *amanyoch* was well-taught leaders who would eventually take responsibility for evangelism, discipline, and nurture.

Twelve *amanyoch* were baptized in Burji on March 1, 1953. They were Masha Bori, his son Boko, Challi, Mamo, Irbo, Bogalä, Guyo, Shägadi, Sodi, Aiymi, Jarso, and Guzu.[127] Dana Mäja and *Ato* Täntu, Wolaitta elders, travelled by mule from Soddo to Burji by way of Arba Minch to conduct the baptism. *Ato* Giorgis, a Koyra by birth but then residing in Lanṭé, Gämo, escorted the two Wolaitta elders to Burji to officiate at the baptism.[128] The baptismal pool was a large rocky basin filled by a stream. The local Burji population believed this area to be inhabited by dreadful spirits. Several days after the baptism, some of onlookers asked nurse Marge Langford, "Are they still alive? Don't you know that the place where those *amanyoch* were dipped is where certain spirits, greatly feared by the Burji, dwell?" Marge replied, "That shows that our God is more powerful."[129]

Buja, residing in the village of Därba, was the first convert among the Koyra. After the March 1953 baptism, Giorgis, the Gämo guide, explained the message of Jesus and Buja believed. Through his testimony, ten of his relatives and friends in Därba and Manana were converted. When Giorgis returned some weeks later from Gämo, he was pleased to discover that the *amanyoch* in Därba and in the surrounding vicinity were increasing. He sent to Burji for help. Evangelists Mäja Adélo, Anjulo Gaga, and Matéwos Shunbulo assisted in establishing the Maze, Gacho, and Manana *sälot bétoch*.[130]

By April 1954 there were eight Wolaitta evangelists serving in the Burji/Koyra districts. These were Ganébo Gaga, Wana Dägalo, Albazo Adaré, Indriyas Gobäna, Matéwos Shunbulo, Anjulo Gaga, Mäja Adélo, Dedana Däkesa, and Giorgis from Gämo.[131] Converts were increasing and

127. Ibid., March 1, 1953.

128. Cotterell, *Born at Midnight*, 137. Wolaitta elders did not always officiate at the first baptism in a new area. In Gämo, Gofa, Aari, and Sidama, the evangelists officiated at the first baptism.

129. Marge Langford, letter to EPB, June 20, 1991.

130. Cotterell, *Born at Midnight*, 138.

131. Burji Log Book, April 11, 1954. It appears that the Wolaitta evangelists and SIM missionaries at Burji were disappointed with evangelist Giorgis's compromising

the baptisms were gaining in frequency. On November 18, 1954, the third baptism in Burji/Koyra was conducted when fifteen were baptized at Därba. Tadässa and Wobala were selected by the group to serve as the elders of the newly established *ṣälot bét*.[132] One year later, another nineteen were baptized at Därba.

There are reports that various miracles took place among the Burji and Koyra through the prayers and preaching of the evangelists. At the Maze *ṣälot bét* near Därba, a young lad, unable to talk, was brought to evangelist Mäja. The parents were adherents of traditional religion. Mäja's advice to them was, "Believe in Christ, put away your false gods and false practices. Let Christ into your hearts and let him perform a miracle for your child."[133] Soon after this their son was able to talk. Because of this miracle, sixteen others became *amanyoch*.

Hardships Endured by the Evangelists and Amanyoch

Kusa Gatiso was the first Wolaitta evangelist in the Burji/Koyra region to be incarcerated in the Kéli prison in 1951. Because there were no *amanyoch* in the Koyra district at that time, no one assisted him with his daily food provisions. While in prison he began weaving mats from palm branches and selling them in the local Kéli market in order to buy daily food.[134]

The intensity of persecution from the Orthodox Church increased after the 1953 baptism at Burji. When Buja and the ten converts around Därba began to explain their faith to others, the clergy in the Därba Mädihin Aläm Church brought charges against evangelists Mäja, Anjulo, and Matéwos. Two of the evangelists were imprisoned in Kéli and were maltreated by the prison officials. In an attempt to make them deny their faith, the evangelists were hung by their feet from the rafters. Burning pepper was placed below their faces which caused sharp irritation to their eyes and lungs.[135] In April 1955 another wave of persecution was instigated at Därba. The local Orthodox clergy had six of the *amanyoch*, including evangelist Albazo Adaré, imprisoned for three months in the Kéli prison. The charge against the *amanyoch* was that they had constructed a *ṣälot bét*

---

relationship with Därba government officials. See Lloyd Stinson and Jarel Nagel, letter to Ed Ratzliff, March 23, 1955.

132. Burji Log Book, November 18, 1954.

133. As reported to Yosef Menna, "*Yätinsaéw Näṣibiraq,*" 220.

134. Alex and Theresia Fellows, personal information to EPB, April 2, 1997.

135. Ibid.

on another person's land without government permission. Again the missionaries had to make three trips to Kéli and one to Yirga Aläm to obtain release papers for the *amanyoch*. The Burji *amanyoch* assisted the Därba prisoners by sending them 83 shillings (US$41) for their upkeep.[136] The prison ordeal was very trying for Albazo, who eventually signed a statement before the prison officials that he would not preach again in the Koyra district. He was released and soon after returned to Wolaitta with his family. It was during this time that *Qés* Wäldé Samayat of the Orthodox clergy in Därba joined the *amanyoch* with a confession of faith. Both he and his wife ably endured bitter resentment from their former colleagues within the Därba Orthodox community. But there were also others from the Orthodox establishment who were converting. Pawlos Dästa, a former monk at the Därba Church, converted in 1955 and was subsequently hired to teach in the SIM elementary school at Burji.[137]

In addition to these hardships, influential traditional religious functionaries made plans to harass the *amanyoch* who had formerly been their clients. As was customary in that area, the *qalichas* could demand payment for their services of providing rain or warding off a pestilence. A special meeting was called by the leaders of the traditional religion. They demanded payment from each household. Because the *amanyoch* were unwilling to make payment, their neighbors decided to punish them. Their goods were to be plundered, their grinding stones to be broken, and no one was to give them coals for lighting fires. When the *amanyoch* heard this they were greatly distressed and spent the night praying. That very night, a sharp disagreement arose between the various clans. They began to break each others' grinding stones and granaries, spill all the grain, plunder, and attempt to destroy each others' houses.[138]

A local Burji official attempted to stop the assembling together of the new *amanyoch*. He arrested *Ato* Burji Durra, tied him to a tree overnight, and ordered him to be beaten for three days. After this he was brought before the judge and asked what the *amanyoch* do in their *ṣälot bétoch* each Sunday. *Ato* Burji replied that they worship God by singing, praying, learning the Bible, and literacy. The judge told him that he could be released if he would sign that he and all the believers would not meet again in their *ṣälot bétoch* and would pay a fine of 10.00 EB. Burji refused

136. Burji Log Book, April 1955.
137. Burji Log Book, October 1955.
138. Burji Durra, personal information to EPB, January 16, 1997.

and asked for an appeal to the higher court. In the Kéli *awraja* court, he explained to the judge why he was accused. The judge released him and thanked him for teaching the citizenry of Ethiopia how to read and write. The judge said that the Ethiopian government should remunerate him and his co-workers for the good work they were doing.[139]

Hunger was the common lot of the evangelists in Burji. The Ganébo Gaga and Wana Dägalo families suffered from lack of daily provisions.[140] The evangelists' 5.00 birr monthly stipend was inadequate so the missionaries assisted the evangelists with produce from their gardens and in other material ways.[141]

The evangelists experienced other hardships of daily life. The language and culture were strange to them. At the outset of their ministry they were dependent on Burji translators.[142] Often they endured sickness. When the Mäja Adélo family made the ten-day journey by mule from Soddo to Burji in 1952, one of their children became ill with a fever. The family had to decide whether to return for medical help to the Soddo Hospital or continue their journey. Before they reached Dilla, the child succumbed and was buried by his parents along the trail.[143]

The evangelists' wives faced deprivation and loneliness in the Burji/Koyra districts. Most of the wives knew no Amharic and had difficulty learning the Burji language. Some of them found daily life in Burji very trying. When they returned to Wolaitta for the annual spiritual life conference in January, some remained. In 1952 Ganébo brought his own wife, Matafai, and children to Burji. Marge Langford commented about Matafai, "a wonderful woman who did a lot for the [Burji] women. These wives must never be forgotten."[144]

Wolaitta Evangelists in Burji/Koyra—Some Concluding Observations

In 1951 a new era was about to open up for the Burji and Koyra in southern Ethiopia. They had suffered for many decades under the heavy yoke of

139. KHC, *"Bäwängél Amanyoch Andinät,"* 84.

140. Marge Langford, letter to EPB, June 20, 1991.

141. Alex and Theresia Fellows, personal information to EPB, April 2, 1997.

142. Burji Durro was Ganébo's main translator within the Burji district from 1952 to 1957. Burji Durro, personal interview with EPB, January 27, 1997.

143. Mäja Adélo, transcribed tape, March 15, 1988 (EPB Collection). See also Yosef Menna, *"Yätinsaéw Näsibiraq,"* 219.

144. Marge Langford, letter to EPB, June 20, 1991.

northern oppression. Menilek II had allowed his soldiers to settle among the local population. *Däjazmach* Balcha, residing in Agärä Sälam, had used the *näftänyoch* to collect taxes for him, much of which was sent off again to Addis Ababa. In post-occupation Ethiopia, the burden of taxes and the impositions made by the Orthodox clergy were stimulus to the Burji and Koyra population to change their religious loyalties. Their former gods had ceased to work for them.

From 1951 to 1960, there were eighteen Wolaitta evangelists who served for different lengths of time in the Burji and Koyra districts. The Burji *amanyoch* look back in appreciation on the sacrificial service of these evangelists and their families. *Ato* Burji Durro identified Ganébo Gaga as the "father of the Burji *amanyoch*."[145] Ganébo has been described as a "preacher with fire." The Burji people loved him because of his passion and compassion. He was appreciated by the Burji because of his identification with them when he bought land and settled his family, began to plough his fields just like one of them, and became involved in the life cycles of their community. When he eventually terminated his ministry in Burji, he is remembered for his effort to say his farewells to each local *sälot bét* prior to leaving with his family in 1962.[146] "He gave each *sälot bét* his blessing, wept over the shoulders of the *amanyoch*, and then returned to Wolaitta."[147]

The Wolaitta evangelists lived very much under the aegis of SIM and were invited to evangelize in partnership with SIM in Burji/Koyra. Under certain government administrators, the evangelists operated under the threat of incarceration in local prisons. When the evangelists were imprisoned, the SIM missionaries, having the backing of higher officials at the provincial and national level for their educational and medical activities, often were able to obtain letters of permission from higher officials that would reverse the decisions of the lesser *wäräda* officials.

The ten-year legacy left by the Wolaitta evangelists in Burji and Koyra may be summed up in the following manner: First, they assisted the Burji/Koyra people to discover in Christ a stronger power than their traditional religion offered. Second, they assisted local communities in establishing their own *sälot bétoch* in which they could worship God with dignity and

---

145. Burji Durro, personal interview with EPB, January 27, 1997.

146. John Cumbers, Burji Bible School teacher, confirmed this, letter to EPB, June 17, 1991.

147. Burji Durro, personal interview with EPB, January 27, 1997.

express their own cultural identity. And, third, the evangelists were the forerunners in establishing literacy centers and elementary schools. From these humble educational beginnings, Burji and Koyra parents were given the option of having their children step into modern Ethiopia.

Aari and Maali

Background

In 1954, when Don and Christine Gray and Bill Carter of SIM arrived in Bako, the population of the Aari people was about 55,000.[148] Bako was the administrative center for the Aari, Bänna, Bodi, Bumé, Dime, Érboré, Gäläb, Hammär, Maali, Mursi, Qaro, and Samai tribal groups (see map 7.4). The Aari are sedentary farmers residing in the semi-tropical *wéne däga* at an altitude around 1700 meters. Coffee, corn, barley, wheat, and ensette are grown in abundance because of ample rain.[149]

The territory of Maali is a large valley floor nestled along the Béto River at an altitude of about 1200 meters. In 1954 the Maali population was estimated at about 5,000.[150] They are grain and cotton producers with an abundance of cattle. This study links together the disparate Aari and Maali because the SIM missionaries and the Wolaitta evangelists, from their center in Bako, began preaching to both the Aari and the Maali.

Origins of the Aari and Maali

Oral history relates that Aari forbears migrated from the Sudan many generations ago. Their Nilotic language affirms that the Aari have historical roots in Sudan.[151] The small ethnic tribe of Maali are of Omotic stock. Aari and Maali legend relates that three brothers wandered from a far country and were found by a chieftain, who took them into his residence as adopted sons. The three sons became the forbears of the Aari, the Bänna, and the Maali. As the Bänna and the Maali increased in number they

148. Fargher et al., "New Churches' Movement in Hammer-Bako," 9. According to an estimate by Summer Institute of Linguistics (SIL), the Aari population had increased to 109,000 by 1990. Mary Breeze, letter to EPB, March 1996.

149. See Willmott, *Doors Were Opened*, 99–104, for a descriptive account of a trek from Bulqi to Bako in 1955.

150. An SIL estimate of the Maale population in 1990 was 12,000. Mary Breeze, letter to EPB, March 1996.

151. Affirmed by Aari elders, Dägu Daqilabu et al., *"Käisat Yätänäṯäqä,"* 5.

eventually fought over grazing land. It was the Aari who were called to arbitrate.[152] This legend affirms that the three ethnic groups, Aari, Maali, and Bänna, all have a common lineage because of their former relationship to the chieftain who adopted them. And the legend acknowledges the incompatibility between the Maali and Bänna as well as the fact that the Aari are great mediators and have lived harmoniously with both the Bänna and the Maali to the present.

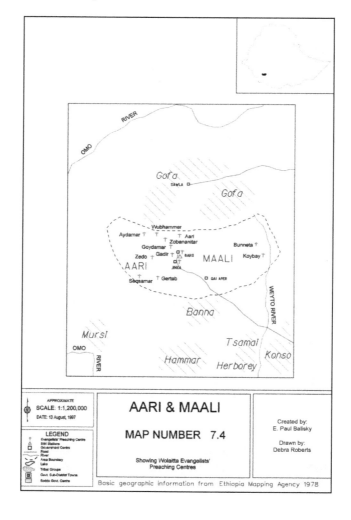

AARI & MAALI

MAP NUMBER 7.4

Showing Wolaitta Evangelists' Preaching Centres

Created by: E. Paul Balisky

Drawn by: Debra Roberts

APPROXIMATE SCALE: 1:1,200,000
DATE: 13 August, 1997

Basic geographic information from Ethiopia Mapping Agency 1978

152. As recorded in Cotterell, *Born at Midnight*, 130–31. See also Tippett, *Peoples of Southwest Ethiopia*, 71–72, regarding a similar myth of origin among the Me'en tribe.

Primal Religious Beliefs of the Aari

The Aari royalty burial custom was to sew the body of their king inside the hide of a recently slain ox. The corpse was hung in a tree for thirty days, after which it was taken down. An undercover raid was then made on a neighboring ethnic group, with the purpose of catching a young man, who was then tied alive to the decaying body of the king. With this activity, the Aari symbolize that they have made provision for the needs of the king in the next life.[153]

The Aari belief in the clan *wuqabé* regulated their social activities. Certain forested areas were said to be the abode of the *wuqabé*, and it was taboo to go near them.[154] The Aari culture has strict prohibitions regarding the activities of menstruating women. When an Aari woman is about to give birth she is placed in a small temporary shelter. Except for a birthing specialist, all others are forbidden to assist her in childbirth. In 1958 Christine Gray wrote to her Canadian family:

> The mother goes into a little hut just prior to the birth of the baby all by herself and none of her relatives come near her. . . . If that type of person [midwife] is not around, no matter how much she calls for help, none of the relatives are allowed to go into the hut. They do not even give the mother proper food.[155]

By 1955 various cultural changes such as education, western medicine, and communication with greater Ethiopia seemed to have influenced the Aari culture. Their traditional religion was no longer functioning as before. The Aari were sacrificing chickens, sheep, and goats to appease the spirits that seemed to be causing sickness, death, and broken relationships. But this did not bring relief. Aari elders recall their neighbors' losing their health and mental equilibrium at that time. Some said that they must go to Bulqi, Gofa, and have the spirit of the ancestors, their *wuqabé*,

---

153. As described by Edna Ratzliff, *Letters*, 284. According to Cotterell's research, mummification of the dead from the royal clans is common among many of the Omo valley ethnic groups. *Born at Midnight*, 132. See also Tippett, *Peoples of Southwest Ethiopia*, 270, where mention is made of the Maji tying the body of the royal dead in a fresh cow hide. Dägu Daqilabu et al., "*Käisat Yätänätäqä*," 15–16, states that when an Aari noble dies, his corpse is wrapped in the skin of an ox.

154. Dägu Daqilabu et al., "*Käisat Yätänätäqä*," 17. The Aari called the forest *doyce*, the abode of their high God, *Bairo*.

155. Fargher et al., "New Churches' Movement in Hammer-Bako," 30. See also Dägu Daqilabu et al., "*Käisat Yätänätäqä*," 7–8.

that was disturbing them "tied by the *färänj*."[156] In 1958 two Aari men, Unsa Shamyé and Baykäda Gaṣa, travelled the two day journey from Bako Gazor in Sedo district to Bulqi. At Bulqi, Dick McLellan introduced them to Wolaitta evangelist Nana Shaga, who taught them for one week about the power of Jesus and introduced them to several Gofa *amanyoch* before they returned to Aari. It was through these two Aari men that the Gospel was to spread throughout the Bako Gazor district.[157]

SIM Missionaries Locate in Bako

On January 18, 1954, Don and Christine Gray and Bill Carter arrived in Bako.[158] They transported their personal and building supplies by three Italian trucks from Addis Ababa to Bulqi. For the remaining five-day trek south to Bako, fifty-two mules and fourteen head-carriers were hired to transport their goods. With much effort, the SIM missionaries were able to erect a clinic, elementary school, and residences. They themselves began an itinerant ministry among the Aari and Maali. There were Wolaitta and Gofa evangelists in the northern section of Aari, but the Grays had little contact with them.

Negative forces were at work attempting to hamper the outreach of the missionaries. Brigadier General Asfaw, Gämo provincial governor based in Chäncha, visited Bako in 1954 and informed the Grays that they were not to go off the mission station to preach or teach. This same restriction, no doubt under pressure from the Orthodox Church clergy, was also imposed upon the SIM stations at Aläta Wändo, Burji, Dilla, and Chäncha.[159]

Aari *amanyoch* leaders Dägu and Täfära recognized the significant contribution of the itinerant medical ministry of Christine Gray in the beginning stages of the gospel outreach in Aari and Maali. Her healing ministry provided an alternative for those who were sick and formerly dependent on the *qalicha*. Through the SIM medical clinic and the medical itineration of the Grays, many heard and accepted the good news, but when they returned to their homes there was no one to teach them, so they

---

156. Dägu Daqilabu, personal information to EPB, February 11, 1992.

157. KHC, "*Bäwängél Amanyoch Andinät*," 142.

158. Fargher et al., "New Churches' Movement in Hammer-Bako," 9.

159. Ibid., 13. Dägu Daqilabu relates that in 1954 the Orthodox Church attempted to convert and baptize the Aari. At that time a scourge of yellow fever swept through Aari, leaving many dead. The Aari interpreted this scourge as the anger of their deities against the Orthodox.

continued to practice their traditional religion.[160] One of the reasons the Wolaitta evangelists were effective with the Aari is that they resided among them. It is to the story of these evangelists that we now turn.

Wolaitta Evangelists in Aari

In May 1957 three Wolaitta evangelists and their wives arrived in Bako to begin their preaching ministry: Ombolé Odiro and his wife, Dukitai, with their three children; Guradé Jägäna, his wife, Dorani, and their two children; and Shanka Boroda and his wife, Halishai.[161] Gofa evangelist Hafta Mar, with his wife and family, also joined the Wolaitta evangelists. But the evangelists had much adjusting to do to a new language and a new culture.[162] To the evangelists, Wolaitta seemed developed and civilized compared to Aari in 1957.[163]

In March 1958 Ed and Edna Ratzliff made a mule trip into Bako from Soddo. They reported:

> The next day the evangelists and their wives came to see us. There are three evangelists from Wolamo and two from Gofa working in the area. Sunday Ed had the joy of preaching to a group of Shanqila.[164] They received the Word but none yet have actually accepted Christ as their Saviour."[165]

Edna commented sympathetically on how difficult it was for the women to live and function in Aari.

Lyda was one of the first places where the Aari began congregating to hear preaching of the good news.[166] Evangelists Guradé and Shanka were

160. Dägu Daqilabu and Täfärä Alles, interview with EPB, February 11, 1992.

161. Halishai is the daughter of evangelist Lolamo Täntu.

162. Aari *amanyoch* leaders *Ato* Dägu and *Ato* Täfärä complimented the Wolaitta evangelists and their families for their ability to learn Aari culture and language, which was unrelated to the family of Omotic languages. Dägu Daqilabu and Täfärä Alles, interview with EPB, February 11, 1992.

163. Fargher et al., "New Churches' Movement in Hammer-Bako," 25.

164. The designation "*shanqila*" was a pejorative word used by Ethiopian highlanders when they referred to black Ethiopians of Sudanese origin.

165. Ratzliff, *Letters*, 284.

166. Mahé Choramo, "Philip," 106–34, describes the evangelists' preaching activity in the northern district of Aari from their base in Gofa. The SIM missionaries and Wolaitta evangelists based in Bako and surrounding areas were not fully aware of this evangelistic initiative from Gofa. Alex and Theresa Fellows, personal interview with EPB, April 2, 1997.

invited by the Lyda community to live among them because of the medical help the Grays were able to administer to a young lad suffering from a spear wound. A local Aari man named Maro gave the evangelists land where they could build their houses and farm on a small scale. The evangelists soon became part of the Lyda community, and a *ṣälot bét* (the first in Aari) was erected next to Maro's thatched-roof house. Soon forty to fifty people were gathering on Sundays to listen to the evangelists preach through an interpreter as well as hear to recordings of Bible stories played on a hand-crank gramophone. In 1957 Shanka preached to a group of men who were ploughing in their fields. His message was that Christ could deliver them from bondage and fear. There was not the immediate response among the Aari that Shanka had experienced among the Gofa, where he had been evangelizing for some five years previously. The evangelists discovered that these initial years among the Aari were years of preparation.

By August of 1957 there were three Gofa evangelists, Hafta Mar, Bushari, and Buzdi, together with their families, commissioned and supported by the Gofa *amanyoch* and assisting the evangelists from Wolaitta and SIM missionaries in Aari.[167] On February 19, 1959, evangelist Ombolé returned the 250 kilometers from Wolaitta to Aari by foot, bringing with him three additional evangelist families. The Sayma and Muné families were invited by the Kuré community to live among them.[168]

Opportunities amid Opposition

In 1959 evangelist Ombolé was arrested by the Bako police and charged with "preaching without a permit."[169] The police also arrested Guradé and Gofa evangelist Bushari, located at Alga, and imprisoned them in the Bako prison. Guradé became very ill with dysentery while in prison. After his recovery, he said, "Bushari and I were able to do more evangelistic work in jail than while we were free."[170] The prison proved to be a meeting place of people from all sections of the Hammer-Bako region. During the three months the evangelists where imprisoned the officials repeatedly offered them release if they would sign a paper stating that they would no longer preach and teach. This the evangelists refused to do.[171]

167. Fargher et al., "New Churches' Movement in Hammer-Bako," 27.

168. Ibid., 34.

169. Ibid., 36.

170. Ibid.

171. Imprisonment was not a new thing for the evangelists. Ombolé Odiro had been

In 1960 persecution continued against the *amanyoch* in Aari. Their crops and *ṣälot bétoch* were burned; *amanyoch* were beaten and imprisoned, and personal property was pilfered. The instigators of this harassment were landlords, descendents of the *näftänyoch* who had settled much of southern Ethiopia at the end of the nineteenth century.

Because Aari was a wealthy coffee producing country, it was attractive for the landlords to live there. Zäläqä Gizaw, residing in the Wuba Hammär district in northern Aari, was one of these landlords who made it very difficult for the evangelists and *amanyoch*. Evangelist Déngo Sana, assigned to the Wuba Hammär district, may have been overly provocative when he told the new *amanyoch* that it was *Bairo*, their high God, who had created all the world and that the land belonged to *Bairo*, not to the landlord. He advised the *amanyoch*, "Don't be slaves of the landlords."[172] As a result, landlord Zäläqa Gizaw retaliated and imprisoned Déngo, Danél Choramo, and two Gofa evangelists, Bango and Käbädä. Zäläqa, known for his cruelty and greed, forced the *amanyoch* chisänyoch to work extra days each week on his personal coffee holdings and, in addition, increased their taxes on their small plots of land.[173] Another landlord, Biyé Godaymär, flogged two evangelists for teaching literacy in the home of *amanyä* Bäradoso Bualäko.[174] Landowner Mäkonän Wärqu stole two sheep from recent Aari convert Unsa.

Evangelist Mahé's Advice to Abaynäh, Aari Convert

In the northern district of Aari, at a place called Baldmär, a small *ṣälot bét* was built for the *amanyoch*. Abaynäh was a recent convert from this *ṣälot bét*, and he asked evangelist Mahé Choramo if he, too, could become an evangelist, for he had been Mahé's interpreter for nearly a year. This was Mahé's advice to him:

> An evangelist must be willing to travel around and tell people about Christ.
> He cannot be a polygamist.[175]
> He must be willing to suffer.

---

imprisoned for one-and-a-half years while serving in Gofa. Personal interview with EPB, December 12, 1995.

172. Mahé Choramo, "Philip," 107.

173. Ibid.

174. KHC, *"Bäwängél Amanyoch Andinät,"* 146.

175. At the time Abaynäh had two wives. Mahé Choramo, "Philip," 115.

He must keep away from politics and teach the way of peace.

The evangelist's business is to teach others, not to meddle in politics, because if he gets involved in politics, the landlord will stir up trouble.

He doesn't get involved in court cases with the landlords.

The evangelist's message must be spread by love not by strife.

The evangelist must not overtly initiate social change in the country. Change will eventually come to the culture through the *amanyoch*.

When an evangelist mixes any other thing with the Gospel he will spoil the truth of the Gospel.

The only way to free people from slavery is to preach the gospel.

Preach only those things that are found in the Bible.

Have no arguments with the landlords or meddle with their business.

Don't get tied up with legal quarrels with landlords.

Preach from the Bible and the landlords will leave you alone.[176]

We have here a succinct statement of how an evangelist should function in a different cultural situation where there is oppression. The evangelists must have faced the temptation to become involved in local litigation procedures. Even if there was no justice in the courts or among the officials, the evangelist must preach and teach. The evangelists were committed to the belief that theirs was a holy calling that must be pursued with purpose and single-mindedness.[177]

Expansion of Evangelistic Activities in Aari and Maali

When Alex and Theresa Fellows arrived in Bako in September 1961, they encouraged several of the Wolaitta evangelists with whom they had worked in Burji/Koyra to join them in the Aari outreach. The *amanyoch* of the Wolaitta *mahibär* were keen to support the ongoing venture in Aari and Maali. Experienced evangelists such as Mäja Adélo, Anjulo Gaga, Minota Mishano, Milkiyas Masoro, Thomas Alaro, Täntu Debana, and Basa Fola, as well as first-timers Kusa Mita and Yamané Madalcho, together with their wives and children, were assigned to various locations in Aari and Maali.[178]

176. Mahé Choramo, "Philip," 115–16.

177. Sawl Salgédo stated that the motivation for an evangelist is "a strong push by the Holy Spirit. We just have to go. For me it was the lost . . . that pushed me out." Personal interview with EPB, December 13, 1995.

178. Alex and Theresia Fellows, personal information to EPB, April 2, 1997.

By 1962 four Wolaitta evangelists, Mäja Adélo, Minota Mishano, Amantä Soso, and Matéwos Ṯeqa,[179] with their families, were located in Maali, where some 5,000 people lived.[180] The evangelists opened an elementary school and began preaching in the market and in Maali homes. A power struggle ensued between the Maali *balabat*, Tolba, and the evangelists. In front of the newly opened school at Koybe, the evangelists flew the Ethiopian flag on a tall bamboo pole. Enraged that these intruders were flying an unknown flag in his territory, Tolba pulled the flag down and severely beat *Ato* Lamé, a Maali elder. Tolba said, "Here I am the *balabat* of Maali and why are you, you poor insignificant people, attempting to fly your flag?"[181] This incident was reported to the Bako officials. *Balabat* Tolba was summoned to Bako by the *awraja* officials, rebuked for insulting the Ethiopian flag, and ordered to support the elementary school. During the next ten years, sixteen *ṣälot bétoch* were established among the Maali.

The first baptism in Aari was conducted on May 24, 1962, when Dana Mäja from Wolaitta and evangelist Ombolé Odiro officiated in baptizing thirty-five Aari.[182] Of these thirty-five *amanyoch*, fourteen were motivated to believe in Jesus because of his love. Eight wanted relief from their sickness (most of them had stomach ailments); seven desired relief from disturbing spirits; two desired comfort because of the recent deaths of their children; and one, a thief, wanted to be free from his evil way of life.[183] A large step forward was made when the Aari women *amanyoch* came together in May 1963 for their first women's meeting. And by 1965 there were thirty-five functioning congregations. By 1970 the number of congregations had increased to forty-four, with around 1500 baptized *amanyoch*.[184] By 1970 most of the Wolaitta evangelists were withdrawn from Aari and Maali and redeployed to new areas by their sending *mahibär*.

179. Ibid.

180. Donham, *Work and Power in Maale, Ethiopia*, 69. Donham, a cultural anthropologist, describes the Wolaitta evangelists as teaching the Maali "hard work, honesty, bettering one's lot, and a certain contempt for traditional ways."

181. KHC, "*Bäwängél Amanyoch Andinät*," 144.

182. Cotterell, *Born at Midnight*, 155. See also Dägu Daqilabu et al., "*Käisat Yätänäṯäqä*," 22.

183. Dägu Daqilabu et al., "*Käisat Yätänäṯäqä*," 22–24.

184. Cotterell, *Born at Midnight*, 156.

Short Biographies of Two Wolaitta Evangelists

Milkiyas Masoro was born and raised in the Fango district of Wolaitta. After an itinerant evangelistic ministry in Kambatta, Arsi, and Wolaitta, he and his wife, Ṣähaynish volunteered for evangelistic service to Aari in 1962. When they arrived in Bako, they were assigned by the monthly *mahibär* gathering of evangelists, Aari leaders, and SIM missionary, Alex Fellows, to a place called Shetär. Milkiyas built a grass-roofed house and planted his garden on a plot of ground given to him by one of the Shetär *amanyoch*. From his Shetär base, Milkiyas itinerated in the district, preaching at markets and funerals and telling the Jesus story in neighboring homes for three years.

In 1965 evangelist Guradé Jägäna, who was serving at Zobänantär *ṣlot bét*, was relocated to Bänna, and Milkiyas was appointed to replace Guradé at Zobänantär by the Aari *mahibär*. During his two years of service at Zobänantär, the attendance at the *ṣälot bét* grew and an elementary school as well as a basic Bible school were established.

In 1967 Milkiyas and his family were again asked to move. Because Ombolé Odiro, based at Sido, was recalled to Wolaitta for re-assignment to Käfa, Milkiyas, Ṣähaynish and their five children transferred to Sido, one of the older established *ṣälot bétoch* in Aari. His assignment at Sido was for two years.

The local leadership at the Zobänantär *ṣälot bét* pled with the Aari *mahibär* leaders to have evangelist Milkiyas return to serve them again, arguing that Milkiyas was taken from them prematurely. The Aari *mahibär* leaders conceded to their request, so Milkiyas returned with his family to the Zobänantär congregation and served as teacher, mentor, counselor, and evangelist to outlying areas.

In 1974, while Milkiyas was serving among the Bänna, news reached him that the former Emperor Haile Sellassie was deposed and that a new military provisional government had been established. In 1975, when the Wolaitta *ṭärapéza* recalled all their evangelists serving beyond the Wolaitta borders, Milkiyas faced a dilemma. Should he return to Wolaitta or remain? The Aari *mahibär* invited Milkiyas and his family to serve with them in Jinka. Up to the present, he serves not only the Jinka *ṣälot bét* but the larger fellowship of the Aari *mahibär*, which presently numbers some eighty-five congregations.[185] Milkiyas, with his family, is appreciated by the Aari *amanyoch* for his ability to integrate and for his spiritual leadership.

185. Milkiyas Masoro, personal information to Ermias Mamo, April 20, 1991. Since

The home district of Minota Mishano was C̲haraqé, Wolaitta. He began his evangelistic career in 1942 in the Kambatta and Hadiya *awraja* without any promise of financial support. Together with Bärata Jabu he preached in Durami, Ambursi, Bobicho, and other places in Kambatta and Hadiya, as well as in Maräqo. In 1949 he married one of Selma Bergsten's trainees, Faränje Buria.

At the 1961 annual conference at Soddo, the speakers challenged the audience for volunteer evangelists. Minota offered himself for ministry to Bako. At that time there were discouraging reports of famine in the Bako *awraja*. There were also reports of famine in the Bako *awraja*.

When Minota and his family first arrived in Aariland, he was assigned to work with evangelist Ombolé Odiro at Sido. This proved to be worthwhile period of orientation for the Minota family. In 1962 he transferred to Maali. There he and his family found the drought very severe and the local practitioners blaming the local *amanyoch* for disturbing the ancestor spirits. Minota and the other evangelists explained how God sends the rain on the unjust and the just, and when the rain began to fall in abundance soon after, the evangelists gained ready listeners.

In 1969 Minota was appointed by the Aari *mahibär* to serve at the Gärtäb *s̲alot bét*, situated near Jinka. In 1975, together with Milkiyas, Minota was recalled to Wolaitta. He chose to remain in Aari, continuing to serve as pastor/teacher at the Gärtäb *s̲alot bét*, as well as travelling out from there on evangelistic ventures among the Aari, the Maali, and the Bänna.[186]

Wolaitta Evangelists to Aari and Maali— Some Concluding Observations

The evangelists preached and taught that the power of Christ was greater than the Aari or Maali *wuqabé*. While the Aari were living in fear, they knew that the evangelists, through the power of Jesus, could "tie the spirits." The Aari *amanyoch* no longer feared the forests. When tax collector Taffäsä Yirga offered the *amanyoch* a large tract of forest to increase their landholdings, they gladly accepted his offer. The unbelievers in the community were horrified, thinking that some great plague would strike first the *amanyoch* and eventually the entire community. But no ill came upon

---

Wolaitta terminated Milkiyas's monthly stipend in 1975, the Aari *mahibär* continue to give him "soap money."

186. Minota Mishano, personal information to Ermias Mamo, April 20, 1991.

anyone. The *amanyoch* benefitted financially from enhanced produce; the tax collector increased his annual tax revenue; and the authority of the local diviner was viewed with skepticism by the community.[187] The preaching of the gospel eventually brought about changes in the society.

The evangelists encouraged the Aari and Maali to attend the Bako Bible School. Soon Aari and Maali evangelists were working in their own districts, supported by the tithes and offerings brought to the monthly *mahibär*.[188]

Evangelists from Wolaitta assisted in organizing the sixty-seven scattered *ṣälot bétoch* to form various district *mahibäroch*, such as at Sido, Arke Shängama, Zodo, Yäbeyé Goydamär, Gudär, and among the Maali. These small, grass-roofed *ṣälot bétoch* located in the countryside served as places of praise, thanksgiving, and confession.[189] The Wolaitta evangelists taught the Aari *amanyoch* that they, like the Wolaitta, must be a "church for others." The evangelists taught the Aari *amanyoch* that they must be willing to give sacrificially—both of their young people and of their funds—for evangelism.

The Wolaitta evangelists modeled Christian virtues that must be evident in the *amanyä's* personal life, family, and *mahibär*. When the evangelists mastered the Aari and Maali languages, they served as teachers and shepherds of the small groups of *amanyoch* that met together in their *ṣälot bétoch*.

When Aari *mahibär* leaders were asked about the significant contribution the Wolaitta evangelists had made in Aari and Maali, they responded:

> They brought a great light to us. And then they assisted in helping us to organize and manage our churches in a good way. They taught us the procedure of electing church officers, establishing regular monthly meetings where we would discuss church business, collect and distribute our tithes and offerings and how to handle discipline matters. We had no idea of how difficult managing a church really was.[190]

187. Mehari Choramo, *Ethiopian Revivalist*, 142–43.

188. See Dägu Daqilabu et al., "*Käisat Yätänäṭäqä*," 44–47, for a 1984 list of forty-seven Aari and Maali evangelists supported by an average monthly stipend of 5.00 EB.

189. See Hastings, *History of African Christianity*, 265, in which he aptly describes these face to face gatherings where the worshippers "create a public liturgy which makes full cultural sense to its participants in terms of symbol, gesture and language it incorporates."

190. *Ato* Dägu and *Ato* Täfärä, personal interview with EPB, February 11, 1992.

These Aari leaders were grateful to both the Wolaitta evangelists and the SIM missionaries for teaching them the scriptures in their many *sälot bétoch* as well as in their Bible schools. Significant changes in cultural practices began to take place among the *amanyoch*. The status of women was enhanced; they were cared for during childbirth. Husbands and wives began to live in harmony, and the wives were no longer treated as slaves. Marriage was made a public contract in a *sälot bét* with elders, while secret marriages were discouraged. One of the great changes that came to society was that the artisans, who were the fringe people of Aari society, were accepted as equals in the Aari *mahibär*: the potters, the metal workers, who sharpened tools and formed metal tips for plows and hoes, the leather workers, who made saddles and bridles—all were fully accepted into the *amanyoch* community. They could now eat and socialize together. Indeed, the Wolaitta evangelists did bring a "great light" to Aari.

Käfa

Background

A Käfa historian has said, "The significance of the Käfa for the history and the cultures of southern Ethiopia and beyond cannot be overestimated."[191] The Käfa trace their origin back to the fourteenth century.[192] In the nineteenth century the kingdom of Käfa was one of the most powerful in all of southern Ethiopia.[193] When Menilek's general *Ras* Wäldä Giorgis Abboyä conquered Käfa in 1897 and defeated the Käfa king, Amhara control was imposed upon Käfa. Käfa king, *Tato* Gaki Sherocho, taken prisoner to Addis Ababa, asked to be bound in chains of gold, which would better fit his dignity.[194]

During the early part of the twentieth century sections of the population of Käfa were devastated by slave raiding. It was reported that *Lij* Iyasu took as many as 40,000 slaves from Käfa in 1912.[195] By 1950 the population of Käfa was approximately 120,000, and statistics for 1990 estimated a population of 250,000.[196]

191. Lange, *History of the Southern Gonga*, 180.

192. Bahru Zewde, *History of Modern Ethiopia*, 16.

193. During the period 1972–1976, the author has seen evidence of many kilometers of hand-dug defense trenches on the southeastern border of Käfa.

194. Bahru Zewde, *History of Modern Ethiopia*, 66.

195. Ibid., 93.

196. Grimes, *Ethnologue*, 266.

Primal Religion in Käfa

The name of the high God in Käfa is *Yero*. It is not conclusively known if the northerners introduced the name *Yero* to the Käfa when Malak Sägad attempted to convert the Käfa toward the end of the sixteenth century. There were probably two factors that assisted in strengthening the sense of a single transcendent divinity among the Käfa: first, the invading Christian army of the Amhara in 1567 and, second, the settlement of migrating Christian northerners in Käfa in the succeeding decades.[197]

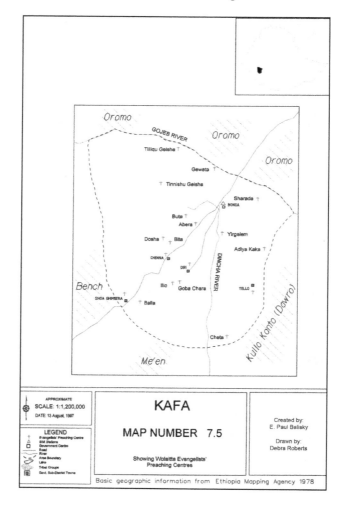

197. See Nicolas, "Dizzu of Southwest Ethiopia," 85.

Incentives for the Käfa to accept Orthodox Christianity in the sixteenth century may well have included a desire to become connected with Abyssinian power and to exploit this connection in order to curtail the advancing Oromo threat from Jimma. Another incentive was internal. Sometime prior to the sixteenth century, Käfa had been conquered by the Minjo, who practiced the Qollo possession cult on the hill of Bonga. For the Minjo, their clan spirits, or *wuqabé*, were legion—as many as their clans. The Käfa may have opted to accept Christianity, which offered them a single high God, in protest against the numerous clan deities honored by the Minjo.[198]

In the beginning of the nineteenth century it appears that the Käfa were abandoning Orthodox Christianity and reverting to the former Minjo Qollo cult. In 1972 researcher Nicolas discovered that within Käfa oral history there was an account of a nineteenth-century Käfa prophet called Shod' Ashelochi, who sounded the clarion to the Käfa to repent. He "shook the country with the thundering eloquence of John the Baptist: 'Repent, the day of judgement is at hand.'"[199]

The apocalyptic message of this Käfa prophet has been kept alive to the present in poetic verse:

> Fresh vegetables as food now you grow;
> One day wild mustard and bulbs you will eat.
> Before your enemy used to be the Galla;
> Behold, now it will be the naked Shanqala.[200]

By the middle of the nineteenth century, Shod' Ashelochi's prophetic message was fulfilled when the Shé and Bench devastated sections of Käfa.

The Roman Catholics in Käfa

The Franciscan order of the Capuchins began missionary work among the Käfa in the 1850s.[201] The Catholics, believing that the Käfa were Oromo, had a similar vision to that of the Protestant missionary J. L. Krapf—that

---

198. Ibid., 86.

199. Ibid., 92. Shod' Ashelochi's message was very similar to that of Ésa Lalé of Gämo, as related in chapter 4.

200. As quoted in Nicolas, "Dizzu of Southwest Ethiopia," 92.

201. Bahru Zewde, *History of Modern Ethiopia*, 25, comments that Antoine d'Abbadie's prolific writing about the Gibe River states caught the imagination of Catholics back in France.

the Oromo of Ethiopia might eventually evangelize central Africa.[202] In the early 1800s, reports from Ethiopia had reached Rome of "the existence of a densely populated area, dominantly pagan, yet containing islands of Christian traces."[203] By papal decree, Bishop Guglielmo Massaja, together with four compatriots, arrived in Käfa. Bishop Massaja insisted on using the Latin rite for the new congregations that began emerging among the Käfa. His reasoning was: "The supreme advantages which implanted the Latin rite and literature in these savage countries . . . [are] to attach themselves to us, and to the Mother Church."[204] Massaja's keen interest to establish a stronghold of Catholicism in Käfa was evidenced by his ordination of local clergy with minimal training. Ordaining clergy who could neither read nor write drew sharp criticism from his Capuchin colleague, des Avanchers, who contended, "It is to throw the sacraments of the Church to the dogs. For how can these indigenous priests dispense of the treasures of the Church?"[205] The debate on this issue continued. But the acute problem that the Catholics faced in Käfa was "staying power" because of political instability in central Abyssinia. Massaja became adept at courting French imperial power to retain a foothold in Käfa. This was to no avail, for by 1860 all Capuchin missionaries were evicted from Käfa. Several Catholic congregations around Bonga remained intact until the Consolata Fathers took up the work in 1920.

Post-Italian Catholic missionary activity in Käfa was initiated by the Vincentian/Lazarist order in 1956.[206] With their base in Bonga, by 1972, there were eight Catholic missionaries serving ten parishes within a limited distance of Bonga and with a combined membership of nearly 2,000.[207]

SIM and Wolaitta Evangelists' Entrance into Käfa

In 1932 SIM missionaries established a base near the *Abba* Jifar center at Jerén, several kilometers north of Jimma, the capital of Käfa province. During this pre-Italian era, they recognized the immensity of the task of evangelizing throughout the province and wrote in the SIM Prayer Guide

202. Arén, *Evangelical Pioneers in Ethiopia*, 72–73.

203. Crummey, *Priests and Politicians*, 60.

204. Crummey, *Priests and Politicians*, 81. Lazarist missionary Justin de Jacobs encouraged the Ge'ez rite in the highlands of central and northern Ethiopia.

205. As quoted by Crummey, *Priests and Politicians*, 85.

206. Ethiopian Catholic Secretariat, *Ethiopian Catholic Directory, 1990*, 142.

207. Ibid., 51.

for 1934, "Pray for God-provided Ethiopian evangelists through whom the unreached people of Jimma Province may be given the Gospel."[208] It was over twenty years later that Ethiopian evangelists were to join the SIM missionaries in Käfa.

After the Italian occupation, in 1948 SIM placed educational personnel, Bill and Iris Wallace, in the Bonga government school. It was unclear as to how SIM's evangelistic goals were to be accomplished in Käfa region. Then in 1950 SIM established an elementary school and a clinic on the southern outskirts of Bonga town, located on the Gädam road. It was through these two institutions that SIM initially attempted to evangelize the Käfa. In 1951 Bud and Doreen Isaacs, recently stationed in Bonga,[209] requested evangelists from the Wolaitta *mahibär*. Around 1955 Wolaitta evangelists Anjulo and Hidaro[210] arrived in Käfa and were placed in the village of Abära, some forty-five kilometers from Bonga, on the road to Ch̲äna.[211]

7.5 Evangelist Mälkamu Shanqo with wife, Gältamé
Säramo. Together they served in Kullo Konta, Käfa and
Jimma
(Lila W. Balisky, 2008)

On December 3, 1958, the two evangelists at Abära were invited to explain the good news to the Bonga SIM school students. Several children indicated that they desired to become followers of Jesus. On November

208. SIM Prayer Guide, 1934 (PG-1), "Jiran," 26.

209. SIM Prayer Guide, 1951.

210. Wolaitta oral history about evangelists Anjulo and Hidaro has yet to be uncovered.

211. Grace Bartja, diary, November 19, 1958, confirms that the two evangelists were located in Abära.

27, 1959, Anjulo and Hidaro returned to Bonga and baptized Salilee and Gäbré Mariyam in the Dén<u>ch</u>a River, some two kilometers west of the SIM station. This first baptism of Käfa *amanyoch* was witnessed by about fifteen SIM elementary school children.[212]

Amantä Soso and his wife, Magdalawet, replaced evangelists Anjulo and Hidaro in the Abära district in late 1959. Grace Bartja, director of the Bonga SIM elementary school, together with three Bonga *amanyoch*, travelled to Abära to visit evangelist Amanta. In January 1960 she writes, "After breakfast we had a lovely informal service to which a number of neighbours dropped in at various stages of the service."[213]

At the end of January, Bud Isaacs, together with evangelist Amanta, made a mule trip over 80 kilometers southwest of Bonga in an attempt to make contact with the Bänch people in the Shoa Ghimeera district.[214]

On May 29, 1965, evangelists Amanta and Ombolé Odiro, recently arrived from Bako, located at Gädam, some thirteen kilometers south of Bonga, where SIM nurse Edith French had established a medical outstation about a year earlier.[215] During the month of June the two evangelists, with the assistance of several Bonga *amanyoch,* constructed their houses. This was an unfortunate choice of location for the evangelists because the nineteenth-century *Qidus* Giorgis Church was located at Gädam. The local Käfa population were staunch followers of Orthodox Christianity. For six years the Ombolé and Amanta families were based at Gädam and itinerated to places as far away as Tiliqu Gésha, a three-day mule trip. Many heard the proclamation of the gospel, but there is no record of any Käfa converts or baptized *amanyoch* beyond the immediate confines of SIM Bonga school and clinic.

Magdalawet Séttana, wife of Amanta, recalled some of the disappointments and hardships they experienced as a family while living at Gädam. One disappointment was the unresponsiveness to the evangelists' message. The Käfa people living in the immediate vicinity of the large Orthodox church at Gädam, which Magdalawet described as the church with forty doors, claimed they had been Christians for generations.[216] The Amanta

212. Ibid., November 27, 1959.

213. Grace Bartja, letter to prayer partners, January 1960.

214. Ibid.

215. Grace Bartja wrote, "In the Gädam area we were able to rent a nice piece of land for 15 years." Ibid., May 29, 1966.

216. Magdalawit Séttana and her husband Amanta Soso said to the Käfa at Gädam, "We have been preaching to you for four years. Because you have not accepted Jesus as

family experienced the hardship of hunger because of famine in the area. The evangelists' meager allowance of ten birr per month was inadequate, and their own limited grain crop and garden hardly produced enough to meet family needs. The Amanta family also experienced the danger of attack by hyenas at night. Magdalawit recalls,

> One night a hyena attempted to break through the walls of our house and eat our children. My husband and I stayed awake all night attempting to guard our children. After we prayed to God, that ferocious animal vanished from the area.[217]

Between 1966 and 1967, three other evangelists' families joined Amanta and Ombolé. The Ṯaso Hébäna, Sawl Salgédo, and Madalcho Gésamo families, all from the Boloso district in Wolaitta, responded to the plea from the Wolaitta *ṯärapéza* for evangelism in Käfa. In April 1967 Bonga elder *Ato* C̱hänäqa accompanied evangelists Ombolé, Ṯaso, and Madalcho to scout out the Sharada district, some twenty kilometers north of Bonga.[218] By September 1967 Ṯaso and his wife, together with the Sawl Salgédo family, established themselves in Sharada.

7.6 Evangelist Tassew Hébäna with his wife, Laloré Ladisa and his family. They served in Sidama, Käfa, Kullo Konta and Bänna.
Lila W. Balisky. 2008)

your Saviour, we now shake the dust off our feet and leave you." Magdalawit Séttana, personal interview with EPB, January 9, 1988. At the American Mission station at C̱häbärä, Bill Muldrow cooperated with the Orthodox clergy at Bachuma from 1968 to 1972. All Me'en converts were baptized by an Orthodox priest from Bachuma.

217. Magdalawit Séttana, personal interview with EPB, January 9, 1988.

218. Grace Bartja, letter to prayer partners, April 5, 1967.

During the latter part of the 1960s, several developmental changes began to take place in Käfa *awraja*. The Ethiopian Ministry of Education began constructing elementary schools through its own department, the Ethiopian School Building Unit, in all ten *wäräda*.[219] Remote district centers such as Chiri, Chäta, Tälo, Shoa Ghimeera, Chäna, Shishinda, Tinishu, and Tiliqu Gésha, Adiya Kaka, Gäwata, and Dämbära now offered grades one to six. Also, the Ethiopian Highway Authority rebuilt the Jimma/Bonga road and extended an all-weather highway from Bonga to Abära. This now made it possible for trucks to transport the lucrative Käfa coffee to the Addis Ababa market. Roads were of such importance to Käfa that the ten district administrators raised adequate local funds to purchase a DC7 Caterpillar to construct additional feeder roads throughout Käfa *awraja*.[220] Another significant development was that the Ministry of Health established small clinics in all ten *wäräda*, and permission was granted to private pharmacists to operate in Käfa *awraja*.[221]

In 1969 experienced evangelists Éqaso Eybära and Mahé Choramo arrived in Bonga. After greeting the Amanta and Ombolé families at Gädam the men began a preaching tour southwest of Bonga towards Chäna. Zewdé and Adito, who were residing in the Beta community, volunteered to serve as guides and interpreters. Both evangelists and the two Käfa men were arrested and imprisoned in the *wäräda* police station at Ginbo. They were then escorted to Bonga and questioned regarding their place of origin and by whose authority they came to Käfa to preach. Mahé and Éqaso responded, "We are evangelists from Wolaitta and have come to preach God's word. We come with the authority of Jesus Christ who told His disciples in Mark 16:15, 'Go into all the world and preach the good news.' The Ethiopian government has not said this is prohibited so we have come here."[222] The Bonga officials were upset with Mahé and Éqaso and after insulting them by calling them troublemakers and other names, said, "Are you not aware that the whole of this province is already Christian? This province does not need any evangelists."[223] After the four

219. Personal observation from July 1972 to March 1976.

220. Käfa *awraja* officials willingly offered to SIM the use of the bulldozer to level the airstrips at Bonga and Shoa Ghimeera.

221. Dresser Käbädä, who had connections with the American Mission in Gatchab, opened a pharmacy near Chäna. In 1971, Wolaitta paramedic Mäsqälé opened a small pharmacy in Balla, near Shoa Ghimeera.

222. Mahé Choramo, "Philip," 145.

223. Ibid., 147.

had been in custody at the Bonga police station for two months, they were sent back to Ginbo where their case was heard by a sympathetic judge. The two evangelists, as well as Zewdé and Adito, were set free and admonished not to preach again in the area. As the two evangelists continued to preach openly in the district, there were further threats against them of possible imprisonment of up to five years. They decided it would be wise to return to Wolaitta. They were also disappointed with the Bonga *amanyoch*, who did not visit them in prison or assist them with prison provisions.[224]

In June 1971 Alex and Theresa Fellows were assigned to Bonga. As stated above, there had been opposition by the Orthodox Church to the preaching of the gospel in the immediate vicinity of Bonga.[225] Alex Fellows, through the cooperation of the local Bonga Ministry of Education, was able to obtain authorization for the evangelists to teach literacy anywhere in Käfa *awraja*. With this permission in hand he assisted placing recently arrived evangelists Mälkamu Shanqo, Séfu Giru, Yohanis Washé, and Mulu Olté in Dosha, near Chäna town. Taso Hébäna was shifted from Sharada to Buta and assisted by Wolaitta newcomers, evangelists Silase Manchika and Wäldé Silase. Sawl Salgédo was reassigned to Shasha in the Goba Chara district, along with new Wolaitta recruits, Yohanis Wanjamo and Mäja Adélo. Tessema Dubé, from Gédéo, was also placed in Shasha. To the lowland area of Chäta, some sixty kilometers south of Bonga, among the Omotic speaking people, travelled Eliyas Kuné, Indriyas Kurpé, Kusa Mita, and Eliyas Andabo, accompanied by Alex Fellows. Long-time evangelist with the Fellows at Burji and Aari, Anjulo Gaga, together with evangelists Olesä and Pétros from the Koyra *mahibär*, were placed in the Shoa Ghimeera district. Fantayé Hébäna and Gizaw Gumago were located among the distant Tara people situated on the north bank of the Omo River. Mulu Ulté was assigned to Tinishu Gésha and Mamo Mäja to Tiliqu Gésha. The Ombolé and Amanta families, residing at Gädam, were recalled to Soddo by the Wolaitta *mahibär*.[226]

There was amiable cooperation between the Bonga government officials and the evangelists and missionaries. For example, *Wotarasha* Kiflé Gäbré Silase, administrator of Shoa Ghimeera, was helpful in placing

224. Ibid., 151.

225. Magdalawit Séttana, personal interview with EPB, January 9, 1988, acknowledged that the Käfa of Gädam threatened not to assist in burying any of the dead from the families of the evangelists. She stated, "Praise God that we left before any of us died in that place."

226. Alex and Theresia Fellows, personal information to EPB, April 2, 1997.

evangelists Olesä and Pétros in his district at Balla. In 1974 he assigned several hectares of land in the administrative centre of Shoa Ghimeera for the construction of an SIM outstation.[227] Also, *Grazmach* Pétros Yosa, secretary of the Bonga *awraja,* assisted in writing letters to *wäräda* officials seeking their cooperation in developing airstrips so that air travel by Missionary Aviation Fellowship (MAF) could be expedited.[228] And both Ibida Goda and Gäro Mänjo, influential traditional religion practitioners in the Käfa region, were befriended by the SIM missionaries and the evangelists. The evangelists were invited and assisted to teach literacy by these local practitioners in the Goba Chara and Adiya Kaka districts.[229] Ibida Goda began prophesying in 1973 that change was imminent. He began to tell the people of Käfa, especially those followers of his cult, to begin following the teaching of the evangelists.[230]

Short Biographical Sketch of Evangelist Sawl Salgédo[231]

Sawl Salgédo was born into a family practicing traditional religion in Boloso *wäräda.* As a young lad he heard the gospel from evangelist Chondo Wola in 1948. After his conversion and baptism, he joined Chondo's evangelistic band, preaching throughout the Boloso *wäräda.* In 1957 Sawl heard of Wolaitta evangelists who were preaching in Sidama. After prayer and Bible reading he felt a divine urge to join the other Wolaitta evangelists in Sidama. After evangelizing in the Aleta and Yanasse districts for three years, he returned to Wolaitta in 1959 and attended the Soddo Bible School for three years. From 1962 to 1966 Sawl again served as an evangelist in both his home *wäräda* of Boloso and in the neighboring Damot Fulasa district. In 1966 he was asked to become the Bible school instructor at the newly established SIM center at Boloso. It was in 1968 that he was commissioned by the Wolaitta *ṭarapéza* to go to Käfa as an evangelist.

---

227. *Wotarasha* Kifle Gäbré Silase stated, "It will be through the preaching of true Christianity that the power of the *qalicha* in Käfa will be overcome." Personal information to EPB, March 15, 1975.

228. The author was accompanied by *Grazmach* Petros during 1972–1975, as he travelled by Toyota and by MAF Cessna 185 to several districts where the evangelists were teaching literacy and preaching.

229. Alex Fellows assisted Gäro Mänjo to repair his four-wheel-drive vehicle and received a milk cow as payment. Alex Fellows, personal information to EPB, April 2, 1997. In 1973 EPB was given a goat by Gäro Mänjo as a gesture of friendship.

230. Ibida Goda, personal information to EPB, November 1974.

231. Condensed from Sawl Salgédo, "*Achir Yähiywäté Tarek.*"

At that time there was only one *s̱älot bét* in the Käfa *awraja*, with only a handful of *amanyoch* meeting on Sundays. This was located on the upper edge of Bonga town. Sawl stayed with one of the Käfa *amanyoch* families at Bonga for several weeks, then established himself at Sharada. His friend and co-worker T̲aso Hébäna had preceded Sawl to Bonga and was already located in the district of Sharada, some eight hours out from the *awraja* center of Bonga. There they attempted to gather the people together and teach literacy. The SIM missionaries at the Bonga station assisted with various kinds of literacy teaching materials. While they were teaching literacy and preaching, the two evangelists were summoned to the *wäräda* police station and were asked what they were doing in Käfa. They replied that they were preachers and were also teaching the Käfa people literacy. They were then asked who had authorized them to teach in Käfa. The officials were not satisfied with their answer and so arrested both T̲aso and Sawl, accusing them of trespassing. While in the local prison awaiting their trial, they read the Bible and preached to the other prisoners. After several months the circuit judge from the *awraja* came to the local village of Sharada to judge various cases. The defense lawyer begged the judge to try the evangelists' case quickly "because I am losing sleep about the injustice done to these men." When the two evangelists were tried, they were judged innocent and set free to return to their homes and workplace at Sharada.[232]

As Sawl was teaching and preaching at Sharada, the people would listen politely, but no one would really accept the truth that Sawl was teaching. As he travelled about the district of Sharada, he would stay overnight with the Käfa. This provided opportunities to tell about Jesus. For example, when a Käfa woman serves a new loaf of bread, she will present it first to her husband, who will break off a piece and eat, and then all may partake. When Sawl received the bread, he asked all to bow their heads as he gave thanks to *Yero*, who gives all good gifts to his people. During and after the meal, Sawl was able to explain how *Yero* is the giver of all good things, and it is he who must be thanked and worshipped. The Käfa gave assent to all that Sawl told them.

Another time Sawl came upon a group of men ploughing their fields with oxen. The man in charge was a *t̲änqway* who was sitting under the shade of a tree. Sawl greeted the man politely and asked if he could have permission to tell the entire group about Jesus. The *t̲änqway* was honored

---

232. Sawl Salgédo, *"Ac̱hir Yähiywäté Tarek,"* 29.

and soon had all the men who were ploughing gathered around to listen as Sawl explained to the *tänqway* and his men the way of Jesus.

Sawl shifted his residence from Sharada *qäbälé* to the district of Yirgaläm, located about two hours south of Bonga. He was located at this place for about two years, but as in Sharada, no one accepted his message. His third move in Käfa was to the district of Goba Chara in 1971, a full twelve-hour journey by foot from Bonga, where he and two Wolaitta evangelists, Mäja Adélo and Yohanis Wanjamo, together with two evangelists from Gédéo, Gizaw Gämägo and Tässäma Dubé, were assigned by the other evangelists, in cooperation with the SIM missionary.

While Sawl was in the Goba Chara district, the local official at Yileyo *qäbälé, Wodorasha* Käbädä, cooperated in constructing a grass-roofed literacy center. He wanted all children in his area to learn to read and write and the adults to hear teaching from the Bible. Again, the SIM missionaries located at Bonga provided the literacy materials, blackboard, and chalk. The evangelists had many opportunities to teach and preach in the seven *qäbäléoch* located in the district of Goba Chara. They had no fear of being arrested by officials because it was known that the evangelists had official permission from Bonga to teach literacy, and the diviner, Gäro Mänjo, encouraged his followers to attend the literacy classes.

But there were those in the Käfa region who were jealous that the gospel was being preached openly by the evangelists. On January 19, 1973, Sawl was falsely accused by the Bonga Orthodox clergy, together with some of the *awraja* officials. The occasion was the annual *timqät* celebration commemorating the baptism of Jesus. At this special holiday, the sacred *tabot* (ark of the covenant) is removed from the church and accompanies the procession down to the Déncha River. Sawl's accusers said he had insulted the *tabot* as it was being carried back to Bonga from the *timqät* celebration.[233] His offense was that he refused to give a nod and genuflect as the *tabot* was carried by in the procession. [234]

233. Lila Balisky, diary, January 19, 1973.
234. See Davis, *Winds of God*, 119, for the same account.

7.7 Evangelist Sawl Salgédo (seated) served in Sidama,
Käfa, Siraro, Bänna and Kullo Konta. His son,
Evangelist Istifanos Sawl (standing) also served in Käfa
(Lila W. Balisky, 2008)

Sawl had no ill feelings against those who had falsely accused him. His imprisonment provided him an opportunity to tell fellow prisoners about Jesus. Bonga prison warden, *Shämble* Basho, allowed Sawl to conduct a Bible study for the prisoners. Through this means, Käfa prisoner Täkälä Marro was converted to Christ. The prison officials reduced his seven-year sentence to five, which he completed several months prior to Sawl's release in April 1974. Täkälä returned to his home in Shishinda, and through his evangelizing activities a *ṣälot bét* was founded.

During the time Sawl served his sentence in the Bonga prison, he was assigned the task of being the prison literacy teacher. SIM Bonga cooperated by providing literacy materials and other teaching aids. Sawl was eventually awarded a special prize for successfully teaching prisoners to read and write. Those who presented him with his literacy teaching award in the public meeting held in the Bonga town hall were the same officials who had falsely accused him the previous year.[235]

After his release from prison, Sawl was transferred to a new location east of Bonga called Adeya Kaka. This was the home of another well known *ṭänqway* of Käfa, Ibida Goda Wido. In former days the people of Wolaitta, Dawro/Konta, Gämo Gofa, and other areas of southern Ethiopia would send their tithes to him. Of recent years these funds had been dropping off. One day Ibida Goda called Sawl and asked him, "Was it not true

235. Lila Balisky, diary, April 13, 1974.

that at one time your people from Wolaitta used to send gifts to me?" Sawl answered in the affirmative, explaining that in former times the people did not know better. Sawl went on to explain that in recent years many in Wolaitta had believed in Jesus and for this reason the tithes were no longer being sent. Ibida Goda responded, "What you say is true. My *wuqabé* informs me that changes are beginning to happen here in Käfa." Sawl was encouraged to hear that this well-known Käfa *ṯänqway* acknowledged that something new was about to be initiated within Käfa.

In February 1974 evangelists Sawl and Arshé Dubé began winning the confidence of the Adeya Kaka people by teaching their children literacy in a building that was erected for them by Ibida Goda. They were given freedom to preach and teach about Jesus from the Bible. By April 1975 Ibida Goda was taken into custody by provincial police and escorted to Addis Ababa. Since then his location has been unknown. In April 1974 Wolaitta evangelists were recalled by the Wolaitta *ṯärapéza* to evaluate their future in light of the *dergue* government land reform decree.

Wolaitta Evangelists in Käfa—Some Concluding Observations

Until 1971 the evangelists had little success in Käfa. Capable and successful evangelists, such as Amanta in Gofa and Ombolé in Ṯämbaro and Kullo Konta, met with little response in Käfa. But around 1970 social and economic changes within Käfa brought about an openness on the part of Käfa officialdom to SIM and the evangelists. This friendliness benefitted both; the officials wanted literacy taught throughout their isolated *awraja*, and the evangelists received official authorization to teach and preach. SIM Bonga attempted to communicate clearly with all levels of Käfa officialdom the activities of the evangelists. The Bonga missionaries assisted the evangelists with their literacy supplies. It was in Käfa that the evangelists befriended two significant diviners. Because external events within greater Ethiopia prevented the development of a long-term relationship with the two diviners, it is impossible to surmise what may have transpired.

Conclusion

This chapter has followed the involvement of the Wolaitta evangelists among peoples of different cultures and languages some distance from Wolaitta. Because the SIM missionaries recognized that their own success in evangelism would be subject to cultural and language limitations, they asked the Wolaitta *ṯärapéza* to supply evangelists. By 1962 the majority of the evangelists who were serving in Arsi, Sidama, and Burji Koyra had been redeployed elsewhere. In 1962 the Wolaitta *mahibär* sent eight to Aari and by 1971, over twenty were sent to Käfa.

Within the Arsi, Sidama, Burji/Koyra, Aari, and Käfa districts, the evangelists operated under the aegis of SIM. Among the communities in which the evangelists lived, they were identified as "mission" workers. The evangelists faced ambiguities in their relationships to their sending body, the Wolaitta *mahibär*, to the SIM personnel residing in the district in which they served, and to the emerging *amanyoch* community that came into being through their evangelizing.

Not all the evangelists were successful. Some returned to Wolaitta because they were unable to adapt to a different culture and language. Some of the wives could not cope with the isolation and loneliness. Incompatibility between evangelists sometimes made it necessary to either relocate one of the families in the same district or to encourage one of them to return to Wolaitta.

The evangelists were able to accomplish what expatriate missionaries could not do on their own. It was an interdependent relationship, as the SIM missionaries provided backup, travel, family and health assistance, transfer of salary, and other logistical benefits, while the Wolaitta evangelists were able to settle among the local residents, erect their own dwellings, learn the local language, become trusted members of the community, and articulate the good news. Those who were converted, upon evidence of a changed life, were baptized and incorporated into a *ṣälot bét*. After about ten *ṣälot bétoch* were functioning, the evangelists organized these into a fellowship or *mahibär*, to which delegates would gather. The main agenda of the *mahibär* would be to discuss how the gospel could be communicated to others. A portion of the tithes and offerings from each local *ṣälot bét* would be gathered and used to support evangelists both within their own district and to other districts. This process came full circle when evangelists from Gofa joined together with the Wolaitta evangelists to preach in Aari. The Burji/Koyra evangelists joined with the Wolaitta evangelists to preach in Käfa. And since 1969, two Aari evangelists have lived and preached with the Wolaitta evangelists among the nomadic Bänna people, whose story, among others, will be told in the following chapter.

8

The Evangelists' Outreach to Several Southern Ethiopia Urban Centers, the Maräqo and Janjäro Tribes, and to the Omo Nomadic People

"The Church exists by mission, just as a fire exists by burning."[1]

Introduction

When SIM missionaries arrived in Ethiopia in 1927, their stated goal was to evangelize "the regions beyond . . . where Christ has never been preached."[2] Because there were Orthodox churches in nearly all the southern administrative centers of Ethiopia, the SIM missionaries initially focused their ministry on the various indigenous populations of the South through the vernacular languages.[3] Several post-occupation SIM stations were established in urban centers of the South. The first section of this chapter will discuss the role and effectiveness of the Wolaitta evangelists in their attempt to preach and teach to several Amhara urban populations.

The second section will deal with evangelistic efforts among two smaller ethnic groups isolated geographically from the larger areas we have thus far considered. The attempt by the Wolaitta evangelists, together with the SIM missionaries, to evangelize the Silṭi Guragé and the Janjäro[4] ethnic groups incurred two new challenges. One evangelist used an innovative method among the Silṭi Guragé, which we will discuss here. On the

1. Brunner, *Word and the World*, 108.

2. Lambie, Thomas, "The Goals of the First Missionary Party of the AFM to Enter Ethiopia," 2, as quoted in Cotterell, *Born at Midnight*, 16–20.

3. See Fargher, *Origins of the New Churches Movement*, 87–93.

4. Since 1975 the former name, "Janjäro," has been changed to "Yäm." In this thesis both names are used.

other hand, the approach the evangelists attempted among the Janjäro was less than satisfactory. The manner in which they attempted to enforce the Wolaitta prohibition of circumcision upon the Janjäro converts will also be explored. In the third section of this chapter, we will explore the evangelistic efforts among several nomadic groups in southwest Ethiopia. When SIM located the Dimika station among the Bänna and Hammer nomadic people of the Omo River valley in 1961, they requested the Wolaitta *mahibär* to partner with them in sending evangelists. This assignment among the Omo nomads challenged the versatility and adaptability of the evangelists. The commitment and resources needed to sustain this operation taxed both the evangelists and their sending *mahibär*. An attempt will be made to understand the initiative launched by the evangelists among the lowland nomads.

Urban Centers

Agaro

In 1946 SIM opened an elementary school and clinic in this coffee producing center (see map 8.1) some thirty kilometers northwest of Jimma. In 1949 the *Ato* Aldada Aṯébo family, initially from Ṯämbaro, was sent and supported by the Wolaitta *mahibär* for Agaro evangelism. Aldada and his wife had been converted in 1945 through the evangelizing efforts of Ombolé Odiro, Godana Gutullo, and Mäja Mädéro.[5] The *Ato* Aiha family from the Kambatta/Hadiya *mahibär* joined together with *Ato* Aldada for evangelism in Agaro. Their efforts made little impact on the Agaro community, composed of Amhara Orthodox and Oromo Muslims. Mina Moen recalls that "*Ato* Aldada's wife had a hard time because she really wasn't in sympathy. It must be very hard on all evangelists' wives, especially if they don't have the same vision as their husbands."[6] Obtaining rental housing in an urban area with the meager stipend the evangelists received was not feasible. The SIM missionaries provided housing on the Agaro for the evangelists.

---

5. Cotterell, *Born at Midnight*, 117. See "Kullo Konta" section in chapter 7.

6. Mina Moen, letter to EPB, June 21, 1991.

Wolaitta evangelists Shunké Shalämo and Atalo Ashängo replaced Aldada and Aiha in Agaro in 1954. Consequently, the Aldada family was asked by the Wolaitta *mahibär* to assist the *amanyoch* in Kullo Konta,[7] and the Aiha family transferred to Jimma for evangelism.[8] Shunké and Atalo stayed in Agaro for only two years. The lack of response among the Oromo and the Amhara of Agaro to the evangelists' preaching was perplexing to them. One of them commented, "If I preached this message to

---

7. Gershon Dilbato, personal information to EPB, July 11, 1997.

8. Mamo G/Mäsqäl, personal information to EPB, August 27, 1997.

Wolamos, hundreds would be saved. Why is it they will not believe?"[9] His statement may well confirm that conversion is a process. The Wolaitta had been on their religious pilgrimage for decades. There was an attempt on the part of both the evangelists and the SIM to give the urban population of Agaro an opportunity to consider the Jesus Way. But the combined efforts of the SIM elementary school and clinic, together with the preaching of the evangelists, produced very little response among the Orthodox and Muslims of Agaro and vicinity.[10]

Goba in Bale Province

Gus and Lois Kayser, together with school teacher Eleanor Neufeld and nurse Chris Lund, opened an SIM elementary school and clinic on the outskirts of Goba town (see map 5.0) in 1950.[11] SIM's goal was to evangelize the Oromo of Bale province through the stations at Goba and Ghineer. According to the chief administrator of Bale province, in 1945 the Oromo were leaving their traditional religion and turning to the Muslim religion. In 1948 he invited SIM to Goba with a specific mandate, "Will you not come in and make Christians of them?"[12] When Gus Kayser, missionary in Goba, requested the Wolaitta *mahibär* for evangelists to assist in the Oromo outreach, the Wolaitta *mahibär* responded by sending two of their successful evangelist families. The Ombolé Odiro family, with experience in Ṯämbaro and Kullo Konta, and the Guradé Jägäna family, who had served in Gofa, arrived in Goba in 1951.[13] There were no local *amanyoch* in Goba at the time who could offer the evangelists hospitality and assist them in getting established. Gus Kayser contracted a hectare of land from Bogale and Elfinish Bäshe, near the SIM station, where the evangelists built their houses and began cultivating small plots of land.[14] Gus Kayser provided them with quality seed potatoes, from which they were able to obtain a bountiful harvest. Through the sale of the surplus potatoes they were able to purchase new clothes for their children.[15]

9. As quoted in Willmott, *Doors were Opened*, 124.

10. Yosef Menna, "*Yätinsaéw Näṣibiraq*," 231.

11. Shepley, "SIM Stations in Ethiopia," 3.

12. Willmott, *Doors Were Opened*, 107.

13. Ombolé Odiro, transcribed tape, October 7, 1988 (EPB collection).

14. Tilahun Haile, personal interview with EPB, April 10, 1997.

15. Gus and Lois Kayser, letter to EPB, May 24, 1991.

In 1953 Borsamo Boké and Oda Ogato replaced evangelist Guradé, whom the Wolaitta *mahibär* assigned to Burji.[16] The three evangelists in Goba then focused their evangelism on two groups of people in Bale province. They trekked through the surrounding districts of Goba, preaching to the Oromo population through an interpreter.[17] After five years of ministry, their one Oromo convert was Lämma Gutu[18] from the village of Gamma. The other group upon whom the evangelists focused was an enclave of potters and freed slaves. They were of Omotic extraction, residing on the outskirts of Goba town. The evangelists were able to communicate with ease with this marginalized group; however, we have no record of any converts among them.[19]

The population in Goba town was predominantly of Amhara extraction. The SIM elementary school attracted the children of this Amhara community. Occasionally the evangelists were asked to teach Bible lessons in the school. Because of their limited facility in Amharic, the Wolaitta evangelists found it difficult to communicate effectively to those from Goba town. "They [Amhara] were very proud of pure language and laughed at people who spoke it poorly."[20] The Jarmans, who were assigned to nearby Ghineer in 1956, commented about the Wolaitta evangelists in Goba:

> I do know that these dear folk, however sincere they may have been, were completely unable to cope with the situation at Goba. . . . They found the people of Goba so tough spiritually as compared with Wolaitta where the people believed so readily upon hearing the Gospel. . . . They were right out of their element in Amhara country and finally took the opportunity to return to their own country.[21]

---

16. Yosef Menna, "*Yätinsaéw Näṣibiraq*," 231.

17. KHC, "*Bäwängél Amanyoch Andinät*," 95.

18. Marge Langford, letter to EPB, July 27, 1991. Lämma Gutu eventually became an effective colporteur of Bibles and Christian books in Bale province.

19. Ombolé Odiro related that he discovered among the Goba potters a cousin of his from Damot Zuriya, Wolaitta. Personal information to EPB, December 12, 1995. See also Yosef Menna's acknowledgement that "because of language limitation in Oromo and Amharic, these evangelists did not have much success with the dominant culture." "*Yätinsaéw Näṣibiraq*," 231.

20. Gus and Lois Kayser, letter to EPB, May 24, 1991. Yosef Menna came to the same conclusion.

21. Bob Jarman, letter to EPB, June 20, 1991.

It was, rather, through the effective preaching and teaching of itinerant evangelists from Addis Ababa that the gospel was communicated effectively to the Amhara of Goba. Tilahun Haile, a former adherent of the Goba Orthodox Church, said of one of these visiting evangelists from Addis Ababa, "Eshätu touched on relevant points pertaining to Ethiopian cultural matters and the Gospel."[22] In June 1957 there were six men and one lady baptized in Goba. Evangelist Ombolé Odiro and missionary Herb Ediger were honored to officiate at the baptism.[23] And in 1965 the Goba *amanyoch*, consisting of high school students, school teachers, police, and various government employees, raised funds to construct their own urban *sälot bét* in Goba town.

The Goba *amanyoch* experienced various kinds of opposition from their relatives and from the Orthodox clergy. The *amanyoch* were denounced for leaving the faith of the country, failing to fast, failing to pray through the mediation of the angels, re-baptizing former Orthodox adherents, and becoming "like those who are against Mary."[24] In an attempt to bring them back into the Orthodox fold, the *amanyoch* were threatened: "When you die, we will not allow you to be buried in the Orthodox Church's graveyard nor will we attend your funerals to sit and mourn with you."[25]

After the Wolaitta evangelists terminated their service in Goba, the local *amanyoch* continued the itinerant preaching in the surrounding area begun by the evangelists. Following Sunday morning services, the Goba *amanyoch* would go out and tell others the gospel within the confines of Goba town as well as in the surrounding districts.[26] They visited small groups of Oromo *amanyoch* in the Gamma district as well as in the towns of Robe and Goro. Although the Wolaitta evangelists had been less than successful in verbalizing the Christian message, they were an example to the Goba community of holy living and steadfast commitment to their faith.

Awassa

In 1970 a group of Awassa *amanyoch* (see map 5.0) contacted the Wolaitta *mahibär*. They requested a Wolaitta evangelist to serve the Wolaitta population in the urban centre of Awassa.

22. Tilahun Haile, personal interview with EPB, April, 10, 1997.
23. KHC, *"Bäwängél Amanyoch Andinät,"* 95.
24. Ibid., 97.
25. Ibid., 98.
26. Ibid., 96.

We are *amanyoch*. How can we and our families retain our faith
if we do not have our own *ṣälot bét* to pray and worship *Tosa*? As
a temporary means, what if we begin to worship in someone's
house until you select and send us an evangelist?[27]

Amanyoch were gathering each Sunday at other places of worship
in Awassa. In 1960 the Swedish Philadelphia Mission established a craft
training center in Awassa, and by 1965 a Pentecostal congregation had
developed. Also, the Southern Synod of the Ethiopian Evangelical Church
Mekane Yesus (EECMY) was based in Awassa, as was Tabor Seminary,
their diploma theological school. Through the impetus of the EECMY, a
growing congregation of Lutherans was formed in Awassa around 1963.
But the *amanyoch* residing in Awassa, with roots in Wolaitta, were not
comfortable with the Amharic language nor the form of worship in either
the Pentecostal church (*Heywet Birhan*) or the EECMY congregations.

In response to the request from Awassa *amanyoch*, Wolaitta recalled
seasoned evangelist Ombolé Odiro from Käfa and assigned him to Awassa.[28]
His ministry was focused on the Wolaitta population of government employees and migrant workers. Because Awassa had replaced Yirga Aläm as
the provincial capital of Sidamo in 1955, job opportunities in government
offices, factories, and state farms drew the Wolaitta people to this urban
center.

Evangelist Ombolé organized the Awassa *amanyoch* into a functioning *ṣälot bét*. Four elders were elected, choirs were formed, offerings were
collected, which were sent back in their entirety to the Wolaitta *mahibär*
each month. In 1973 Ombolé was replaced by Israél Okoyé, a younger
man who could better relate to the urban congregation, although they
still worshiped in the Wolaitta language. Under the leadership of evangelist Israél, an elementary school was also launched on the premises of
the newly established *ṣälot bét*. Like his predecessor, Israél was under the
authority, not of the recently elected Awassa *ṣälot bét* elders, but of his
sending *mahibär* in Wolaitta, which was paying his salary.

The new factor in Awassa for the Wolaitta *mahibär* was the extended
control they assumed through their evangelists over a congregation outside
the geographic borders of Wolaitta. In other geographic areas of Ethiopia

27. Soka Asha, transcribed tape, September 21, 1987 (EPB Collection).

28. KHC, "*Bäwängél Amanyoch Andinät,*" 150. Soka Asha, transcribed tape, September 21, 1987 (EPB Collection), comments that the Wolaitta KHC sent *Ato* Markina
Mäja, accompanied by Alex Fellows, to review the Awassa request.

where Wolaitta evangelists were placed, the Wolaitta *mahibär* had no aspirations to manage or control the *amanyoch* who were the fruit of their
evangelists' labor. As has been described in chapters 6 and 7, after an initial baptism, elders were elected who assumed full responsibility of the
nascent *ṣälot bét*. But the Wolaitta leaders saw the dynamics of the Awassa
situation somewhat differently. The members of the Awassa congregation
were almost exclusively of Wolaitta extraction. Because they were sons and
daughters of the Wolaitta *mahibär*, the leaders at Wolaitta accepted the
Awassa *amanyoch* as an extension of the Wolaitta *mahibär*. But the result
of a Wolaitta-language *ṣälot bét* in Awassa was that the door was closed
to other *amanyoch* from non-Wolaitta areas such as Kambatta, Sidama,
Hadiya, and Arsi. In the Awassa *ṣälot bét*, the language of prayer, singing,
and Biblical instruction was Wolaitta.[29]

In 1979 there was growing dissatisfaction among the elders of the
Awassa *ṣälot bét* with the control the Wolaitta *mahibär* retained over them.
When the Awassa elders requested the freedom to be autonomous from
the Wolaitta *mahibär*, the response from the *mahibär* was to call for an
election of new elders to replace "those who were causing disagreement."[30]
This was only a temporary solution. The attempt to maintain loyalty both
to the Awassa congregation and to his sending Wolaitta *mahibär* produced
tension for evangelist Israél Akoyé.[31] He was replaced by evangelist Soka
Asha in 1981.

The role of the Wolaitta evangelists in Awassa was ambiguous to the
Awassa *amanyoch*, to the sending *mahibär* in Wolaitta, and to the evangelists. In actuality the evangelists functioned as shepherds of Wolaitta
amanyoch residing in Awassa. Unlike their Wolaitta counterparts serving
in other places of southern Ethiopia, the evangelists in Awassa spent little time preaching the good news to the unconverted. A solution for the
Awassa *amanyoch* came from an unusual quarter. In 1982 the *dergue* officials confiscated the Wolaitta sponsored *ṣälot bét* and elementary school in
Awassa.[32] The Awassa *ṣälot bét* was re-opened in 1991 under the direction

29. Soka Asha, transcribed tape, September 21, 1987 (EPB Collection).

30. KHC, "*Bäwängél Amanyoch Andinät*," 152–53.

31. Soka Asha stated that "there was no conflict between the Wolaitta evangelist
and the Awassa elders" because they both followed the Wolaitta pattern of worship and
organizational structure. Transcribed tape, September 27, 1987 (EPB Collection). The
recorded history of the Awassa church in KHC, "History of the Kale Heywet Church,"
152, seems to indicate otherwise.

32. The Awassa *ṣälot bét* was one of many that were closed. Between 1982 and 1984,

of a local board of elders representing *amanyoch* from many ethnic groups of the South. The Awassa experience taught the Wolaitta *mahibär* that their former practice of relinquishing authority and control over *amanyoch* outside their geographic boundaries was sound and practical.

Jimma

Non-Orthodox Ethiopian evangelists first reached Jimma in 1884. The Swedish Evangelical Mission based in Imkullu, Eritrea, sent Nigusé and his wife to *Abba* Jifar, the sultan of Jimma, who was residing in Jirén. Nigusé's mandate was to "rescue young people from slavery and if possible to restore them to their full dignity by leading them to Christ."[33] Even though Nigusé developed a good relationship with *Abba* Jifar,[34] his evangelistic effort to convert the Oromo population met with resistance from a fanatical sector of the Muslim community in Jimma. By 1895 the evangelical community had grown to sixty adherents, the majority being liberated slaves. Due to the lack of reinforcements from the North to sustain the evangelical community in Jimma, together with a growing contingent of militant Muslims, *Abba* Jifar and the people of Jimma remained Muslim.[35]

When SIM began mission activity at Qochi, near Jirén, Jimma, in 1931,[36] there was no evidence of the former evangelical community established by the Swedish Evangelical Mission evangelist, Nigusé. And in December 1936, when the Italians forced the SIM missionaries to leave Qochi by expropriating their property, again there were no Jimma converts left behind.

SIM made another attempt to evangelize the Oromo in Jimma and vicinity in 1946. Their means of entry was through elementary school education and a medical clinic near Jirén. Bob and Hazel Thompson pioneered the Jimma outreach but after one year were replaced by Fred

---

1,700 Kale Heywet Churches were closed by the *dergue* regime. See Eide, *Revolution and Religion in Ethiopia*, 122.

33. Arén, *Evangelical Pioneers in Ethiopia*, 266.

34. Nigusé became *Abba* Jifar's personal secretary in 1890, handling all correspondence with Menilek II. See Arén, *Evangelical Pioneers in Ethiopia*, 272.

35. The five Oromo states of Limu-Enarya, Jimma, Gera, Goma, and Gummu became Muslim by the middle of the nineteenth century because of the influence of northern Muslim traders and the desire of the Oromo states to retain their cohesion. See Markakis, *Ethiopia*, 54, and Lewis, *Galla Monarchy*.

36. See "Wayside Jottings," 11, for Rhoad's account of his overland trip to Jimma with the Piepgrasses, Schneck, and Seally. They were warmly received by *Abba* Jifar.

and Betty Zabel, Nelda Palmer, and Marion Scott.[37] From 1946 to 1948 Markina Mäja enrolled in the Miaziya 27 Teacher Training School in Jimma. On Saturdays and Sundays, Markina, together with Wolaitta evangelist Bädacho Anato, would preach to the Kullo Konta traders and travelers who spent the night in Jimma.[38]

8.1 Ato Markina Mäja, son of Dana Mäja Madäro, served as the General Secretary of the Wolaitta KHC in the early 1960s. He was a strong advocate of the Wolaitta evangelists. Ato Markina assisted in pioneering the Wolaitta Bible translation project
(Lila W. Balisky, 1989)

In 1965 Wolaitta evangelists Yayinya C̲hagiso, Indriyas Darécho, and Yayna Mégeso arrived in Jimma, focusing their preaching upon the Kullo Konta who had migrated to the urban center of Jimma because of work opportunities. It was among the Kullo Konta *amanyoch* residing in Jimma that a *s̲älot bét* was founded. The Jimma *amanyoch* made a decision that their *s̲älot bét* would serve all ethnic groups residing in Jimma; therefore, Amharic was the language used in their worship services. By 1975 there were 150 *amanyoch* meeting each Sunday in the Jirén *s̲älot bét*. Evangelist Indriyas Darécho has continued his ministry assisting the Jimma *s̲älot bét* elders in urban evangelistic activities.[39]

37. SIM Prayer Guide, 1946 and 1947.

38. Markina Meja, *Unbroken Covenant*, 38. Markina was an enthusiastic evangelist among his fellow students. The school director, Kreble, accused Markina of "making all the students Catholics [non-Orthodox]. You must stop this or you will be dismissed from school." Markina was dismissed from Miaziya 27 School in 1948.

39. Clarence Ely, personal letter to EPB, May 21, 1991.

The Janjäro and Maräqo Ethnic Groups

Saja/Janjäro

The Janjäro[40] reside on the west bank of Gibe River. The Janjäro report that the indigenous dynasty of the Mowa was replaced in the eighteenth century by the Dida or Gamma, who were of northern origin.[41] The Janjäro society was hierarchical, with the *ammo* (king) serving as both king and priest. Under the *ammo* were the state council, the provincial governors, and district chiefs. An economy based on agricultural, from which tribute was gathered, supported the system. From their highland fortress, the Janjäro retained their independence throughout most of the nineteenth century in spite of the invading Oromo. It was the military might of Menilek's army that subdued the Janjäro. By the beginning of the twentieth century, many from the elite class of Janjäro had been baptized into the Orthodox Church and given Amhara names. The ordinary Janjäro continued their practice of primal religion.

In 1948 SIM launched a station at Saja (see map 8.1) with the intention of evangelizing the surrounding Oromo population. Godébo Adamo, Shunké Shalämo, and Éliyas Därgasu, evangelists from Wolaitta, were invited to assist.[42] The evangelists discovered that the Janjäro,[43] located some twenty kilometers south of Saja station, were willing to hear the gospel. Unlike the Oromo surrounding the Saja station, who were Muslim, the Janjäro claimed they were Orthodox Christians. The three evangelists used recent convert Täklä Mängäsha's residence for their base as they preached in the Janjäro district. In 1952 the first Janjäro *s̱älot bét* was built at Gannita.[44] The building served as both a worship center for a growing group of Janjäro *amanyoch* and an elementary school for some two hundred students. In January 1953 an opposing element burned the *s̱älot bét* to the ground. Undeterred, the small group of Janjäro *amanyoch* rebuilt, and soon two other congregations were formed—one at Wargu, the other at Gogware.

---

40. Since 1975, the Janjäro prefer to call themselves "Yäm."

41. Bahru Zewde, *History of Modern Ethiopia*, 18.

42. KHC, *"Bäwängél Amanyoch Andinät,"* 16. Cotterell, *Born at Midnight*, 120, reports that the Wolaitta *mahibär* initially sent Shunké Shalämo and Éliyas Därgaso to Janjäro.

43. The 1994 Ethiopian government census records that the combined Janjäro population (Jimma and west of the Omo River) was 165,180.

44. Cotterell, *Born at Midnight*, 140.

The matter of circumcision surfaced in Janjäro. Wolaitta evangelists Shunké and Éliyas[45] insisted on the Wolaitta prohibition of circumcision among the *amanyoch*.[46] This led to a conflict between the Janjäro *amanyoch* and the Wolaitta evangelists. The Wolaitta evangelists serving in other districts also experienced conflict with the local *amanyoch* regarding circumcision. The Intalla *ṣälot bét* in Kullo Konta debated the issue in 1955 when one of the leading elders, *Ato* Molisso, was circumcised. For reasons of hygiene, other Kullo Konta men chose to be circumcised.[47] The circumcision debate took on a broader dimension among the *amanyoch* of southern Ethiopia. Circumcision was on the agenda at the annual *Bäwängél Amanyoch Mahibär* held in Hosanna in 1954 and at Shashämänä in 1955. Ayällä Waldé Mikaél, one of the leaders of the Janjäro *amanyoch*, pled with the delegates "not to add any further burdens upon us. We *amanyoch* are already being isolated from our communities because we no longer drink intoxicating *bordé* and *ṯälla* with our neighbours."[48] At the Shashämänä meeting it was decided that the circumcision of *amanyoch* should not be linked to any religious ceremony or belief, rather it was to be viewed as a personal matter of hygiene.[49] The Wolaitta *mahibär* did not fully support the *Bäwängél Amanyoch Mahibär* decision on circumcision and so withdrew their two evangelists from Janjäro. Ted Veer, missionary at Saja station at the time, together with the Janjäro *amanyoch*, felt the loss of the two. He described them as "older men, very gracious and well accepted. They were a real help to the young church. Their position was more to be a support and teacher to the new believers and this was well accepted."[50]

By 1956 two Kambattan evangelists were invited by Janjäro to assist in their evangelistic outreach. The evangelists were to be under the supervision of Kambattan evangelist *Ato* Aiha, formerly based in Agaro but transferred to Jimma in 1952. The two Kambatta evangelists, under the direction of *Ato* Aiha, decided that the Janjäro *amanyoch* should come under

45. Godébo returned to Wolaitta in 1953.

46. See chapter 3, where reference is made to circumcision as part of the initiation rite within Wolaitta traditional culture. The Wolaitta *amanyoch* and their evangelists took a strong stand against the practice of any kind of circumcision.

47. Cotterell, *Born at Midnight*, 142.

48. Ayällä Waldé Mikaél, personal interview with EPB, April 10, 1997.

49. Nathan Barlow was reprimanded by the Wolaitta *mahibär* when he circumcised a teenage Wolaitta lad for medical reasons in the Soddo Hospital. Nathan Barlow, personal information to EPB, June 6, 1997.

50. Ted Veer, letter to EPB, May 17, 1991.

the control and authority of the Kambatta/Hadiya *mahibär*.[51] Because Janjäro would not agree to this, they asked the Kambatta evangelists to leave.[52] The Janjäro *amanyoch* decided to form their own *mahibär*, at which delegates from their four local *ṣälot bétoch* would meet each month to discuss matters relating to discipline, evangelism, finances, and elementary school matters.

Silṭi and Maräqo

Menilek's troops attempted to incorporate the northern and western Guragé (see map 5.0) through several military campaigns from 1875 to 1876. The northern Guragé, known as the Kestane, submitted peacefully to Menilek's Shoan army for several reasons. First, they had a religious affinity to Orthodox Shoa. Second, they were geographically close to one another, and third, both southern Shoa and northern Guragé had a common enemy in the hostile Oromo.[53] Western Guragé, on the other hand put up stiff resistance to Menilek's troops. *Ras* Gobana finally subjugated the western Guragé in 1888, but not before they had become staunchly Muslim, inspired by a revivalist movement led by Hassan Enjamo around 1885.[54]

SIM's evangelism in Maräqo goes back to 1928, at which time SIM established their first station south of Addis Ababa.[55] The Maräqo population of Silté Guragé includes both Orthodox Christians and Muslims. Charlie and Elsie Barton, Daisy MacMillan, and Freda Horn befriended *Ato* Dembel, residing at Goggeti, near the mission station. *Ato* Dembel had come to Christian faith some ten years before by reading his Amharic Bible, which had been given to him by an Orthodox priest.[56] When SIM returned to Ethiopia in the post-occupation era, Silṭi was selected as the Amharic language and culture learning center in 1947. Silṭi was some thirty kilometers south of the former SIM Maräqo station in a strong

---

51. Lois Bixby recalls that "the Kambatta wanted authority, but the Janjero would have none of it. They [Janjäro] said, 'We have been translating for them but now we can do it [preach] as well ourselves.'" Letter to EPB, May 14, 1991.

52. Cotterell, *Born at Midnight*, 141.

53. Bahru Zewde, *History of Modern Ethiopia*, 61.

54. Ibid.

55. Duff, *Cords of Love*, 138.

56. Cotterell, *Born at Midnight*, 88–89, describes how *Ato* Dembel heroically guided the SIM missionaries to Addis Ababa in May 1936, when law and order had broken down among the tribes of the South.

Muslim Guragé area. In 1951 evangelist Minota Mishano and his wife Faränj Buriya, together with evangelist Israél Anjulo and his wife Astér, began their ministry in Silṭi.

Shortly after evangelists Minota and Israél arrived in Silṭi to assist in evangelizing, they discovered the evangelical leanings of *Ato* Dembel's family, located at Goggeti. Soon a relationship developed between evangelist Minota and *Ato* Dembel's son, Nega. Minota assisted Nega in ploughing his fields and harvesting his crops. They visited neighbors as well as studying the Bible and praying together.[57] Minota cultivated this close relationship with Nega for some ten years, after which he was transferred to Arsi.

In February 1995, at the burial of Nega Dembel in Goggeti, where some two thousand attended, it was acknowledged publicly that it was evangelist Minota (*Abba* Minji) who had taught and baptized *Ato* Nega some forty years before.[58] *Ato* Nega retained a strong evangelical faith until his death, although he was residing in a Muslim and Orthodox community. At his funeral, *Ato* Nega's neighbours chanted this eulogy: "He was a strong man, a man of peace, a man who brought unity to our community and reconciled us to one another. He was a man who did not favour race or colour."[59] During his life time he built a small *sälot bét* near his home at Goggeti where other Guragé converts gathered together for worship.

The carriers of the gospel to Nega Dembel were many. The Orthodox Church and the Bible played a significant part in the spiritual pilgrimage of Nega's father, *Ato* Dembel. The pre-occupation SIM missionaries had observed *Ato* Dembel's evangelical pilgrimage. That Nega was well taught by Minota is affirmed by Ruth Cremer, who was stationed at Silti, Maräqo, from 1955 to 1959.

> *Ato* Nega has been a faithful and fearless witness over the years and has won twenty-five others to the Lord of which eighteen stand true to this day. . . . If *Abba* Minji [Minota] only won this person to the Lord, his going out [from Wolaitta] was worthwhile.[60]

After 1960, other evangelists from Hadiya, Kambatta, and Sidama were assigned to Maräqo. They continued to build on the foundation of the evangelists who had gone before them. In 1981 there were five local

57. Minota Mashamo, personal interview with Ermias Mamo, April 21, 1992.

58. Coleman and Cremer, "Testimony and Funeral," 1.

59. Murray Coleman and Ruth Cremer, "Testimony and Funeral," 2.

60. Ruth Cremer, letter to EPB, May 14, 1991.

şälot bétoch, in which some 210 baptized *amanyoch* were meeting together for worship, teaching, and fellowship in the district of Maräqo.[61]

Omo Valley Nomads

Background

Contiguous to the east bank of the Omo River reside the nomadic Bänna, Hammär, Şamai, Bodi, Mursi, and Demi tribal peoples (see map 8.2). The Bänna and the Hammär had been contacted by the Wolaitta evangelists from their northern base in Aari in the late 1950s. But these excursions were of short duration because of the harshness of living conditions among the nomads. Don and Christine Gray, living in Bako, made the following diary entry on April 13, 1959:

> Two of our Ethiopian missionaries left to visit a village in the Banna tribe. An inter-tribal murder [reciprocal killing] had taken place and they had to return [to Bako] because of the trouble. Since then two men from this village visited our home and invited us to their village again.[62]

The Bob Swart family from the American Mission established a station among the nomadic Dasaanich of southern Ethiopia in 1956.[63] And in 1968 the Swedish Philadelphia Mission began an outreach to the Qaro at a location called Kibish, west of Turme, on the east side of the Omo River.[64] (See map 8.2.)

The Wolaitta Initial Evangelistic Advance

The Wolaitta evangelists serving among the Aari were the first to attempt to evangelize the Bänna.[65] From 1967 to 1971 Milkiyas Masoro was assigned to Bänna, first to Qorké, then to the small government center at Kako, where he taught literacy mainly to the children of highlanders who were in government employment and to children of traders.[66] Ombolé

61. KHC, *"Bäwängél Amanyoch Andinät,"* 108–9.

62. As quoted in Fargher, "New Churches' Movement in Hammer-Bako Area," 35.

63. Dick Swart, personal information to EPB, May 1994.

64. David Strand, personal information to EPB, February 1969.

65. The Bänna and Hammer, two distinct ethnic groups, are often confused by outsiders because they speak the same language.

66. Milkiyas Masoro and Minota Mashamo, personal interview with Ermias Mamo, April 20, 1991.

Odiro joined Milkiyas in 1970 in his attempt to evangelize the Bänna. Their efforts produced no converts among the Bänna but sensitized the Wolaitta evangelists to the complexity of evangelism among nomadic people. Among the Aari, the evangelists were confronted with a different language, but the Aari agrarian lifestyle was similar to that of Wolaitta. The nomads residing along the Omo River did not engage in the same kind of communal activities that the highland Wolaitta were accustomed to. The nomads lived in scattered clusters of temporary shelters where they could find adequate grazing and water for their cattle. Movement was a way of life for them.

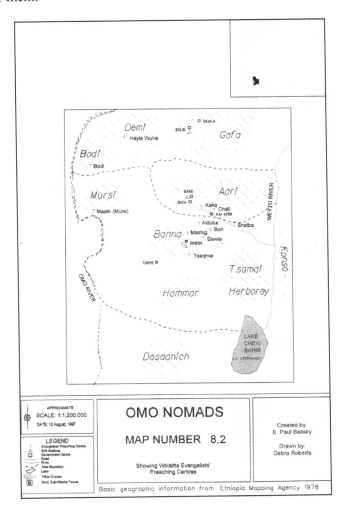

SIM Establishes the Dimika Station

In 1968 SIM launched the Dimika station on the border between the Bänna and the Hammär. With five truck loads of building supplies from Addis Ababa, builder Charles Bonk, accompanied by his wife Marion, constructed missionary dwellings, a clinic, and a school.[67] The Dimika station became a base for evangelism chiefly to the Bänna, the Hammär, and the Samai. The SIM missionaries were dependent upon the Wolaitta, Aari, and Gämo evangelists to communicate the gospel to the nomads, as no attempt was made by the SIM personnel to learn any of the nomadic languages.[68] Ruth McCoughtry described the relationship that developed between the evangelists and the missionaries at Dimika.

> Without the evangelists the missionaries would not be able to communicate with the Bänna and without the missionaries the evangelists would have a difficult time attempting to stay among the Bänna.[69]

Itinerant evangelist Mahé Choramo left his residence in the Gofa mountains in 1970 and surveyed among the Omo nomadic people of Demi, Bänna, Hammär, and the Samai for several months. He eventually settled among the Bänna at Alduba and received his monthly stipend from Wolaitta through the SIM missionaries based at Dimika. This was a new cultural experience for him as well as for his Aari and Wolaitta co-workers. He realized this new assignment was dangerous. Cattle raids and inter-tribal wars often took place between the nomadic groups. And then there was the possibility of being murdered by a young Bänna warrior out to prove his manhood. An evangelist armed only with his Bible would be easy prey. Mahé made full preparations for death by writing out his last will and testament regarding his family and the distribution of his meager resources.[70]

Mahé admitted that he and other evangelists often made mistakes while living among the Bänna.

---

67. Charles Bonk, personal information to EPB, July 1969, related that it was impossible to hire day laborers from among the Bänna. He eventually had to depend on imported help from Wolaitta and Gämo.

68. Charles and Marion Bonk, letter to EPB, July 9, 1991. John Chan, located at SIM Alduba, has been preparing Bänna literacy materials since 1995.

69. Ruth McCoughtry, letter to EPB, August 28, 1991. Jonathan and Barbara Geddes, living among the nomadic Mursi, 130 kilometers northwest of the Bänna, are in the process of mastering the Mursi language.

70. Mahé Choramo, "Philip," 152.

Sometimes they would get angry with us because we did things which offended them, especially in the early days when we did not know any of their language. Then we would talk to them through an interpreter and become friends again. We learned to eat their food with them and to drink milk with them. . . . We became friends.[71]

By 1974 there were ten Wolaitta, two Gämo, and three Aari evangelists residing among the Bänna. The Wolaitta and Gämo found it easier to settle among the Bänna than did the three Aari evangelists. The Gämo and Wolaitta ethnic groups were located far from the Bänna; historically there had been no land competition between them. Historically there had not been land competition between them. This was not the case with the Aari. Because of occasional Bänna border skirmishes with the Aari landholders, the Aari evangelists, Girma and Petros, were sometimes under pressure to leave Bänna territory or face the possibility of being killed.[72] In 1974 at Alduba, the Bänna warriors threatened the lives of two other Aari evangelists based among them. Girisho,[73] one of the first Bänna *amanyä*, stood with the Aari evangelists and attempted to convince his tribesmen that the two Aari were not spies and should not be killed. When Bänna guns were

8.2 Evangelist Éqaso Eybéro with his wife, Bāqalāch Chama. They served in Sidama, Kāfa, and Bänna.
(Kay Bascom, 1994)

71. Ibid., 153.

72. Aari evangelist Petros was murdered by a Bänna warrior in 1991. See Davis, *Winds of God*, 101–3, and Mahé Choramo, "Philip," 155–56.

73. Malcolm Hunter, personal information to EPB, March 16, 1991.

pointed at him to force a change of mind, Girisho refused. In Bänna culture there must be unanimity among the warriors before they kill. Girisho convinced the warriors, but they were annoyed with him and punished him by stealing some of his personal effects.[74]

Girisho first heard the gospel from Gämo *amanyoch* who were imprisoned with him in the Chäncha prison. He was serving a long-term prison sentence for murdering another Bänna. While serving his twelve-year prison sentence he became conversant and literate in Amharic. Girisho understood the gospel and believed. Soon after his conversion, while still in custody in the Chäncha prison, he married a young Gämo woman. After his release from prison and return to Bännaland in 1974, he refused the customary Bänna marriage rite of running over the backs of a herd of cattle.[75] His response was that he was already married and had children. Was this not adequate proof that he was married? Girisho and his family were not fully accepted as Bänna. It was felt by the other Bänna that Girisho had left the customs of his fathers by marrying a non-Bänna and by changing his religion.[76]

From the SIM Dimika base the evangelists began to trek among the Bänna. Mahé and evangelist Birhanu Haile lived in the Bänna village of Ebsheda. Other evangelists were based at Bori. As the evangelistic force from Wolaitta, Gämo, and Aari increased, other centers were opened at Shanko and Lala. An outpost at Shala, among Samai people, was staffed with two evangelists. These outposts among the semi-nomads of the plateau were easier for the evangelists to operate from because the plateau nomads practiced a more stable family and community life. The Bänna of the lowlands, because of limited water resources, were of necessity migratory, herding their cattle from one water hole to another. This made it difficult for the evangelists to live among them and build friendships. Because the Bänna lowlanders had minimal communal activities, the evangelists used a different approach. They established a center and tried to encourage the Bänna to come to it for the teaching of their children and for preaching. This strategy was not entirely successful. The stationary approach of the SIM center in Dimika may have influenced the evangelists' outreach strategy.

74. Mahé Choramo, "Philip," 153.

75. According to the Bänna, the ritual of running across the backs of the cows insured the future virility of the tribe. See Mahé Choramo, "Philip," 168.

76. Girisho, personal information to EPB, March 13, 1983.

Mention has been made above of Girisho, the Bänna prison convert. He served as an able friend and translator to evangelist Mahé.[77] But Girisho was ridiculed by other Bänna and accused of being a traitor for assisting the evangelists. The Bänna looked upon all those who were outside their tribal group as spies. One day when Girisho was with evangelist Mahé, a Bänna man said:

> Garisho, why do you teach this man our language so that he can hear all our secrets? Why do you show him our trails? Why do you protect him? He is our enemy. Probably one day he will be found dead.[78]

The evangelists lived with the threat of death both from the Bänna and from enemy attacks against the Bänna by the Bodi or Mursi. The evangelists occasionally witnessed Bänna warriors dying from bullet wounds after an enemy raid.

Sustaining the evangelists among the nomads proved to be a challenge to the SIM staff at Dimika. At other SIM stations, such as Bako, Bulqi, Waqa, and Bonga, transferring the evangelists' salaries, dispensing some medical treatment, offering counsel and encouragement, and distributing literacy material was the extent of the SIM assistance. However, because markets were nonexistent among the Bänna and the Samai, basic food supplies such as grain, sugar, salt, cooking oil, and clothing were sold to the evangelists at the Dimika station.[79] By 1974 a small mechanized farm was established near the SIM station, and most of the grain supplies for the evangelists and their families were grown on the farm. Boarding facilities for the evangelists' children were provided, and Wolaitta teacher Gäbré Silasse Assa had some twenty-five students in a small classroom.[80]

---

77. Mehari Choramo says, "We quickly became friends; we were as close as David and Jonathan." *Ethiopian Revivalist,* 184–85.

78. Mahé Choramo, "Philip," 157.

79. Ruth McCoughtry, letter to EPB, August 28, 1991. McCoughtry described the stock supplies for the evangelists: besides food stuffs there were canvas and plastic shoes, spices, batteries for torches, kerosene, shirts, shorts, tea kettles, pots, envelopes, airforms, pens, pencils, and a steamer trunk filled with used clothing for "shop-hungry warriors in from the plains." Letter to prayer partners, 1979.

80. Malcolm Hunter, personal information to EPB, March 16, 1991.

8.3 *Evangelist Kusa Mita who served in Aäri, Käfa and Bänna. He is teaching the gospel story to Käfa listeners/viewers from flip charts (Lila W. Balisky, 1973)*

SIM missionary Ruth McCoughtry describes the evangelistic band working out of Dimika as follows:

> The 20 evangelists working here are fully supported by their sending churches from Wallamo, Bako, and Gämo. With them they have four Bänna guides. These are in the front line of the battle, out in lonely places, getting acquainted with the people, setting up their preaching posts, as they make their first contacts with the message of God's light and truth. Along with them (after they get a house built) are their gallant little wives with younger children. The older ones have to be left in school, some across in Wallamo, others, 20 of them, in the small school we have on the compound, grades one to four.[81]

As the evangelists expanded in number, new recruits were placed at Mäshig and Dawila, in the southern section of Bänna.

In 1977 another Bänna, by the name of Gumzaro, said he believed the message of the evangelists. It became evident, not only to the evangelists but also to the people in his community, that he was a "changed person." He began to be insulted for his "anti-social behavior." It was thought that his behavior would bring bad fortune to his community. He was told:

> You are becoming just like these foreigners who have come to us from another country. Either you go live with them or you

81. Ruth McCoughtry, letter to prayer partners, February 1976.

observe the traditions of our ancestors. We don't want you in our community if you are going to be different.[82]

Gumzaro refused to leave his community or revert back to his former Bänna ways. His wife also become an *amanyä* and had the metal bracelets that were around her ankles, wrists, and neck cut off.[83] She began to wash her body. She was also sending their children to the school in Dimika. When her friends scolded her for leaving the Bänna customs, she replied, "These old customs have not brought us peace and happiness. Our hearts have not found rest by doing all these things. There is a better way of life from that which our ancestors taught us."[84]

When Gumzaro and his wife declared their change of religion, Gumzaro was beaten up by a group of young warriors. In order to make peace, the Bänna community leader, *Grazmach* Adinew, and his elders brought Gumzaro and the young warriors together. Evangelist Mahé, Gumzaro's spokesman, asked the community leaders why this brutal action had been taken against Gumzaro who, together with his wife, were making every attempt to live at peace with all in the community. One of the elders expressed the thinking of the group in this manner to evangelist Mahé:

> Let me give you five reasons why this person was beaten up. Mind you, I personally have nothing against him. I'm only speaking on behalf of those who beat him up.
>
> First, the foreigners came and built some houses at Dimika. They began to teach new things about God. They lived in a different way. This man, he accepted their teaching. He began to dress like them. Now, where are the foreigners? They have all gone away.[85] This man, he belongs to them. He should go with them; he is not one of us any longer.
>
> Second, he tells us that God's book says that we shouldn't fight and kill people. If we don't fight and kill people, how can we defend our houses, our families, our cattle and our country?
>
> Third, he knows that there are special places set aside for those who are diviners, those who can tell us which are good days and bad days to attack our enemies. He knows that certain areas of

82. Mahé Choramo, "Philip," 164.

83. Davis, *Winds of God*, 106, records that it was Charles Bonk who removed her bracelets in his workshop at Dimika.

84. Mahé Choramo, "Philip," 164.

85. Malcolm Hunter, personal information to EPB, April 11, 1997. In 1977 SIM personnel abandoned the Dimika station for security reasons and because MAF terminated their Ethiopian operations.

land belong to these people. But what does he do? He went and cut the grass on the land. Then he ploughed it and sowed some guinea corn. He knows that we have a custom that we wait until the diviner tells us that it is the right time to sow grain before we sow. He did not ask; he did not wait for us; he went ahead and sowed his grain as soon as the first rains came.

His grain was ready before ours. He knows that it is the custom to take the first ear of corn to the diviner in order to acknowledge his wisdom in telling us the right time to sow. This man, Gumzaro, he refused to do this. He says that the diviner doesn't bring the rain. Then he went ahead and broke of the first heads of grain and roasted them over his own fire. He refused to take any of his grain to the diviner.

Fourth, there are many other traditions and customs of our fathers that he is failing to observe. Not observing these will bring bad luck on the community.

And now I will bring the fifth reason. It is our custom to pour our honey on the graves of our deceased chiefs. He says, "the deceased chiefs have no authority to bless or curse us. We need not waste our honey by pouring it onto their graves." This is contrary to our customs. The ancestors will be angry and they will bring bad luck upon us.[86]

The elders discussed the matter for some time, recognizing that they were not only residents of Bännaland but that they were also residing in "greater Ethiopia" and were subject to the higher laws of the country. Their decision was a compromise. Gumzaro had to apologize for becoming angry with the warriors when they had attacked him and stolen his goats. The warriors in turn were punished for stealing Gumzaro's goats and were made to replace Gumzaro's clothes that were torn in the scuffle. Peace was restored to the community, but not without stressing the fabric of Bänna primal belief and social custom.

This account indicates the kind of cultural tensions the evangelists experienced among the converted nomads. It was inevitable that the preaching of the gospel would bring cultural conflict among the Bänna. Certain cultural practices such as retaliatory killing must be stopped. The process caused Mahé to question to what extent an evangelist should become involved in the inner debates and arguments of the Bänna. It appears that Mahé realized that for the Bänna, understanding the gospel was a much longer process than it was for the Qucha, Gofa, or Aari. Breaking

86. Mahé Choramo, "Philip," 164–65.

down barriers that hindered Bänna belief in the evangelists' message was an important part of this process. But change was impacting the Bänna from other quarters. For example, by 1976 able young Bänna men were being recruited to serve in the Ethiopian National Army to defend the "Motherland." The Bänna elders had no choice but to allow their warriors go, even if the Bänna ability to defend themselves from outside enemies was weakened. Through the process of time and the continued evangelizing activities of the Wolaitta, Aari, Gämo, and Gofa evangelists, together with the SIM support base at Dimika, by 1975 there were twenty-five Bänna *amanyoch* meeting in four *s̠älot bétoch*.[87]

Evangelizing among the Mursi

In 1977 evangelists Mahé C̠horamo, Mahé's son-in-law Gäbré Silasse Assa, and Israél Anjulo traveled to the Mursi, who reside along the eastern banks of the Omo River. In October and November the receding waters of the Omo River leave a moist, rich soil, in which the Mursi plant their corn. The evangelists stayed among the Mursi for six months.[88] This was not an easy assignment for the three evangelists. They were unable to sustain themselves on the daily diet of the Mursi, which consisted of a mixture of blood and milk drawn from their animals. The evangelists' store of food transported in by MAF to the Haile Wuha landing strip was exhausted in several weeks because they were forced to share it with the hungry Mursi. With some effort Mahé was able to send a messenger to Bako, where missionary Bark Fahnestock was able to replenish the evangelists' food supplies. Evangelist Mahé reported no lasting evangelistic results among the Mursi after their six-month stay. His reason: "We have not yet been here long enough for the people to get to know us."[89]

Towards the end of 1977 the Wolaitta *mahibär* council was becoming impatient with their five or six evangelists who remained in life-threatening nomadic ministry.[90] Mahé recalls this conversation:

---

87. By 1984 there were about sixty Bänna meeting in the same four *s̠alot bétoch*. See Davis, *Winds of God*, 108. According to Fred VanGorkem, personal information to EPB, July 20, 1997, the number of Bänna *amanyoch* has remained at about sixty.

88. Mahé C̠horamo, "Philip," 162.

89. Ibid., 163.

90. Mahé C̠horamo, personal information to EPB, April 24, 1997. Those who remained in Bänna and Demi were: Tomas Alaro, Éqaso Eybéro, Gétahun Dalé, Mahé C̠horamo, Nana Shaga, and one other.

8.4 Evangelist Mahé Choramo reminiscing with the author in Soddo.
Evangelist Mahé served with success in Qucha, Gofa, Aäri, Bänna, Käfa,
Bodi, Mursi and Borana
(Lila W. Balisky, 1995)

They said to me, "You are getting old. You have been sick many
times. It is time for you to have a rest." I told them that the Lord
had told me to go but he hadn't told me to return, so how could I
retire to my land? At this they permitted me to return.[91]

Evangelist Mahé left his wife and children in Wolaitta. He and other
evangelists returned to Bänna to encourage the young Bänna *amanyoch*.
In 1982 the four Bänna *sälot bétoch* were confiscated by the government
cadres who were attempting to teach the Omo nomads Marxist-Leninist
ideology and Amharic literacy

An Attempt to Evangelize the Bodi and Demi

Nana Shaga of Wolaitta, together with one or two Gofa evangelists, established a base among the Bodi around 1972. Over time, Nana and the
Gofa evangelists learned the Bodi culture and language and were accepted
by the Bodi as friends.

In 1976 the Bodi attacked Gofa highlanders, stealing cattle and clothing and killing those who attempted to resist. Gofa refugees fled to the
SIM Bulqi station for assistance.[92] Back in Bodiland, Nana and the Gofa

91. Mahé Choramo, "Philip," 169.

92. In February 1996 the author witnessed the devastation of a similar attack by Podi
warriors at Chätta, sixty kilometers south of Bonga.

evangelists were present when the Bodi warriors returned with their loot of Gofa animals, blankets, and clothing. When a number of animals were ritually slaughtered and offered as praise sacrifices to the Bodi ancestor spirits for the successful victory, the evangelists were invited to partake in this Bodi celebratory feast. The evangelists refused. Feelings of anger and contempt ran high against the evangelists. Nana became the spokesman for the evangelists to the Bodi. He told his compatriots that he was an old man, and if the Bodi killed him it wouldn't matter as his family were grown. The Gofa evangelists were able to leave Bodi as Nana diplomatically appeased the Bodi by giving them some of his personal clothes and blankets.[93]

In April 1977 the Gofa *mahibär* council made representation to the Gofa government officials at Sawla regarding the massacre of many Gofa. Soon after this, sixteen Bodi chiefs were flown in from Bodi to Sawla to meet with Ethiopian officials from the Gofa *awraja,* several *wärädas,* and the Gofa police. Ruth McCoughtry wrote, "They [the government officials] gave the evangelists great commendation, after hearing Nana's story, the final summing up was to tell them [the evangelists] to go back [to the Bodi] and preach and teach."[94] A promise was made by the Sawla government officials that after the evangelists regained the confidence of the Bodi people, the government would travel to Bodiland and set up a market, a clinic, and an agricultural project![95] In early 1977 the following Gofa evangelists were working together with Nana Shaga at Bodi: Ali, Desta, Kassa, Tamiru, Ermiyas, and Matusel.[96]

Nana reported in late 1977 that, with the coordination of the government officials at Hanna, farmer associations had been formed among the Bodi, Demi, and Mursi. Two fertile areas that could be ploughed by oxen were identified. Among the Demi, the literacy center operated by the evangelists was upgraded into a government elementary school. With peace and stability among the Bodi and Demi, there were opportunities for the evangelists to function in seven Demi farmer associations. Evangelist Nana had written three times to the Gofa *mahibär* council for more recruits among the Demi, because "people want us but the preachers are in short supply. So we are praying."[97]

93. Nana Shaga, personal information to Ruth McCoughtry, March 1976.
94. Ruth McCoughtry, letter to prayer partners, April 1976.
95. Ibid.
96. Dick and Vida McLellan, letter to prayer partners, May 10, 1977.
97. Nana Shaga, letter to Dick McLellan, November 16, 1977.

In 1978 evangelist Nana again wrote from Bodi to Dick McLellan:

> From the time we came to Podi, with much prayer until today, the Podi people have, by the power of prayer, stopped murdering people and pillaging and have become like ordinary men. They are trading in the market places and farming land, and for this we praise God. All men here are praising God. They are building houses together, trading together, eating together and mixing together. They have left their former raiding and oppression and united are talking with and living with other people.[98]

This account reflects the ideals to which the Wolaitta evangelists committed themselves. They desired to see industry, harmony, and a change in lifestyle among the nomads. Nana is grateful, not only because the Bodi are now eating and mixing together, but that "all men here are now praising God."[99]

Summary and Assessment

The Wolaitta evangelists were less than successful in urban and nomadic evangelism. The evangelists' efforts in Janjäro foundered somewhat when they insisted on imposing Wolaitta legalism regarding circumcision upon the recent converts. The Awassa experiment in which Wolaitta attempted to control at a distance was untenable. Minota's focused ministry for nearly a decade on the Nega Dembel family in Maräqo could well be assessed as significant. The five *sälot bétoch* among the Orthodox and Muslim of Maräqo are witness to the fact that deep evangelical roots were planted.

We have observed in this chapter that the evangelists were undaunted by various kinds of evangelism assignments. When the Wolaitta *mahibär* attempted to give the evangelists an opportunity to secure land for themselves in 1975, a number of them chose to return to their places of evangelism. Veteran evangelist Sawl Salgédo expressed the motivation for evangelism thus: "Telling others about Jesus is like breathing to me. If I do not speak about Jesus to others, I will die spiritually."[100]

---

98. Nana Shaga, letter to Dick McLellan, November 8, 1978.

99. Nana Shaga's untimely death on October 18, 1990, was wrongly reported in "World Scene, People and Events," *Christianity Today* 35, no. 5 (April 29, 1991) 46, as "stabbed to death near the remote community of Alduba in southwestern Ethiopia." The cause of his death was self-inflicted. See also Phillips, *Peoples on the Move*, 201, and McLellan, *Warriors of Ethiopia*, 51.

100. Sawl Salgédo, personal information to EPB, December 13, 1995.

Conclusion

WOLAITTA WAS INITIALLY EVANGELIZED in the sixteenth century by evangelists from monasteries founded by Täklä-Haymanot and his followers in northern and central Ethiopia. It is difficult to ascertain how deeply Christianity took root among the primal religionist people of the South. Hagiographies of these early evangelists indicate a prolonged struggle between the evangelists and the functionaries of primal religion. During the sixteenth and seventeenth centuries the advance of the Oromo into the central highlands of Ethiopia cut off effective communication between northern and southern Ethiopia. Because of this isolation, much of the South reverted to primal religion. But northern Christianity had reshaped the religious terrain of the South. Information about the South gleaned by nineteenth century geographers and travelers, for instance, indicated that remnants of Christianity survived.

During the last two decades of the nineteenth century, Ethiopian imperialism again began to assert its domination of southern Ethiopian societies that had formed themselves into small yet prestigious and self-contained kingdoms. In 1894 Menilek II marched his imperial army against the Wolaitta. Their defeat and subsequent colonization by the northerners inflicted a severe blow to Wolaitta identity. Social change was initiated by the introduction of towns, use of currency in the markets, northern administration, and the re-introduction of Christianity. Unfortunately, rampant slavery and exploitative taxes imposed upon the Wolaitta made northern Christianity unattractive to the majority of the Wolaitta.

In 1919 several prophets of renown from within primal religion, such as Ésa of Gämo and Albé of Humbo, became active in calling the Omotic people of the South to repentance. Their message, spoken with authority and passion, was a call to repent from worshipping the deities and to focus their worship only upon *Tosa*. They directly addressed social issues such as slavery, as well as the issue of Amhara domination and ownership of land. Prophet Albé predicted that one day all in Wolaitta would eat around one table; there would be no difference between various ethnic groups or clans, no disparity between the despised artisans and the ordinary Wolaitta. The prophets dealt with ethical issues such as integrity, marriage, and divorce —matters with which the Wolaitta and others were struggling. They heralded a new kind of society; however, in order to obtain it, they insisted, there must be repentance. In 1924 officials in C̲h̲ӓncha, capital of Gӓmo Gofa, classified Ésa as a dangerous element within southern society and marched him off to Addis Ababa under police escort, where he died an anonymous death. A dozen years later both the Sudan Interior Mission as well as the Roman Catholic Capuchins were able to harvest where these prophets had sown. They found the Wolaitta responsive to their message.

The SIM evangelists put the following principles into practice in establishing new religious communities in Wolaitta: they told the good news to anyone who would listen, expecting some listeners would be converted; they taught the converts the rudiments of Christianity; they baptized the converts and celebrated the Eucharist with them; and they assisted the new believers to establish a new religious community. It was this pattern that the evangelists later replicated throughout southern Ethiopia.

The Italian occupation of the South in 1936 brought about irreversible transformation within a section of Ethiopian society. When the Italians established their administration and military base in Soddo, December 1936, they initially attempted to meet the social expectations of the Wolaitta population. Public proclamations announced equality, an end to taxes, and the establishment of schools in all districts of Wolaitta.

The occupation brought about three important changes to Wolaitta society that assisted in transforming the imported model of Christianity into a Wolaitta Christian movement. First, the Amhara hegemony was removed from Wolaitta as northern landholders left for their ancestral homelands of northern Shoa, Gondar, and Gojam. Facing an uncertain future in the South, they traveled north either to join the patriotic front or to find a safe haven for themselves and their families. With the Amhara gone, the Wolaitta began to experience their freedom; they were regaining their land as well as their dignity. Second, the Italians made a concerted effort to eradicate traditional religious practitioners from the country. A void was created by the disappearance or overt removal of the former traditional religious functionaries. And third, the imprisonment in Soddo of about seventy *amanyoch* leaders in 1940 by the Italians brought a certain solidarity to the movement, as families and friends assisted in bringing food to their fathers in prison. These seventy leaders sang, prayed, and studied portions of the Bible together and told other prisoners the Jesus story.

It could be asked why the Italians incarcerated so many of the Wolaitta leaders. The Italian military no doubt thought there was a link between the Wolaitta *amanyoch* and the patriotic fighters hiding in adjacent mountain strongholds and the Omo River valley of neighboring Kullo Konta. Through the intensive preaching by converts, the Wolaitta *amanyoch* were growing in numbers and gaining a sense of their own identity. The Wolaitta *whodooga* (paid informers) provided information to the Italians about this growing *amanyoch* community, who baptized at night and who seemed to the Italians to have the characteristics of a clandestine operation. Leaders of the *amanyoch* community, however, were unafraid to show that their religious loyalty was to a higher authority.[1] There is no evidence within Wolaitta that the *amanyoch* movement had any direct connection with the Ethiopian Patriots. It appears that the *amanyoch* gained their boldness from religious inspiration.

So, while in prison, the *amanyoch* created a new mythology that was entirely their own. They were finding a new identity and regaining their center—not a political centre, but a religious one.

The Wolaitta have good cause to think that Haile Sellassie himself planted the seed for the existence of the Wolaitta community of *amanyoch* independent from the Ethiopian Orthodox Church. He visited Soddo in May 1945with an entourage of officials. Because of an apparent conflict among the newly appointed Soddo officials regarding the growing number of *amanyoch*, the matter of imprisoning them was brought to the attention of the emperor. It was here he made the pronouncement that became very significant to the *amanyoch*: "*Haymanot yägil, inje, agarachin yägara näw*" (Religion is a private matter; our country is that which we share together). Haile Sellassie was hereby affirming the potential for other religious bodies within Ethiopia. This statement was picked up by the Wolaitta *amanyoch* and has been echoed by her evangelists in government offices and courtrooms throughout southern Ethiopia.

---

1. It is not clear from my research if indeed the Wolaitta *amanyoch* leaders were anti-Italian prior to their incarceration. Pre-occupation SIM missionary Earl Lewis taught Wolaitta *amanyoch* from his Scofield Bible in 1937. Lewis wrote to Raymond Davis on September 12, 1961, "Many of them thought that when the Italians came in that the Roman Empire was being restored and they expected the Lord to come any time." Could this represent the Wolaitta view of the occupation, from Lewis's perspective?

In March 1945, Laurie and Lily Davison became the first SIM return-ees to take up post-occupation residence in Soddo. Lily Davison recalls, "We found such a change in the people. . . . The people were different in their minds."[2] Even women, whom the men thought were unable to learn, became literate. Laurie Davison stated in a 1945 report, "The desire for education has been created by the Gospel among the tribal peoples."[3] The *amanyoch* developed their own literacy schools in local *şälot bétoch*. The Davisons were replaced by Walter and Marcella Ohman, Selma Bergsten and Bernice Barnard in August 1945. There was a strong emotional bond between the Wolaitta *amanyoch* and the returning missionaries. Every week hundreds of *amanyoch* would visit the missionaries living in Soddo. By 1945 the *amanyoch* community had exceeded 25,000 meeting together in 200 *şälot bétoch* each Sunday.[4] An Ohman prayer letter describes some of the social changes that were taking place within Wolaitta:

> The gospel has greatly affected the social status of the whole tribe. . . . The power of witch doctors has been almost entirely broken. The various classes within the tribe, many who could not inter-marry, nor eat and drink with each other, now take each other in marriage and also meet around the same communion table.[5]

The *amanyoch* movement was impacting the Wolaitta society at large. The *amanyoch* were a renewed community bringing richness and whole-ness to Wolaitta.

The Wolaitta *amanyoch* leaders requested the Ohmans to teach them the Bible, with the result that the Soddo Bible School was opened on April 1, 1947, with a total of seventy-nine students. Ohman, fluent in the Wolaitta language, struggled to teach, in his limited Amharic, those who were attempting to learn in Amharic.[6] The post-occupation Decree for Mission Societies stated that all instruction in Ethiopia must be in Amharic, and the Wolaitta willingly accepted this language stipulation because they were eager to participate in greater Ethiopia. The pattern set at that time of SIM involvement in the Bible school was maintained until 1975. SIM was responsible for the instruction; the students paid for their books and writing materials. In 1975 the Wolaitta *amanyoch* took full

---

2. Davison, "Re-entry of SIM to Ethiopia," 11.

3. Davison, "Notes on the Situation in Walamo," 4.

4. The estimated population of Wolaitta in 1945 was approximately 150,000.

5. Walter and Marcella Ohman, letter to prayer partners, December 15, 1945.

6. Walter and Marcella Ohman, letter to prayer partners, August 18, 1947.

responsibility for their Bible school program, which had grown to seventeen institutions.

SIM's contribution through the medical services at the hospital was much appreciated by the Wolaitta. In 1946 Dr. Barlow launched the Soddo Dresser Training Program. In the first class of students, sixteen men were trained, one from each of the sixteen districts of Wolaitta. They provided an important substitute for the traditional religious practitioners who were disappearing from Wolaitta. Through the medical service at the hospital and the contribution of the recent graduates from the Dresser Training Program now posted in the Wolaitta districts, the belief that all sickness is related to some spiritual cause began to be undermined. SIM also assisted the *amanyoch* in formalizing their educational programs throughout Wolaitta. What began as literacy schools during the occupation now became church elementary schools with grades one to three. In 1963 there were 13,450 students learning in 325 church schools.[7]

The post-occupation Ethiopian government began to initiate large-scale development projects in southern Ethiopia. Through the World Bank a multi-phased agricultural development project, the Wolaitta Agricultural Development Unit (WADU), was launched in Wolaitta in the early 1970s. Over 1.5 million birr a year was poured into this project, to the benefit of Wolaitta agriculture. The use of commercial fertilizer and the introduction of crop rotation and other improved farming methods enhanced the production of local farmers. From 1978 to 1983 the WADU project focused on rural artisan training. The goal was to upgrade the quality of products produced by the local artisans and enhance the dignity of those who were considered second-class citizens. Prior to initiating the WADU project, the World Bank made a study of various agricultural regions of southern Ethiopia.[8] Their study revealed that the Wolaitta society was open to new ideas. They were willing to make changes in their farming methods, their eating habits, and their attitude towards the artisans. The World Bank research also brought to light that there were very few northern landlords, known for resisting change, residing within Wolaitta. The WADU project helped the Wolaitta develop their own resources. This directly benefited the Wolaitta *amanyoch*, for their increased resources could be invested in

7. SIM Soddo Station report to SIM Ethiopia Field Council, June 1963.

8. See Tesfai Tekle, *Evolution of Alternative Rural Development Strategies in Ethiopia*, 24–37, for a report of the WADU project. "The World Bank found Wolamo *awraja* to be very suitable for its financing . . . and the target population was believed to be very enthusiastic about the proposed development effort." Ibid. 25.

their evangelists who were sent to other areas of Ethiopia. The following song, popular after the eviction of the Italians in 1941, expresses the growing Wolaitta awareness of the significance of their own country:

> The country blessed of God,
> Walamo, the flower like Galilee
> There is Jesus' preaching place.
> Men, come to the teaching place.
> Everyone come to the teaching place.[9]

To the Wolaitta *amanyoch*, it was evident that God's blessing was upon them. Because of what they had experienced, they believed that they were now a preaching and teaching center. Evangelists began to move out from the Wolaitta religious center to other Omotic speaking people like the Gämo, the Qucha, the Gofa, and the Kullo Konta. It was not the intention of Wolaitta to control the new groups of *amanyoch* that came into existence through the preaching of their evangelists. However, there are some instances of individual evangelists who overstayed in their preaching localities. The evidence presented in chapters6, 7, and 8 reveals that the basic policy of the Wolaitta *mahibär* was for evangelists to strive to organize a *mahibär* within each ethnic group that would exist in fellowship with, yet independent from, Wolaitta. These were allowed freedom to reflect their own identity. After this came about, the evangelists were to move to yet another location and repeat the process. The shared background of the evangelists enabled them to establish a consistent pattern that was simple and reproducible.

The *amanyoch* Sunday worship service was different from that of the Orthodox Church, which consisted of a liturgy performed by one or more of their functionaries in the Ge'ez language (since the 1970s much of the liturgy has been changed to Amharic). In the new churches movement, the vernacular language is used. Amharic is used for the Bible reading and then interpreted into the vernacular for all to hear and understand. The Amharic Bible came into use in Wolaitta soon after the eviction of the Italians. Former SIM missionary Laurie Davison, attached to the British army to assist in repatriating Italian and Ethiopian troops to their homelands, was able to send nine hundred Wolaitta copies of the Gospel of John to Soddo in 1942.[10] According to Wolaitta informants, these were

9. As quoted in Davison, *News from Ethiopia*.

10. Marcella and Walter Ohman letter to prayer partners, September 17, 1945 (written from Doro, Sudan).

not as well accepted as Amharic portions of Scripture.[11] After the publication of the Haile Sellassie Bible of 1962, the Wolaitta *amanyoch* willingly purchased these. It appears that the new *amanyoch* within Wolaitta felt that it was important to be part of greater Ethiopia and were making a statement by learning to read and write Amharic and by carrying their Amharic Bibles with them to their *ṣälot bétoch*. For the many of the evangelists, the Amharic Bible became an object of power, as they prayed and placed it on the sick.

Throughout the years, Wolaitta and SIM have maintained an amiable and healthy relationship as two independent organizations functioning with similar goals and ideals but with two distinct identities. They have assisted one another in various ways. When SIM would open a new mission station in Ethiopia, the Wolaitta *mahibär* would usually respond positively to the SIM request for evangelists. SIM, in turn, continued to provide Bible school education at no cost to Wolaitta, except for school fees paid by the students, until 1974. The SIM presence in Wolaitta since the handing over of the Soddo hospital to the Ethiopia Ministry of Health in 1977 has included no more than several missionaries at a time; these are involved with Wolaitta Bible translation, clean water supply to Wolaitta communities, and Bible teaching in seminars. In 1987 Wolaitta *mahibär* leader Markina Mäja paid tribute to the SIM for their fifty years of service within Wolaitta. His concluding remarks were, "And in faith we anticipate serving together as one [closely knit] in various projects to accomplish even greater results."[12]

SIM missionaries opened doors for the evangelists by establishing SIM mission stations. The Haile Sellassie government looked upon missions as purveyors of the government's policy of modernization and development for Ethiopia. Generally, the evangelists were countenanced by the officials because of the social benefits accrued through SIM. The missionaries encouraged the evangelists by visiting them and passing on their monthly salaries as well as their mail from Wolaitta. The mission stations served as literacy depots as well as places where Bibles could be purchased. Limited supplies of anti-malaria medicine and some antibiotics were also sold to the evangelists, who in turn would sell them to eager customers in their areas.

11. Laliso Täntu traded his jacket for an Amharic New Testament in 1943. Personal information to EPB, December 13, 1995.

12. Markina Mäja, "*YäÉs Ay Ém läWolaitta*," 6.

As the evangelists moved outside of Wolaitta into various ethnic districts of southern Ethiopia, they encountered four major social challenges. The need for land reform was primary. Nearly every peasant family in the South was negatively affected by northern colonialism. It was common practice for greedy landlords to evict small tenant farmers and give their land to a better resourced tenant with strong plowing oxen and able-bodied sons, so that both landlord and the new tenant farmer might gain greater profit. The evicted tenants had no recourse but to relocate on an uncultivated hillside and begin the process of slashing and burning the forest, rebuilding their houses, ploughing their fields, sowing seeds, and fending off the baboons and wild pigs from their crops. Even though the evangelists were unable to do anything about this directly, they did advise the *amanyoch* not to waste their time with litigation in corrupt courts. At times the only recourse for the evangelists was to pray with the oppressed.

In chapter 7 reference was made to Wolaitta settlers encroaching on Arsi grazing land. It is significant that the Wolaitta evangelists had no difficulty obtaining small plots of land from Arsi landowners in a share-cropping arrangement. One evangelist had an amiable relationship with his Arsi landlord for over ten years. Most of the settlers in Arsi from other ethnic areas of Ethiopia were forced out, some violently, during the turbulent 1970s. The Arsi community perceived the evangelists for what they were—messengers of *Waq*.

The second social problem encountered by the evangelists was the integration of the artisans into the mainstream of society. In order to implement this, the evangelists took an active role in socializing with this segment of society and teaching them. After the artisans were converted and baptized, they were incorporated into the life of the *amanyoch* community. Their dead were buried beside their homes, as was common practice in the community. Formerly, it had been thought that the spirit of a dead body of a *fuga* (potter) and *faqi* (leather worker) would contaminate the ground, causing crops to fail and cattle to be barren. It was expected that the artisans would bury their dead in an unmarked shallow grave in the forest, where the corpse was likely to be molested by wild animals.

The third challenge for the evangelists was the control the diviners exercised over the local population. Through the preaching of the gospel and the eventual support of the Ethiopian government, the influence of the diviners has been diminished.

And the fourth challenge they faced was the debased society that needed to be cleaned up. This was the mission of Prophet Ésa in the 1920s. The evangelists practiced monogamy and insisted that the dignity and integrity of family life be honored and respected. For this reason they and their sending *mahibär* in Wolaitta were unwilling to baptize polygamists. The evangelists also took a stand against intoxicating drink because of the negative effects it had on relationships. Drunken brawls at southern markets were a scourge on society. The evangelists spoke out against dancing because of the immorality connected with this cultural practice. Change was effected within the society of the South not only through the evangelists' preaching against certain perverse practices, but through the positive example of their lives. The evangelists were unwilling to pay bribes when brought to court. Because the low-salaried officials were dependent on bribes to supplement their monthly salaries, it was customary to bribe any and all who were involved in the courts of justice. The honesty and integrity of the evangelists' lives was in marked contrast to the local population, where deviousness and duplicity were lauded.

Unlike their counterparts within the Orthodox Church, who confined their religious activities to the precincts of their buildings, the evangelists were communicating to all segments of society: with the Amhara in courts, with the traditional religious functionaries at their places of worship, with the marginalized—the *fuga,* the *faqi,* and the *qächqachi.* They intermingled with the common people and preached wherever and whenever they had an opportunity. They were not interested in any kind of personal promotion. They left their homes in Wolaitta because they believed in what they were doing. They had experienced the encouraging changes that were taking place within Wolaitta.

The evangelists did not see themselves as permanent fixtures of the local *sälot bétoch* they assisted in establishing. They were as pilgrims who continued to move along. They preached, baptized, and trained leadership. After this process they would move to another location. Some evangelists did stay on as pastors, but the general pattern has been for them to continue moving to the frontiers. It was never easy for an evangelist to move location after a functioning *sälot bét* came into existence. The process of establishing new relationships would have to begin again. There was the insecurity of the unknown. Then there would be the physical expenditure for a new residence as well as the process of securing land from another *amanyä* in the new district. The evangelist was dependent on the goodwill of the new community to which he went and the willingness of a local tenant to allow him the option of sharecropping a small plot of land.

This thesis has attempted to present evidence that Wolaitta has discovered her own identity through religion and, through the instrumentality of her evangelists, has been the means of bringing the reality of a new religious identity to others in southern Ethiopia. Because religion touched the deepest part of her society, the Wolaitta evangelists were motivated to initiate and sustain social change through the advocacy of religion.

One of the conundrums of Ethiopian history is that the social change that prophets, Wolaitta evangelists, expatriate missionaries, and others yearned and strived for was implemented by the atheistic Marxist *dergue* regime when they came to power in 1974. Ethiopia land reform came about through the *dergue* edict of February 1975. Again, it was the *dergue* who declared the equality of all ethnic groups and classes of people. The marginalized were officially invited to take part in greater Ethiopia. Every Ethiopian citizen was given the opportunity to become literate. Unfortunately, the *dergue* began to suppress Christianity within Ethiopia. This may well have contributed to the *dergue*'s undoing.

As the evangelists trekked the mountains of southern Ethiopia and preached the good news, they insisted that they were non-political. The sons and daughters of those who were initially evangelized in the post-occupation era now serve as government officials in offices that once sentenced the evangelists to prison.[13]

The Christian movement described in this thesis eventually became structured into the Ethiopian Kale Heywet Church, which numbers over three million members and adherents. This national church is now co-operating with others from the new churches movement in Scripture translation, together with the Ethiopian Orthodox and Catholic churches and the Ethiopian Bible Society. Full Bibles are now available in Wolaitta and Chaha Gurage. New Testaments are available in Aari, Bench, Burji, Kafa, Maali, Arsi, and Sidama. Work on the New Testament is in progress in Basketo, Kullo Konta, Hamer/Bunna, Koyra, Me'en, and Mursi. And full Bible translation projects are under way in Aari, Gamo, Gofa, Kafa, Maali, Arsi, and Sidama.[14] To the delight of the evangelists, biblical preach-

---

13. *Ato* Mulu Mäja, son of Wolaitta *mahibär* leader Dana Mäja, was appointed Addis Ababa High Court judge during the *dergue* regime. Markina Mäja, oral information to EPB, March 4, 1991.

14. Mary Breeze, SIL Africa consultant, e-mail to EPB, March 23, 2009.

ing is now being blared out over loudspeakers in a language understood by the listeners from Orthodox churches in nearly every major town of southern Ethiopia.

The central argument of this thesis may be summarized as follows. If the evidence presented is correct, then the Wolaitta have made a significant contribution to social and religious change in southern Ethiopia. Not the least significant feature of this contribution is the fact that it was made through the work of her evangelists.

Over a half a century ago the imprisoned Wolaitta fathers were inspired by the fire they saw spreading down from Damota Mountain. Will future generations of *amanyoch* continue to be motivated and driven by this founding vision of the new churches movement within southern Ethiopia? It is a vision that has brought renewal, innovation, and liberation to the Wolaitta and, through their evangelists, to multitudes of others.

Epilogue[1]

THE STORY OF THE Wolaitta evangelists did not end in 1975. This short epilogue recounts the trials faced by the Wolaitta *amanyoch* during the communist regime and the church's ongoing endeavor to support cross-cultural evangelists. Rather than retrench, the Wolaitta church developed bold plans that streamlined the process of financially supporting its own evangelists. As of 2008, a younger generation of over sixty-five well-trained cross-cultural Wolaitta evangelists/missionaries are serving within Ethiopia and beyond the country's borders. The following is a brief summary of this development over a span of 33 years.

In 1974 the former Haile Sellassie government came under siege from revolutionary Marxist-Leninist usurpers in the Ethiopian military who called themselves the *dergue*.[2] The ancient Ethiopian empire was now crumbling, and the execution of fifty-nine high-ranking government officials in November 1974 sent shock waves as far as the smallest mountain villages.[3] The Christians of Ethiopia, those within the Orthodox tradition and those of the new churches movement, were not immune to pressure from the newly established communist government. In July 1979 Patriarch Theophilos, of the Ethiopian Orthodox Tewahido Church, was martyred. Soon to follow in martyrdom was Rev. Gudina Tumsa,[4] secretary general of the Ethiopian Evangelical Church Mekane Yesus.

By 1980 hundreds of congregations from the new churches movement in southern and western Ethiopia were being closed. The annual Spiritual Life Conference held at Wolaitta Soddo in February 1983 was

1. The material for the "Epilogue" was researched in Ethiopia from January to June of 2008 and subsequently compiled in Grande Prairie, Alberta, in September 2008.

2. Markakis and Nega Ayale, *Class and Revolution*, 77–101.

3. Bascom, *Hidden Triumph*, 31.

4. Eide, *Revolution and Religion*, 178.

disrupted. When armed soldiers in several military vehicles arrived at the conference site where over 10,000 *amanyoch* were gathered, the large crowd was not intimidated. These *amanyoch* held their Bibles high, and someone from the crowd shouted, "You might have your guns, but our Bibles are much more effective weapons."[5] Though the conference concluded peacefully, people left with anxiety about what the future would hold, in light of the day's events. And the communist officials of Wolaitta were not to be outdone. In October 1984, all 748 of the local Wolaitta *ṣälot bétoch* were closed overnight and expropriated by the revolutionary youth organizations and local farmers' associations. Seven WKHC leaders were imprisoned in the nearby regional government center of Awassa, with an additional forty-five incarcerated locally in Wolaitta.[6]

The Mengistu government continued to report to the outside world that there was freedom of religion within Ethiopia. But the reality was otherwise, as reported by the Lutheran World Federation in Geneva:

> The military government has repeatedly claimed that there is freedom of religion in Ethiopia. But it refuses to take responsibility for repressive measures and allows its administrators to act against the church in contradiction to its own declaration. The local administrators again escape their responsibility by referring to directives they say they have received from the provincial representatives of the Party.[7]

It appeared that the dynamic impetus of the Wolaitta evangelists launched in 1937 among contiguous tribal groups was about to wane because of the collapse of the WKHC structure. These evangelists were dependent on the WKHC for their monthly stipend.[8] Previously, these funds had been collected from offerings given by each Wolaitta *ṣälot bét*.[9]

In 1989 an American funding agency received information about the 1984 closure of all the Wolaitta *ṣälot bétoch* and the resultant negative impact on the financial support for evangelists, the majority of whom, by this time, had been serving among the Bunna and Hammer nomadic

5. Markos Hébena, personal information to EPB, March 10, 1983.

6. Cumbers, *Living with the Red Terror*, 243–44.

7. Lutheran World Federation *News Analysis*, as found in Cumbers, *Living with the Red Terror*, 252.

8. See chapter 6, n. 163, for details of the previous financial support of the WKHC evangelists. In 1975 the annual Wolaitta contribution for their cross-cultural evangelists was US $19,500.

9. See chapter 5, n. 179, and Markina Meja, *Unbroken Covenant*, 82–85.

cattle herding groups scattered in the lowlands bordering the Omo River. This agency made a generous offer to the WKHC to support fifty evangelists, each at US$50, with the condition that the WKHC also commit to finance another 50.[10] This offer would facilitate the deployment of one hundred evangelists from Wolaitta at a salary of US$50 per month. These evangelists were to be selected and assigned by the WKHC. This agreement was put into effect and continued for three years, after which time, the reasons being somewhat unclear, the US agency severed the support agreement. Rumours within Wolaitta seem to indicate that not all the agency funds had gone to the evangelists' salaries. The WKHC and the fifty evangelist families who had been supported by the agency found themselves in a financial crisis.

In 1991 the communist regime of Mengistu Haile Mariam collapsed quite suddenly in the wake of events in Eastern Europe.[11] The hundreds of WKHC *ṣälot bétoch* began to re-open, and the administration of the WKHC was gradually restructured. The newly elected WKHC leadership faced to the difficulty of supporting the fifty evangelists whose salaries had been terminated. It was decided to recall the majority of them back to Wolaitta. In order to continue raising support for the remaining evangelists, each Wolaitta *ṣälot bét* was to collect an additional offering for mission outreach on the Sunday when monthly communion was celebrated. These funds were to be handed over to the WKHC central office, located at Otona, near Soddo town, for distribution to the evangelists. But this method placed undue pressure on the local *ṣälot bétoch* as they were struggling with rebuilding their own houses of worship and paying local salaries. The WKHC leadership began discussing among themselves, "How can each individual Wolaitta believer become involved in mission?"[12]

Wolaitta church member Yosef Menna was concerned about the post-communist spiritual life of the WKHC, as many of the *amanyoch* had become complacent and others had compromised their faith by accepting Marxist-Leninist atheist propaganda. Yosef also sought to solve the conundrum of how best to fund the Wolaitta evangelists. From 1990 to 1991 Yosef spent time drafting a book dealing with self-sustainability.[13]

10. Séta Wotango, "*Ades Zädé*," 3.

11. Donham, *Marxist Modern*, 181–82.

12. Timoteos Lerra, personal interview with EPB, June 24, 2008; Mälkamu Shanqo. "*Käfitiya Wängél Alälak Zädé*."

13. Yosef Menna, *Bäaṭibeya Bétä Kristeyan*.

The core verses that nurtured his mind were Ephesians 4:15 and 16, which speak of growing in love together in Christ. The vision statement that was developed read thus: "The purpose of a disciple-making church is to spread the Good News to all who have not heard the Gospel."[14]

WKHC leaders such as Markina Mäja, Waja Kabäto, Danél Ganébo, Desalegn Enaro, Bassa Anjulo, and Yaiqob Shanka arranged that a four-month teaching program, using the material prepared by Yosef Menna, be presented on consecutive Sundays in two local congregations, Mäbrat Haél and Woganä, near Soddo. The *amanyoch* were so receptive that the Wolaitta church leadership decided this teaching should be implemented for the entire twelve months of 1992 in each of the 613 re-opened local *sälot bétoch*. Some 20,000 training manuals were printed by the Addis Ababa EKHC office and sent to Wolaitta. This year-long teaching in each *sälot bét* kindled spiritual renewal and deepened commitment to mission.

Soon after these teaching sessions, in 1993, Yosef Menna developed a further vision on how better to raise funds for the Wolaitta evangelists.[15] He determined that the local *sälot bét* was the key to supporting evangelists—not the coordinating office of the WKHC located in Soddo. After the year-long teaching mentioned above, there was a renewed sense of commitment, cooperation, and contribution to cross-cultural evangelism. Individual churches were now willing to support their own evangelists. A method was put into place whereby individuals in each local *sälot bét* could voluntarily make a financial commitment to support a particular evangelist. Previously, funds for the evangelists were collected from local church offerings and from church district conferences. Under the new system, a local Wolaitta congregation may sign an agreement with an evangelist family and entirely support that family for a designated period of time. Several large urban Wolaitta *sälot bétoch* such as the Soddo Mäbrat Haél and Stadium congregations now each support up to three evangelist families. The two urban *sälot bétoch* in Areka town each support up to three evangelist families. In some instances, rural Wolaitta *sälot bétoch* with limited financial resources have yoked together to support one missionary family. Each month the local *sälot bét* deposits the evangelist's funds into a personal bank account. The evangelist may then withdraw these funds from a bank in the Ethiopian district where he is serving.

14. Ibid., iii.

15. His teaching was later compiled into a ninety-one-page manual. See Yosef Menna, *Bädäqä Mäzmurinät*, ii, where he clearly spells out the EKHC vision statement.

Experienced Wolaitta church leader Séta Wotango commends this caring manner for supporting the evangelists:

> Today, this new method of bringing the Wolaitta evangelist in a close relationship to the local *şälot bét* by signing a formal contract has enhanced the prayer support, the financial giving and personal responsibility between the members of the *şälot bét* and the evangelist family. This method is now being endorsed by other non-Wolaitta KHC districts and streamlines the sending out of many more evangelists.[16]

Several factors fostering individualism and private enterprise were set in motion in 1989 when the Mengistu regime, soon to collapse, began to encourage limited private business. To the Ethiopian evangelical churches, this trend now signalled a certain freedom that would allow the opening of closed *şälot bétoch* and the possibility of experimenting with a more democratic church structure. The WKHC office realized that the pre-*dergue* hierarchical church administration based in Soddo must change. Formerly, the administrative office of the WKHC bore the responsibility for all matters concerning the affairs of the more than 800 *şälot bétoch*. Under the new structure, nine regional centers within Wolaitta have authority to decide on the spiritual and financial affairs of the *şälot bétoch* within their jurisdiction. The regional centers, called *hibrätoch* in Amharic, are: Boloso/Soré, Damot Galé, Damot Wédé, Humbo, Ofa, Soddo Town, Kindo Käwésha, Kindo Wämära, and Siraro.[17] *Qätäna*, the coordinating Wolaitta office in Soddo, serves the nine districts in communicating with the national EKHC[18] office in Addis Ababa and other international agencies.

Another factor that has promoted a creative missional mindset within the WKHC is the provision of quality post-secondary theological and missionary training by the national EKHC, in partnership with SIM. A door has been opened for dozens of committed Wolaitta men and women to avail themselves of theological and mission studies within Ethiopia at appropriate levels. Since 1989 diploma-level training colleges have been

16. Séta Wotango, "New Method," 4.

17. Elsabét Gäbayähu, personal interview with EPB, June 24, 2008. During the reign of *Kawo* Gobé (1845–1886), his officials, called *Hospan Dana*, assisted the king in administering eight Wolaitta districts. [See the text on page 25 of chapter 1: "During the forty years that Kawo Gobé (1845–1886) ruled Wolaitta, there was peace and justice."]

18. "KHC" throughout the body of the thesis indicated the national Kale Heywet Church. More recently, the national church is known as EKHC (Ethiopian Kale Heywet Church).

established at Dilla, Hosanna, Soddo, Jimma, and Durame. Many of the graduates from these regional schools, located in the heartlands of the Ethiopian KHC, feed into the accredited degree-level Evangelical Theological College (ETC) in Addis Ababa, which is owned by the national EKHC of Ethiopia. Since 2002, theological study at the master's level is now available at the Ethiopian Graduate School of Theology (EGST) located in Addis Ababa. Several Wolaitta scholars have availed themselves of this program.[19]

An innovative two-year missionary training college, the Ethiopian Kale Heywet School of Missions, was launched in Durame in 2003. This college provides quality classroom instruction as well as supervised practicums in cross-cultural and communication skills. At present, nine Wolaitta evangelists with previous missions experience are enrolled at this institution.

As of June 2008, there are sixty-two WKHC evangelists serving in sixteen geographic areas, the majority among the Southern Nations people of Ethiopia. The monthly salaries of evangelists are organized into three categories, according to the challenges of the geographic area to which they are assigned. For evangelists in category 1, where food and transportation are readily available, the salary is approximately US$50. Category 2, for those evangelists sent further afield and who might need to rent their living quarters, provides US$62. And evangelists being salaried at US$76 in category 3 serve the more remote nomadic hunters and gatherers along the Omo River valley or among the Gumuz, residing along the Blue Nile gorge.[20]

A recent initiative in which the WKHC evangelists/missionaries are involved is the sending of foreign missionaries to serve in Pakistan and South Sudan. In 2006 a Wolaitta missionary family, Abera Ayele and Desta Yohanis, were sent to Pakistan under the auspices of a tri-partite partnership with WKHC, SIM Ethiopia, and the national EKHC office. Under the same agreement, two other couples, Yaikob Aga and Tibarek Wondimu together with Hizkiyas Faku and Fireheywet Tomas, are now serving in Southern Sudan.[21] The US$550 monthly salary for each of these couples is borne by the Wolaitta *amanyoch*. SIM provides transportation to and from the Wolaitta missionaries' service locations. The national EKHC

19. Steve Hardy, "Report on Ethiopian Kale Heywet Church," 8–11.

20. Mälkamu Shanqo, personal interview with EPB, June 25, 2008.

21. Eyob Denio, e-mail information to EPB, July 25, 2008.

office coordinates the transfer of salaries to these missionaries, as well as providing counsel, spiritual uplift, and encouragement. Wolaitta's obedience to the great commission, "Go into all the world," has created yet another Jerusalem from which the gospel emanates.

Mahé Choramo was one of the pioneer Wolaitta cross-cultural evangelists.[22] Now in retirement at eighty-seven years of age, Evangelist Mahé continues to prayerfully recruit and encourage a new generation of Wolaitta evangelists. His vision for outreach is that which one of the Wolaitta fathers, Wändaro Däbäro, saw in his dream some seventy years ago: that the gospel would spread like a fire being carried by a strong wind sweeping down the gullies of Damota Mountain.[23] This dream continues to develop, as the fire of the gospel, deeply rooted within Wolaitta, continues to spread not only throughout Ethiopia but beyond its borders.

22. McLellan, "Memories of Mahae: A Biography"; Mehari Choramo, *Ethiopian Revivalist*; Fargher, "Mahay Choramo." See also pages 177–80 of this thesis.

23. See page 150 in chapter 5: "One night in 1941, Wändaro Däbäro had a dream that the gospel would spread throughout Wolaitta like a fire sweeping down Damota Mountain."

Appendix I

Wolaitta Clans and Deities[1]

Clan	Deity/Spirit (Wuqabé)	Origin
Adda	lightning bolt	Kullo
Agarshuwa	thunder/lightning	Kullo
Agowa	Giorgisan[2]	Shoa
Aguwaa	stone	Shoa
Amaara	Giorgisan	Shoa
Angotiya	Giorgisan	Shoa
Araachiya	monkey	Shoa
Argammaa	Awa-kada	Gämo Gofa
Auguraa	monkey	Tambaro
Awureetaa	land	Shoa
Ayfarssuwaa	Kitosa	Sidama
Badaadriya	Giorgisan	Shoa
Badigadalaa	Giorgisan	Shoa
Bohaliya	Wärqa	Kambatta
Booshiya	sun/moon	Kindo
Boroda Mallaa	open plains	Gämo Gofa
Boshasha	Chaqa Qesse	Kindo
Boyna Tegré	sun/moon	Tegré
Bubulaa	Mulu Gusho	Shoa
Chinasha (potters)		
Damotaa	Hambaza	Kullo
Degella (tanners)[3]		

1. Sources: Mälkamu Shanqo, "*Hulum Ades Honwal*," 6–9; Bogalä Walälu, *YäWolamo Hizb Tarik*, 23–24; and Chiatti, "The Politics of Divine Kingship," 114–18.

2. All proper names are spirits/deities. Items in English are lesser protective spirits that are in continuous change.

3. Some clans were reluctant to disclose this information; some rely on the deities of other clans.

327

Dogalla (tanners)		
Dohayaa	Hambaza	Gämo
Dongaa	monkey	Tämbaro
Faṭegaraa	Giorgisan	Shoa
Gäddaa	thunder	Kambatta
Gajja	plain	Tämbaro
Gämo Mallaa	shola tree	Gämo Gofa
Gänzia	Halla/Godala	Janjäro
Gareno	prosperity	Shoa
Gauraruwa	lake	Shoa
Gézo Mallaa	large tree	Gämo Gofa
Gishshaa	pumpkin	Käfa
Godabishuwa (slave)		
Goqa (common people)		
Golla	Aulachuwa	Quchа
Gollo Mallaa	sun/moon/Dubush	Gämo Gofa
Gonduwaa	rainbow	Quchа
Gudareettaa	cow/ensette	Boroda
Gurmallaa	Ashélo	Shoa
Hérgära	Aulachuwa	Quchа
Hili Mallaa	Aulachuwa	Quchа
Hiraytwa	Kitosa	Sidama/Guji
Hiziya	buffalo/sun	Kullo
Huduga		Kullo
Innigara		Shoa
Kalisiya		Shoa
Kanchachiliya	great tree	Gämo Gofa
Kauka	monkey	Dawro
Komineya	nobility	Kindo
Lonto Mallaa	tree/bird	Käfa
Maka	big tree	Gämo Gofa
Maraqua	Giorgisan	Kambatta
Martoqa	cow	Gämo Gofa
Masha	Giorgisan	Shoa
Masireya	Hambaza	Kambatta
Mayla	dogs	Kambatta
Moghiya[4]	Aljanuwa	Momogotua
Monicha		Gämo Gofa
Mugaréta	cow	Kullo
Onogotuwa	Aborda	Gämo Gofa

4. Place of origin was not identifiable for some tribes.

Qalicha	monkey	Kullo
Qésiga	Ajora waterfall	Shoa
Qogo Mallaa	crow	Gämo Gofa
Taradua		Gämo Gofa
Taradwaa		Hadiya
Tata		Darwro
Tegré	sun/moon	Tegré
Wageshwa	Worika	Kambatta
Walsa		Kullo
Wallaqa		Tämbaro
Warareta	Aborda	Kullo
Woguwa (royalty)		Ghimeera
Wojuwa	plain	Amaaro
Wolaitta Mallaa		Wolaitta
Womanaqa	Dumbube	Kenya
Womghira	Hambaza	Dawro
Woshesha	Ighlala	Käfa Gomära
Wucha	Yaffero	Kullo
Yagayia	Dosha	Tämbaro
Zagotadiy	Landiya	Kullo
Zambocha	Hauzula	Kambatta
Zaminiya	Gammana	Kambatta
Zantala	Andya	Qucha
Zirgo Mallaa	Anka tree	Kullo
Zatuma	Aborda	Käfa
Zatuwa	Aborda	Kambatta

Some details about Wolaitta clans and deities:

a) Largest clan to least

      Mallaa (10 sub-clans)

      Dogalla

      Amaara

      Gofa

      Godabishuwa

      Chinasha

      Degella

      Masha

      Maiyla

b) Mallaa clans

    Boroda Mallaa
    Gämo Mallaa
    Gezo Mallaa
    Golomallaa
    Hilimallaa
    Lonto Mallaa
    Qogomallaa
    Tegré
    Wolaitta Mallaa
    Zirgo Mallaa

c) Origin of clans
From:

Shoa	17
Kullo	14
Gämo Gofa	12
Kambatta	9
Qucha	4
Wolaitta/Kindo	4
Tämbaro	4
Käfa	4
Sidama	2
Other	18
Total	88

d) Clan deities unique to Wolaitta

    Aborda
    Aljanuwa
    Ashé
    Auwlachuwa
    pumpkin
    Gamana
    Hambaza
    Hauwsula
    Ingilla
    Kitosa
    Mulugusho
    monkey
    Wombo
    Worika
    Yafero

Names of Wolaitta Evangelists, 1937–1975

Wolaitta Districts:

1. Balé Koysha	6. Damot Galé	11. Humbo
2. Boloso	7. Damot Wédé	12. Kindo
3. Bosa Abäla	8. Damot Zuriya	13. Koysha
4. Chiraqé	9. Duguna	14. Ofa
5. Damot Fulasa	10. Fango	15. Oforé
		16. Soré

Code: "d"—evangelist died
"re"—evangelist remained in area
"dk"—evangelist was killed
"dr"—evangelist drowned in river
"dp"—evangelist died in prison

Evangelists and Years of Places of Service:
District Number: Service:

Abära Asha–14	1975–85	Borana
Abära Héramo–13	1970–74	Kullo Konta
Abebo Ataro–12	1958–71	Maräqo, Burji/Koyra
Abota Anjulo–12	1960–75	Kullo Konta
Abraham Toma–12	1965–75	Jimma
Agébo Aläto–13	1942–47(d)	Gämo
Ajabo Anjajo–2	1970–74	Kullo Konta
Alaho Éna–5	c.1942–44	Kambatta
Alaro Gutulo	1947–94(d)	Sidamo
Alaro Hardedo–10	1946–85(d)	Sidama, Kullo Konta
Albazo Adaré–5	1945–55(d)	Kullo Konta, Burji/Koyra
Albé Acha, Goda–11	1942–45(d)	Gämo, Gofa
Aldabo Anshébo–7	1952–59(d)	Kullo Konta, Sidama
Amanta Soso–5	1942–88(d)	Gofa, Käfa, Aari/Maali, Bänna,
Amoné Aba, W/o–8	1950–55(d)	Gofa

Anamo Anjaja–4	1952–74	Qucha, Aari, Bänna
Andabo Aymalo–14	1953–92	Qucha, Gofa
Anébo Adamo–6	1951–70(d)	Arsi, Kullo Konta, Qucha, Gofa
Anja Asale–3	1955–62	Sidama
Anjébo Alaho–11	1950–52(d)	Gofa
Anjulo Adbo–2	1953–76(d)	Kullo Konta
Anjulo Aqamo–6	c.1954–65	Qucha, Gofa
Anjulo Asa–10	c.1960–70(d)	Sidama, Awassa
Anjulo Gaga–4	1955–75	Qucha, Koyra, Käfa
Anjulo Galso–6	1960–70	Maali, Bänna
Anjulo Masébo–10	c.1965–78	Sidama, Awassa
Arshé Dubé–8	1965–97	Käfa, Jimma
Asanaqé Alolo–13	c.1950–65	Gofa
Asha Alänbo–2	1952–65	Kullo Konta
Atalo Ashängo–5	1954–56(d)	Agaro
Atangé Adaré–11	1949–90(dp)	Gofa
Ayälä Toru–8	c.1955–65	Sidama
Ayällä Alato–13	1953–97(d)	Qucha, Kullo Konta
Ayällä Alito–8	1945–97(re)	Arsi,Kullo Konta,Gofa
Bädacho Anato–6	1948–55	Jimma
Badébo Banté–11	1948–60	Gofa
Balcha Bala–3	1937–55	Gämo, Gofa, Qucha
Baloté Aymalo,W/o–8	1952–65	Gofa
Bäqälo Qelto–10	1945–63	Sidama
Bärata Jabu–5	1941–53	Kambatta/Hadiya, Gofa
Barato Disa–9	c.1945–65(d)	Silti, Jimma
Basa Albato–5	1947–53	Arsi
Basa Fola–8	1955–70	Gofa, Aari, Bänna
Bäza Bakalo–9	1946–97(re)	Kambatta, Arsi
Birhanu Bukato–10	1970–85	Jimma, Aari, Zway, Awassa
Birhanu Haile–?	1969–74(dk)	Bänna
Biru Dubalä–8	1934–46(d)	Gofa, Kullo Konta
Bogalä Shené–15	1972–77	Kullo Konta
Boltana Borécho–8	1947–65(d)	Gofa
Bonga Boroda–11	1952–57	Gofa
Bonja Albé–11	1936–40	Gämo, Qucha
Borana Darébo–2	1953–73	Kullo Konta
Boré Sana–13	c.1945–57	Gämo
Borsamo Boqé–16	1949–90(d)	Gofa, Bale, Ghinir, Kullo Konta
Bosha Dinato–9	1968–76	Kullo Konta
Bunaro Sumago–8	1948–85	Sidama, Arsi, Käfa, Kullo Konta
Busharé Adaré–16	1955–65(d)	Aari

Chama Tumato–11	1950–60	Gofa
Chäramo Gäläso–8	1946–50(d)	Arsi
Charé Ashango–13	1973–75	Wällo
Chondo Wola–2	c.1952–68(d)	Kullo Konta
Choramo Cholo–14	1941–65	Gämo, Arsi, Gofa, Kullo Konta
Däbisa Iligo–6	1969–81	Asälla, Arsi
Dadu Chakiso–9	c.1948–55	Sidama
Dägoya Dändu–2	c.1954–60	Kullo Konta
Däjäné Dura–16	c.1955–65	Arsi, Kullo Konta
Daka Borana–4	1950–65	Kullo Konta
Dama Hémacho–14	1952–75(d)	Gofa
Däme Génbéro–5	1952–60	Burji/Koyra
Dana Anjajo–6	1939–43	Gämo
Dana Jallo–14	1957–71(d)	Gofa
Dana Känido–3	1950–63	Gofa, Aari, Bänna
Dana Lanbébo–3	1950–56	Gofa
Dana Léncho–13	1948–53	Gofa
Danél Choramo–8	1948–74	Gofa, Aari, Bänna
Danél Madalcho–11	1965–96(re)	Käfa, Kullo Konta
Daqeto Anato,W/o–15	1955–65	Kullo Konta
Dästa Amato–4	1949–65(d)	Arsi
Dästa Dayésa–8	c.1945–55	Gämo, Qucha
Dawet Anato–15	1972–77	Kullo Konta
Dawet Batamo–4	1949–91	Qucha, Burji/Koyra, Bale, Arsi
Dedana Däkesa–5	1941–65	Kambatta, Burji/Koyra, Maräqo
Dema Génbéro-5	1952–58	Burji/Koyra
Déngo Datamo–6	1945–65	Qucha, Kullo Konta
Déngo Sana–4	1950–92(d)	Gofa, Aari, Bänna
Deta Mandoyé–4	1970–77(d)	Maräqo
Didana Dilbato–14	1942–80(d)	Qucha
Dima ? –?	1952–54	Burji/Koyra
Doda Gémbéro–15	1948–65	Arsi, Sidama
Dola Alabo–5	1942–55	Maräqo/Silti
Dulata Mandoyé–11	1952–55	Qucha, Maräqo, Siraro, Butajira
Dumicho Durésa–2	c.1952–55(dr)	Kullo Konta
Éliyas Andabo–16	1971–74	Käfa
Éliyas Därgasu–9	1950–58	Janjäro, Dugda
Éliyas Kuné–9	1971–74	Käfa
Enaro Tumato–9	c.1963–75	Aari, Bänna
Éqaso Eybéro–10	1960–92	Sidama, Käfa, Bänna
Érmias Dolao–6	1968–74	Siraro
Ersado Kuké–2	1952–67	Gofa, Kullo Konta

Esayas Wada–14	1965–75	Jimma
Eyob Ololo–2	c.1950–97(re)	Kullo Konta
Falaha Olo–4	1953–62(d)	Gofa
Fanta Hébäna–10	1972–74	Käfa (born in Gofa)
Fanta Iltamo–15	c.1955–60(d)	Sidama
Färacho Chalalo–13	1953–66(d)	Qucha, Gofa
Faränjé Buré–3	W/o 1946–56	Gofa
Filimon Bakalo–4	1949–70	Gofa, Burji/Koyra, Aari, Bänna
Fola Gidébo–9	c.1965–75	Siraro, Arsi
Fola Tämbalo–4	1946–60(d)	Arsi
Folata Mobalo–4	1946–65	Arsi, Siré
G/Silasse Assa–9	1965–75	Hammär, Mursi
Gäfäto Jagiso–13	1941–43	Qucha
Gäfäto Gäbré–1	c.1945–55	Qucha
Gagébo Mäna–14	1951–67	Qucha, Gofa
Gälaso Adamo–6	c.1960–70	Siraro
Gälasu Gaga–9	1968–74	Ari, Bänna
Galcha Girmamo–16	1968–96	Kullo Konta, Käfa, Jimma
Galoré Guradé–4	1946–65	Arsi
Gamo Gabeso–9	1950–60	Arsi
Ganamo Dokilé–5	1944–55(d)	Qucha
Gänébo Gaga–9	1951–62	Burji/Koyra
Ganta Gäbirä–10	1965–85	Bänna
Gateso Gaga–14	1955–65	Kullo Konta
Géta Halala–1	c.1946–65(d)	Qucha
Gétahun Dalé–8	1957–97	Bänna, Kullo Konta
Gina Léra–15	1972–74	Kullo Konta
Gizaw Adamo–13	c.1945–65	Qucha, Gofa
Gizaw Gimago–2	1977–81	Käfa, Kullo Konta
Godana Gutullo–?	1944–48	Tämbaro, Kullo Konta
Godébo Adamo–6	1952–70	Janjäro, Assela, Siraro, Dugda
Gola ?–13	c.1944–50	Qucha
Gopilo Golo–13	1945–97(re)	Gämo, Kamba
Guja ? –10	c.1953–59	Sidama
Guradé Jägäna–11	1945–85(d)	Gofa, Goba, Burji, Aari, Bänna, Kullo Konta
Hadaro Dokilé–5	1952–60	Qucha
Hadaro Hantuka–9	1946–97(re)	Arsi
Hardedu Hatiyé–13	1943–75	Qucha, Gofa
Harkéso Halé–16	1968–74	Kullo Konta
Hatäro Aramo–14	1944–55	Gofa
Héläna Débesa–14	1940–55(d)	Gämo

Héliso Kuké–2	1952–84(d)	Gofa, Kullo Konta
Hiloré Nadabo–9	c.1970–75	Siraro
Hirboro ? –11	1936–46	Gämo
Hirboro Halabo–2	1958–72(d)	Kullo Konta
Indriyas Darécho–8	1960–96	Jimma
Indriyas Gobäna–6	1952–57(d)	Burji/Koyra
Inga Sharécho–2	1968–74(d)	Kullo Konta
Indriyas Kurfé–8	1971–75	Käfa
Indriyas Täntu–14	1969–75	Kullo Konta, Jimma
Ingäshaw Re<u>ch</u>o–16	c.1965–75	Kullo Konta
Irgado Babiso–11	1947–67(d)	Gofa
Israél Akoyé–6	1975–80	Awassa
Israél Anjulo–14	1950–65	Maräqo/Sil<u>t</u>i, Käfa, Bänna, Mursi
Israél Däkesa–4	1943–45(d)	Kullo Konta
Israel Soso–5	1952–55	Sil<u>t</u>e
Jara Bakalo–11	1940–79(d)	Gämo, Qu<u>ch</u>a, Gofa
Jore Urqé–9	1956–70	Asäla
Kasa Babecho–13	c.1940–55(d)	Gämo
Kasa Koyra–13	c.1970–97(re)	Kullo Konta
Kora Sana–13	c.1940–70	Gämo, Kullo Konta
Korga Zäläqä–9	1950–65	Arsi
Koroto ? –5	c.1942–50	Kambatta
Kusa Anamo–5	1950–56	Qu<u>ch</u>a, Kullo Konta
Kusa Gatiso–6	1951–53	Burji/Koyra
Kusa Mita–6	1969–77	Aari, Käfa, Bänna
Labéna Bonjo–6	1952–65	Arsi
Lalamo Boké–8	1942–87	Kambatta, Arsi, <u>T</u>ambaro, Kullo Konta, Gämo
Lalé Aymalo–2	1967–74	Kullo Konta
Laliso Täntu–ll	1937–60	Gämo, Gofa, Qu<u>ch</u>a
Läma Alqamo–9	1959–58	Amaro, Burji
Läma Hemacho–14	1948–60(d)	Gofa
Läma Olqamo–6	1956–59	Burji/Koyra
Lateno Lachoré–5	1950–65(d)	Qu<u>ch</u>a, Gofa
Lén<u>ch</u>a Lorato–14	1945–60	Gofa
Léra Guje–10	1946–90(d)	Sidama
Léra Legamo–14	1954–58	Gofa
Libabo Wabilo–8	c.1948–64	Gofa
Libabo Wobelo–3	1950–63(d)	Gofa
Lolamo Ébéro–7	1940–60	Sidama, <u>T</u>ämbaro, Kullo Konta
Madalcho Gésamo–7	1950–70(d)	<u>T</u>ämbaro, Gofa, Kullo Konta
Madalcho Maldayé–4	1950–57	Gofa

Madébo Boké–12	1948–50	Qucha, Gofa
Mahé Choramo–8	1945–97	Qucha, Gofa, Aari, Bänna, Käfa, Bodi, Mursi
Mäja Adélo–8	1946–83	Kullo Konta, Qucha, Burj/ Koyra, Aari, Bänna, Käfa
Mäja Mädéro–7	1940–55	Tämbaro, Kullo Konta
Mala Kurqé–9	1948–58	Arsi
Mälaqo Dana–8	1971–75	Käfa, Kullo Konta
Mälkamu Shanqo–2	1967–97	Kullo Konta, Käfa
Mamo Meja–9	1972–75	Käfa
Mäna Ako–3	1946–97(re)	Arsi
Matéwos Dora–2	1968–70	Kullo Konta
Matéwos Shunbulo–2	1952–55	Burji/Koyra
Matéwos Téqa–14	c.1943–65(dk)	Gofa, Maali
Matéwos W/Mädhin–15	1967–77	Siraro, Kullo Konta
Matusal Gebäyähu–2	1969–74	Kullo Konta
Mégaro Mégeso–9	1953–57	Burji/Koyra
Milkiyas Mamré–7	1965–75	Kullo Konta
Milkiyas Masoro–9	1945–97(re)	Kambatta, Arsi, Aari, Bänna
Minota Mishano–5	1942–97(re)	Kambatta/Hadiya, Maräqo, Gofa, Aari
Mola Urqé–9	1945–65	Arsi
Moleso Hitiso–2	c.1968–74(d)	Kullo Konta
Mulu Ulté–2	1965–75	Gofa, Käfa, Bänna
Muné ?–9	1948–55	Arsi, Burji/Koyra, Aari
Muné Gambéto–14	1965–97	Gofa, Käfa, Bänna, Kullo Konta
Muné Shano–8	1955–65	Silti
Nana Shaga–14	1954–91(d)	Gofa, Demi, Mursi
Oda Ogato–16	1944–60	Gofa, Qucha, Goba
Oida Odire–7	1947–55	Arsi
Ombolé Odiro–8	1944–92	Tämbaro, Kullo Konta, Goba, Aari, Käfa, Awassa
Omoché Ukulo–3	1944–55(dk)	Gofa
Pawlos Asärat–8	1969–90	Gofa, Bänna
Pawlos Dogeso–15	1972–84	Kullo Konta
Pawlos G/Maryam–2	1968–91	Käfa
Pawlos Gumago–2	1970–85	Kullo Konta
Pawlos Luga–2	1952–69	Kullo Konta
Pawlos Milkano–2	1969–79	Kullo Konta, Bänna
Pétros Asha–12	1968–80	Kullo Konta
Qaba Dedo–9	1952–75	Alaba, Wonji, Arsi
Sadébo Gundé–9	1952–60	Sidama

Sälasé Manchika–14	1970–95	Käfa
Sämago Galto–4	1955–86	Qucha, Aari, Bänna
Samuél Babeso–12	1960–70	Kullo Konta
Samuél Dido–9	1969–74	Kullo Konta
Samuél Galata–4	1967–97	Kullo Konta, Bänna
Samuél Sälasé–16	1968–77	Kullo Konta
Sawl Salgédo–2	1956–97	Sidama, Käfa, Siraro, Bänna, Kullo Konta
Séfu Giru–8	1971–97	Käfa, Siraro, Jimma
Seqa ? –4	1955–60	Burji/Koyra
Séta Wogaso–16	1968–74	Kullo Konta, Käfa
Shanka Alolo–4	1955–65	Gofa
Shanka Boroda–11	1949–60	Gämo, Gofa, Aari, Kullo Konta
Shanka Séto–13	1959–97(re)	Gofa
Shanka Shamébo–13	c.1950–60	Gofa
Shanka Tada–13	1950–61	Qucha, Gofa
Shano Borago–10	1945–55	Sidamo
Shonga Sadébo–15	1947–65	Sidama
Shonké Dilaba–13	1950–60	Gämo, Gofa
Shunké Shalämo–9	1945–65	Arsi, Gofa, Agaro, Janjäro
Silase Manchika–14	1969–97	Käfa
Soka Asha–7	1967–87	Bale, Burji/Koyra, Awassa
Soka Gateso–4	1951–74(d)	Burji/Koyra, Bänna
Sorsa Sumamo–9	1949–97(re)	Arsi, Sidama, Käfa, Sidama
T/Yohanis Bänta–11	1950–62	Gofa
Tadäsa Witango–9	1948–50(dk)	Gédéo
Tadewos Hatéso–2	1969–74(d)	Kullo Konta
Tadewos Yota–4	1970–74	Kullo Konta
Tadiwos Borago–16	1968–74	Käfa
Takiso Täntu–6	1969–71	Arsi, Siraro
Taltamo Saboré–2	1953–66(d)	Sidama
Tanga Dedo–9	1942–55	Gofa, Arsi
Tanga Lorato–9	1949–91	Sidama
Tanga Täntu–5	1941–60(d)	Kambatta, Maräqo
Täntu Debana–10	1946–85(re)	Arsi, Aari, Maali
Täntu Débéra–15	1945–55	Sidama
Täntu Mandoyé–15	c.1955–65	Sidama
Täntu Shasharo–4	1968–72	Kullo Konta
Täntu Yardo–7	1944–77	Qucha, Kullo Konta
Taso Hébäna–2	1953–97	Sidama, Kullo Konta, Käfa, Bänna, Käfa
Tola Tala–9	c.1950–60	Siraro

Toma Dana–16	1968–74	Kullo Konta
Tomas Alaro–8	1952–90	Sidama, Siraro, Kullo Konta, Aari, Bänna
Toramo Leqa–13	c.1945–55	Kullo Konta
Toro Dubusho–13	1942–44	Qucha
Toro Gadimo–7	1951–64	Sidama
Tumébo Tala–1	c.1953–75	Kullo Konta
Wachalé Kasamo–4	1955–60	Maräqo/Silti
Wada Damana–14	1951–61	Qucha, Gofa
Wadébo, Goda–14	1937–60	Qucha, Gofa
Waga Dilgato–5	1955–66	Kullo Konta
Wana Dägalo–5	1951–85	Burji/Koyra, Goba, Kullo Konta
Wäldé Silase–4	1971–75	Käfa
Wanté Walela–13	1944–48	Gämo
Wogaso Däbana–16	1975–80	Kullo Konta
Wogaso Walila–13	1944–49	Gämo, Qucha, Kullo Konta
Wogaso Womago–5	1969–75	Käfa
Yada Ejaju–6	c.1942–55	Gämo
Yaiqob Chunfuré–16	1972–97(re)	Kullo Konta
Yaiqob Fältamo–9	c.1965–75	Bänna, Kullo Konta
Yaiqob Larébo–5	c.1960–91	Kullo Konta
Yamané Madalcha–7	1950–69	Aari, Bänna, Gofa
Yayinya Chagiso–12	1965–80	Jimma
Yayna Mégéso–12	1965–75	Jimma
Yinoré Hadaro	1968–74	Siraro
Yohanis Adéto–4	1952–60	Kullo Konta
Yohanis Bäqälä–12	1965–80	Kullo Konta
Yohanis Basana–5	1970–73	Kullo Konta
Yohanis Dado–15	1970–90	Kullo Konta
Yohanis Darota–13	1945–97(re)	Gofa
Yohanis Ukulo–4	1949–55	Gofa
Yohanis Wanjamo–16	1969–97	Käfa
Yohanis Washé–4	1971–97	Käfa, Kullo Konta
Yoséf Mäna–8	1969–76	Kullo Konta
Yosha Shämäna–6	1952–97(re)	Gofa
Zäkéwos Malaqo–5	1945–67	Qucha, Kullo Konta

There were 295 Wolaitta cross–cultural evangelists, listed above, who served two years or more from 1937 to 1975.

Official Permission Letter for the Fellowship of Evangelical Believers' Association

Number 0/9251/56

Säné 28, 1955 E.C.
[July 4, 1963]

To the President of the Fellowship of Evangelical Believers' Association,
Addis Ababa

The Fellowship of Evangelical Believers' Association has been granted permission to be established according to the constitution they have duly submitted.

1st/ In the future, if the Association's purpose is to be presented in a different form or changed according to your thoughts to suit your work, according to Article #476 of the Feteha National Code, the reason for altering [the Constitution] must be stated in writing to the Ministry of Interior Public Security Department 15 days prior to the change becoming effective.

2nd/ If the Association is found to be operating outwith or contravening your [own] constitution, we caution [warn you] from the outset that what is stated in the Feteha National Code Article #461, section "A" and Article #462, sub-section #1 will be the basis for action [against you].

We notify [you] that 15 days prior to a general meeting of the Association, you are to inform us [of such a meeting] in writing.

With peace,
Ato Tilahun Belete

(See Amharic copy next page.)

የሕዝብ · ደኅንነት · ጠባቃ ።
MINISTRY OF INTERIOR
PUBLIC SECURITY DEPT.

ቁጥር :

አ/ል .....

 የፖስታ · ጥ · ቁ ·
P. O. Box

የስልክ · ቁ · ጥር ·   13
Tel. No.   13

ለወንጌል አገኝች አንድነት ማህበር   ግፈዳሪት ግ

አዲስ አበበ ::

የወንጌል አማኝች አንድነት ወረፃ ማህበር ለባጀቱ እንዲታደ በተደረጉ
ግጣስኝ፦ የማህበሩ የወጡ ዶገብ መሠረቶ እንዣሬ ቲ ቀፃደስ ::

1ኛ / ለወደረት የማህሩረን ዓላፃ በአነ ወሰከ ለማሽከል ወይፀ ለወለፃ
በአበቡ ዝፍ፦ ሠይ ከጣዊሳ፥ አስተፀ ናቹ በጨር ሕን ጥር 476 እነደተገለ
አው የማሽሺልበ እነ ቀከ1ገት ከ15 ቀነ እስተፀ ሰ ስባሰ ፀፃ ቀበ ጸ / በ
በጽፍ እነ ፎ ተ ርበ ::

2ኛ / ከእተረ ነ የማበ መ ደ የወስ ፀ ነበ ወ .ሠር ተ ቢ ፦ ና ፦
ኞ ር ዘ ጥር 461 በ ., ከ ፀ ጀ በ ጥር 462 ገ ስ እ ተ በ 1 በ ተ ፀ
ገ ወ ት የ ፎ ዎ ሆ አ አ ስ ተ ፀ እ ረ ስ ነ ተ ::

ማህ ፀ መ ስ ስ ስ በ ፀ ገ ት ዝ ስ ስ ከ ረ ረ ከ ፦ ተ
ክ ፀ እ ፎ ተ በ ጽ አ ዲ ግ ለ ለ እ ስ ተ

APPENDIX 4

Wolaitta *Mahibär* Response to 1975 Land Reform Bill

The Woleyta *mahibär* recalled all their evangelists at the time of the Land Reform Bill in [of] February, 1975.[1] We had plane load after plane load of men, wives and children land on us at Otona. It took some arranging to get them all a place to sleep and some *kurso* (breakfast or snacks) to eat until they could get their families settled for the time of planning and discussions with the *mahibär* elders over the future of evangelism.

The essence of the Land Reform Bill was that everyone who wanted land would be given a plot large enough for his family but that no one could have two sources of income. This meant that if one chose land as his means of livelihood he had to be present to work his land and could not have another job. This had tremendous consequences for the evangelists from Woleyta because most kept tracts of land that others farmed for them while they were away in evangelism. They even had cattle that others kept for them.

The Woleyta elders wanted to discuss these implications with their evangelists so that all could make the wisest choice possible for the future. Discussions were held and all the implications of continuing as evangelists were considered. Then, the question was put to the group of some 50 evangelists, "Do you want to continue as evangelists, or do you want to return to your home areas and claim land?"

The evangelists asked for time to pray and discuss among themselves. When they gave their answer it was a unanimous "Yes," for evangelism. They said in essence, "God has cared for us 'til now. He will continue to provide our needs until we die. We're going [giving] our lives to Him and if we lose our land, we lose it."

1. The evangelists actually returned home in March and April. Lila Balisky, diary, entry for March 26, 1975, records that MAF transported Wolaitta evangelists from Bonga to Soddo. (Note by EPB.)

While the evangelists answered with a resounding affirmative to continue their evangelism work, the elders still felt some practical concern for them. They feared it might be too difficult for many to continue on their meagre allowances (33.00 Eth. at that time) if they didn't have their land and crops to fall back on. So the elders decided to set the following guidelines for all who wanted to be evangelists under the Woleyta *mahibär*:

1. A family could not have more than 7 children.
2. All evangelists should have completed 4 years of Bible School. Those who had not completed up to this level should stay at home in Woleyta and finish to at least the 4th year.
3. All must have medical clearance from the local mission hospital, both wives and men.

This eliminated about 1/3 to 1/2 of the previous evangelists. Some 20–25 were back in the areas where they had labored. As others became eligible, they were sent out to new areas or helped to fill the gaps in the former areas.

A refresher course was held for a week for all before they returned to their field.

(Drafted by Merle Dye)
SIM Soddo Station Manager, n.d. [May 1975?]

APPENDIX 5

Graph of Wolaitta Evangelists

Commissioned and Supported by the Wolaitta Mahibär for 45 Years

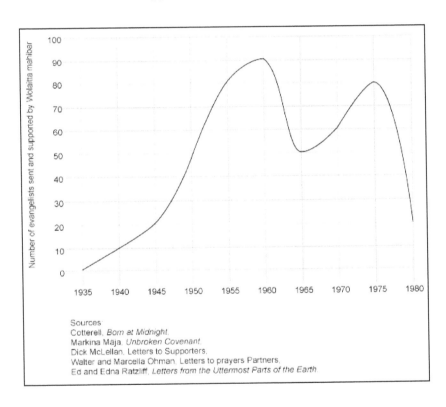

SOURCES:

Cotterell, *Born at Midnight.*
Dick McLellan, letters to prayer partners.
Markina Meja, *Unbroken Covenant.*
Walter and Marcella Ohman, letters to prayer partners.
Ratzliff and Ratzliff, *Letters from the Uttermost Parts of the Earth.*

Glossary

abbal Clerical title meaning "father."

adärash Reception hall used for large feasts and important assemblies. An essential building for all meetings in every Ethiopian town.

aläqa An ecclesiastical title referring to the chief priest. Also may mean: head, chief, doctor of theology.

amanyä A believer within the new churches movement.

amanyoch Believers in Jesus who identify with the new churches movement.

antiränya Metal worker. Also known as *qächqachi*.

aqwamä hig The official KHC constitution, which contains the governing doctrine and practice recognized by all member churches.

arämawiyan Those who have no religion; pagans.

ashkir A servant or retainer that serves the overlord.

asrat Annual tithe paid to the church, usually 10 percent.

ato A courteous address that precedes the name of a man, similar to the English "Mr." It is a contraction of *abéto*.

awaj Public proclamation of an official law.

awraja Previously, an administrative sub-province. The present government has modified the meaning.

ayana Among most ethnic groups of southern Ethiopia, spiritual power that resides within a leader. Wolaitta royalty usually are endowed with this when they received the ring of authority. Individuals with *ayana* are highly respected by the community.

bäjirond Treasurer of the imperial finances or keeper of the patron's wardrobe. A most influential official of the court who enjoyed the confidence of the ruler.

balabat Literally, "One who has a father." In southern Ethiopia he was an indigenous official providing the chief administrative link between his own ethnic population and the central government. The administrative unit is called a *balabatänät*.

bätäwodäd A senior adviser to the imperial court.

bétä kristeyan Literally, "Christian house"; used originally by the EOC for their places of worship. Now it is commonly used by both the EOC and the new churches movement to designate the church building.

birr Ethiopian currency. From 1946 to 1975 US $1 was worth about 2 EB.

buluqo A thick, hand-woven garment made of cotton—a specialty of the Dorzé weavers—used extensively by southern highlanders for keeping warm. Often given as a farewell gift.

chäwa A free-born person; a gentleman who speaks with dignity. A trait found among Amhara nobility.

chiqa shum A village headman.

chisänya A tenant farmer; literally, "one who is the owner of the smoke from a grass-roofed house."

däga The highlands of Ethiopia above 2,000 meters.

däjazmach A military title that corresponds to a general; literally, "commander of the gate to the king's tent." During the reign of Menilek II and Haile Sellassie, the title *Däjazmach* was connected with holding the important position of governor of a province.

dana Wolaitta title of honor for one who has performed an exploit. Has become a common name within Wolaitta.

danya Usually a judge of a lower court. In southern Ethiopia, often means anyone in a position of authority or rule who metes out judgment. Title given to lesser officials; written *dana* in Wolaitta.

dergue Appellation used by the Mengistu Haile Mariam regime to designate the executive of that military government. Root meaning is "to act," "to do something."

dubusha Wolaitta term for the place where the *mäsqäl dämära* is ignited each year in September.

endärasé A deputy or representative; literally, "just as if [he is] my head."

ensette edulis A leafy plant that looks very much like the banana. The starchy pulp, served in a variety of ways, is the staple food of the Cushitic peoples of southern Ethiopia.

faqi A tanner of hides.

färänj A non-Ethiopian. Probably originated when contact was made with Europeans from Florence.

faseka Ethiopian Easter, celebrated according to the Julian calendar.

fetawrare A military title; literally means, "one who goes before."

firdibét The government courthouse; literally, "house of judgment."

fuga A potter.

gäbbar A peasant landholder who is responsible to pay taxes to the government. He is always in a client status to his landlord.

gänna Ethiopian Christmas, celebrated on January 6 according to the Julian calendar.

gasha A unit of land measuring about 60 x 60 meters. The size varies according to productivity and the number of peasant farmer residents.

gibär Government tribute or taxes collected annually.

gibär shum A client chosen to collect taxes from his peers.

goda A Wolaitta honorific title ascribed to a highly respected elder.

gomé; *gomeata* Wolaitta word used to describe a prohibition that is religiously adhered to in order to ward off malevolent spirits.

grazmach A military title; literally, "commander of the left flank."

gudit A primal designation for all witches. Northerners refer to Gudit as a cruel queen from the South who destroyed much of northern Christianity in the tenth century.

gult Extensive land-use rights given to high ranking Ethiopian officials responsible to administrate a given area. Because of the land-use benefit, these officials are not salaried but are allowed to collect taxes from the peasants residing on the *gult* holding. The Orthodox Church was also allotted *gult* land. The Ethiopian Revolution of 1974 set in motion the Land Reform Act, which abolished this exploitative system of land use.

hamsa aläqä A military term; literally, "leader of 50 soldiers."

kätäma An Ethiopian town, but traditionally used to designate a fortified garrison populated by soldiers that was strategically located for military purposes.

kawo Wolaitta word for "king." The original Wolaitta rulers originated from the northern province of Tegré.

mahibär Originated as a religious self-help association within a local Orthodox church, meeting each month to commemorate a saint. The members of the new churches movement of southern Ethiopia adapted the *mahibär* for their own use. For example, the 825 local Wolaitta KHC are structured geographically into sixteen districts, or *kifil mahibär*. Each of the sixteen *kifil mahibär* meet regularly every month to discuss matters pertaining to the local churches. Usually three or four elders represent each local church at a *kifil mahibär*.

marcha Metal bar (3 cm. x 1 m. long) used for currency prior to 1920 only in Wolaitta. Was replaced by the Austrian Maria Theresa *thaler*, which in turn was replaced by the *birr* after Haile Sellassie's victorious return to Ethiopia in May 1941.

mäsqäl Annual celebration on September 21 of the finding of the true cross by St. Helena, mother of Constantine; one of the significant Christian holidays in Ethiopia. This term is also used to designate "cross."

matäb A special cord tied around the neck of every new adherent of the Ethiopian Orthodox Church.

näftänya A northern soldier allocated a piece of land in the South as reward for his military service to the imperial government.

nägarit A large drum sounded to announce a call to war or some significant government decree.

nigus Amharic word for king. Formerly, the highest ranking official of an ethnic group.

nigusä nägäst Emperor. Literally, "king of kings."

qädus qurban Lord's Supper, in which all baptized *amanyoch* are invited to participate each month.

qalad A piece of land that has been officially surveyed; literally, "the rope used to measure."

qalicha Literally, "possessor of the spirit." May be linked to the Oromo *qallu,* a traditional man of religion or one who slaughters (ritually); a magician-priest common in Islamized Oromo populations. In Wolaitta the *qalicha* clan fast from Thursday evening until Friday evening, during which time prayers of blessing and cursing are made. It is customary to chew *chat,* a narcotic leaf, for the duration of this fast.

qänyazmach A military title now of lesser rank; literally, "commander of the right."

qätäna A sub-district within a city or a province. Also, a group of churches cooperating together for fellowship or a project.

qés Historically, a priest in the Orthodox Church. Pastors in the Mekane Yesus denomination are called "*qés.*" In Wolaitta a derivative word, *qésiga,* is used to designate either a traditional priest or a cleric within the EOC.

qola Ethiopian lowlands below 1,500 meters; usually malaria infested.

ras By the nineteenth century, a high ranking military title designating one who commands the army; literally, "head." In battle the *ras* was positioned next to the king. There was a proliferation of these officials during the militaristic reign of Menilek.

rist A piece of land, as well as land-use rights, involving privileges and obligations; in principle, hereditary. The obligation was the payment of an annual tax either to the local landlord or a government official. The privilege was the right to transfer the deed to one's descendants. *Rist* was claimed by both peasant and landlord.

säbake Preacher. Sometimes used by the Amharas to designate an evangelist.

sälot bét Literally, "house of prayer." Used within the new churches movement to designate the church building.

sämint danya In former days referred to the eight coordinators/elders/judges of the Wolaitta kingdom representing the eight districts of the *awraja.* They are called *hospän dana* in Wolaitta and now refer to the twenty-four Wolaitta KHC elders who represent the districts to the monthly KHC *tärapéza* meeting held at the Anka center.

shämagälé A respected elder in the community. A church leader is called *yäbétä kristeyan shämagälé.*

shambäl Formerly, the title designating a commander of a garrison containing up to 300 soldiers; now is used to mean a prison official.

shängo A regular meeting of local officials (church or community) to discuss business matters.

shänqäla Literally, "a black one." Used traditionally to refer to the Nilotic inhabitants of the western Ethiopian periphery, such as the lowlands of the Blue Nile or Omo River basins. The word now has a pejorative connotation.

sharechewa Wolaitta word for a diviner who can predict the future by reading the entrails of an animal or by throwing stones on a board. In Amharic, *tänqway* is equivalent.

shifta An outlaw or bandit; a word of Arabic derivation common to East Africa.

sidama The appellation given the Cushitic population of South-Central Ethiopia by the Oromo. The invading sixteenth century Oromo called all non-Oromo and those who had a Christian orientation "*sidama.*" Now used to designate the ethnic people residing south of Lake Awassa and north of Lake Abbaye.

sidamo Formerly, one of the fourteen provinces of Ethiopia. Broadly speaking, could mean any of the diverse ethnic groups residing in Sidamo province.

tabeya A station or center from which activities emanate.

tabot A wooden replica of the Solomonic ark of the covenant found in every Eastern Orthodox church. It is the object of that church's patron saint, whose name is carved on the *tabot*. KHC evangelists were often falsely accused and incarcerated for calling the *tabot* a "meaningless block of wood."

täj An alcoholic drink made from honey water.

tälähéya The Omotic goddess of the Omo River. Since the Menilek II conquest, *tälähéya* has become, to the Omotic peoples, a malevolent spirit. The people of Gädicho Island honor the crocodile by offering various kinds of sacrifices; they call this ritual *tälähéya*. The Wolaitta interchange the words *tälähéya* and *saytan* to mean "that which is evil."

taléya The Wolaitta pronunciation of "Italian" during the occupation.

tänqway A diviner who foretells the future by interpreting signs or omens. This is usually done by reading the entrails of a goat, sheep, or chicken. The word is derived from the Amharic "*tänäqola*," which means the practice of the occult or to deceive. A soothsayer.

ta'ot An idol or object that is worshipped.

tärapéza Literally, "table." Because pre-Italian SIM missionaries discussed important business matters with Wolaitta church leaders around a table in the evening, subsequent Wolaitta monthly church business meetings held at Otona were called "*tärapéza.*" All Wolaitta church districts are represented at this meeting. Other KHC areas such as Kambatta/Hadiya and Gédéo call this regular meeting of church leaders "*shängo.*" The Wolaitta KHC center at Anka is referred to by many as *tärapéza*.

täskär Literally, "remembrance." This memorial celebration for the dead is usually celebrated forty days after burial. After this it is celebrated annually. The
outlay of food, drink, and cash for this celebration is considerable.

ṭimqät In the EOC, an annual holiday on January 12 that commemorates the
baptism of Jesus by John the Baptist. Among Kale Heywet Church members,
it is the occasion for baptizing converts who have been taught the basics of
the Christian faith for at least six months.

Ṭosa Name of high God for most of the Omotic-speaking people.

wähine bét A prison where convicts are detained and where the Wolaitta evangelists were once incarcerated.

wängélawe An evangelist who is involved in an itinerant ministry of preaching
the gospel. Those serving within a KHC area were called *wisṭ wängélawe*.
Those ministering in "unreached" ethnic areas were the *wiche wängélawe*.

wäräda A sub-district within an *awraja* with its own administrative structure.

wéne dägä The fertile plains of Ethiopia between 1500 and 2000 meters.

Wézäro (W/o) The title that precedes a married woman's name, similar to the
English "Mrs."

wogésha Herbalist, healer, or bone setter. A helpful medical specialist in
Ethiopian society.

wuqabé Protective spirit of the ancestor that must be honored and appeased
with food offerings and libations.

yäsimänt danya Literally, "the eight judges." Now refers to the ruling body of
elders in traditional Wolaitta society. Many Wolaitta KHC members use this
term for the *ṭärapéza* elders. These elders (at one time up to twenty-four)
fulfill the role of spiritual leaders in the Wolaitta KHC.

zämächa Ordinarily, a military campaign, but could designate any organized
group foray to accomplish a stated objective, such as a literacy or evangelism
campaign. The verb form is *zämätä*.

zar A spirit-possession cult. Also, a kind of spirit.

zär Literally, "seed." Used to designate clan. There are over 130 clans within
Wolaitta. *Gosa* has the wider meaning of "tribe."

(Note: Ethiopic script does not utilize a capital form; therefore, in this glossary all entries
are made in lowercase Latin letters. In the text, however, Amharic words are capitalized
when they would be capitalized in English.)

Bibliography

Published Articles

Abéles, Marc. "La guerre vue d'Ochollo" (Éthiopie méridionale). *Canadian Journal of African Studies* 11 (1977) 455–70.

Abir, Mordechai. "The Emergence and Consolation of the Monarch of Enarea and Jimma in the First Half of the Nineteenth Century." *Journal of African Studies* 6, no. 2 (1965) 205–19.

Abir, M. "Southern Ethiopia." In *Pre-Colonial African Trade: Essays on Trade in Central and Eastern Africa before 1900*, edited by Richard Gray and David Birmingham, 119–37. London: Oxford University Press, 1970.

Adams, Bruce. "The Strange Prophecy of the Golden Book." *Africa Now* 39 (July–August 1968) 10–11.

Almeida, Manoel de. "The History of High Ethiopia." In Beckingham and Huntingford, *Some Records of Ethiopia*, 145–66.

Athill, L. F. I. "Through South-Western Abyssinia to the Nile." *Geographical Journal* 56, no. 2 (1920) 347–70.

Bähäré. "History of the Galla." In Budge, *History of Ethiopia, Nubia & Abyssinia*, 2:603–17.

Bairu Tafla. "Four Ethiopian Biographies." *Journal of Ethiopian Studies* 5, no. 2 (1969) 133–50.

Balisky, E. Paul. "Birru Dubale." *Dictionary of African Christian Biography*. No pages. Online: htpp://www.dacb.org/stories/ethiopia/dubale_birru.html.

————. "Esa Lale, a Prophet of Religious Innovation in Southern Ethiopia." In Baye Yiman et al., *Proceedings of the XIVth International Conference of Ethiopian Studies*, 568–81.

Bartels, Lambert. "Studies of The Galla in Wälläga." *Journal of Ethiopian Studies* 8, no. 1 (1970) 135–59.

Bartnicki, Andrzej, and Joanna Mantel-Niecko. "The Role and Significance of the Religious Conflicts and People's Movements in the Political Life of Ethiopia in the Seventeenth and Eighteenth Centuries." *Rassega di Studi Etiopici* 24 (1969) 5–39.

Beckingham, C. F., and G. W. B. Huntingford. "The Ethnology and History of South-West Ethiopia." In Beckingham and Huntingford, *Some Records of Ethiopia*, l–lxxviii.

Bediako, Kwame. "Christ in Africa: Some Reflections on the Contribution of Christianity to the African Becoming." In *African Futures: Conference: Papers*, 449–58. 25th Anniversary Conference, December 9–11, 1987. Seminar Proceedings—University of Edinburgh Centre of African Studies 28. 1988.

Beidelman, T. O. "Social Theory and the Study of Christian Mission." *Africa* 44, no. 3 (1974) 235–49.

Beke, Charles T. "On the Countries South of Abyssinia." *Journal of the Royal Geographical Society* 13 (1843) 254–69.

———. "On the Languages and the Dialects of Abyssinia and the Countries of the South." *Philological Society* 2, no. 33 (April 25, 1845) 89–107.

———. "Routes in Abyssinia" *Journal of the Royal Geographical Society* 14, no. 1 (1844) 1–75.

Bingham, R. V. "Long Live the King—A Coronation in Ancient Abyssinia." *Evangelical Christian,* October 1930, 575–76.

Blackhurst, Hector. "Ethnicity in Southern Ethiopia: The General and the Particular." *Africa* 50, no. 1 (1980) 55–65.

Blundell, H. Weld. "Exploration in the Abai Basin, Abyssinia." *Geographical Journal* 27, no. 6 (1906) 529–58.

———. "A Journey through Abyssinia to the Nile." *Geographical Journal* 15, no. 2 (1900) 96–120.

Boff, Leonard. "Theological Characteristics of a Grass-roots Church." In *The Challenge of the Basic Christian Communities,* edited by Sergio Rorres and John Eagleson, 124–42. Maryknoll, NY: Orbis, 1981.

Bonk, Jonathan. "Church Growth in Ethiopia." *Africa Now* 75, July/August 1974, 18.

Braukämper, Ulrich. "Aspects of Religious Syncretism in Southern Ethiopia." *Journal of Religion in Africa* 22, no. 3 (1992) 194–207.

———. "The Correlation of Oral Tradition and Historical Records in Southern Ethiopia: A Case Study of the Hadiya/Sidamo Past." *Journal of Ethiopian Studies* 11, no. 2 (1973) 29–50.

———. "The Ethnogenesis of the Sidama." *Journal of Ethiopian Studies* 14 (1978) 123–30.

Bridges, Roy C. "Book Review of *Black Evangelists: The Spread of Christianity in Uganda 1891–1914,*" by M. Louise Pirouet, London: Rex Collins, 1978. *Journal of Religion in Africa* 10, no. 2 (1979)143–45.

Brunner, Emil. *The Word and the World.* London: SCM, 1931.

Bureau, Jacques. "The 'Tigre' Chronicle of Wollaita; A Pattern of Kingship." In Pankhurst et al., *Proceedings of the First National Conference of Ethiopian Studies,* 49–64.

Caulk, R. A. "Religion and the State in Nineteenth Century Ethiopia." *Journal of Ethiopian Studies* 10, no. 1 (1972) 23–53.

Clapham, Christopher. "Centralization and Local Response in Southern Ethiopia." *African Affairs* 74, no. 294 (1975) 72–81.

Coleman, Robert E., "The Authority of the Great Commission." *Trinity World Forum* 16, no. 2 (1991) 1–3.

Cotterell, F. Peter. "The Case of Ethiopia." In Shenk, *Exploring Church Growth,* 12–23.

———. "Dr. T. A. Lambie: Some Biographical Notes." *Journal of Ethiopian Studies* 10, no. 1 (1972) 43–53.

———. "An Indigenous Church in Southern Ethiopia." *Bulletin for African Church History* 3, no. 1–2 (1970) 68–104.

Crummey, Donald E. "Book Review of *Fire on the Mountains* by Raymond J. Davis." *Journal of Religion in Africa* 1 (1968) 156–57.

———. "Shaikh Zakaryas, an Ethiopian Prophet." *Journal of Ethiopian Studies* 10, no. 1 (1972) 55–66.

———. "The Violence of Téwodros." *Journal of Ethiopian Studies* 9, no. 2 (1971) 107–25.

Donham, Donald. "Old Abyssinia and the New Ethiopian Empire: Themes in Social History." In Donham and James, *Southern Marches of Imperial Ethiopia*, 3–48.

Duff, Clarence W. "The Gospel in Ethiopia." *Evangelical Christian*, March 1938, 145–46.

Edwards, Jon R. "Slavery, the Slave Trade, and the Economic Reorganization of Ethiopia." *African Economic History* no. 11 (1982) 3–14.

Ellis, Gene. "The Feudal Paradigm as a Hindrance to Understanding Ethiopia." *Journal of African Studies* 14, no. 2 (1976) 275–95.

Eyayu Luseged. "Why do the Orthodox Christians in Ethiopia Identify Their Faith with Their Nation?" In Pankhurst et al., *Proceedings of the First National Conference of Ethiopian Studies*, 3–11.

Fargher, Brian. "Mahay Choramo." "Dictionary of African Christian Biography," http://www.dacb.org/stories/ethiopia/choramo_mahay.html

Fasholé-Luke, Edward W. "Ancestor Veneration and the Communion of Saints." In Glasswell and Fasholé-Luke, *New Testament Christianity for Africa and the World*, 209–21.

Fernandez, James W. "African Religious Movements." *Journal of Modern African Studies* 2, no. 4 (1964) 531–49.

Fleming, Harold C. "Omotic Overview." In *The Non-Semitic Languages of Ethiopia*, edited by M. Lionel Bender, 299–313. Occasional Papers Series—Committee on Ethiopian Studies 5. East Lansing, MI: African Studies Center, Michigan State University, 1976.

———. "Recent Research in Omotic Speaking Areas." In Marcus et al., *Proceedings of the First United States Conference on Ethiopian Studies*, 261–78.

Garretson, Peter P. "Vicious Cycles: Ivory, Slaves, and Arms on the new Maji Frontier." In Donham and James, *Southern Marches of Imperial Ethiopia*, 196–218.

Gatatchew Haile. "Power Struggle in the Medieval Court of Ethiopia: The Case of Bätärgela Maryam." *Journal of Ethiopian Studies* 15 (1982) 37–56.

Gheddo, Piero. "A New Church is Born under Persecution." *Religion in Communist Lands* 9, no. 1–2 (1982) 156–66.

Gray, Richard. "Christianity and Religious Change in Africa." *African Affairs* 77, no. 306 (1978) 89–100.

———. "Problem of Historical Perspective: The Planting of Christianity in Africa in the Nineteenth and Twentieth Centuries." In Baëta, *Christianity in Tropical Africa*, 18–29.

Gwynn, C. W. "A Journey in Southern Ethiopia." *Geographical Journal* 38, no. 2 (1911) 113–34.

Haberland, E. "The Influence of the Christian Ethiopian Empire on Southern Ethiopia." *Journal of Semitic Studies* 9 (1964) 235–38.

"Haile Selassie: Man of the Year." *Time* 27, no. 1 (1936) 13–17.

Haliburton, G. "The Calling of the Prophet: Sampson Oppong." *Bulletin of the Society for African Church History* 2, no. 1 (1965) 84–96.

Hallpike, C. R. "The Origins of the Borana Gada System." *Africa* 46 (1976) 48–55.

———. "The Status of Craftsmen among the Konso of South-West Ethiopia." *Africa* 38, no. 2 (1968) 258–68.

Hamer, John H. "Myth, Ritual and the Authority of Elders in an Ethiopian Society." *Africa* 46 (1976) 327–39.

———. "Rivalry and Taking Kinsmen for Granted: Factors in the Development of Voluntary Associations." *Journal of Anthropological Research* 38, no. 3 (1982) 303–14.

————. "Sidamo Generational Class Cycles: A Political Gerontocracy." *Africa* 40 (1970) 50–70.

Hamer, John, and Irene Hamer. "Spirit Possession and Its Socio-Psychological Implications among the Sidamo of Southwest Ethiopia." *Ethnology* 5, no. 4 (1966) 392–408.

Harbeson, John W. "Socialism, Traditions, and Revolutionary Politics in Contemporary Ethiopia." *Canadian Journal of African Studies* 11, no. 2 (1977) 217–34.

Harrison, James J. "A Journey from Zeila to Lake Rudolf." *Geographical Journal* 18 (1901) 258–75.

Heldman, Marilyn E. "Christ's Entry into Jerusalem in Ethiopia." In Baëta, *Christianity in Tropical Africa*, 43–60.

Hodson, Arnold. "Southern Abyssinia." *Geographical Journal* 52, no. 2 (1919) 65–83.

Hooper, E. Ralph. "The Wail of the Walamo." *Evangelical Christian,* July 1932, 317–18.

Horton, Robin. "African Conversion." *Africa* 42, no. 2 (1971) 85–108.

————. "Of the Rationality of Conversion." *Africa* 45, no. 3 (1975) 219–35.

Horvath, Ronald J. "The Wandering Capitals of Ethiopia." *Journal of African History* 10, no. 2 (1969) 205–19.

Hultkrantz, Ake. "An Ideological Dichotomy: Myths and Folk Beliefs among the Shoshone Indians of Wyoming." *History of Religions* 2 (1972) 339–53.

Huntingford, G. W. B. "The Lives of Saint Täklä Haymanot." *Journal of Ethiopian Studies* 4, no. 2, (1966) 35–40.

————. "Saints of Mediaeval Ethiopia." *Aba Salama* 10 (1979) 257–341.

Iwarsson, I. "A Moslem Mass Movement towards Christianity." *Moslem World* 14 (1924) 286–89.

Jessen, B. H. "South-Western Abyssinia." *Geographical Journal* 25 (1905) 158–71.

Kaplan, Steven. "The Africanization of Missionary Christianity: History and Typology." *Journal of Religion in Africa* 16, no. 3 (1986) 166–86.

————. "The Ethiopian Holy Man as Outsider and Angel." *Religion* 15 (1985) 235–49.

————. "Ezana's Conversion Reconsidered." *Journal of Religion in Africa* 13, no. 2 (1982) 101–9.

————. "Hagiographies and the History of Medieval Ethiopia." *History in Africa* 8 (1981) 107–23.

Keller, Edmond J. "Ethiopia: Revolution, Class, and the National Question." *African Affairs* 80, no. 321 (1981a) 519–49.

————. "The Revolutionary Transformation of Ethiopia's Twentieth-Century Bureaucratic Empire." *Journal of Modern African Studies* 19, no. 2 (1981) 307–35.

Kobishchanov, Y. M. "Aksum: Political System, Economics and Culture, First to Fourth Century." In UNESCO, *General History of Africa*, 381–99.

Kraft, Charles H. "Ideological Factors in Intercultural Communication." *Missiology* 2, no. 3 (1974) 295–312.

Lambie, T. A. "Impasse." *Evangelical Christian,* October 1930, 596–97.

Lass-Westphal, Ingeborg. "Protestant Missions during and after the Italo-Ethiopian War, 1935–1937." *Journal of Ethiopian Studies* 10, no. 1 (1972) 89–101.

Lebel, Philip. "Oral Tradition and Chronicles on Gurage Immigration." *Journal of Ethiopian Studies* 12, no. 2 (1974) 95–106.

Leslau, Wolf. "An Ethiopian Argot of People Possessed by a Spirit." *Africa* 19, no. 3 (1949) 204–12.

————. "The Influence of the Sidamo in the Ethiopic Language of Gurage." *Language* 27, no. 1 (1952) 63–81.

Levine, Donald D. "Ethiopia: Identity, Authority, and Realism." In *Political Culture and Political Development,* edited by Lucian W. Pye and Sidney Verba, 245–81. Studies in Political Development 5. Princeton: Princeton University Press, 1965.

Levine, Donald. "On the History and Culture of Manz." *Journal of Ethiopian Studies* 9, no. 1 (1964) 204–11.

Lewis, Herbert S. "Neighbors, Friends, and Kinsmen: Principles of Social Organization among the Cushitic-Speaking Peoples of Ethiopia." *Ethnology* 13, no. 2 (1974) 145–57.

———. "A Reconsideration of the Socio-Political System of the Western Galla." *Journal of Semitic Studies* 9 (1964) 139–43.

Loewen, Jacob A. "Mission Churches, Independent Churches, and Felt Needs in Africa." *Missiology* 4, no. 2 (1976) 405–25.

———. "Myth and Mission: Should a Missionary Study Tribal Myths?" In *Readings in Missionary Anthropology II*, edited by William A. Smalley, 287–332. South Pasadena, CA: William Carey Library, 1978.

Mafeje, Archie. "The Ideology of 'Tribalism.'" *Journal of African Studies* 9, no. 2 (1971) 253–61.

Marcus, Harold G. "Imperialism and Expansion in Ethiopia from 1865–1900." In *Colonialism in Africa: 1870–1960*, edited by L. H. Gann and Peter Duignan, 2:420–59. London: Cambridge University Press, 1969.

———. "The Last Years of the Reign of the Emperor Menilek, 1906–1913." *Journal of Semitic Studies* 9, no. 1 (1964) 229–34.

Markakis, John, and Asmelash Beyene. "Representative Institutions in Ethiopia." *Journal of Modern African Studies* 5, no. 2 (1967) 193–219.

McCann, James. "The Ethiopian Chronicles: An African Documentary Tradition." *Northeast African Notes* 1, no. 2 (1979) 47–61.

McClellan, Charles W. "Land, Labor, and Coffee: The South's Role in Self-Reliance, 1889–1935." *African Economic History* no. 9 (1980) 69–83.

McLellan, Dick. "Daybreak for the People of the Mountains." *Africa Now* no. 64, September–October 1972, 3–4.

———. "Rainy Season Evangelistic Campaign." *Africa Now*, November–December 1970, 13.

Meinardus, Otto. "The Zequala, the Holy Mountain of Ethiopia." *Orientalia* 13 (1964) 34–47.

Messing, Simon D. "Group Therapy and Social Status in the Zar Cult of Ethiopia." *American Anthropologist* 60 (1958) 1120–26.

Montandon, George. "A Journey in South-Western Abyssinia." *Geographical Journal* 40, no. 4 (1912) 372–91.

Negaso Gidada with Donald Crummey. "The Introduction and Expansion of Orthodox Christianity in Qélém Awraja, Western Wälläga, from about 1886 to 1941." *Journal of Ethiopian Studies* 10, no. 1 (1972) 103–12.

Neumann, Oscar. "From the Somali Coast through Southern Ethiopia to the Sudan." *Geographical Journal* 20, no. 4 (1902) 373–401.

Ohman, Walter. "Africa, a Dark Picture." *Evangelical Christian*, September 1929, 360–61.

Olmstead, Judith. "Agricultural Land and Social Stratification in the Gamu Highlands of Southern Ethiopia." In Marcus et al., *Proceedings of the First United States Conference on Ethiopian Studies*, 223–34.

Pankhurst, Richard. "The Ethiopian Slave Trade in the Nineteenth and Early Twentieth Centuries: A Statistical Inquiry." *Journal of Semitic Studies* 9 (1964) 220–28.

————. "The Great Ethiopian Famine of 1888–1892: A New Assessment." Pts. 1 and 2. *Journal of the History of Medicine* 21 (1966) 95–124; 271–94.

————. "Menelik and the Utilization of Foreign Skills in Ethiopia." *Journal of Ethiopian Studies* 5, no. 1 (1967) 29–86.

Paton, William, and W. W. Underhill. "Survey—Roman Catholic Church." *International Review of Missions* 26 (1937) 99–105.

Pawlikowski, John T. "The Judaic Spirit of the Ethiopian Orthodox Church: A Case Study in Religious Acculturation." *Journal of Religion in Africa* 4 (1971) 178–99.

Peel, J. D. P. "The Christianization of African Society: Some Possible Models." In Fasholé-Luke et al., *Christianity in Independent Africa*, 243–454.

Powles, Cyril H. "Christianity in the Third World: How Do We Study Its History?" *Studies in Religion* 13, no. 2 (1984) 131–44.

Ranger, Terence. "The Churches, the State and African Religion." In Edward Fasholé-Luke et al., *Christianity in Independent Africa*, 479–502.

————. "Introduction." In Petersen, *Religion, Development and African Identity*, 29–57.

————. "Conclusion." In Petersen, *Religion, Development and African Identity*, 154–62.

Reminick, Ronald A. "The Structure and Functions of Religious Belief among the Amhara of Ethiopia." In Baëta, *Christianity in Tropical Africa*, 25–42.

Rhoad, G. H. "To the Uttermost Parts." *Evangelical Christian*, December 1931, 653–54, 702.

Roberts, Violet. "The Story of Wandara (Wolamo)." *Evangelical Christian*, February 1936, 79–80.

Savard, George Clovis. "The Peoples of Ethiopia." *Ethiopia Observer* 5, no. 3 (1961) 216–21.

Sergew Hable-Selassie. "The Expansion and Consolidation of Christianity." In Sergew H/Selassie and Taddesse Tamrat, *Church of Ethiopia*, 7–9.

Sergew Hable-Sellassie, and Belaynish Mikael. "Worship in the Ethiopian Orthodox Church." In Sergew H/Selassie and Taddesse Tamrat, *Church of Ethiopia*, 63–71.

Shack, William A. "The Mäsqal-Pole: Religious Conflict and Social Change in Gurageland." *Africa* 38, no. 4 (1968) 457–68.

————. "Occupational Prestige, Status, and Social Change in Modern Ethiopia." *Africa* 46 (1976) 167–81.

————. "Religious Ideas and Social Action in Gurage Bond-Friendship." *Africa* 23, no. 1 (1963) 198–208.

Shank, David A. "African Christian Religious Itinerary: Toward an Understanding of the Religious Itinerary of African Traditional Religion(s) to That of the New Testament." In Walls and Shenk, *Exploring New Religious Movements*, 143–62.

————. "The Legacy of William Wade Harris." *International Bulletin of Missionary Research* no. 10 (1986) 170–76.

Shenk, Calvin E. "The Demise of the Church in North Africa and Nubia and Its Survival in Egypt and Ethiopia: A Question of Contextualization?" *Missiology* 21, no. 2 (1993) 131–54.

————. "The Ethiopian Orthodox Church: A Study in Indigenization." *Missiology* 16, no. 3 (1988) 259–78.

————. "The Ethiopian Orthodox Church's Understanding of Mission." *Mission Studies* 4, no. 1 (1987) 4–20.

————. "The Italian Attempt to Reconcile the Ethiopian Orthodox Church: The Use of Religious Celebrations and Assistance to Churches and Monasteries." *Journal of Ethiopian Studies* 10, no. 1 (1972) 125–35.

Singleton, Michael. "Asa—Pagan Prophet or Providential Precursor?" *Afer* 2 (1978) 82–89.

Smith, A. Donaldson. "Expedition through Somaliland to Lake Rudolf." *Geographical Journal* 8 (July to December 1896) 120–37.

Staiger, W. "Abyssinia." *Church of Scotland Home and Foreign Missionary Record* 5 (July 2, 1866) 85–86.

Staiger, W., and F. W. Brandeis. "Jewish Mission." *Church of Scotland Home and Foreign Missionary Record* 4 (Dec. 1, 1865) 224–25.

Sundkler, Bengt. "African Church History in a New Key." In Petersen, *Religion, Development and African Identity*, 73–83.

———. "Worship and Spirituality." In Fasholé-Luke et al., *Christianity in Independent Africa*, 545–96.

Taddesse Tamrat. "The Abbots of Däbrä-Hayq 1248–1535." *Journal of Ethiopian Studies* 8, no. 1 (1970) 87–117.

———. "Ethiopia, the Red Sea and the Horn." In *Cambridge History of Africa*, edited by J. D. Fage and Roland Oliver. Vol. 3, 1977, 98–182.

———. "Ethnic Interaction and Integration in Ethiopian History: The Case of the Gafat." *Journal of Ethiopian Studies* 21 (November 1988) 121–45.

———. "Hagiograghies and the Reconstruction of Medieval Ethiopian History." *Rural Africana* 10 (Spring 1970) 12–20.

———. "Revival of the Church (1200–1526)." In Sergew H/Selassie and Taddesse Tamrat, *Church of Ethiopia*, 17–25.

———. "A Short Note on the Traditions of Pagan Resistance to the Ethiopian Church (14th and 15th Centuries)." *Journal of Ethiopian Studies* 10, no. 1 (1972) 137–50.

Tekle Tsadik Mekuria. "Christian Aksum." In UNESCO, *General History of Africa*, 401–22.

Thesiger, Wilfred. "The Awash River and the Aussa Sultanate." *Geographical Journal* 85, no. 1 (1935) 1–23.

Tsehai Berhane Selassie. "Individual Leadership and Grass-Roots Resistance to the Italian Occupation of Ethiopia: Bulga, 1935–41." In Pankhurst et al., *Proceedings of the First National Conference of Ethiopian Studies*, 383–93.

———. "The Life and Career of *Dejazmach* Balcha Aba Näfso." *Journal of Ethiopian Studies* 9, no. 2 (1971) 173–89.

———. "The Question of Damot and Walamo." *Journal of Ethiopian Studies* 13, no. 1 (1975) 37–45.

———. "The Wolayta Conception of Inequality, or Is It Inclusive or Exclusive?" In *Proceedings of the Eleventh International Conference of Ethiopian Studies, Addis Ababa, April 1–6, 1991*, edited by Bahru Zewde et al., 2:341–58. Addis Ababa: Institute of Ethiopian Studies, 1994.

Turner, Harold W. "African Independent Churches and Education." *Journal of Modern African Studies* 13, no. 2 (1975) 295–308.

———. "The Contribution of Studies on Religion in Africa to Western Religious Studies." In Glasswell and Fasholé-Luke, *New Testament Christianity for Africa and the World*, 169–78.

———. "Patterns of Ministry and Structure within Independent Churches." In Fasholé-Luke et al., *Christianity in Independent Africa*, 44–59.

———. "Tribal Religious Movements, New." *Encyclopedia Britannica* 18:697–705, 1974.

———. "A Typology for African Religious Movements." *Journal of Religion in Africa* 1, no. 1 (1967) 1–34.

———. "The Way Forward in the Religious Study of African Primal Religions." *Journal of Religion in Africa* 12, no. 1 (1981) 1–15.

Turner, Victor W. "Witchcraft and Sorcery: Taxonomy versus Dynamics." *Africa* 34, no. 4 (1964) 314–24.

Ullendorff, Edward. "Gurage Notes." *Africa* 20, no. 4 (1950) 335–44.

Vansina, Jan. "Once upon a Time: Oral Traditions as History in Africa." *Daedalus* 2 (1971) 442–68.

Verstraelen-Gilhuis, G. M. "The History of the Missiological Movement from the Perspective of the Third World." In *Missiology: A General Introduction,* edited by F. J. Verstraelen et al., 253–62. Grand Rapids, MI: Eerdmans, 1995.

von Allmen, Daniel. "The Birth of Theology." *International Review of Missions* 64 (1975) 37–55.

Wallace, Anthony. "Revitalization Movements." *American Anthropologist* 58 (1956) 264–81.

Walls, Andrew F. "Africa and Christian Identity." In *Mission Focus, Current Issues,* edited by Wilbert R. Shenk, 212–21. Scottdale, PA: Herald, 1980.

———. "Primal Religious Traditions in Today's World." In *Religion in Today's World,* edited by Frank Whaling, 250–78. Edinburgh: T. & T. Clark, 1987.

———. "The Significance of Christianity in Africa." Friends of St. Colm's Public Lecture, Church of Scotland St. Colm's Education Centre and College, 1989.

———. "Some Recent Literature on Missionary Studies." *Evangelical Quarterly* 42 (1970) 213–29.

———. "Towards Understanding Africa's Place in Christian History." In *Religion in a Pluralistic Society: Essays Presented to Professor C. G. Baëta,* edited by J. S. Pobee, 180–89. Leiden: Brill, 1976.

———. "The Translation Principle in Christian History." In *Bible Translation and the Spread of the Church: The Last 200 Years (Studies in Christian Mission),* edited by P. C. Stine, 24–39. Leiden: Brill, 1990.

Wellby, M. S. "King Menelik's Dominions and the Country between Lake Gallop (Rudolf) and the Nile Valley." *Geographical Journal* 16, no. 3 (1900) 292–306.

Wilson, Monica. "To Whom Do They Pray?" *The Listener,* November 1956, 692–93.

Wood, Adrian P. "Rural Development and National Integration in Ethiopia." *African Affairs* 82, no. 326 (1983) 509–39.

Worku Nida. "The Traditional Beliefs of the Sebat-Bet Gurage, with a Particular Emphasis on the *Bozhah* Cult." In Pankhurst, et al., *Proceedings of the First National Conference of Ethiopian Studies,* 109–23.

Published Books

Abbie Gubegna. *Defiance.* Oxford: Oxford University Press, 1975.

Abir, Mordechai. *Ethiopia: The Era of the Princes. The Challenge of Islam and the Re-Unification of the Christian Empire, 1769–1855.* London: Longmans, 1968.

Abraham Babanto. *The Origin of Wollaita and Revolutionary Modern Ethiopia.* Addis Ababa: (Private Printing) 1976 EC.

Achebe, Chinua. *Things Fall Apart.* New York: Knopf, 1984.

Allen, Roland. *Missionary Methods: St. Paul's or Ours?* London: World Dominion Press, 1927.

———. *The Spontaneous Expansion of the Church.* London: World Dominion Press, 1927.

Alpers, Edward A. *Ivory and Slaves in East Africa: Changing Patterns of International Trade to the Later Nineteenth Century.* Berkeley: University of California Press, 1975.

Alvarez, Francisco. *The Prester John of the Indies.* Translated by Lord Stanley of Alderley. Revised and edited by C. F. Beckingham and G. W. B. Huntingford. Cambridge: The Hakluyt Society, 1961.

Anderson, David M., and Douglas H. Johnson, eds. *Revealing Prophets.* London: Currey, 1995.

Andersson, Ephraim. *Churches at the Grass-Roots: A Story in Congo-Brazzaville.* London: Lutherworth Press, 1968.

Arén, Gustav. *Envoys of the Gospel in Ethiopia: In the Steps of the Evangelical Pioneers, 1898–1936.* Stockholm: EFS-förlaget, 1999.

———. *Evangelical Pioneers in Ethiopia: Origins of the Evangelical Church Mekane Yesus.* Stockholm: EFS-förlaget, 1978.

Baëta, C. G., ed. *Christianity in Tropical Africa: Studies Presented and Discussed at the Seventh International African Seminar, University of Ghana, April 1965.* London: published for the International African Institute by the Oxford University Press, 1968.

———. *Prophetism in Ghana.* World Mission Studies. London: SCM, 1962.

Bahru Zewde. *A History of Modern Ethiopia: 1855–1974.* East African Studies. Addis Ababa: Addis Ababa University Press, 1994.

Bakke, Johnny. *Christian Ministry: Patterns and Functions within the Ethiopian Evangelical Church Mekane Yesus.* Atlantic Highlands, NJ: Humanities Press, 1987.

Barrett, David B., ed. *African Initiatives in Religion. African Initiatives in Religion; 21 Studies from Eastern and Central Africa.* Workshop in Religious Research, University College, Nairobi, 1967–1968. Nairobi: East African Publishing House, 1971.

———. *Schism and Renewal in Africa: An Analysis of Six Thousand Contemporary Religious Movements.* Nairobi: Oxford University Press, 1968.

Bartels, Lambert. *Oromo Religion: Myths and Rites of the Western Oromo of Ethiopia—an Attempt to Understand.* Berlin: Reimer, 1983.

Bartleet, E. J. *In the Land of Sheba.* Birmingham: Cornish Brothers, 1934.

Bascom, Kay. *Hidden Triumph in Ethiopia.* South Pasadena, CA: William Carey Library, 2001

Baye Yiman, et al., editors. *Proceedings of the XIVth International Conference of Ethiopian Studies, Addis Ababa, 6–11 November 2000.* Addis Ababa: Institute of Ethiopian Studies, 2002.

Baylis, Philippa. *An Introduction to Primal Religions.* Edinburgh: University of Edinburgh, 1988.

Beckingham, C. F., and G. W. B. Huntingford, eds. and trans. *Some Records of Ethiopia, 1593–1646, Being Extracts from the "History of High Ethiopia or Abassia," by Manoel de Almeida, together with Bahrey's "History of the Galla."* Works issued by the Hakluyt Society, 2nd ser., 107. London: Printed for the Hakluyt Society, 1954.

Bediako, Gilliam M. *Primal Religion and the Bible: William Robertson Smith and His Heritage.* Sheffield: Sheffield Academic, 1996.

Bediako, Kwame. *Christianity in Africa: The Renewal of a Non-Western Religion.* Edinburgh: Edinburgh University Press, 1995.

———. *Jesus in African Culture: A Ghanaian Perspective.* Accra, Ghana: Asempa Publishers, 1990.

———. *Theology and Identity: The Impact of Culture upon Thought in the Second Century and Modern Africa.* Oxford: Regnum, 1992.

Beke, Charles T. *An Enquiry into M. Antonine D'Abbadie's Journey to Kaffa in the Years 1843 and 1844 to Discover the Source of the Nile.* London: Hakluyt Society, 1850.

Bender, M. L., et al., eds. *Language in Ethiopia.* Ford Foundation Language Surveys. London: Oxford University Press, 1976.

Bergsma, Stuart. *Rainbow Empire: Ethiopia Stretches Out Her Hands.* Grand Rapids: Eerdmans, 1932.

Bogalä Walälu. *Yäwälamo Hizb Tarik ina Barnätim Indét Indätäwägädä* [A history of the Wolaitta people and how slavery was eliminated]. Addis Ababa: Berhan and Selam Printing Press, 1956 EC.

Bosch, David J. *Believing in the Future: Toward a Missiology of Western Culture.* Valley Forge, PA: Trinity, 1995.

———. *Transforming Mission: Paradigm Shifts in Theology of Mission.* Maryknoll, NY: Orbis, 1991.

Brant, Albert E. *In the Wake of Martyrs.* Langley, BC: Omega, 1992.

Bruce, James. *Travels to Discover the Source of the Nile, in the Years 1768, 1769, 1770, 1771, 1772, 1773.* Edinburgh: Edinburgh University Press, 1790.

Brunner, Emil. *The Word and the World.* London: Student Christian Movement, 1931.

Budge, E. A. Wallis, trans. *The Book of the Saints of the Ethiopian Church: A Translation of the Ethiopic Synaxarium: Made from the Manuscripts Oriental 660 and 661 in the British Museum.* 4 vols. Cambridge: Cambridge University Press, 1928.

———, ed. and trans. *A History of Ethiopia, Nubia & Abyssinia.* 2 vols. London: Methuen, 1928.

———, trans. *The Life and Miracles of Täklä Haymanote: Version of Waldäbrä.* London: Griggs, 1906.

———, trans. *The Life of Täklä Haymanote: In the Version of Däbra Libanos.* London: Private Printing for Lady Meux, 1906.

———, trans. *The Queen of Sheba and Her Only Son Menyelek.* London: Methuen, 1922.

Caraman, Philip. *The Lost Empire: The Story of the Jesuits in Ethiopia (1555–1634).* London: Sedgwick & Jackson, 1985.

Cerulli, Enrico. *The Folk Literature of the Galla of Southern Abyssinia.* Cambridge, MA: Harvard African Studies, 1922.

Cerulli, Ernesta. *Peoples of South-West Ethiopia and Its Borderland.* London: International African Institute, 1956.

Chadwick, Henry. *The Early Church.* London: Penguin, 1984.

Clapham, Christopher. *Haile Sellassie Government.* New York: Praeger, 1969.

———. *Transformation and Continuity in Revolutionary Ethiopia.* African Studies Series 61. Cambridge: Cambridge University Press, 1988.

Coleman, Robert E. *The Master Plan of Evangelism.* Old Tappan, NJ: Revell, 1963.

Cook, Guillermo. *The Expectation of the Poor: Latin American Basic Ecclesial Communities in Protestant Perspective.* Maryknoll, NY: Orbis, 1985.

Costas, Orlando. *The Integrity of Mission: The Inner Life and Outreach of the Church.* New York: Harper & Row, 1979.

Cotterell, F. Peter. *Born at Midnight.* Chicago: Moody, 1973.

Crawford, O. G. S. *Ethiopian Itineraries 1400–1524.* London: Hakluyt Society, 1958.

Crummey, Donald C. *Priests and Politicians: Protestant and Catholic Missions in Orthodox Ethiopia, 1830–1868.* Oxford Studies in African Affairs. Oxford: Clarendon, 1972.

Cumbers, John. *Count it All Joy.* Kearney, NE: Morris, 1995.

———. *Living with the Red Terror.* Kearney, NE: Morris, 1996.

Darkwah, R. H. K. *Shewa, Menelik and the Ethiopian Empire, 1813–1889.* London: Heinemann, 1975.

Darley, Henry. *Slaves and Ivory: A Record of Adventure and Exploration in the Unknown Sudan and among the Abyssinian Slave-Raiders.* New York: McBride, 1926.

Davis, Raymond J. *Fire on the Mountains.* Grand Rapids: Zondervan, 1966.

———. *Winds of God.* Toronto: SIM International Publications, 1984.

DeBrunner, Hans W. *A Church between Colonial Powers: A Story of the Church in Togo.* London: Lutterworth, 1965.

Del Boca, Angela. *The Ethiopian War, 1935–1941.* Translated by P. D. Cummins. Chicago: Chicago University Press, 1969.

Donham, Donald L. *Marxist Modern: An Ethnographic History of the Ethiopian Revolution.* Berkeley and Los Angeles: University of California Press, 1999.

———. *Work and Power in Maale, Ethiopia.* Ann Arbor, MI: UMI Research Press, 1985.

Donham, Donald, and Wendy James. *The Southern Marches of Imperial Ethiopia.* African Studies Series 51. Cambridge: Cambridge University Press, 1986.

Duff, Clarence W. *Cords of Love.* Phillipsburg, NJ: Presbyterian & Reformed Press, 1980.

Eide, Oyvind M. *Revolution and Religion in Ethiopia: The Growth and Persecution of the Mekane Yesus Church, 1974–1985.* Oxford: Currie, 2000.

Eliade, Mircea. *Images and Symbols: Studies in Religious Symbolism.* London: Harvill, 1952.

———. *Myth and Reality.* New York: Harper, 1963.

Emmanuel Abraham. *Reminiscences of My Life.* Oslo, Norway: Forlag Og Bokhandel A/S, 1995.

Ethiopian Catholic Secretariat. *The Ethiopian Catholic Directory.* Addis Ababa: self-published, 1990.

Fargher, Brian L. *Bivocational Missionary Evangelist: The Story of the Itinerant Evangelist Sorsa Sumamo of Northern Sidama.* Edmonton, AB: Enterprise Publications, 2002.

———. *The Origins of the New Churches Movement in Southern Ethiopia, 1927–1944.* Leiden: Brill, 1996.

Fasholé-Luke, Edward, et al., eds. *Christianity in Independent Africa.* London: Collings, 1978.

Fields, Karen. *Revival and Rebellion in Colonial Central Africa.* Princeton, NJ: Princeton University Press, 1985.

Forsberg, Malcolm. *Land beyond the Nile.* New York: Harper, 1958.

Foster, William, ed. *The Red Sea and Adjacent Countries at the Close of the Seventeenth Century.* London: Hakluyt Society, 1949.

Fuller, W. Harold. *Mission Church Dynamics: How to Change Bicultural Tensions into Dynamic Missionary Outreach.* South Pasadena, CA: William Carey Library, 1980.

———. *Run While the Sun Is Hot.* New York: Sudan Interior Mission, 1967.

Gäbrä Sellassie Wäldä Arägai. *Tarek Zemen Za-Dagmawi Minilik Nigus Nägäst Zä-Etyopia* [*Chronicles of the Reign of Menilek II*]. Addis Ababa: Berhan & Selam, 1959 EC.

Geddes, Michael. *The Church History of Ethiopia.* London: R. Chriswell, 1696.

Getachew Haile, et al., editors. *The Missionary Factor in Ethiopia.* Frankfurt: Peter Lang, 1998.

Getz, Gene A. *The Measure of a Church.* Glendale, CA: Regal, 1975.

Gidada Salon. *The Other Side of Darkness.* New York: Friendship, 1972.

Gilks, Patrick. *The Dying Lion: Feudalism and Modernization in Ethiopia.* London: Friedmann, 1975.

Gilliland, Dean. *Pauline Theology and Mission Practice.* Grand Rapids: Eerdmans, 1983.

Glasswell, Mark E., and Edward W. Fasholé-Luke, eds. *New Testament Christianity for Africa and the World.* London: SPCK, 1974.

Gray, Richard. *Black Christians and White Missionaries.* New Haven: Yale University Press, 1990.

Green, E. Michael B. *Evangelism in the Early Church*. Grand Rapids: Eerdmans, 1970.

Greenfield, R. *Ethiopia: A New Political History*. London: Pall Mall, 1965.

Grenstedt, Staffan. *Ambaricho and Shonkolla: From Local Independent Church to the Evangelical Mainstream in Ethiopia*. Uppsala: Uppsala University, 2000.

Grimes, Barbara F., ed. *Ethnologue—Languages of the World*. 13th ed. Dallas: SIL, 1996.

Grubb, N. *Alfred Buxton of Abyssinia and Congo*. London: Lutterworth, 1942.

Gruhl, Max. *The Citadel of Ethiopia: The Empire of the Divine Emperor*. London: Jonathan Cape, 1932.

Gutiérrez, Gustavo. *We Drink from Our Own Wells: The Spiritual Journey of a People*. Translated by M. J. O'Connell. Maryknoll, NY: Orbis, 1984.

Haberland, Eike. *Untersuchungen zum Äthiopischen Königtum* [Studies on Kingship in Ethiopia]. "Summary of 'Kingship in Ethiopia,'" by Wolfgang Weissleder, 317–22. Studien Zur Kulturkunde 18. Weisbaden: Steiner, 1965.

Haliburton, Gordon Mackay. *The Prophet Harris: A Study of an African Prophet and His Mass-movement in the Ivory Coast and the Gold Coast*. London: Longmans, 1971.

Hamer, John H. *Humane Development, Participation and Change among the Sidama of Ethiopia*. Tuscaloosa: University of Alabama Press, 1987.

Harbeson, J. W. *The Ethiopian Transformation*. Boulder, CO: Westview, 1988.

Harris, W. C. *The Highlands of Ethiopia: Described During Eighteen Months of Residence at a British Embassy at the Christian Court of Shoa*. 3 vols. London: Longman, Brown, Green and Longmans, 1844.

Hastings, Adrian. *Church and Mission in Modern Africa*. London: Burns and Oates, 1967.

Hess, Robert L. *Ethiopia: The Modernization of Autocracy*. Africa in the Modern World. Ithaca, NY: Cornell University Press, 1970.

Hesselgrave, David J. *Communicating Christ Cross-Culturally: An Introduction to Missionary Communication*. Grand Rapids: Baker, 1978.

Hodges, Melvin L. *The Indigenous Church and the Missionary: A Sequel to "The Indigenous Church."* South Pasadena, CA: William Carey Library, 1978.

Hodson, Arnold. *Where Lions Reign: An Account of Lion Hunting and Exploration in South-West Ethiopia*. London: Unwin, 1928.

Horn, L. Freda. *Hearth and Home in Ethiopia*. London: Sudan Interior Mission, 1960.

Howell, Allison M. *The Religious Itinerary of a Ghanaian People: The Kasena and the Christian Gospel*. Studies in the Intercultural History of Christianity 102. Frankfurt: Lang, 1997.

Huntingford, G. W. B. *The Galla of Ethiopia: The Kingdoms of Kaffa and Janjero*. Ethnographic Survey of Africa: North Eastern Africa, pt. 2. London: International African Institute, 1955.

———, trans. and ed. *The Glorious Victories of Amdä Seyon*. Oxford: Clarendon, 1965.

Hyatt, Harry Middleton. *The Church of Abyssinia*. London: Luzac, 1928.

Idowu, E. Bolaji. *African Traditional Religion: A Definition*. London: SCM, 1973.

Isenberg, C. W., and J. L. Krapf. *The Journals of C. W. Isenberg and J. L. Krapf, Missionaries of the Church Missionary Society*. London: Cass, 1843.

Isichei, Elizabeth. *A History of Christianity in Africa: From Antiquity to the Present*. Grand Rapids: Eerdmans, 1995.

Jesman, Czeslaw. *The Ethiopian Paradox*. London: Oxford University Press, 1963.

Johnson, Aubrey R. *Sacral Kingship in Ancient Israel*. Cardiff: University of Wales Press, 1967.

Johnston, Charles. *Travels in Southern Abyssinia through the Country of Adal to the Kingdom of Shoa*. 2 vols. London: Hakluyt Society, 1844.

Jones, A. H. M., and E. Monroe. *A History of Ethiopia*. Oxford: Clarendon, 1965.

Kaplan, Steven. *The Monastic Holy Man and the Christianization of Early Solomonic Ethiopia*. Studien zur Kulturkunde 73. Wiesbaden: Steiner, 1984.

Kassate Berhan Tessema. *Yamarinya Mazgaba Qalat* (Amharic dictionary). Addis Ababa Artistic Printing Press: 1951 EC.

Kato, Byang H. *Theological Pitfalls in Africa*. Kisumu, Kenya: Evangel Publishing House, 1975.

Knutsson, K. E. *Authority and Change: A Study of the Kallu Institution among the Macha Galla of Ethiopia*. Etnologiska studier 29. Göteborg: University of Göteborg, 1976.

Kobishchanov, Y. M. *Axum*. Edited by J. W. Michaels. Translated by L. T. Kapitanoff. Pittsburgh: Pennsylvania State University Press, 1979.

Kraemer, Hendrik. *The Christian Message in a Non-Christian World*. London: Edinburgh House Press, 1938.

Kraft, Charles H. *Christianity and Culture: A Study in Dynamic Biblical Theologizing in Cross-Cultural Perspective*. Maryknoll, NY: Orbis, 1979.

Krapf, J. L. *Travels, Researches, and Missionary Labours during an Eighteen Years' Residence in Eastern Africa*. 2nd ed. London: Cass, 1968.

Lambie, T. A. *Boot and Saddle in Africa*. New York: Revell, 1943.

———. *A Doctor Carries On*. New York: Revell, 1941.

———. *A Doctor without a Country*. New York: Revell, 1939.

———. *A Doctor's Great Commission*. Wheaton, IL: Van Kampen, 1954.

Lange, Werner J. *Domination and Resistance: Narrative Songs of the Kafa Highlands*. East Lansing, MI: UMI Research Press, 1979.

———. *History of the Southern Gonga (Southwestern Ethiopia)*. Studien zur Kulturkunde 61. Wiesbaden: Steiner, 1982.

Latourette, Kenneth S. *A History of Christianity: The First Five Centuries*. Grand Rapids: Zondervan, 1971.

Launhardt, Johannes. *Evangelicals in Addis Ababa (1919–1991): With Special Reference to the Ethiopian Evangelical Church Mekane Yesus and the Addis Ababa Synod*. Uppsala: Lit, 2005.

Levine, Donald N. *Greater Ethiopia: The Evolution of a Multi-ethnic Society*. Chicago: Chicago University Press, 1974.

———. *Wax and Gold: Tradition and Innovation in Ethiopian Culture*. Chicago: Chicago University Press, 1965.

Lewis, H. S. *A Galla Monarchy: Jimma and Abba Jiffar, Ethiopia, 1830–1932*. Madison: University of Wisconsin Press, 1965.

Lipsky, George A. *Ethiopia: Its People, Its Society, Its Culture*. Survey of World Cultures 9. New Haven, CT: H.R.A.F. Press, 1962.

Ludolf, J. *A New History of Ethiopia: Being a Full and Accurate Description of the Kingdom of Abyssinia, Vulgarly and Erroneously Called the Empire of Prester John*. London: Samuel Smith, 1683.

Luther, Ernest W. *Ethiopia Today*. Stanford, CA: Stanford University Press, 1958.

Luzbetak, Louis. *The Church and Cultures: New Perspectives in Missiological Anthropology*. Maryknoll, NY: Orbis, 1989.

Lydall, Jean, and Ivo Strecker. *The Hamer of Southern Ethiopia*. 3 vols. Work Journals. Gutenberg: University of Gutenberg, 1979.

MacGaffey, Wyatt. *Modern Kongo Prophets: Religion in a Plural Society*. Bloomington: Indiana University Press, 1983.

Madge, John. *The Tools of Social Change*. New York: Longmans, Green, 1965.

Malinowski, B. *Magic, Science and Religion*. Garden City, NY: Doubleday, 1955.

Marcus, Harold G. *The Life and Times of Menelik II, Ethiopia 1844–1913*. Oxford: Clarendon, 1975.

Marcus, Harold G., et al., eds. *Proceedings of the First United States Conference on Ethiopian Studies, Michigan State University, 2–5 May, 1973*, Occasional Papers Series—Committee on Ethiopian Studies 3. East Lansing: African Studies Center, Michigan State University, 1975.

Markakis, J. *Ethiopia: Anatomy of a Traditional Polity*. Oxford: Clarendon Press, 1974.

Markakis, John, and Nega Ayele. *Class and Revolution in Ethiopia*. Trenton, NJ: Red Sea, 1986.

Markina Meja. *Unbroken Covenant with God: An Autobiography in the Context of the Wolaitta Kale Heywet Church, Ethiopia*. Translated by Haile Jenai. Belleville, ON: Guardian, 2008.

Mbiti, John S. *The Crisis of Mission in Africa*. Mukumo, Uganda: Church of Uganda Press, 1971.

McLellan, Dick. *Warriors of Ethiopia: Ethiopian National Missionaries*. Kingsgrove, Australia: Kingsgrove, 2006.

Mehari Choramo. *Ethiopian Revivalist: Autobiography of Evangelist Mehari Choramo*. Annotated by Brian L. Fargher. Edmonton, AB: Enterprise Publications, 1997.

Mohammed Hassen. *The Oromo of Ethiopia: A History 1570–1860*. Trenton, NJ: Red Sea Press, 1994.

Molyneux, K. Gordon. *African Christian Theology: A Quest for Selfhood*. Lewiston, NY: Mellen, 1993.

Mosley, Leonard. *Haile Selassie: The Conquering Lion*. London: Weidenfeld & Nicolson, 1964.

Murdock, G. P. *Africa: Its People and Their Culture History*. New York: Macmillan, 1959.

Ndiokwere, Nathaniel I. *Prophecy and Revolution: The Role of Prophets in the Independent African Churches and in Biblical Tradition*. London: SPCK, 1981.

Neill, Stephen C. *Colonialism and Christian Missions*. London: Lutterworth, 1966.

———. *Salvation Tomorrow: The Originality of Jesus Christ and the World's Religions*. London: Lutterworth, 1976.

———. *The Unfinished Task*. London: Lutterworth, 1957.

Newbigin, Lesslie. *Truth to Tell: The Gospel as Public Truth*. Grand Rapids, MI: Eerdmans, 1991.

Nyamiti, Charles. *African Tradition and the Christian God*. Eldoret, Kenya: Gaba Publications, n.d.

Oliver, Richard. *The Missionary Factor in East Africa*. London: Longmans, 1965.

Pankhurst, Richard, ed. *Economic History of Ethiopia, 1800–1935*. Addis Ababa: Haile Sellassie University Press, 1968.

———. *The Ethiopian Royal Chronicles*. Addis Ababa: Oxford University Press, 1967.

———, ed. *Letters from Ethiopian Rulers (Early and Mid-Nineteenth Century)*. Translated by David L. Appleyard and A. K. Irvine. Oriental Documents 9. Oxford: Oxford University Press, 1985.

Pankhurst, Richard, et al. *Proceedings of the First National Conference of Ethiopian Studies, Addis Ababa, April 11–12, 1990*. Addis Ababa: Institute of Ethiopian Studies, 1990.

Pankhurst, Sylvia. *Ethiopia: A Cultural History*. London: Lalibela House, 1955.

Parkyns, Mansfield. *Life in Abyssinia: Being Notes Collected During Three Years' Residence and Travels in That Country*. London: Murray, 1853.

Parrinder, Geoffrey. *African Traditional Religion*. London: Faber & Faber, 1974.

Peel, J. D. Y. *Aladura: A Religious Movement among the Yoruba*. London: Oxford University Press, 1968.

Perham, Margery. *The Government of Ethiopia*. London: Faber & Faber, 1969.

Peters, George L. *A Biblical Theology of Missions*. Chicago: Moody, 1972.

Petersen, Kirsten Holst, ed. *Religion, Development and African Identity*. Uppsala: Scandinavian Institute of African Studies, 1987.

Phillips, David J. *Peoples on the Move*. Nottingham: Piquant, 2001.

Pirouet, M. Louise. *Black Evangelists: The Spread of Christianity in Uganda 1891–1914*. London: Rex Collins, 1978.

Playfair, Guy W. *Trials and Triumphs in Ethiopia*. Toronto: Sudan Interior Mission, 1943.

Plowden, Walter C. *Travels in Abyssinia and Galla Country: With an Account of a Mission to Ras Ali in 1848*. London: Longmans, Green, 1868.

Prouty, Chris. *Empress Taitu and Menelik, Ethiopia 1883–1910*. Trenton, NJ: Red Sea, 1986.

Quinton, A. G. H. *Ethiopia and the Evangel*. London: Marshall, Morgan & Scott, 1949.

Ratzliff, Ed and Edna. *Letters from the Uttermost Parts of the Earth*. Abbotsford, BC: Private Publication, 1987.

Rey, Charles F. *The Romance of the Portuguese in Abyssinia*. New York: Negro University Press, 1969.

Rice, G. Ritchie, and E. Ralph Hooper. *Ethiopia*. New York: Sudan Interior Mission, 1933.

Roke, Alfred G. *An Indigenous Church in Action*. Auckland, New Zealand: Scott & Scott Ltd., 1938.

Rosenfeld, Chris Prouty. *A Chronology of Menilek II of Ethiopia, 1844–1913*. East Lansing, MI: African Studies Center, 1976.

Rubenson, Sven. *King of Kings: Tewodros of Ethiopia*. Addis Ababa: Haile Sellassie University Press, 1966.

Saeverås, Olav. *On Church-Mission Relations in Ethiopia 1944–1969 with Special Reference to the Evangelical Church Mekane Yesus and the Lutheran Missions*. Uppsala: Studia Missionalia Uppsalien, 1974.

Sahle Sellassie. *The Afersata*. London: Heinemann, 1970.

Sandford, Christine. *Ethiopia under Hailé Selassié*. London: Dent, 1946.

Schwab, Peter. *Ethiopia: Politics, Economy and Society*. London: Francis Printer, 1985.

Sergew Hable Sellassie. *Ancient and Medieval Ethiopian History to 1270*. Addis Ababa: United Printers, 1972.

———. *Bibliography of Ancient and Medieval Ethiopian History*. Addis Ababa: United Printers, 1968.

Sergew Hable Sellassie, and Taddesse Tamrat, eds. *The Church of Ethiopia: A Panorama of History and Spiritual Life*. Addis Ababa: United Printers, 1970.

Shank, David. *Prophet Harris: The "Black Elijah" of West Africa*. Abridged by Jocelyn Murray. Leiden: Brill, 1994.

Shack, W. A. *The Gurage: The People of the Ensette Culture*. London: Oxford University Press, 1966.

Shenk, David W., and Ervin R. Stutzman. *Creating Communities of the Kingdom*. Scottdale, PA: Herald, 1988.

Shenk, Wilbert R., ed. *Exploring Church Growth*. Grand Rapids: Eerdmans, 1983.

———. *The Vision: The Church Renewed*. Harrisburg, PA: Trinity, 1995.

SIM Publication. *Ethiopia is Stretching Out Her Hands to God*. Toronto: Sudan Interior Mission, 1944.

Singleton, Michael. *Ethiopia Tikdem—Ethiopia First.* Brussels: Pro Mundi Vita, 1977.

Smith, W. Robertson. *The Religion of the Semites.* London: A. & C. Black, 1927.

Spencer, John H. *Ethiopia at Bay: A Personal Account of the Haile Selassie Years.* Algonac, MI: Reference Publications, 1984.

Stigand, C. H. *To Abyssinia through an Unknown Land.* London: Pringle, 1910.

Stott, John R. W. *Christian Mission in the Modern World.* Downers Grove, IL: InterVarsity Press, 1975.

Strayer, Robert W. *Making of Mission Communities in East Africa, 1875–1935.* London: Heinemann, 1978.

Sumner, Claude. *Ethiopian Philosophy.* Vol. 2, *The Treatise of Zär'a Ya'eqob and of Wäldä Heywät; Text and Authorship.* Addis Ababa: Addis Ababa University, 1976.

Sundkler, B. G. M. *Bantu Prophets in South Africa.* London: Oxford University Press, 1961.

———. *The Christian Ministry in Africa.* London: SCM, 1960.

Taber, Charles R., ed. *The Church in Africa.* South Pasadena, CA: William Carey Library, 1977.

Taddesse Tamrat. *Church and State in Ethiopia, 1270–1527.* Oxford: Clarendon, 1972.

Taylor, John V. *The Go-Between God: the Holy Spirit and the Christian Mission.* London: SCM, 1972.

Tayyä Gäbrä Maryam (*Aläqa*). *History of the People of Ethiopia.* Translated by Grover Hudson and Tekeste Negash. Uppsala Multiethnic Papers 9. Uppsala: Centre for Multiethnic Research, Uppsala University—Faculty of Arts, 1987.

Tesfai Tekle. *The Evolution of Alternative Rural Development Strategies in Ethiopia: Implications for Employment and Income Distribution.* East Lansing, MI: UMI Research Press, 1975.

Thompson, Leonard. *Survival in Two Worlds: Moshoeshoe of Lesotho 1786–1890.* Oxford: Clarendon, 1975.

Thompson, Robert N. *Liberation—the First to be Free.* Fort Langley, BC: Battleline, 1987.

Tippett, Alan R. *Peoples of Southwest Ethiopia.* South Pasadena, CA: William Carey Library, 1970.

Trimingham, J. S. *The Christian Church and Missions in Ethiopia.* London: World Dominion Press, 1950.

———. *Islam in Ethiopia.* London: World Dominion Press, 1965.

Triulzi, Alessandro. *Salt, Gold and Legitimacy: Prelude to the History of a No-Man's Land Bela Shangul, Wallagga, Ethiopia.* Naples, Italy: Oriental University Press, 1981.

Turner, H. W. *Commentary on a Shortened Version of Rudolf Otto's "The Idea of the Holy": A Guide for Students.* Aberdeen: University of Aberdeen Press, 1974.

———. *History of African Independent Church.* 2 vols. Oxford: Clarendon, 1967.

Ullendorff, E. *Ethiopia and the Bible.* London: Oxford University Press, 1968.

———. *The Ethiopians.* London: Oxford University Press, 1960.

UNESCO International Scientific Committee for the Drafting of a General History of Africa. *General History of Africa.* Vol. 2, *Ancient Civilizations of Africa*, edited by G. Mokhtar. London: Heinemann Educational Books, 1981.

Van Engen, Charles. *God's Missionary People: Rethinking the Purpose of the Local Church.* Grand Rapids: Baker, 1991.

Vansina, Jan. *Oral Tradition as History.* Madison: University of Wisconsin Press, 1985.

Verstraelen, Frans J. *Christianity in a New Key: New Voices and Vistas through Intercontinental Communication.* Gweru, Zimbabwe: Mambo, 1996.

Verstraelen, Frans J., et al., eds. *Missiology: An Ecumenical Introduction. Texts and Contexts of Global Christianity*. Grand Rapids: Eerdmans, 1995.

Verstraelen-Gilhuis, Gerdien. *A New Look at Christianity in Africa*. Gweru, Zimbabwe: Mambo, 1992.

Walker, C. H. *The Abyssinian at Home*. London: Sheldon, 1933.

Walls, Andrew F. *The Cross-Cultural Process in Christian History*. New York: Orbis, 2002.

———. *The Missionary Movement in Christian History: Studies in the Transmission of Faith*. Maryknoll, NY: Orbis, 1996.

Walls, Andrew F., and Wilbert R. Shenk, eds. *Exploring New Religious Movements: Essays in Honour of Harold W. Turner*. Elhart, IN: Mission Focus, 1990.

Wand, J. W. C. *The History of the Early Church to A.D. 500*. London: Methuen, 1989.

Wanderheym, J. G. *Une Expédition Avec Le Négous Ménélik, Vingt Mois in Abyssinie*. Paris: Librarie Hachette, 1896.

Watson, David C. *I Believe in Evangelism*. Grand Rapids: Eerdmans, 1979.

Wellby, M. S. *Twixt Sidar and Menelik*. New York: Harper, 1901.

Whaling, Frank. *Christian Theology and World Religions: A Global Approach*. Hants, UK: Marshall, Morgan & Scott, 1986.

Whiteway, R. S. *The Portuguese Expedition to Abyssinia in 1541–1543 (Translations of the Narratives of Castanhosa and Bermudes)*. Works Issued by the Hakluyt Society, 2nd series, 10. London: Hakluyt Society, 1902.

Willmott, Helen M. *The Doors Were Opened: The Remarkable Advance of the Gospel in Ethiopia*. London: Sudan Interior Mission, n.d.

Wilson, Monica. *Religion and Transformation of Society*. Scott Holland Memorial Lectures 15. Cambridge: Cambridge University Press, 1971.

Yoder, John H. *The Politics of Jesus*. Grand Rapids: Eerdmans, 1992.

Yosef Menna. *Bäaṭibeya Bétä Kristeyan Däqämäzamurtin Bämafrat Yätämäsärätä Yäwängél Mahibärtänyanät Säbat Däräjawoch* [Seven steps to build self-sustainable disciples in the local church]. Addis Ababa: EKHC Publishing Department, 1992 EC.

———. *Bädäqä Mäzmurinät Yätämäsärätä Bihérawena Além Aqäfawe Läwängél Täliko Mahibärtänyanät Yämanqäsqäs Manuwal* [The EKHC disciple-making based national and global missions mobilization commission manual]. Addis Ababa: EKHC Publishing Department, 1999 EC.

Zewde Gabre-Sellassie. *Yohannes IV of Ethiopia: A Political Biography*. Oxford: Clarendon, 1975.

Dissertations and Theses

Adams, Bruce A. "The Tagmemic Analysis of the Wolaitta Language." PhD thesis, University of London, 1983.

Altaye Alaro. "The Political History of Wolayita in the Eighteenth and Nineteenth Centuries." BA thesis, Addis Ababa University, 1982.

Balisky, E. Paul. "Church Growth in Southern Ethiopia (and other essays)." MTh thesis, Fuller Theological Seminary, 1972.

Bediako, Kwame. "Identity and Integration: An Enquiry into the Nature and Problems of Theological Indigenization in Selected Early Hellenistic and Modern African Christian Writers." PhD thesis, University of Aberdeen, 1983.

Berry, Laverne B. "The Solomonic Monarchy at Gondar, 1630–1755: An Institutional Analysis of Kingship in the Christian Kingdom of Ethiopia." PhD diss., Boston University Graduate School, 1976.

Chiatti, Remo. "The Politics of Divine Kingship in Wolaita (Ethiopia), 19th and 20th Centuries." PhD diss., University of Pennsylvania, 1984.

Crummey, Donald E. "European Religious Missions in Ethiopia, 1830–1868." PhD thesis, University of London, 1967.

Debela Birri. "History of the Evangelical Church Bethel." ThD diss., Lutheran School of Theology, 1995.

Fargher, Brian L. "The Origins of the New Churches Movement in Southern Ethiopia, 1927–1944." PhD thesis, University of Aberdeen, 1988.

Fekadu Gadamu. "Ethnic Associations in Ethiopia and the Maintenance of Urban/Rural Relationships: With Special Reference to the Alem Gana—Wolamo Road Construction Association." PhD thesis, University of London, 1972.

Garreston, Peter P. "A History of Addis Ababa from its Foundation in 1886–1910." PhD thesis, University of London, 1974.

Hubbard, David A. "The Literary Sources of the *Kebra Nagast*." PhD thesis, St. Andrews University, 1956.

Lange, Werner J. "Gimira (Remnants of a Vanishing Culture)." PhD thesis, Johann Wolfgang Goethe University, 1975.

McClellan, Charles W. "Reaction to Ethiopian Expansionism: The Case of Darasa, 1895–1935." PhD diss., Michigan State University, 1978.

Merid Wolde Aregay. "Southern Ethiopia and the Christian Kingdom 1508–1708: With Special Reference to the Galla Migrations and Their Consequences." PhD thesis, University of London, 1971.

Mikre-Sellassie Gabre Ammanuel. "Church and Missions in Ethiopia in Relation to the Italian War and Occupation and the Second World War." PhD thesis, University of Aberdeen, 1976.

Mohammed Hassen. "The Oromo of Ethiopia, 1500–1850: With Special Emphasis on the Gibe Region." PhD thesis, University of London, 1983.

Nicolas, Gildas E. "The Dizzu of Southwest Ethiopia: An Essay in Cultural History Based on Religious Interaction." PhD diss., University of California, Los Angeles, 1976.

Okorocha, Cyril C. "Salvation in Igbo Religious Experience: Its Influence on Igbo Christianity." PhD thesis, University of Aberdeen, 1982.

Quiren, James Arthur. "The Beta Israel (Felasha) in Ethiopian History: Caste Formation and Culture Change, 1270–1868." PhD diss., University of Minnesota, 1977.

Shenk, Calvin. "The Development of the Ethiopian Orthodox Church and Its Relationship with the Ethiopian Government from 1930 to 1970." PhD diss., New York University, 1972.

Tienou, Tite. "The Problem of Methodology in African Christian Theologies." PhD diss., Fuller Theological Seminary, 1984.

Tsehai Berhane Selassie. "The Political and Military Traditions of the Ethiopian Peasantry (1800–1941)." DPhil thesis, Oxford University, 1980.

Udoh, Enyi Ben. "Guest Christology: An Interpretive View of the Christological Problem in Africa." PhD diss., Princeton Theological Seminary, 1983.

Vecchiato, R. L. "Culture, Health, and Socialism in Ethiopia: The Sidama Case." PhD diss., University of California, Los Angeles, 1985.

Unpublished Sources

Awäqä Amzayé. *"Silä Koré Bihéräsäb Ac̱ẖir Mägiläc̱ẖa"* [The Koré ethnic group: a short description]. A paper read at the Democratic Cultural Conference convened at Amaro Kéli town, Sidama, November 5–6, 1991.

Balisky, E. Paul. "The Expansion of the Ethiopian Orthodox Church through the Centuries: The Role of the Monasteries in Evangelism." Paper presented at the Religion in Ethiopia colloquium, Addis Ababa, December 4–8, 1995, 16 pp.

Balisky, Lila W. "Ethiopia Diaries, 1967–1997." Private collection.

Bartja, Grace. Diary and correspondence. EG-2, SIM Archives, Charlotte, NC.

Bassa Däa. *"Yätämärätä Tiwild: Ac̱ẖir yäQuc̱ẖa Qalä Hiywät Béta Kristeyan Tarek"* [A chosen generation: a short history of the Quc̱ẖa Kale Heywet Church]. Mimeographed copy, 43 pp., Addis Ababa, 1977 EC.

Beckingham, C. F. "The Achievements of Prester John: An Inaugural Lecture Delivered on 17 May, 1966." School of Oriental and African Studies, University of London, 1966.

Bediako, Kwame. "Cry Jesus! Christian Theology and Presence in Modern Africa." Laing Lecture at London Bible College, February 5, 1993. Transcript, 12 pp. Centre for the Study of Christianity in the Non-Western World library, New College, University of Edinburgh.

———. "The Primal Imagination and the Opportunity for a New Theological Idiom." Mimeographed copy, 12 pp. Duff Lectures, New College, University of Edinburgh, 1990.

Bentwich, Professor Norman. *Progress in Ethiopia.* Pamphlet no. 21, 8 pp. Speech given at Westminster Abbey, London, 1994.

Bergsten, Selma, and Earl Lewis, interview with Raymond Davis, Soddo, December 16, 1961. Transcription, 66 pp. Source material for *Fire on the Mountains*, EE-2, SIM Archives, Charlotte, NC.

Bergsten, Selma. Interview with Charles Anderson, January 1961. Transcription, 90 pp. Source material for *Fire on the Mountains*, EE-2, SIM Archives, Charlotte, NC.

Brant, Howard. "Ethiopian Mission and Church in a Time of Revolution." Paper submitted for D.Miss. to Trinity Evangelical Divinity School, Deerfield, IL, 1984.

Burji Log Book, 1947–1956. Information entered by Theresia Fellows, 12 pp. SR-37, SIM Archives, Charlotte, NC.

Coleman, Murray, and Ruth Cremer. "Testimony and Funeral of Ato Nega Dembel." Typed copy, 2 pp. February 8, 1995.

Couser, Norman C. "Seeds of Sacrifice." Photocopied document, 102 pp. SIM Archives, Charlotte, NC, c. 1962.

Dägu Daqilabu et al. *"Käisat Yätänätäqä Tintag"* [A burning stick snatched from the fire: the story of Aari]. Mimeographed copy, 64 pp. Bako, 1976 EC.

Danél Ganébo. *"YäWolaitta Béta Kristeyan Tarik"* [Wolaitta Church History]. In KHC, *"Bäwängél Amanyoch Andinät,"* 5–8.

Davis, Raymond J. Correspondence. EE-2, SIM Archives, Charlotte, NC.

———. "Over My Shoulder; Some Incidents in the Lives of Raymond and Evelyn Davis." Photocopied document, Sebring, FL, 1989.

———. Source material for *Fire on the Mountains*, EE-2, SIM Archives, Charlotte, NC.

Davison, Laurie. "News from Ethiopia." November 26, 1941. 4 pp. EC-1 (folder 4), SIM Archives, Charlotte, NC.

———. "Notes on the Situation in Walamo," May 1945. Photocopy, 6 pp. EE-2, SIM Archives, Charlotte, NC.

———. "The Re-entry of the SIM to Ethiopia," May 1, 1961. Transcription, 5 pp. Source material for *Fire on the Mountains*, EE-2, SIM Archives, Charlotte, NC.

Davison, Laurie, and Lily Davison. Correspondence. EE-2, SIM Archives, Charlotte, NC.

Donald, Mel. Correspondence and SIM Administration Reports. ED-2, SIM Archives, Charlotte, NC.

Eshetu Abate. "*Ato* Birru Dubale." Photocopy, 9 pp. Personal interview by Eshetu Abate, Addis Ababa, August 20, 1979.

———. "Origin and Growth of Evangelical Christianity in Wollayta." 49 pp. Research paper presented to Mekane Yesus Seminary, Addis Ababa, 1980.

Fargher, Brian L., with Don Gray and Christine Gray. "The New Churches' Movement in Hammer-Bako Area, 1954–1961." 44 pages of duplicated text and 23 pages of photographs. Edmonton, AB, 1996.

Forsberg, Malcolm, and Enid Forsberg. Letters to family. EE-1, SIM Archives, Charlotte, NC.

Fyfe, Christopher. "Race, Empire and Decolonization in Africa." Mimeographed copy, 16 pp. Paper presented at conference, Rethinking African History: Interdisciplinary Perspectives, University of Edinburgh, Centre for African Studies, May 22–23, 1996, Edinburgh.

Hardy, Steve. "Report on the Ethiopian Kale Heywet Church Theological Education Programs." 17 pp. Paper presented to EKHC leadership, May 20, 2007, EKHC central office, Addis Ababa.

Ishätu Gäbré. "*Yäwängél Amanyoch Andinät Mahibär Achir Tarek*" [The Fellowship of Evangelical Believers: a short historical account]. Mimeographed copy, 37 pp. Addis Ababa, 1985 EC.

Jackson, R. T., et al. "Report of the Oxford University Expedition to the Gamu Highlands of Southern Ethiopia, 1968." Mimeographed copy, 112 pp. University of Edinburgh Main Library, 1969.

Jacobs, Donald R. "Christian Theology in Africa." Mimeographed copy, 65 pp. Mount Joy, PA, 1966.

Kale Heywet Church. "*Bäwängél Amanyoch Andinät Mahibär Yäqalä Heywät Bétä Kristeyan Tarek*" [A history of the Kale Heywet Church (which is a member of) The Fellowship of Evangelical Believers]. Mimeographed copy, Addis Ababa, 1978 EC.

———. "*Qalä Heywät Bétä Kristeyan Bäsilsa Hulät Amätat Gezé Wist*" [The Kale Heywet Church during the past 62 years]. Mimeographed copy, 78 pp. Addis Ababa, 1982 EC.

Kayser, Gus. "Chapter 11, Waka SIM Station and Kullo Konta." Unpublished autobiography, Abbotsford, BC, 1996.

Lambie, Thomas. Miscellaneous papers. EA-2, SIM Archives, Charlotte, NC.

———. Reports and correspondence. EA-1, SIM Archives, Charlotte, NC.

Lewis, Earl. Correspondence. EE-2, SIM Archives, Charlotte, NC.

———. Letter to R. J. Davis, September 12, 1961. 14 pp. Source material for *Fire on the Mountains*, EE-2, SIM Archives, Charlotte, NC.

Mahé Choramo. "Philip: An Ethiopian Evangelist." Autobiography of Evangelist Mahé Choramo, transcribed by Brian L. Fargher. Mimeographed copy, 176 pp. Addis Ababa, 1985.

Mäkonin Magato. "*Wängélawena Yäwängél Sirichit*" [The Evangelist and the Spread of the Gospel]. Photocopy, 5 pp. Addis Ababa, 1988 EC.

Mälkamu Shanqo. "*Hulum Ades Honwal: YäBoloso Qalä Hiywät Bétä Kristeyan Aҫhir Tarek*" [All has become new: a short history of the Boloso Kale Heywet Church]. Mimeographed copy, 56 pp. Addis Ababa, 1978 EC.

———. "*Käfitänya Wängél Alälak Zädé*" [A better method of spreading the gospel]. 15 pp. June 25, 2001 EC.

Mamo Bälätä. "*YäSidama Qalä Hiywät Bétä Kristeyan Aҫhir Tarek*" [A Short History of the Sidama Kale Heywet Church celebrating their 50th anniversary]. Mimeographed copy, 6 pp. Aläta Wändo, Ethiopia, 1975 EC.

Markina Mäja. "*YäÉs Ay Ém läWolaitta Hizb Yäbäräkätut Agälgilot*" [The blessed service of the SIM among the people of Wolaitta]. Typewritten copy, 6 pp. Soddo, Wolaitta, 1988.

Matéwos Gäbrä Mariam. "Report of a Visit to Goppa Manja Church." Translated into English by Ruth Cremer. Typewritten copy, 4 pp. Addis Ababa, 1995.

McCoughtry, Ruth. Correspondence. EG-2, SIM Archives, Charlotte, NC.

McLellan, R. J. "Memories of Mahae: A Biography." Mimeographed copy, 39 pp. Addis Ababa, 2006.

———. "The Wallamo Church." Photocopied document, 12 pp. Soddo, Ethiopia, 1972.

Mekane Yesus Seminary—Theological Education by Extension Department. "History of Christianity in Ethiopia." Mimeographed textbook, 151 pp. Addis Ababa, 1989.

Mitchell, Myrtle. Prayer letters. EE-1, SIM Archives, Charlotte, NC.

Neal, Alan. "The Arsee Story." Photocopy of chapters 2, 5, 9, and 10. Klemzig, Australia, 1957.

———. "Lecture to SIM Language Students." January 3, 1972. ED-2, SIM Archives, Charlotte, NC.

Ohman, Walter, and Marcella Ohman. Correspondence. EE-2, SIM Archives, Charlotte, NC.

———. Letter to Raymond Davis, February 15, 1961. 12 pp. Source material for *Fire on the Mountains*, EE-2, SIM Archives, Charlotte, NC.

———. Prayer letters. EE-2, SIM Archives, Charlotte, NC.

Playfair, Guy W. Post-Italian war correspondence, EC-1, SIM Archives, Charlotte, NC.

Pauswang, Siegfried. "Participation in Social Research: An Experience in Rural Ethiopia." Derap Working Paper, 20 pp. Bergan, Norway, 1987.

"Religion in Ethiopia." Compilation of papers presented at a colloquium, December 4–8, 1995, Addis Ababa.

Rhoad, George W. "'Wayside Jottings' Being a Personal Account of the Second Advance Towards the Frontiers on the Southwesterly Route through Jimma Province, March–June 1931." 45 pp. EE-1, SIM Archives, Charlotte, NC.

Roberts, Percy, and Violet Roberts. Correspondence. EE-2, SIM Archives, Charlotte, NC.

Roberts, Violet. "Soddo Diary," 1934–1937. 45 pp. DD-3, SIM Archives, Charlotte, NC.

———. "Soddo News." EE-2, SIM Archives, Charlotte, NC.

Roke, Alfred G. "They Went Forth: Trials and Triumphs of a S.I.M. Missionary in Ethiopia," 412 pp. New Zealand, 2002. [A record of Alfred Roke's experiences in Ethiopia and the Anglo-Egyptian Sudan during the period of 1929–1947.]

Sawl Salgédo. "*Aҫhir Yähiywäté Tarek*" [My short life story]. Amharic handwritten document, 112 pp. Boloso, Wolaitta, 1977 EC.

———. "*Birhan Anṣäbaräqä: YäDawro Konta Tarik*" [Let the light shine: the Dawro/Konta story]. Handwritten document, 12 pp. Soddo, Wolaitta, 1978 EC.

Séta Wotango, "*YäWolaitta Kalä Heywät Bétä Kristeyan Yäwängélaweyan Alälak Ades Zädé*" [The new method of supporting the WKHC evangelists]. 5 pp. May 7, 2001 EC.

Sergew Hable Sellassie. "Ethiopian Church Manuscripts." Lecture at Evangelical Theological College, Addis Ababa, July 26, 1990.

Shenk, Calvin E. "African Traditional Religion." Mimeographed textbook for Mekane Yesus Seminary—Theological Education by Extension Department, 72 pp. Addis Ababa, 1975.

Shepley, Gladys. "SIM Stations in Ethiopia." Typed document, 4 pp. Addis Ababa, 1979.

SIM Ethiopia. Ethiopia Field Council Minutes. Convened in Soddo, December 2–6, 1933. 5 pp. ME-2, SIM Archives, Charlotte, NC.

SIM Prayer Guide (1928–2008). SIM Archives, Charlotte, NC.

Tesfaye Tole, "*YäGamo Bétä KristeyanTarik*" [The Church History of Gamo]. In KHC, "*Bäwängél Amanyoch Andinät,*" 21–38.

Toews, J. B. "Excerpts from Notes on a Visit to Ethiopia in July of 1959." EE-2, SIM Archives, Charlotte, NC.

Yosef Menna. "*Yätinsaéw Näṣibiraq Achir yäWolaitta Qal Hiywät Bétä Kristeyan Tarek*" [The glory of the resurrection: a short history of the Wolaitta Kale Heywet Church]. Mimeographed copy, 279 pp. Addis Ababa, 1978 EC.

Index